The English Penal System
in Transition

The English Penal System
in Transition

by

J. E. HALL WILLIAMS, LL.M. (Wales)

of the Middle Temple, Barrister-at-Law
Reader in Criminology in the
University of London

LONDON
BUTTERWORTHS
1970

ENGLAND:	BUTTERWORTH & CO. (PUBLISHERS) LTD.
	LONDON: 88 KINGSWAY, W.C.2
AUSTRALIA:	BUTTERWORTH & CO. (AUSTRALIA) LTD.
	SYDNEY: 20 LOFTUS STREET
	MELBOURNE: 343 LITTLE COLLINS STREET
	BRISBANE: 240 QUEEN STREET
CANADA:	BUTTERWORTH & CO. (CANADA) LTD.
	TORONTO: 14 CURITY AVENUE, 374
NEW ZEALAND:	BUTTERWORTH & CO. (NEW ZEALAND) LTD.
	WELLINGTON: 49/51 BALLANCE STREET
	AUCKLAND: 35 HIGH STREET
SOUTH AFRICA:	BUTTERWORTH & CO. (SOUTH AFRICA) LTD.
	DURBAN: 33/35 BEACH GROVE

©
Butterworth & Co. (Publishers) Ltd.
1970

ISBN – Casebound : 0 406 59310 8
Limp : 0 406 59311 6

Printed in Great Britain
by Billing & Sons Limited, Guildford and London

To my students, for whom this is written, and my wife, without whom it would not have been completed.

Preface

This is a book which grew out of the needs of my students for an up-to-date account of the English penal system. Several important developments have taken place in that system since Sir Lionel Fox's classic study in 1952. The Royal Commission on the Penal System was the occasion for a kind of stocktaking by all those concerned in the treatment of offenders, and the publication of four volumes of Written Evidence in 1967 provided a great deal of valuable material upon which the author has freely drawn. The Commission was wound up but was followed by the comprehensive investigation carried out by the Estimates Committee and published in its Eleventh Report on Prisons, Borstals and Detention Centres. This too provided useful information for the author's purpose.

The penal system is in transition, but how far it is being transformed and into what it is changing is not altogether clear. Do we witness the transition from punishment to treatment? From ancient out-moded methods to modern sophisticated techniques? From an irrational accumulation of sentiment and tradition to a scientific and well thought out variety of régimes and measures? From bumbledom to efficiency? There are clearly several levels of conflict and stress here, for example, between staff and inmates, between different levels of staff, and between the community's expectations and the actual resources and provisions made.

We cannot resolve these queries but it is hoped that the book will help the reader, by giving him vital information about developments in the system, and the materials upon which an informed assessment of the situation can be made.

This is not only a book about prisons, and other custodial measures for dealing with offenders, though much of the space is necessarily devoted to these matters. The non-custodial measures are also fully discussed. There are also special chapters dealing with the offenders under twenty-one and with recidivist prisoners, mentally disordered offenders and female offenders. The section on Sentencing does not profess to provide a complete philosophical guide to the discussion of

vii

punishment, but the more important aspects are dealt with, and the limitations and strengths of each theory of punishment are examined. There is also some discussion of the different goals of sentencers and penal administrators. The chapter on the Sentencing Process is not intended as a complete guide to the business of sentencing, but the main sentencing stages are considered, together with the information available to the courts, and some of the more interesting and important problems surrounding the sentencing stage are reviewed.

The book takes account of developments up to 31 October 1969. A final chapter reviews the White Paper "People in Prisons", published in November 1969, and the Report of the Probation and After-Care Department published in December 1969.

The author's sincere thanks are due to his friends J. J. Tobias, Police College, Bramshill House, and Eric Stockdale, barrister-at-law, for kindly reading the manuscript and making numerous suggestions. Their acute observations and criticisms were invaluable. Any faults which remain are the author's sole responsibility. The author's thanks are also due to his research assistants T. J. Lewthwaite, LL.B., and J. P. W. Cartwright, LL.M.

Writing about an on-going series of inter-related social systems, such as are represented in the treatment of offenders, "from the outside", as it were, presented the writer with several problems. The Prison Department very kindly provided facilities for visits and supplied such information as was requested, but they have no responsibility for what has been said. To preserve his independence the author chose to rely mainly on published sources of information and his own personal knowledge or inquiries. In other words, this is not an "authorised" version of the penal system. As such it has no doubt many limitations, and may be less than complete. It is offered humbly in the belief that it is better to chronicle the known developments than to seek that degree of perfection of vision which can only come from "inside" experience.

J. E. HALL WILLIAMS

London School of Economics
  and Political Science
1 *November* 1969

Table of Contents

Part III

SPECIAL CLASSES OF OFFENDER

Part IV

NON-CUSTODIAL MEASURES FOR DEALING WITH OFFENDERS

Part V

OFFENDERS UNDER TWENTY-ONE

Part VI

FUTURE TRENDS

INDEX

Acknowledgments

The author's thanks are due to the following for permission to quote from published work:

Dr. Charlotte Banks
Miss Ann Duncan and Mrs. Sarah McCabe
Lady Fox
Professor H. L. A. Hart (and the Clarendon Press)
The Rev. R. S. E. Hinde
Dr. Roger Hood
Mr. F. V. Jarvis
Mrs. Joanna Kelley (and the Longman Group Ltd.)
Miss Joan F. S. King
Dr. Hermann Mannheim
Mr. R. L. Morrison
Professor R. B. Pugh (and the Cambridge University Press)
Dr. A. Gordon Rose
Dr. Nigel Walker
Mr. John A. F. Watson, C.B.E., J.P.
The Controller of Her Majesty's Stationery Office, for permission to quote from H.M.S.O. publications, and to reproduce the table from *The Sentence of the Court* in Chapter 13.

Abbreviations

B.J.C.	= *British Journal of Criminology*
B.J.D.	= *British Journal of Delinquency*
Crim. L.R.	= *Criminal Law Review*
Estimates Committee, Eleventh Report	= Eleventh Report from the Estimates Committee, Session 1966–67, Prisons, Borstals and Detention Centres, H.C. 599, 27 July 1967
Fox	= Lionel W. Fox, *The English Prison and Borstal Systems*, 1952
F.R.D.	= *Federal Rules and Decisions*
Jo. Crim. L., Criminology and Pol. Sc.	= *Journal of Criminal Law, Criminology ond Police Science*
Jo. S.P.T.L.	= *Journal of the Society of Public Teachers of Law*
L.Q.R.	= *Law Quarterly Review*
M.L.R.	= *Modern Law Review*
U. of Penn. L.R.	= *University of Pennsylvania Law Review*

Table of Statutes

References in this Table to "Stats." are to Halsbury's Statutes (3rd Edn.) showing the volume and page at which the annotated text of the Act will be found

Table of Cases

In the following Table references are given where applicable to the English and Empire Digest where a digest of each case will be found

PART I

Sentencing

CHAPTER I

The Aims of Punishment

USE OF THE TERM "PUNISHMENT"

As a preface to this discussion, it should be made clear that the term "punishment" is not being used here in any pejorative sense but simply as a convenient word by which to describe the various methods available for dealing with offenders upon conviction of crime. By no means all these methods are punitive in intent or in their practical application. However, it is not easy to find another term to replace "punishment" as a description of the compulsory measures ordered by a court to take effect in regard to a convicted offender. The term "treatment" is not really apposite to many of the measures adopted, and it is too clumsy to speak of both "punishment" and "treatment". Perhaps the most neutral way of putting the matter would be to say that we are discussing the aims of sentencers at the disposition stage. Even this solution raises yet another problem, viz. that the aims of sentencers at the disposition stage are not necessarily identical with the aims of penal administrators and others concerned in the actual execution of the orders of the court. We shall return to this subject later.

THE AIMS OF SENTENCERS

Several research studies have revealed how divergent are the aims of different courts and judges in sentencing offenders.[1] These differences are not simply the result of different opinions concerning the best means of achieving particular goals, they are also the result of different beliefs about what the goals should be. In other words, entirely different philosophies are often followed by different courts and sometimes by separate

---

1. E. Green, *Judicial Attitudes in Sentencing*, 1961; R. Hood, *Sentencing in Magistrates' Courts*, 1962; H. Mannheim, J. Spencer, G. Lynch, "Magisterial Policy in the London Juvenile Courts" (1957–58), 8 *B.J.D.* 13, 119.

members of the same court. The solution to the problem of sentencing, as the late Robert Kennedy once said when he was Attorney-General, "does not rest in making sentences equal, but in making sentencing philosophies agree".[2]

With this in mind, there have been some attempts to bring judges and magistrates to meet with experts and discuss these matters in sentencing conferences and courses. The Lord Chief Justice in 1963 started the practice of convening the high court judges, recorders and chairmen of quarter sessions, and in September 1968 and 1969 the Lord Chancellor arranged a one-week course for all new judges and recorders and the like. The Magistrates' Association has sponsored many similar activities in different parts of the country, and universities and other educational bodies have contributed towards the provision of these organised opportunities for the exchange of information and knowledge. In October 1969 the Bar Council instituted some informal discussion meetings with criminologists and persons with administrative responsibilities for convicted offenders.

One matter on which all agree today is that sentencing has become a much more complicated task, as so many different matters have to be considered, and there are so many different choices available. As the Streatfeild Committee said, in the past, sentencing was a comparatively simple matter because (i) the choice was limited, and (ii) the purpose was restricted. The primary objective was to fix a sentence proportionate to the offender's culpability and this could be done on the basis of very limited information, according to the "tariff" system of punishment. All that the court needed to know was the facts of the offence and the details of the offender's past record, together with information about any aggravating or mitigating circumstances. The court could sentence according to the culpability or blameworthiness of the offender, and take in its stride such questions as the need to protect society, to deter other potential offenders, and the question of the reform of the individual offender.[3]

---

2. Address by Attorney-General Robert F. Kennedy, Highland Park, Illinois, Seminar and Institute on Disparity of Sentences, For Sixth, Seventh and Eighth Judicial Circuits, October 1961, 30 *F.R.D.* 401 at p. 426.
3. Report of the Interdepartmental Committee on the Business of the Criminal Courts, Cmnd. 1289, February 1961, p. 76, paras. 257 *et seq.*

Nowadays it is not so straightforward. Sentencing has become a much more complex task, and for this to be adequately performed much more information about the offender is needed. We shall discuss in the next chapter how the courts and the authorities have responded to this situation. (See Chapter 2: The Sentencing Process.)

Now we shall describe the main aims of punishment for crime, viewed from the sentencer's standpoint, and consider some of the arguments concerning the relative merits of each, and the difficulties encountered in their application. So much has been written about the aims of punishment by philosophers and lawyers that it would be tedious and indeed quite impossible to do more than give a brief and rather concentrated summary. The reader is referred to the vast literature on the subject for "further and better particulars", as the lawyers say. The following aims of punishment will be discussed:

1. Deterrence;
2. Protection of society;
3. Reform of the offender;
4. Retribution;
5. Justice;
6. Reparation.

I DETERRENCE

One of the principal aims of punishment for crime is to deter the individual offender and also others who may be minded to commit similar offences and hence to prevent further crime. There is clearly a double aspect to deterrence—individual deterrence must be distinguished from general deterrence, the former looking to the individual offender before the court, the latter considering the deterrence of the public at large, or particular sections of it.

Individual deterrence

There is a great deal of doubt concerning the effectiveness of punishment as a deterrent on the individual offender. While common experience in child-rearing habits, at school, and in adult life[4] suggests there must be something in it, deterrence is

---

4. Punishments may be used to discipline mental patients: see "Rewarding and punishing mentally ill", *The Times*, 26 May 1969.

often ineffective as regards the individual offender for a number of reasons:

(*i*) *The nature of the crime involved.*—The threat of punishment is more likely to be effective as a deterrent in the case of property crimes than in the case of crimes of a more impulsive nature, such as violence and most homicide. The experience of Denmark in 1944 provides some evidence for this view.[5] The German authorities deported the whole of the Danish police force in September 1944, and for seven months Denmark had no police. The result was a sharp rise in crimes of dishonesty, robbery and crimes against property, but the figure for murder, sexual crimes and crimes of violence remained fairly stable.

(*ii*) *The character and personality of the individual.*—This clearly comes into the question, since punishment is more likely to deter some individuals than others, depending on their social and economic status, family background and educational attainment, etc. Margery Fry described most delinquents as being inclined to short-run hedonism, immediate gratification of personal needs, and she described them as "present-dwellers", whereas most normal human beings, or most normal middle-class human beings, have aspirations and long-range goals, and are willing to postpone satisfaction in order to achieve those goals; they are essentially "future-dwellers".[6] How often do the courts transfer their own modes of thought and moral standards to those appearing before them, and blame offenders for having little foresight or treat them as if they had more than they have got!

(*iii*) *The certainty and celerity of punishment.*—One important factor in deterrence is the risk of being caught and swiftly dealt with. Jeremy Bentham stressed this nearly two hundred years ago,[7] and in our time it has been stressed by both the Lord Chancellor and the Lord Chief Justice.[8] It is said that it is more important that punishment should be swift and sure, "like a

---

5. S. Hurwitz *Criminology*, 1952, p. 303; J. Andenaes, "The General Preventive Effects of Punishment" May 1966, 114 *U. of Penn. L.R.*, No. 7, 949 at p. 962.
6. Margery Fry, *Arms of the Law*, 1951, pp. 82–83. Tony Parker and Robert Allerton, *The Courage of His Convictions*, 1962.
7. Jeremy Bentham, *The Rationale of Punishment*, 1830, p. 39.
8. Gerald Gardiner, "The Purposes of Criminal Punishment" (March, May 1958) 21 *M.L.R.* 117, 221 at p. 124; Lord Parker of Waddington, House of Lords Debates, Vol. 220, col. 728, 27 January 1960, *The Times*, 28 January 1960.

seal to hot wax", to use Stephen's metaphor,[9] than that it should be condign or severe (though Stephen might have dissented on the question of severity).

Unfortunately, the degree to which detection is certain varies enormously from one crime to another and even within the same crime category there are considerable differences in the rate of detection, in different circumstances. The general rate of "clear-up" of indictable offences is given in the annual criminal statistics, and is currently (1968) 41·9% of the indictable offences known to the police.[10] But some crimes carry a very high clear-up rate, like murder, and rape. Other crimes, like robbery, are much more difficult to solve, and, to give an extreme case, it is said that four out of five robberies in the open remain unsolved.[11]

So we can say, with regard to individual deterrence, that a great deal depends on the person and upon the crime.

General deterrence

This is an even more difficult concept to investigate and understand. While there can be no doubt about the allegiance which it commands among sentencers and the general public, the effectiveness of general deterrence may well be influenced by the following considerations:

(*i*) *It requires the public to be informed of the offence and the penalty imposed for it.*—This is one good reason for having the press report trials, and for the activities of that Sunday newspaper which gives a great deal of space to such matters. General deterrence depends on the widespread dissemination of knowledge of what happens to offenders who are caught and convicted. Roger Hood found that more reliance was placed on general deterrence by magistrates' courts in small towns with a strong local press, than in large amorphous metropolitan communities, whose inhabitants possessed few local loyalties.[12]

(*ii*) *The public must be in general sympathy with the law and the*

---

9. J. F. Stephen, *History of the Criminal Law of England*, 1883, Vol. II, p. 81. Stephen was speaking of the close relation of the moral sentiments of the public to the sentence of the law in relation to any offence.
10. Home Office, Criminal Statistics, England and Wales, 1968, Cmnd. 4098, July 1969, p. x.
11. F. H. McClintock and Evelyn Gibson, *Robbery in London*, 1961. Preface by Leon Radzinowicz, pp. xi and xii.
12. R. Hood, *Sentencing in Magistrates' Courts*, 1962, pp. 73–74.

way it is being administered.—If the courts and Parliament do not take the public with them, in their law-making and law enforcement policies, then however severe the penalties, the general deterrent effect will be weak. Examples are the difficulties experienced over enforcing the road traffic laws, particularly concerning dangerous driving and drunken driving.

In a case at Middlesex Sessions in 1959[13] the then Chairman, Mr. Ewen Montagu, Q.C., remarked:

> "The question of deterrence by savage sentences, such as people who sit not far from here often speak about, is utter nonsense when dealing with this type of case."

The case concerned a baker's roundsman who had pleaded guilty to driving while under the influence of drink, and was fined £10 and disqualified from driving for twelve months. A doctor's evidence showed he had consumed the equivalent of $2\frac{1}{2}$ pints of beer.

Lord Parker said in 1960 in a House of Lords debate that it was a sound principle that the certainty of punishment was a greater deterrent than its severity.[14] Lord Reid, in another debate in the House of Lords,[15] in discussing motoring offences, had something similar to say:

> "This I would say with all the emphasis that I can command: the answer is not increased penalties. All history shows that once you increase penalties beyond what public opinion will support you do more harm than good and the frequency with which juries acquit in cases where the evidence seems almost overwhelming shows that already public opinion is strained to the limit on that matter."

Shortly before these statements, the law concerning death by dangerous driving was altered, but the law concerning compulsory disqualification of motorists remains severe. In 1959 the Magistrates' Association had called for heavier penalties for serious road traffic offences, but the Automobile Association had objected that the imposition of the heavier sentence irrespective of the circumstances of a particular case would be contrary to the principles of British justice. Both organisations agreed that serious motoring offences required deterrent penalties.[16]

---

13. *The Times,* 12 December 1959.
14. House of Lords Debates, Vol. 220, col. 728, 27 January 1960.
15. House of Lords Debates, Vol. 223, col. 360, 4 May 1960.
16. *The Times,* 21 November 1959.

Professor Andenaes has demonstrated the continuing validity of the concept of general deterrence, writing in terms not only of Norwegian experience, but taking a broad cross-cultural view, and he has answered many of the complaints made about the concept, and rehabilitated it in penological thought.[17] He calls for more research into the working of deterrence, a plea which has been made in several quarters. In the United Kingdom there has been some study of the matter carried out by the Government Social Survey, at the request of the Home Office.[18] Clearly it is a very complicated matter to study, and we should avoid sweeping conclusions based on limited observation or isolated experiences.

While we may, along with Professor Andenaes, subscribe to a realistic belief in the effectiveness of general deterrence we should be cautious about claiming too much for it. Illustrations which are frequently used by English judges as evidence to justify deterrent penalties are:

1. The decline in post-office fraud following the harsh penalties adopted by the judges in the immediate post-war years;
2. The decline in racial violence following the severe sentences passed in the cases of the Notting Hill disturbances;
3. The decline in telephone kiosk thefts following the tough line taken with offenders by the Birmingham courts.

It may be true that the harsh penalties inflicted contributed to controlling each of these situations, but close analysis reveals that there were in each situation other factors which affected the situation equally strongly, such as, in cases 1 and 3, changes in post-office techniques and equipment and in case 2 a falling off in racial tension which preceded the actual sentences.[19]

These *post-hoc, ergo propter hoc* arguments in favour of deterrent sentences need to be viewed with suspicion. There are few certainties where human behaviour is concerned, and it would

17. J. Andenaes, "General Prevention—Illusion or Reality?" (July–August 1952), 43 *Jo. Crim. L.*, Criminology and Pol. Sc., No. 2, p. 176; "The General Preventive Effects of Punishment" (May 1966), 114 *U. of Penn. L.R.*, No. 7, p. 949; "Does Punishment Deter Crime?" (November 1968), II *The Criminal Law Quarterly*, No. 1, p. 76.
18. H. D. Willcock and J. Stokes, *Deterrents to Crime amongst Youths aged 15 to 21* Government Social Survey Report No. SS 356, 1968.
19. See discussion in E. Stockdale, *The Court and the Offender*, 1967, p. 37.

be better to say frankly that although we may respond with harsh measures we simply do not know whether these are likely to be effective in controlling any given situation. Moreover, all history points to the futility of increasing the severity of punishment; at least there is a point at which this reaction to a situation becomes counter-productive.

This is not the place to argue the merits of capital punishment as a deterrent. The point should be made, however, that there is no convincing statistical evidence about the effectiveness of capital punishment as a deterrent.[20] In the absence of such evidence we are thrown back on strongly held opinions based on experience, or views based on fundamental moral standpoints. It is hardly surprising that the question is so difficult to resolve. We must content ourselves with the observation that whatever is decided about capital punishment does not necessarily govern the decision about other punishments in terms of their deterrent effects. As Andenaes says:

"Some people tend to jump to the conclusion that since the severity of punishment has no effect on murder rates, the same applies to other crimes. It may be necessary, therefore, to stress the limitations of these findings."[1]

(iii) The public are not moved to compassionate sympathy in the individual case, for some special reason, e.g. some physical disability or mental condition.—What we mean here is that if the particular case excites strong public sympathy on compassionate grounds, little purpose will be served by trying to carry out the general policy of "making an example". The case of *Moodie* in 1959 showed that very well. Here a prison officer killed his imbecile child, and was sentenced to three years' imprisonment for manslaughter. On appeal this was reduced to twelve months, the Lord Chief Justice saying that while nothing the courts did should lead the public to believe that a killing of this sort was other than a grave offence, there were special circumstances, which led the Court to feel it could reduce the sentence.[2]

"Persons such as the applicant were not criminals in the ordinary sense; they often acted in what they considered were the best of

---

20. Royal Commission on Capital Punishment, Report, Cmd. 8932, 1953, pp. 18–24, and Appendix 6, pp. 328 *et seq.*
1. J. Andenaes, "Does Punishment Deter Crime?" (November 1968), 11 *The Criminal Law Quarterly*, No. 1, p. 76 at p. 83.
2. [1959] Crim. L.R. 373; *The Times*, 13 January 1959.

motives and the real deterrent, if deterrent there were, was not a question of how many years' imprisonment they would get."

We shall return to the question of exemplary punishment later, in discussing justice as one of the aims of punishment. We may conclude this section by referring to the Report of the Ingleby Committee on Children and Young Persons, which gave striking recognition to the principle of deterrence:

"Although it may be right for the court's action to be determined primarily by the needs of the particular child before it, the court cannot entirely disregard other considerations such as the need to deter potential offenders. An element of general deterrence must enter into many of the court's decisions and must make the distinction between treatment and punishment even more difficult to draw."[3]

2 PROTECTION OF SOCIETY

It is right for the courts to seek by their sentences to protect society from the danger of repetition of the offence. This extends beyond mere deterrence and comprehends the removal of the offender from society for a period, as a means of public protection. Some scholars describe this as incapacitation.[4] The need to remove the offender from his environment at least for the time being is frequently an important consideration by courts in deciding on a custodial sentence. In some cases, for example, murder and sexual assaults, especially on young children, it would not be wise to release the offender immediately to circulate again in the free community whence he came.

English law does not provide for any form of protective custody or preventive detention, such as is known in some jurisdictions, as a measure of social defence. Even the "habitual criminal" label which before 1948 led to the sentence of preventive detention could not be applied unless a serious crime had been committed, and the preventive detention which replaced it under the Criminal Justice Act 1948 involved proof of previous offences as well as a present offence of a serious nature and provided for a fixed term of imprisonment. But it is clear that the sentence of preventive detention was intended

---

3. Home Office, Report of the Committee on Children and Young Persons, Cmnd. 1191, October 1960, p. 41, para. 110.
4. Paul W. Tappan, *Crime, Justice and Correction*, 1960, p. 255. Bentham used the term too, *The Rationale of Punishment*, 1830, p. 32.

for the protection of society: the section says so.[5] In fact, it is
now recognised that the sentence of preventive detention failed
to protect us from the more dangerous offenders, and fell
harshly on many minor feckless and inadequate thieves and
housebreakers.[6] It has since been replaced by the "extended
term" under the Criminal Justice Act 1967, which also speaks
of the protection of the public.[7] This measure is likely to be
equally unsuccessful as a measure of social protection. Corrective training under the 1948 Act was never intended solely as
a social defence measure, but was conceived more as a last ditch
training and rehabilitation effort to prevent a person from
becoming a persistent adult offender. (See Chapter 14:
Recidivist Prisoners.)

The Mental Health Act 1959 does enable the criminal courts
to order the detention of convicted offenders in hospital under
a hospital order, with or without a restriction order. (See
Chapter 15: Mentally Disordered Offenders.) This kind of
detention can be regarded as intended for the protection of
society, in so far as the person is removed from public circula-
tion, and may have difficulty in obtaining his discharge. The
restriction order which criminal courts frequently couple with
a hospital order is clearly designed to protect society.

Whether the long sentences imposed on spies in recent years
were necessary to protect society from their activities is debatable. Blake's 42 years and the sentences on Lonsdale, the
Krogers, and Britten were partly justified in these terms. Mr.
Justice HILBERY said with regard to Blake: "The sentence had
a threefold purpose. It was intended to be punitive, it was
designed and calculated to deter others and it was meant to be
a safeguard to this country."[8] These severe sentences can be
justified in terms of the possible value to the Soviet Union of the
information the offenders might possess, if they were released
too soon, a point which has been stressed recently in the discussion

---

5. Criminal Justice Act 1948, s. 21 (now repealed). A sentence of preventive detention could be passed: "if the court is satisfied that it is expedient for the protection of the public that he should be detained in custody for a substantial
   time, followed by a period of supervision if released before the expiration of
   his sentence."
6. See Chapter 14: Recidivist Prisoners.
7. Criminal Justice Act 1967, s. 37(2): "if the court is satisfied, by reason of his
   previous conduct and of the likelihood of his committing further offences, that
   it is expedient to protect the public from him for a substantial time, the court
   may impose an extended term of imprisonment" under the section.
8. *R.* v. *Blake*, [1962] 2 Q.B. 377, at p. 383; [1961] 3 All E.R. 125, at p. 128.

concerning the release of the Krogers. But the danger to the country of such persons being able to repeat their offence is nil, and the sentences were seen by many as retributive.

A better case can be made for the long sentences imposed on such clever and violent criminals as the celebrated mail-train robbers and dangerous criminals like the Richardsons and the Kray brothers. They do represent a real threat to society, and we are entitled to be protected from them for a considerable period. The question whether there should be a special law designed to deal with dangerous offenders is a matter for separate discussion. (See Chapter 14: Recidivist Prisoners.)

3 REFORM OF THE OFFENDER

The reform of the offender and his rehabilitation in society is widely canvassed in modern times as one of the principal aims of the penal law. It is certainly a most desirable objective, but it cannot be wholeheartedly embraced at the present time as the sole aim, as some would suggest,[9] for several reasons:

1. The state of our knowledge about how to achieve reform is extremely limited, and even if we knew how to reform offenders, the necessary resources in terms of men and equipment would probably not be available;
2. The nature of the offence may be too trivial for reform of the offender to be seriously considered;
3. The other objectives of punishment must also be pursued, and sometimes they will outweigh the arguments for reform.

Having said this, we must stress our view that it is of the utmost importance that as many of the cases as possible should be disposed of with reform as the main aim, and that as much of the community's resources as possible should be allocated for this purpose. This is because in the long run, reform of the offender is the surest way of protecting society from crime. All that we are saying above is that, despite the claims of certain criminologists, reform of the offender cannot be the exclusive goal.

The point about the lack of the necessary knowledge is a

9. See L. Hall and S. Glueck, *Cases on Criminal Law and Its Enforcement*, 1958, pp. 14–22. Even these authors admit that would-be reformers of the penal law must be realistic.

B

general one, and it must clearly be qualified by saying that we have certain bits of information and experience which provide a more or less reliable guide to the choice of the method of disposal, and we know or suspect that certain courses of action are harmful and others beneficial. We may express it this way: that we are beginning to learn how to maximise the chances of reform of the offender. Having said that, it must be admitted sorrowfully that the results in terms of the crime figures are not very promising. But these require careful interpretation before we draw only melancholy conclusions. (See Chapter 13: Results of Prison Custody (and other Measures.))

That some offences are too trivial to merit the reformative approach may be illustrated by reference to parking offences. Simply because my car was illegally parked does not warrant an attempt to reform me (other than as a car parker!). Sometimes the social cost of an all-out effort to reform is one which society is not yet prepared to meet, as witness our attitude to offences of persistent and public drunkenness. Gradually we are beginning to see that repeated short prison terms for drunkenness are wasteful and destructive, and more effort is being made to approach the problems of alcoholism constructively.

One might add, as a footnote to this discussion of reform, the simple point that whenever capital punishment is ordered and execution takes place, the object is prevention of repetition of the offence, rather than reform of the offender.

4 RETRIBUTION

There are many meanings to the term retribution. The ancient meaning was close to the idea of vengeance, but mixed up with the notion of restoring the balance in society by proportionate punishment of the offender—a kind of judicial "tit-for-tat". It was Bernard Shaw who pointed out that the Biblical phrase: "Vengeance is mine, saith the Lord" does not mean the Lord Chief Justice![10] Even before Shaw's day, there were many who doubted whether retribution in this ancient form was a proper aim of punishment for crime. Unfortunately it got mixed up with yet another notion, that of Expiation, or cleaning the slate, the purifying through suffering which

---

10. Preface to Webb's *English Local Government*, 1963, revised edn., Vol. 6, *English Prisons Under Local Government*, p. lv.

Christianity has often regarded so highly. It has taken us many centuries to realise that there is little that is purifying about suffering except for saints.

The ancient idea of retribution in terms of legalised vengeance is now somewhat unfashionable and discredited. It has been pointed out that even the Hebraic law concerning "an eye for an eye" was really expressing a limitation on primitive vengeance, saying "this far you may go, no further". Over the centuries, especially in the western world, the idea of limiting punishment has gained momentum. So we begin to reach a more modern and sophisticated and perhaps even a more acceptable notion of retribution.

The more modern notion is that punishment should be proportionate to the offence and the culpability or blameworthiness of the offender. The community is entitled to expect the courts to reflect its own disapproval of the crime, and to punish accordingly. But it must condemn the guilty and not the innocent, and punish in proportion to the individual responsibility of the wrongdoer, taking into account various factors such as his age, previous offences, mental condition, etc. Herein lies the origin of the tariff system of punishment which still lies at the heart of our system of sentencing.

Closely linked with the idea of retribution as described in this modern sense is the notion of denunciatory punishment, the feeling, for that is what it often is, that the community must somehow by the sentence chosen mark its displeasure with the conduct of the offender, and place a value on it, in negative terms. This is perhaps no more than a sense of emotional outrage. However, many learned judges and reverend prelates have supported the denunciatory theory of punishment,[11] but more recently it has received pretty rough handling from, among others, Professor H. L. A. Hart.[12] He links this attitude with the moral indignation expressed by Stephen in the nineteenth century, who claimed that it was right to hate criminals. Hart argues that the denunciatory theory of punishment should be dismissed for a number of reasons. It is a

---

11. William Temple, "The Ethics of Penal Action": Clarke Hall Lecture, No. 1, 1934; Lord Denning, quoted in Report of the Royal Commission on Capital Punishment, Cmd. 8932, para. 53. See H. L. A. Hart, *Punishment and Responsibility*, 1968, p. 170.
12. H. L. A. Hart, "Punishment and the Elimination of Responsibility", Hobhouse Memorial Lecture, No. 31, 1962.

distraction from serious thinking and the acquisition of knowledge about what one is doing. It is deceptive about a common
morality. It is better subsumed under the head of the need to
seek justice and fairness in choosing the appropriate sentence.[13]

5 JUSTICE

Hart's claim that the law should not in its scale of punishments flout any well-marked common moral distinctions is
developed into a sophisticated modern view of the needs to treat
offenders justly and fairly, to treat like cases alike, and so on.[14]
He points out that the retributive approach seems to conflict
with the notion of individualisation of treatment to meet the
needs of the offender, which has developed strongly since the
1895 Report of the Gladstone Committee. (See Chapter 3:
the History of Imprisonment.)

What Professor Hart seems to be saying is that the old
classical theory that the punishment should fit the crime should
be replaced by the modern notions of a fair proportion between
offence and punishment, which is basic to the very idea of
justice itself. While the old-fashioned retributive doctrine may
be regarded as backward-looking, the modern notion of the
claims of justice sets a limitation upon what may be done to
the offender which coincides closely with the current interest in
human rights, and modern developments in the theory of
criminal responsibility. We may agree with Professor Hart that:

> "There is . . . at this point something to defend, a moral position
> which ought not to be evacuated as if the decay of retributive
> ideas had made it untenable. There are values quite distinct
> from those of retributive punishment which the system of respon-
> sibility does maintain, and which remain of great importance
> even if our claims in punishing are the forward-looking aims of
> social protection."[15]

Professor Radzinowicz has acknowledged that this notion of the
demands of justice is "still firmly entrenched",[16] and it was
recognised and accepted by the Ingleby Committee.[17] "Criminal

---

13. *Ibid.*, pp. 7–8. See also H. L. A. Hart, *Punishment and Responsibility*, 1968, pp.
　　170–173.
14. *Ibid.*, p. 27.
15. *Ibid.*, p. 27.
16. Leon Radzinowicz, Preface to *Robbery in London*, F. H. McClintock and E.
　　Gibson, 1961, p. xvii.
17. Report of the Committee on Children and Young Persons, Cmnd. 1191,
　　October 1960, p. 42.

punishment", says Hart in his Israel lectures, "is not mere social hygiene whatever the more progressive critics say".[18]

Two situations frequently arise in practice where the courts refer to the claims of justice in regard to the choice of sentence.

The first is where an exemplary punishment is imposed. This is a punishment which goes beyond what is normal for an offence of the kind but is chosen for special reasons such as the prevalence of offences of the kind in the neighbourhood or at that particular time; or the special responsibility of the offenders as public officials, or the special risk to public funds of fraudulent claims, *e.g.* in post office savings accounts, social security benefits, etc. In other words the courts may pay lip-service to the principle that sentences should be proportionate by justifying their departure from the norm in these particular cases. Professor Hart puts the matter thus:

> "when a crime has become exceptionally or dangerously frequent judges have defended punishing an offender more severely than previous offenders on the ground that this step is necessary to check a major evil. It is well that this and other sacrifices of principles of equality between different offenders should be made only with hesitation and with full explanation; for there is always great danger that they may be made in moments of panic or without reliable evidence that they will prevent a worse evil."[19]

The departure from the principle of equality or proportion involved in such exemplary punishments has worried several authorities. The Cadogan Committee on Corporal Punishment, in 1938, doubted whether it was ethically justifiable to make an example of one person for the benefit of the community, especially in the case of a young offender where the punishment chosen was not the most appropriate one for the needs of the individual offender.[20] Professor Rupert Cross has also expressed his doubts about exemplary punishments,[1] and it may well be that the bad luck suffered by the offender who happens to be sentenced as an example to others cannot be put right later on, either by the use of the prerogative power or in the granting of early parole where other indications were favourable.

The second situation where considerations of justice in regard

18. H. L. A. Hart, *The Morality of the Criminal Law*, 1965, p. 42.
19. H. L. A. Hart, *Punishment and Responsibility*, 1968, p. 172.
20. Home Office, Report of the Departmental Committee on Corporal Punishment, Cmd. 5684, February, 1938, p. 23.
1. Rupert Cross, "Indeterminate Prison Sentences", *The Listener*, Vol. 68, p. 289, 15 February 1962, at p. 290.

to the sentence frequently arise is where the offence is committed by several offenders jointly. Here D. A. Thomas has examined the principles which apply.[2] He points out that it is not considered to be inconsistent with the principle of equality to pass a lighter sentence on one co-defendant than the other where there is some factor in the history of the first offender or in the circumstances which justifies such differentiation. The important thing is for those factors which justify such discrimination to be recognised by the courts and given their appropriate weight in such cases. The principles were well explained by HILBERY, J., in *R. v. Ball*.[3]

Much of the concern about the provisions of the new Children and Young Persons Act arose from the suggestion that two joint offenders might be dealt with differently under the Act, and only one of them might be brought before the juvenile court because the other had a good home: this would appear to be discriminatory. The answer given to these criticisms was that the present practice was in need of improvement since it appeared to discriminate against the working-class child. Few middle-class children were brought before the juvenile courts, as compared with working- class children. Under the new law only those who needed official intervention through the juvenile court would be dealt with in that way.[4]

The critics were clearly not satisfied with the official explanations of the provisions of s. 1. Amendments were moved, and lost in the House of Commons, but succeeded in the House of Lords, to ensure that two offenders charged with a joint offence should not be treated differently. The House of Commons eventually restored the words of the Bill.[5]

6 REPARATION

There is a sense in which one can say that this is at once the oldest and the newest aim of punishment for crime. Our primitive ancestors applied this idea that the wrongdoer and his

---

2. D. A. Thomas, "Sentencing Co-Defendants—When is Uniform Treatment Necessary?" [1964] *Crim. L.R.* 22.
3. [1951] 2 K.B. 109.
4. Rt. Hon. James Callaghan, moving the Second Reading, House of Commons Debates, 11 March 1969, Vol 779, cols. 1190 *et seq.*
5. Quintin Hogg, *loc. cit.*, col. 1202; M. Carlisle, House of Commons Debates, 9 June 1969, Vol. 784, col. 1020; Earl Jellicoe, House of Lords Debates, 7 July 1969, Vol. 303, col. 796.

family must pay compensation for his crime, in goods or money.[6] Today many penal reformers believe that it would contribute to the reform of the offender and the reduction of crime if the offender were made to pay compensation to the victim for the injury or loss he has caused him.

As we shall see, legal powers exist which the criminal courts do occasionally use, to order the convicted offender to pay his victim money compensation. (See Chapter 20: Compensation and Restitution.) In recent years some countries, including Britain, have provided schemes for the compensation of victims of crimes of violence, the money being paid out of public funds. There seems little hope of providing that a prisoner should pay compensation out of his earnings, which are at present pitifully small. But the possibility of using some kind of bankruptcy procedure, in order to get hold of the "loot" or the money he has salted away, is seriously advocated by some, and many other devices whereby non-prisoners might be enabled to repay their debt to society by voluntary work and in other ways are often discussed, and are currently being examined by the Advisory Council on the Penal System. Community Service Volunteers do now provide limited social service opportunities for selected offenders.[7] One may comment that it is easy to dream up a sentimental scheme of reparation to the community, but the practical problems raised in its implementation are serious and deep-seated. For example, forced labour cannot be expected to do "voluntary" work satisfactorily, and may not always be suitable for the tasks involved, and there are problems in arranging for supervision and enforcement. Nevertheless, it is to be hoped that somewhere in this direction lies the essential thread of inspiration and application which will one day make this interesting idea a practical reality.

THE AIMS OF PENAL ADMINISTRATORS

Sir Lionel Fox, whose views on the aims of penal administrators carry great weight, maintained that the answer to the question "What is prison for?" was that

---

6. Welshmen will remember that such provisions are to be found in the laws of Hywel Dda. See *The Welsh History Review*, Special number, 1963: "The Welsh Laws".
7. C.S.V. Annual Report 1968-69; *The Scotsman*, 10 November 1969, "Borstal boys on parole" Report by Julie Davidson.

"three main purposes can be distinguished, which may conveniently be defined as (1) custodial, for the unconvicted, (2) coercive, for those who can secure release by paying what they owe (or we might add, by other prescribed conduct, *e.g.* where a person is committed for contempt), (3) correctional, for the convicted."[8]

We shall be exploring later the use the courts make of prison along the lines indicated by Sir Lionel Fox. (See Chapter 5: The Use the Courts Make of Prison.) It is sufficient for the present to note that the prime aims of the prison authorities are necessarily slightly different from the objectives which the courts may have in mind when sentencing offenders. The prison authorities necessarily lay great emphasis on *Safe Custody* as an aim. They are charged with the duty to contain or hold those committed to their care, whether pending trial, or for coercive reasons, or after trial during sentence. This objective has primacy for two reasons, firstly, because the public and the courts expect it; secondly, because it is only through this that any other objectives such as training and treatment can be achieved (as Duncan Fairn has often pointed out, you cannot train a man who isn't there). *Training and Treatment* are therefore secondary aims of the penal administrator, to be pursued in the context of the primary aim of Safe Custody. Since the Report of the Gladstone Committee in 1895, these, along with deterrence, have become the official goals of the prison authorities with regard to most of those in custody. The Prison Rules continue to speak of these twin concepts of Training and Treatment as expressing the essence of the system. The 1964 Prison Rules express the matter thus:

"The purpose of the training and treatment of convicted prisoners shall be to encourage and assist them to lead a good and useful life."[9]

This statement of aims comes very close to that adopted in 1955 by the United Nations in the Standard Minimum Rules for the treatment of prisoners, and this was a matter of which Sir Lionel Fox was very proud.

Some criminologists would make a distinction between "training" and "treatment", maintaining that "training" is concerned more with teaching a person good habits of cleanli-

---

8. Fox, pp. 15–16.
9 Rule 1.

ness, regular work, and self-respect, whereas "treatment" involves helping the prisoner to understand his own personality and character and enabling him to make adjustments and modifications by means of this greater self-knowledge. It is sometimes said that our prison system places undue emphasis on the training aspects at the expense of the treatment situation. This may in fact be a misplaced criticism, for much treatment does undoubtedly take place within the training situation. A skilled prison officer or workshop foreman or assistant governor, indeed any one of the many officials within the prison setting, can use the opportunity for personal contact with a prisoner to develop a personal relationship with him, as well as to elicit certain facts and explore certain attitudes in a constructive manner. Moreover, the knowledge acquired in this way can be fed in to the pool of knowledge about the offender so that in the end better judgments can be made about him and his needs and problems. While it will remain true that some situations are more treatment oriented than others, it would be wrong to make a sharp distinction between training and treatment, as each is inextricably bound up with the other.

The points made so far are excellently illustrated in a passage from Mrs. Joanna Kelley's book on female prisoners:

"The punishment of imprisonment consists in deprivation of liberty for a certain period and the first duty of everyone in the prison service, therefore, is to see that the prisoners remain in custody in accordance with the sentence of the court. Subject to this, however, the prison staff have a fairly free hand in deciding how the period of imprisonment shall be spent. Prison officers are told when they receive their training that people are sent to prison *as* a punishment and not *for* punishment; the Prison Department has laid it down that the treatment of prisoners shall be rehabilitative as far as possible, curative rather than punitive. These statements simply give recognition to a development of long standing and they undoubtedly accord with the wishes of the great majority of those whose work is closely connected with prisons."[10]

It is necessary to emphasise in regard to the use of prison that although the prison staff may wish to make a positive creative contribution to prisoner's reform and rehabilitation, this is not always, indeed not often, the purpose for which the

10. Joanna Kelley, *When the Gates Shut* (Longmans), 1967, pp. 5–6.

courts have committed the offender.[11] Prison is increasingly used as a last resort by courts, for persons who have failed the other more positive types of measure such as probation. Or else prison has been ordered because of the nature and gravity of the offence, but without any views being formed about what should be done with the prisoner while he is in custody. It is one of the great merits of the system that it does not involve such close liaison between courts and prison authorities that the latter are obliged to carry out the wishes of the former. The prison authorities are responsible to Parliament and not to the courts, though they are naturally sensitive to the views of the judiciary and anxious to be held in high regard by them as well as by the public. But no court can tell the prison governor, "this man is to be punished, that man is to be trained, this one is to be treated". It is left to the complete discretion of the prison authorities, subject to the Prison Act and the Rules, how to deal with those whom they receive into custody. It is to the credit of those authorities that they so often strive to induce change in prisoners, even when others have failed and it seems a hopeless undertaking.

---

11. In *R.* v. *Ford*, [1969] 3 All E.R. 782, the Court of Appeal said that "sentences of imprisonment, except where an element of protection of the public is involved, or in special cases such as those involving drugs, are normally intended to be the correct sentence for the particular crime, and not to include a curative element". This was applied in *R.* v. *Moylan*, [1969] 3 All E.R. 783.

CHAPTER 2

The Sentencing Process

Sentencing is a complicated business involving much legal skill and knowledge of human nature. It cannot be regarded simply as a technical branch of social science, as some would maintain,[1] since it requires much legal skill and experience as well as knowledge of human behaviour and some scientific knowledge. It is an emergent branch of the law.[2] Sentencing is seen at its best in the work of the Court of Appeal in dealing with criminal appeals, especially appeals against sentence. Through its decisions, both reported and unreported, the Court of Appeal has developed a jurisprudence of sentencing which should govern the activities of all courts of trial but which is specially applicable to courts of quarter sessions and assizes, for these are the courts from which appeal lies to the Court of Appeal. It is true that there is an appeal on points of law from the magistrates' courts to a Divisional Court of the Queen's Bench Division, but this rarely concerns the exercise of sentencing powers. The High Court also exercises supervisory powers over the decisions of magistrates by means of the prerogative orders. But it is the decisions in sentence appeals from assizes and quarter sessions which provide a code for the guidance of sentencers, one which is now gradually being explored and articulated by scholars like D. A. Thomas.[3]

The sentence stage of a trial is one which follows upon conviction or a finding of guilt. In the English procedure these two stages are kept quite separate, and the information which is relevant to sentencing is not always supplied to the court before conviction takes place since it might be prejudicial to the trial of the issue of guilt. Lists of previous convictions of the accused

---

1. Terence Morris, "Strange paradox of penal reform", *The Observer*, 23 July 1961.
2. Report of the Interdepartmental Committee on the Business of the Criminal Courts, Cmnd. 1289, p. 86, para 299.
3. See D. A. Thomas, "Theories of Punishment in the Court of Criminal Appeal" (September 1964), 27 *M.L.R.* 546.

person are prepared in advance, and are supplied to the judge
in many cases together with the trial calendar, it being left to
his discretion whether to look at them. Some years ago when
this came out in public there was something of an outcry, but
the two views about this matter were not reconciled. One view
is that it is essential that the judge should know about the previous convictions of an accused person so that he may properly
conduct the trial and be able to warn defence counsel of the
dangers he may be running in pursuing a line of questioning
which brings the accused's character in issue. For if the judge
rules that this has been put in issue, he may allow the prosecution to bring in evidence of the accused's character including
his previous convictions. The other view is that it is quite unnecessary to know about the previous convictions in order to
safeguard the accused by warning him or his counsel of the
dangers, and it is better for the judge not to know of the
prisoner's record. Some judges said they made a point of not
looking at the information which was supplied to them about
the prisoner's record. It may well be that a change will be recommended in this matter. Perhaps it is better for justice to appear
to have been done by not supplying judges with this information until after conviction. Where there is a plea of guilty, the
question does not arise. The prosecution will outline the facts,
and the court will proceed straight to the sentence stage.

This part of the court's work has in the past too often been
performed rather hastily and inadequately, and on the basis of
insufficient or incomplete information. It was said by Professor
R. M. Jackson in 1953 that a criminal trial properly conducted
represents one of the finest products of English law, but this
statement only held good provided one walked out of court
before the sentencing stage. If the observer should stay to the
end of the proceedings, he might well find that it takes far less
time and inquiry to settle a man's prospects in life than it has
taken to find out whether he took a suitcase out of a parked
motor-car.[4]

Such a statement, while it contained an element of truth,
was more provocative than informative, and is certainly further
from the truth today that it was in 1953, for the modern court

---

4. R. M. Jackson, *The Machinery of Justice in England*, 2nd Edn., 1953. The statement is repeated in the 3rd Edn., 1960, p. 211. Professor Jackson also made the
same statement in his first edition of 1940.

often goes to very great lengths indeed to puzzle over a man's prospects in life and decide what is the best way of dealing with him. It is unfortunately still the case, however, that at a busy quarter sessions or magistrates' court, sentences are imposed on many cases in a very short space of time, and one cannot but marvel at the confidence of those who can find speedy and final answers to these difficult problems, final, that is, subject to the right of appeal. Better choices could undoubtedly be made if there were (a) more time, and (b) more information available.

THE STREATFEILD REPORT

The Interdepartmental Committee on the Business of the Criminal Courts, which reported in February 1961, was charged with the duty

"to review the present arrangements in England and Wales (a) for bringing to trial persons charged with criminal offences and (b) for providing the courts with the information necessary to enable them to select the most appropriate treatment for offenders. . . ."

THE ORGANISATION OF THE CRIMINAL COURTS

The Committee in the first part of the Report was largely concerned with the increasing pressure of business in the criminal courts, which was leading to long delays in bringing persons to trial at the higher criminal courts. It laid down the acceptable standards for the time taken in bringing persons to trial, being greatly assisted by the research which the Home Office Research Unit had done on Time Spent Awaiting Trial.[5] The Committee found that in nearly a quarter of the cases there was a waiting period of longer than eight weeks, and they regarded it as "indefensible" for so many to wait longer than twelve weeks and some more than sixteen weeks. Recent information suggests that delays of seven weeks or more are to be expected.[6] The Committee recommended various changes in the organisation of the higher criminal courts, most of which have been

---

5. Home Office, Studies in The Causes of Delinquency and The Treatment of Offenders, No. 2, "Time Spent Awaiting Trial", 1960.
6. H.C., Written Ans. Vol. 780, cols. 265 and 351, 25 March 1969, 27 March 1969. See also figures in the Beeching Report, Cmnd. 4153, September 1969.

implemented. But there is now once again mounting concern about the delays, and the long period spent awaiting trial, often with the accused person being detained in custody during this period. Thus it is said not to be unusual for a borstal boy to have spent four months in custody before reaching a training institution (two months awaiting trial, a month in the classification and allocation centre, and another month waiting for a place in the institution).[6A]

The Beeching Report (September 1969) made recommendations concerning the organisation of the work of the higher courts which, if they are accepted, will improve their efficiency.[7] Since the Streatfeild Report courts have been sitting more frequently, and with more judges, than ever before, but the continuing crime wave has made the situation very difficult for all concerned. This affects not only the provision of courts and judges, but the manning of courts by clerks and shorthand writers, and the availability and diligence of prosecutors and defence lawyers, as well as the police, on whom the main force of the crime wave falls.

We are not here concerned to spell out all the changes made in legal procedure and court organisation consequent upon Part A of the Streatfeild Report. The main changes were introduced by the Criminal Justice Administration Act 1962. We might simply note here that the Act provided that time spent by a prisoner in custody waiting for trial after committal by a magistrates' court was to be counted as time served in calculating the length of any sentence of imprisonment.[8]

Part B of the Streatfeild Report is of greater importance to our present theme, since it examined the arrangements for providing the courts with the information necessary for sentencing offenders, and made certain recommendations, many of which have since been implemented.

The Sentencing Task

This part of the Report is prefaced by a discussion of the aims of "sentencers", to use the new word coined by the Committee to describe persons vested with sentencing powers. Here, cer-

---

6A. See comments of the Recorder of Bath, *The Times*, 7 January 1970.
7. Report of the Royal Commission on Assizes and Quarter Sessions, 1966–69, Cmnd. 4153, September 1969 (The Beeching Report).
8. Criminal Justice Administration Act 1962, s. 17(2).

tain rather dogmatic assertions were made concerning the changes which have taken place in sentencing practice and in the aims of sentencers over the last few decades. It is said that:

> "Sentencing used to be a comparatively simple matter. The primary objective was to fix a sentence proportionate to the offender's culpability, and the system has been loosely described as the 'Tariff system'. The facts of the offence and the offender's record were the main pieces of information needed by the court, and the defence could bring to notice any mitigating circumstances. The information was about past events which could normally be reliably described; and it was readily available."[9]

Of course, the courts also have always borne in mind the need to protect society from the persistent offender, to deter potential offenders, and to deter or reform the individual offender, but the Committee says these were objectives which they could take in their stride, as it were, in following the "tariff system".[10]

The Report goes on to explain how courts have come to give increased weight to the needs of the offender as a person, and to examine his social and domestic background more closely. We are led to believe that the "tariff system" is giving way to a system of sentencing based far more on the offender's character and needs. This leads very properly to the conclusion that more information is necessary to enable the courts to carry out the much more complicated task now expected of them in regard to sentencing:

> "In short, sentencing is becoming a more complex task. In many cases, particularly those appearing at the superior courts, the court can still do little more than punish the offender for what he has done, and in every sentence the offender's culpability has to be taken into account. But in a considerable and growing number of cases the tariff system can no longer be relied on to fit all the considerations in the court's mind."[11]

While we have no deep quarrel with these statements, the impression may be gathered that the situation has changed more dramatically than it has, especially in the higher courts. It has been argued elsewhere by the author that the change which has taken place is not from a "tariff system" to one based

---

9. Report of the Interdepartmental Committee on the Business of the Criminal Courts, Cmnd. 1289, February 1961, p. 76, para. 257.
10. *Ibid.*, p. 76, para. 258.
11. *Ibid.*, p. 77, para. 262.

on the needs of the offender, but from a strict tariff system towards a modified tariff system, which recognises the need to
take into account the offender's previous record and the nature
and circumstances of the present offence, because justice requires this to be done, but which at the same time allows courts
to depart from tariff considerations where they decide that this
is a case for individualisation of the sentence to meet the particular needs of the offender.[12] Much nonsense is spoken about the
"tariff system" being backward-looking and therefore presumably not progressive, in so far as it is partly based on a
consideration of past events, in contrast to the reformative/
treatment-oriented system which is forward-looking and therefore regarded as progressive, because it is mainly concerned
with the future behaviour of the offender.[13] The fact is that the
past events may be the best guide to the future conduct of the
offender. Prediction studies suggest strongly that this is so.[14]
There is nothing necessarily retrogressive in considering the
whole of the offender's record together with all the facts and
circumstances of the offence when sentencing an offender.

Often it is the tariff which prevails. The offence is such and
the offender's record is so that the court does not feel able to
adopt any of the more individualised and reformative measures
available to it, such as probation, suspended sentence, discharge,
etc. Indeed, many offenders might be said to sentence themselves. For these there is little point in providing the courts with
elaborate case-histories and social background reports. Under
the present system it is clear that they are to be sent to a
custodial sentence, and the only question very often is to decide
for how long.

On the other hand, there are clearly many cases where the
court may feel able to depart from "tariff" considerations in
order to provide for the offender's mental treatment, or to give
him an opportunity to reform, or for some other reason, *e.g.*
the protection of society. A sentence of preventive detention

---

12. J. E. Hall Williams, "Sentencing in Transition", *Criminology in Transition,*
Essays in Honour of Hermann Mannheim, ed. T. Grygier, H. Jones, J. C.
Spencer, 1965, pp. 23 *et seq.*, especially p. 25.
13. See, for example, Barbara Wootton, "Contemporary Trends in Crime and Its
Treatment", The Nineteenth Clarke Hall Lecture, May 1959, especially at
pp. 16 *et seq.*
14. See, for example, H. Mannheim and Leslie T. Wilkins, *Prediction Methods in
Relation to Borstal Training*, 1955, and the Home Office pamphlet *The Sentence
of the Court*, 2nd Edn., 1969, p. 64.

was in the past viewed in this way as replacing the sentence indicated by the "tariff", so that a longer term would be justified. The concept of the "extended term" introduced by the Criminal Justice Act 1967 was necessitated by the desire to impose long terms of a preventive kind in circumstances where the sentence indicated by the "tariff" would be a term of much shorter duration.

The first task of any court in sentencing is to make up its mind how far this is a case where the tariff prevails. If it is, then there are fairly well-known rules to enable the right choice of sentence to be made. If it is a case for imprisonment, the rules suggest the maximum period, in the light of the legal nature of the offence. This maximum figure may not be exceeded even where it is the wish to protect society from the offender. Then the various mitigating factors must be considered, including age, previous good or bad record, the gap since any previous offence, and the role of the offender in relation to others involved in the crime, and his co-operation with the police and the prosecution, and his genuine repentance. In the light of these "mitigating" factors, the theoretical maximum for the offence may be reduced. But there may be other factors which the court has in mind, such as the need for a deterrent sentence, the position of the offender as a public official (stealing by a postman, burglary by a policeman) and the general crime situation in the neighbourhood.

If the alternative approach is adopted, and the offender is not to be sentenced on a "tariff" basis, then clearly the court will need a probation report and possibly other evidence in order to assist it in finding the best solution, in terms of the offender's needs and the prognosis of his behaviour. The aim now may be to discover what is most likely to stop this offender from offending again.[15]

The matter was well put by an experienced sentencer, in an unpublished paper, as follows:

"very largely, although not exclusively, the indications for a tariff sentence are the circumstances of the offence which establish its intrinsic gravity, assessed in terms of its danger to society; those for an individualised sentence are the circumstances personal to the offender, which constitute the criteria for assessing the

---

15. The Hon. Sir Roger Ormerod, "The Developing Relations Between The Law and The Social Sciences", *B.J.C.*, Vol. 4, No. 4, April 1964, p. 320, at p. 328.

likely effectiveness of the various alternative courses available. Because these two sets of criteria are intrinsically so different, . . . it is necessary, in cases where the tariff indications are not overwhelming, to treat the answer (in favour of a tariff sentence) as a provisional one, and to review it in the light of the offender's personal circumstances in order to see whether the latter are such that a tariff sentence can and should be avoided. This, in turn, may well mean weighing the likely effect of a number of individualised sentences, both upon the offender and upon the public, before the first question is finally resolved."[16]

The same source goes on to explain how in practice these separate questions will frequently become merged with one another so that a judge will frequently answer them both without detailed step-by-step consideration.

Before leaving this topic, one matter calls for discussion, viz. whether the different sentencing aims can always be satisfactorily harmonised when they are in conflict. Different views have been expressed about this. The Streatfeild Report recognises that sentencers have to resolve competing claims and that one objective may suggest a different sentence from another.[17] The courts adopt a philosophy of compromise rather than of synthesis, as Nigel Walker has pointed out.[18] In this compromise it may sometimes be possible to harmonise the conflicting claims satisfactorily. A sentence which is tariff-based and deters others may also serve to meet the needs of the offender and promote his reform. But too often the different approaches cannot be reconciled as they point to totally different sentences.[19] Then the courts have to choose, and it is here that there is so much room for differences between judges and between different courts.

It will be seen that to judge the success of sentences in terms of the question whether the offender is reconvicted may be to ignore the question whether his sentence was designed and intended to prevent further offences. Sometimes the intention is neither preventive nor rehabilitative: often the kind of human flotsam washed up in the reception wings of our prisons is prognostically the least hopeful material, and these offenders

---

16. An experienced sentencer in an unpublished paper, September 1969.
17. Report of the Interdepartmental Committee on the Business of the Criminal Courts, Cmnd. 1289, February 1961, p. 77, para. 260.
18. Nigel Walker, *Crime and Punishment in Britain*, 2nd Edn., 1968, p. 223.
19. D. A. Thomas, "Theories of Punishment in the Court of Criminal Appeal", (September 1964) 27 *M.L.R.* 546, at p. 563.

are not sent there in order that the prisons may reform them and with little hope they will be deterred. It speaks highly of the dedication and determination of many of the prison staff that they look so optimistically upon their charges, but there would be no great harm in a frank recognition by the community (including the community of prison and penal reformers) that in many cases reform is not the purpose for which prisoners have been sent to prison. A realistic appraisal of the situation would be beneficial for all concerned.

INFORMATION FOR THE COURTS

It should be clear from what has been said that in order to discharge their sentencing responsibilities today courts need much more information than they had in the past. Moreover, this information must be comprehensive, reliable and relevant, as the Streatfeild Report said.[20] Over the years, the arrangements for collecting and feeding this information to the courts developed in a more or less haphazard fashion, empirically and piecemeal.[1] The Report recommended that a more systematic approach should be adopted, and outlined various steps which could be taken to improve the situation. We shall summarise these recommendations, and indicate how far they have been implemented.

(1) Pre-Trial Reports

The committee considered that more use should be made of the practice of obtaining probation reports and other information about the offender prior to the trial itself, particularly where the superior courts were concerned, since in those courts sentence has to follow immediately or soon after the finding of guilt, and "the collection of the information needed cannot wait until the court decides what it wants".[2] If the necessary information were available at the trial, post-conviction adjournments would be kept to a minimum, but where they were necessary, it should be made easier for them to be ordered.[3]

---

20. Report of the Interdepartmental Committee on the Business of the Criminal Courts, Cmnd. 1289, February 1961, p. 84, para. 292; Recommendation (9)(e).
1. *Ibid.*, p. 77, para. 265.
2. *Ibid.*, p. 88, para. 309.
3. *Ibid.*, pp. 89–90, paras. 314–320.

The probation service should be permitted to make enquiries about a person accused of an offence before conviction, provided that the accused person is given the opportunity to object and does not do so. In the event that he does object, there may be a delay after conviction before sentence can be imposed, but this possibility should not be held over his head when he is given the opportunity to object.[4]

Many probation officers feel uneasy about the pre-trial report on the ground that it is an invasion of the presumption of innocence, and may prejudice any future relationship should the accused be convicted and placed on probation. These arguments are considered by the Streatfeild Committee but were not found to be persuasive.

The Committee recommended that a probation report should be available in the following cases:

1. Where the defendant has not previously been convicted of an offence punishable with imprisonment;
2. Where the defendant is not over 30 years old;
3. Where the defendant has recently been in touch with the probation service, *e.g.* on probation or for aftercare.

These categories should be regarded as minimum categories, to which individual courts might wish to add.

These recommendations were brought into effect by a Home Office circular, as from 1 August 1963.[5] They have now been extended by virtue of the Criminal Justice Act 1967, s. 57, under which further Home Office circulars were issued in August 1968.[6]

The courts are now recommended to obtain a social enquiry report as a normal practice in the case of any offender aged 17 or over, before sentencing to any sentence in the following categories:

1. Detention in a detention centre;
2. Borstal training;
3. A sentence of imprisonment of two years or less, imposed on an offender who has not received a previous sentence of imprisonment or borstal training. "Imprisonment" here includes a suspended sentence;

---

4. *Ibid.*, pp. 99–100, paras. 353, 355.　　　5. Home Office Circular No. 84/1963.
6. Home Office Circular No. 189/1968. Home Office Circular No. 188/1968 relates to reports in the magistrates' courts. See Cmnd. 4233, December 1969, p. 30.

4. Any sentence of imprisonment on a woman.

With regard to persons under the age of 17 who appear before higher courts, the Circular points out that normally the courts will have available a social enquiry report made under the existing arrangements for a person of that age. But the courts should not impose a sentence of borstal training or make an approved school order, a fit person order, or a detention centre order in respect of a person under 17 without considering a social enquiry report.

The Home Office Circular points out that most of those mentioned in the list above will already be the subject of pre-trial reports under the existing arrangements. The only categories which are added effectively to the previous list are:

1. Men over 30 who have one or more previous convictions but have not received a previous custodial sentence, and for whom the court has in mind a sentence of two years imprisonment or less;
2. Women over 30 who have one or more previous convictions of an offence punishable with imprisonment.

These new arrangements were to apply from 1 October 1968.

Probation officers and administrators had been consulted about the desirability of these innovations and had agreed to co-operate. Nevertheless there is an undercurrent of opinion among persons in the field that much time is wasted preparing reports for courts who then do not use them properly.[7] Research is now beginning to throw some light on the value of reports to the courts and the use the courts make of them.[8]

(2) Contents of the Reports, and Co-ordination of Information

The Streatfeild Committee recommended that steps should be taken to co-ordinate the information supplied to the court for the purpose of sentencing. The police should supply the probation officer with an advance copy of the antecedents

---

7. F. V. Jarvis, "Inquiry before Sentence", in *Criminology in Transition*, Essays in honour of Hermann Mannheim, ed. T. Grygier, J. C. Spencer, H. Jones, 1965, p. 43.
8. See John Hogarth, "Sentencing Research—Some Problems of Design" (January 1967), 7 *B.J.C.*, No. 1, p. 84; Roger Hood and Ian Taylor "Second Report of the Study of the Effectiveness of Pre-Sentence Investigations in Reducing Recidivism" (October 1968), 8 *B.J.C.*, No. 4, pp. 431 *et seq.* See also Roger Hood (July 1966) 6 *B.J.C.*, No. 3, p. 303.

report, and the probation officer should avoid' so far as is possible, duplicating the police enquiries or repeating information.[9] Reports should be supplied to the court at least 24 hours before the hearing.[10] The liaison probation officer at the court should be promptly notified whenever a person is committed for trial or sentence[11]. The probation service should supply all the information they can about the offender and his background which is relevant to his culpability and his reform. They should be free to express an opinion as to the likely effect of probation or some other form of sentence.[12]

Administrative arrangements have been introduced to implement the recomendations about the content of the reports so far as possible. The intention is to submit a composite report, assembled from various sources. The police supply information about the accused's criminal record, if any, the prison governor assesses his suitability for particular types of custodial sentence, and the probation officer will be concerned to give the court full information about the offender's personal history and characteristics.[13]

(3) Confidentiality of the Report

There has been much discussion in Britain and America concerning the question whether the contents of a probation report should be revealed to the offender.[14] The attitude of English law is that a copy of the report must be supplied to the offender or his legal representative, but this does not mean that the contents of the report need be revealed in open court. The Streatfeild Report affirmed this policy, and said that it is for the court to decide, in the interests of justice, what parts, if any, of a written report should be read aloud in open court.[15]

---

9. Report of the Interdepartmental Committee on the Business of the Criminal Courts, Cmnd. 1289, February 1961, p. 95, para. 338, and Recommendations, p. 124.
10. *Ibid.*, pp. 102 and 103, paras. 367 and 369, and Recommendations p. 124.
11. *Ibid.*, p. 103, para. 371, and Recommendations, p. 124.
12. *Ibid.*, paras. 335 and 344. But the Morison Committee doubted this: Cmnd. 1650, pp. 15–18.
13. Home Office Circular No. 84/1963.
14. See for example, Sol Rubin, "What Privacy for Pre-Sentence Reports?" (December 1952), 16 *Federal Probation*, 8: Chute and Bell, *Crime, Courts and Probation*, 1956, pp. 149–151.
15. Report of the Interdepartmental Committee on the Business of the Criminal Courts, Cmnd. 1289, February 1961, p. 118, para. 426.

In the juvenile courts, since 1933, it has been provided that any parts of the report bearing on the person's character or conduct which is material to the court's decision should be explained to the offender, and the parent or guardian likewise must be told of those matters and additionally must be informed of the substance of any comments upon his own character or conduct, as well as the home surroundings, and the health of the child concerned. Both child and parent or guardian have the opportunity to dispute the information in the report if they wish.[16]

F. V. Jarvis comments on the conflict of interests involved in these situations, as follows:

"It is clearly in the interest of the accused that he should not be sentenced upon information about which he knows nothing and which he therefore cannot challenge. It is also clearly in the public interest that justice should not only be done but be seen to be done. On the other hand, it is not in the child's interest to hear in detail the inadequacies of his home and the deficiencies of his parents. Nor is it usually in his interests to hear opinions as to his physical and mental disabilities and the prospects of their treatment. . . . There are some who think that the legislature in permitting written reports which are not read out and limiting the matters which need to be conveyed to the accused, has defiled the pure stream of English criminal procedure. Others, however, think that the legislature has acted in the light of common sense."[17]

As to the desirable practice in the matter, the Court of Appeal recently condemned as undesirable the practice of insisting that the whole report be read out in criminal cases.[18]

(4) Submission of the Report

The report is supplied to the court and not to the defendant or his legal representative, and it is the officer of the court, not the probation officer, who has the responsibility of supplying the defendant or his legal representative with a copy. This serves to emphasise that the report is made for the court and not for the defence.[19]

---

16. Summary Jurisdiction (Children and Young Persons) Rules 1933, rule 11.
17. F. V. Jarvis, "Inquiry before Sentence", in *Criminology in Transition*, ed. T. Grygier, J. C. Spencer, H. Jones, pp. 56–57.
18. *R.* v. *Smith* (1967), 111 Sol. Jo. 850. See also Joan F. S. King, *The Probation Service*, 3rd Edn., 1969, p. 193.
19. Joan F. S. King, *The Probation Service*, 2nd Edn., 1964, p. 193.

The law requiring copies of any reports to be made available to the defence is limited in its terms to probation reports, but the same general policy applies to medical and other reports received by the court. Sometimes, as in the case of a court receiving evidence relating to the use of its powers under Part V of the Mental Health Act 1959, special rules apply as to the manner in which the evidence may be received.

Prison governors are expected to supply reports to the courts in some cases, though the occasions where this is required are now less frequent than previously. In the past, all persons eligible for preventive detention, corrective training or borstal training were the subject of a suitability report from the remand prison if they were remanded in custody. Following publication of the Streatfeild Report, the opportunity was taken to limit the obligation of prison governors to prepare pre-trial reports. Prison governors are now expected to prepare pre-trial reports only on those who are eligible for borstal training AND have previously served a custodial sentence.[20] Of course, nothing precludes the courts remanding an offender in custody in order that a report should be prepared on him by the prison authorities, and the figures show that many cases are so remanded annually. (See Chapter 5: The Use the Courts Make of Prison.) The appeal court hearing an appeal against a sentence of borstal training expects to receive a report from the prison authorities as to where the applicant is in custody, and whether or not he has commenced training, and if he has, the date upon which the training commenced.[1] The court also desires to receive an up-to-date probation report and a report from the borstal governor or housemaster.[2]

The Streatfeild Report contained some discussion of prison governors' reports to courts, and what they should contain. Once again it is emphasised, as with probation reports, that the prison governor's opinion about the likely effects of any particular form of sentence should be welcomed provided it is based on experience and what is known about the results of research studies, etc. The prison governor's opinion, since it will only relate to the likelihood of the sentence diverting the offender from crime, cannot be said to be usurping the court's

20. F. V. Jarvis, *loc. cit.*, p. 49.
1. *R.* v. *Harris (Trevor)*, Practice Note [1969] 1 W.L.R. 1302.
2. *R.* v. *Weekes (Ricardo)*, Practice Note [1969] 1 W.L.R. 403.

function since it will not purport to cover the other possible considerations in the court's mind.[3]

(5) A Handbook on Sentencing for the Courts

The Streatfeild Report recommended that a booklet on sentencing should be prepared, describing the different types of penal treatment available and dealing with every form of sentence, what it involves, what it is designed to achieve, and what it in fact achieves, together with information about research into the results of sentences.[4] The first booklet was published in April 1964 under the title *The Sentence of the Court*. A revised edition was published in 1969, and it represents a very useful short manual or handbook. If it is somewhat disappointing concerning research findings, this is mainly because of the paucity of material. We know very little indeed about the results of what we are doing in sentencing offenders.

(6) Other Steps for Informing Judges

The Streatfeild Report recommended that there should be machinery whereby a sentencer periodically can obtain reports about the progress of particular offenders in whom he is interested.[5] Arrangements have now been made for sentencers to be supplied with such information on request, but it is understood that very few requests are in fact received. We are reminded on Lady Wootton's metaphor that sentencers were like children patiently and conscientiously working out sums with no one to check the answers.[6] Now that the opportunity has been provided to check at least some of the answers, sentencers ought to be willing, if not eager, to find out exactly what happened to some of their more interesting and difficult cases.

Another means by which sentencers may be informed concerning their sentencing duties is by making visits to penal and

---

3. Cmnd. 1289, p. 107, para. 382. In the past, some courts resented the making o recommendations by prison governors with regard to the choice of sentence See report in *The Evening News*, 18 November 1958, "Prison Chiefs are Attacked by Court: Don't Try to Do Our Job".
4. P. 86, para. 299, and Recommendation (10), p. 123.
5. P. 87, paras. 304–305.
6. Barbara Wootton, *Contemporary Trends in Crime and Its Treatment*, The Nineteenth Clarke Hall Lecture, May 1959, p. 18.

other institutions, and the Streatfeild Report recommended that all sentencers, and in particular those newly appointed, should be reminded that such visits are important and that the necessary facilities are readily available.[7] Yet again, although these facilities exist, there seems to be a noticeable reluctance on the part of sentencers to take advantage of them. It is good to learn that the Bar Council is now taking steps to enable members of the bar exercising judicial functions in a part-time capacity to make visits to penal institutions, as well as engaging in "extended discussions" at week-end meetings.

THE SENTENCING DECISION

The actual sentencing decision is taken after the court has received the police antecedents report,[8] the oral testimony of police and the probation officer, if necessary, and any other special reports. The choice before the court is fixed in two ways. Firstly, the law prescribes in a general way the limits within which the sentence is to be fixed, and defines the powers available to the sentencer. In some cases it leaves no discretion to the court, as where the penalty is fixed by law. This is so in murder, in some road traffic offences where compulsory disqualification applies, and in some minor regulatory offences where a fixed penalty applies.[9] Usually, however, the law confers a wide discretion on the court within a stated maximum penalty, a period of so many years' imprisonment or a fine of a certain amount. The court is then free to choose, within the stated maximum, and it need not impose any penalty at all, and if it prefers it may place the offender on probation or give him an absolute or conditional discharge. Where the law permits a sentence of imprisonment, it is not the practice for the law to specify a minimum sentence. English law knows the minimum sentence only in connection with young offenders and offences against the Official Secrets Act.[10] Magistrates' courts have

---

7. P. 87, para. 302.
8. For details concerning the police antecedents report, see Streatfeild Report, pp. 92–94, paras. 326–331.
9. A good example is the penalty for pulling the communication cord in a train without reasonable cause.
10. For example, Borstal training (minimum six months), detention centre orders (minimum three months, exceptionally one month for youth of school age), and approved school orders (see Chapter 28).

limited powers when sentencing offenders, which affect the maximum period of imprisonment or fine, and in some circumstances, under the Criminal Justice Act 1967, the sentence of imprisonment *must* be suspended. All courts are supposed to avoid sending young offenders under 21 and first offenders to prison if there is some reasonable alternative.[11]

The second restraint upon the powers of sentencers, which applies particularly in the superior courts, where the trial has taken place before a jury, is that the jury, by their verdict concerning the category of offence or offences which they find proved, have to some extent controlled or circumscribed the powers of the sentencing judge. For the judge can only sentence to the penalties appropriate to the category of offence which has been found proved. For example, the jury may have decided that a person accused of murder is guilty only of manslaughter, for various reasons such as provocation, diminished responsibility, etc. The sentencer then has to choose his sentence accordingly. Another example would be a charge of a serious offence of wounding where the verdict is guilty of a less serious offence of wounding (Offences against the Person Act 1861, ss. 18 and 20). Where the same body decides both the question of guilt and fixes the sentence, as in the magistrates' court, there is not such a serious restraint.

There are certain rather curious but logical rules about the sentence which may be imposed for attempt or conspiracy, which provide limits on the court's sentencing power. Thus a person cannot be sentenced for attempt to a sentence greater than the maximum for the completed crime which he has attempted.[12] The same rule applies in conspiracy except in special circumstances.[13]

Subject to these restraints, the sentencing court is free to choose whatever sentence it pleases, subject only to limitations imposed by the principles of punishment spelled out in decided cases and the generally accepted conventions governing sentencing. The sentence may be reviewed on appeal, however, and in English law this provides, at least in respect of the superior courts, a substantial measure of control over bad sentencing decisions. However, the power of the Court of Appeal, in deal-

---

11. Criminal Justice Act 1948, s. 17; First Offenders Act 1958.
12. Criminal Law Act 1967, s. 7 (2).
13. *Verrier* v *Director of Public Prosecutions*, [1967] 2 A.C. 195; [1966] 3 All E.R. 568.

ing with sentence appeals from courts of quarter sessions and assizes, is limited to cases where the original sentence appears to have been wrong in principle.

A TREATMENT TRIBUNAL?

There are many who believe that the judge is not the best person to decide what to do with the offender, and even if he were, the necessary information cannot be made available at the time of the trial, as careful and prolonged study of the offender may be necessary. So it is suggested that the whole business of making decisions about the sentence should be transferred to a body of "experts", sitting as a tretment tribunal.

This idea has a fairly long pedigree,[14] but in recent years it has gathered weight and been supported by eminent scholars. Professor Rupert Cross[15] has argued that all sentences over five years should be indeterminate, and Dr. Nigel Walker[16] has said that judges should be limited to deciding whether the sentence should be custodial or non-custodial, leaving it to others to decide, in the case of a custodial sentence, where and for how long the offender should be detained and under what conditions.

These are very attractive and seductive arguments, and this is not the place to consider their full implications.[17] We may merely note that in the United States some jurisdictions, in particular the state of California, have entrusted decisions about the length of penitentiary sentences to a sentencing board, called the Adult Authority, which also decides on the date of a prisoner's parole. In the juvenile offender field, the Youth Authority in California is an example of a more comprehensive transfer of power over an offender to an administrative board.[18] These experiments are of great interest, but so far have attracted few imitators. Although there are some in Britain who favour

---

14. Hermann Mannheim suggested it in *The Dilemma of Penal Reform*, 1939; see also Leo Page, *The Sentence of the Court*, 1948.
15. Rupert Cross, "Indeterminate Prison Sentences" (15 February 1962), 67 *The Listener* 289 *et seq.*
16. Nigel Walker, "The Sentence of the Court" (28 June 1962), 67 *The Listener* 1099 *et seq.* See now his *Sentencing in a Rational Society*, 1969.
17. For the author's views, see "Alternatives to Definite Sentences" (January 1964), 80 L.Q.R. 41.
18. See Paul W. Tappan, *Crime, Justice and Correction*, 1960, Chapter 16, "Improving the Dispositions Process".

some partial transfer of decision-making power in regard to sentence to an administrative body, so far there is little general support for such drastic innovations. If they come, it is more likely to be in the field of young adult offenders (17–21 or over) where it has already been suggested that there should be special courts dealing with the sentencing problems,[19] and some would like to see a new department to deal with youth problems.[20]

COURTS TO GIVE REASONS FOR SENTENCE

A minimum reform which seems to be called for is that courts should give reasons for their sentence decisions. This not only accords with civil law practice and the rules of natural justice but seems to be a beneficial requirement, leading to greater rationalisation of sentencing practice. As the Franks Committee put it (dealing with administrative tribunals and their decisions):

> "a decision is apt to be better if the reasons for it have to be set out in writing because the reasons are then more likely to have been properly thought out."[1]

This idea is supported by Professor Rupert Cross, Dr. Nigel Walker and D. A. Thomas, and was favoured by Dr. Mannheim.[2] There seems to be no great difficulty about insisting on courts giving reasons for their sentence choices. The law of Israel so provides.[3] What is important is that we should not imagine that this would necessarily reveal or cure defects in sentencing practice. Such research as has been done on the reasons for magistrates' decisions does not exactly hold out much hope in this direction.[4]

---

19. Hermann Mannheim, *Courts for Adolescents*, I.S.T.D. pamphlet, 1958; Labour Party's Study Group, "Crime—A Challenge to Us All", June 1964, pp. 26–27; Home Office, "The Child, The Family and The Young Offender", Cmnd. 2742, August 1965, p. 10.
20. At present the responsibility is divided between the Prison Department and the Children's Department in the Home Office, and the Ministry of Education.
1. Report of the Committee on Administrative Tribunals and Inquiries, Cmnd. 218 (1957); Tribunals and Inquiries Act 1958, s. 12.
2. H. Mannheim, "Some Aspects of Judicial Sentencing Policy" (May 1958), 67 *Yale L. J.*, No. 6, p. 981; Rupert Cross "Paradoxes in Prison Sentences" (April 1965), 81 *L.Q.R.* 205, at pp. 212 *et seq.*; D. A. Thomas, "Sentencing—The Case for Reasoned Decisions", [1963] Crim.L.R. 243; Nigel Walker, *Crime and Punishment in Britain*, 2nd Edn., 1968, p. 231.
3. David Reifen (October 1962), 3 *B.J.C.*, 130, at p. 139.
4. Roger Hood and Ian Taylor, "Second Report of the Study of the Effectiveness of Pre-Sentence Investigations in Reducing Recidivism" (October 1968), 8 *B.J.C.*, No. 4, pp. 431 *et seq.* See also Eric Stockdale, *The Court and the Offender*, 1967, pp. 200–201.

REVISION OF SENTENCES

A better solution to the problem of sentencing might be found in easier procedures for the revision and reassessment of sentences after a certain period.[5] The latest proposed solution to the sentencing problem is that all sentences of custody should be made provisional in the first instance. The American Law Institute's Draft Model Penal Code provides that every sentence for felony shall be provisional for one year. In that time the Commissioner of Correction may if he wishes petition the Court to resentence the offender. This applies where he is satisfied that the original sentence is based on a misapprehension as to the history, character, physical or mental condition of the offender. The Court may resentence an offender to any sentence which might have been imposed originally, whether greater or less.[6]

The idea that there should be some procedure to correct wrong choices of sentence apart from the normal avenue of redress by way of appeal by the prisoner is an attractive one. It has found some support in the Labour Party, where Leslie Hale, M.P., and Niall MacDermot, M.P., suggested that all first and second prison sentences should be reviewed after a time, during which there would be a full diagnostic investigation at a special remand centre. A Review Board would then have to confirm the sentence or substitute a lesser sentence.[7]

One solution would be a Sentence Review Board, to which both the prisoner and the authorities could refer the case after an initial period of, say, six or twelve months in custody. This would only apply to long sentences of, say, twelve months or more. The parallel case of the Mental Health Review Tribunals offers a possible model for this type of development.

---

5. See the author's article, "Alternatives to Definite Sentences" (January 1964), 80 *L.Q.R.* 41.
6. The American Law Institute, Model Penal Code, May 1962, Section 7.08.
7. House of Commons Debates, Vol. 687, cols. 1352 *et seq.*: Mr. Leslie Hale, M.P., at col. 1382, Mr. Niall MacDermot, M.P., at col. 1384.

PART II

Imprisonment for Adults

CHAPTER 3

The History of Imprisonment

It is not proposed to do more than provide a brief sketch of the history of imprisonment in England and Wales. Others have covered the subject adequately, and the story of the eighteenth- and nineteenth-century penal reformers is well known.[1] The history of imprisonment may be considered in relation to three periods of time:

1. Up to 1898;
2. 1898 to 1948;
3. 1948 to the present day.

1 UP TO 1898

It has been the fashion to begin any historical account of imprisonment by pointing out that prisons were originally simply places for holding suspects pending investigation and trial, and they were not used as places of punishment under sentence. Sentences were mainly physical in character, involving execution, banishment, branding or mutilation. The Roman law appears to have regarded prison as simply a place of safe custody not a place of punishment, and some of this philosophy carried over to England and is reflected in the writings of Bracton. But recent historical research has revealed that in Saxon times prison was used coercively if not punitively, but as a penal sanction it had marginal significance, and to a modern observer the significant thing would be the absence of prison as punishment.[2]

"From Henry II's time conditions began to alter", we are told in Professor Pugh's important study.[3] "The prisons main-

---

1. The best accounts are to be found in M. Grunhut, *Penal Reform: A Comparative Study*, 1948; Sir Lionel Fox, *The English Prison and Borstal Systems*, 1952; R. S. E. Hinde, *The British Penal System 1773–1950*, 1951. See also T. Sellin, *Pioneering in Penology*, 1944; D. L. Howard, *The English Prisons, their Past and Future*, 1960.
2. Ralph B. Pugh, *Imprisonment in Medieval England*, 1968.
3. *Ibid.*, pp. 385–386.

tained by the King's own officers multiplied, while the crown did nothing to restrict the continuance of prisons" kept by lay barons enjoying franchises. These "liberty" prisons seem to wither away towards the end of the thirteenth century, but municipal and ecclesiastical prisons appeared to take their place. They were used coercively and as places of punishment, and statute law and municipal regulation began to provide authority for punishment, hitherto derived from the prerogative power.

Prisons were essentially local places, and there were to be found in them persons of all ages and both sexes, in conditions of great squalor and degradation. Men, women and children, debtors and murderers, mingled freely, and extensive corruption and exploitation was practised. "Prison was not intended to be barbarous", says Professor Pugh, but "it was nevertheless intended to be nasty".[4] Although some efforts were made to maintain and even improve standards, and the Elizabethans in the latter part of the sixteenth century tried to provide an alternative method of punishment, the position by the late eighteenth century was appalling, and led to John Howard's disclosures and to the beginning of serious reform efforts.

The Elizabethan alternative was the House of Correction. Although originally not intended for criminals but for vagrants, and idle persons, it came to be run side by side with the common gaols and provided work for the prisoners in much better conditions than anything which had been available hitherto. The first Bridewell was opened in 1552 in the palace of that name given by Edward VI to the city of London, situated near to Blackfriars Bridge. Within less than a hundred years the experiment had failed, and Acts were passed incorporating the bridewells in the prison system.[5]

John Howard wrote his famous book, *The State of the Prisons*, in 1777. He spent his whole life travelling in England and on the Continent visiting gaols and writing about the conditions he discovered. The story of corruption and filth which he

---

4. *Ibid.*, pp. 388.
5. Fox, pp. 24–25. In 1961 a Ministry of Housing and Local Government Inquiry heard an appeal by the governors of the Bridewell Royal Hospital (now a charity) against the refusal of the City of London to permit erection of offices and shops. The corporation's reason for refusing the application was that the buildings to be demolished were of historical interest. If the site were now cleared the historic atmosphere of the site would be lost for ever. *The Times*, 16 February 1961.

revealed led to reforms which eventually included taking all prisons out of local control, and placing them in the care of the central administration. Ever since, our prison system has suffered from excessive centralisation which it is only now learning to overcome.

The increasing use of capital punishment did little to alleviate the state of the prisons. Its application was capricious and of marginal significance. Even adding indignities and further suffering to the mode of execution did not reduce the number of offences.[6]

It was left for the authorities to develop and to mould prison as a deterrent and reformative instrument. Signs of a trend in this direction were found in some of the early houses of correction, especially on the continent of Europe. Beccaria's essay "On Crimes and Punishments" in 1764 "stirred the penal systems of Europe"[7] and Jeremy Bentham began his ceaseless fight for better conditions and a more rational use of punishment.[8] Elizabeth Fry began her famous prison visits at the beginning of the nineteenth century.[9]

Certain marginal improvements resulted from this pressure. Segregation of the sexes was assured and sanitation was improved. A paid staff was employed under the supervision of the local magistrates. Chaplains were appointed, and efforts were made to provide work for prisoners.[10] But administrative inertia and the reactionary mood of the general public prevented great changes until later.

Meanwhile transportation had been introduced and was widely used for prisoners as an alternative to the death penalty. At first this was to America, but following the Declaration of Independence the prisoners were confined in old ships or hulks lying in the mouth of the Thames. In 1784 transportation to Australia began, and this system endured for nearly eighty years. All further transportation was forbidden in 1857 and the system ended in 1867, but not before Australia had become the scene of the most enlightened and daring penal experiments. The progressive stage system and early release on parole have their origins in the work of Sir George Arthur and Sir Alexander

6. Fox, pp. 22–23.
7. Fox, p. 26.
8. Fox, p. 31.
9. Fox, p. 28.
10. Fox, pp. 26–27.

Maconochie, the latter while he was in charge of the famous penal colony on Norfolk Island, in the Pacific off the Australian coast.[11]

The ending of transportation necessitated the building of new convict prisons in England. Following the building of Pentonville in 1842, fifty-four new prisons were built in six years under the inspired leadership of Major (later Colonel) Jebb,[12] and they have endured to this day and look like being with us for the rest of the twentieth century. Prison design became standardised on the basis of three-tier wings radiating from a central control point—a development of Bentham's Panopticon idea which still appeals to many prison officers as more practical than much present-day prison design.

Penal servitude to be served in convict prisons was substituted for transportation, the convicts having more privileges than ordinary prisoners, but being released on licence and subject to supervision and recall, a variant of the old "ticket-of-leave" system of the days of transportation. Local prisons remained essentially a local responsibility until they were brought under central control and "nationalised" in 1877. But inspectors of prisons were appointed in 1835, and, starting with Peel's reforms, consolidating legislation was passed, in 1823 and 1865.[13] The prison system was to be based on reform through deterrence, "hard labour, hard fare and a hard bed", to use the phrase of the House of Lords Committee of 1863.[14] Their report reflected the stern Victorian morality which saw in punishment something redemptive as well as retributive.

Meanwhile since 1850 the convict prisons had been brought under the administrative control of a Director of Convict Prisons, and new prisons at Portland and Dartmoor had replaced the old hulks.

In the period between 1790 and 1825 there had been considerable argument over the merits of the separate system of confinement as opposed to the system of classified association. This was eventually resolved by Peel's Gaol Act in favour of classified association, which system remained in force until the

---

11. Fox, pp. 31 *et seq.* The story of transportation is to be found in the *Encyclopaedia Britannica.* See also J. V. Barry, *Alexander Maconochie of Norfolk Island: a study of a pioneer in penal reform,* 1958.

12. Fox, p. 38.

13. See R. S. E. Hinde, *The British Penal System,* 1951.

14. Fox, p. 46.

Prison Act 1835. There followed a further period of argument concerning the relative merits of the separate system as against the silent system, which was finally resolved, in favour of the separate system, by the House of Lords Committee of 1865. But elements of the silent system were grafted on to the separate system, so that we can hardly see the difference. What is quite clear, however, is that the English penal system rejected solitary confinement except as a punishment, and developed a mixture of the separate and silent systems.

The separate system permitted a degree of freedom of association in work and chapel, but with severe restrictions such as separate exercise yards, and boxes or cubicles in the prison chapel in which the prisoners were placed when attending divine service. Relics of both of these features are to be seen today in various old prisons, *e.g.* Trenton, New Jersey. The silent system, sometimes known as the Auburn System, from the name of the New York state prison where it was first invented, involved separate cells for the prisoners for sleeping, but association in workshops and leisure activities, subject to the strict rule that silence be maintained, and various other indignities such as turning to face the wall when visitors passed by. It is only recently that the rule forbidding prisoners to converse with one another in workshops (a relic of the silent system) was finally abolished. There are prisoners today who will tell you how they removed their false teeth so as to be better able to talk to one another without the prison warder's noticing.

In what Sir Lionel Fox has termed "the battle of the systems",[15] we must not lose sight of the "Irish system", so named because it was developed by Sir Walter Crofton in Ireland in 1854–1862. This involved the use of progressive stages in the sentence, through which the prisoner could pass, earning corresponding privileges, until his eventual release on licence. Under this system some prisoners were employed in circumstances of considerable freedom from supervision. The influence of the early Australian experiments was evident here.[16]

English prisons were run on the basis of a combination of the separate system, and the progressive stage system, for many years, the latter being particularly noticeable in connection with

---

15. Fox, pp. 32 *et seq.*
16. Fox, p. 45.

the régime for preventive detention prisoners (abolished in 1967) and borstal training. It is a somewhat chilling thought that so much of what we do today in so-called modern treatment and training of prisoners had been anticipated if not prescribed by the early nineteenth-century penal administrators.

Hard labour and strict conditions led to an outcry in 1895. The whole responsibility for prison administration had been transferred to a central board as from 1 April 1878. The first chairman of this board, which was known as the Prison Commission, was Edmund du Cane, who superintended the system so rigorously and meticulously that, to use Sir Lionel Fox's memorable passage:

> "the lights that had been lit in Newgate by Elizabeth Fry, on Norfolk Island by Captain Maconochie, and at Portland by Colonel Jebb, went out: for twenty years our prisons presented the pattern of deterrence by severity of punishment, uniformly, rigidly and efficiently applied. For death itself the system had substituted a living death."[17]

The Gladstone Committee, set up in 1895, to inquire into complaints against the prison administration, marked the end of an era, and provided a Report which, as Sir Lionel Fox puts it, "remains the foundation stone of the contemporary prison system".[18] Reading the Report today it is difficult to appreciate how courageous and radical were the recommendations and the general approach adopted, but it is a surprisingly modern view which echoes through its dreary pages.[19]

The main objection to the system previously operating, in the Committee's view, was its excessive uniformity in treating offenders. Much more elasticity was called for, more adaptation to the needs of individual prisoners, more effort at training and rehabilitation. The Committee's emphasis on reclamation of prisoners, says Fox, "was not incompatible with the maintenance of the deterrent aspect of imprisonment".[20]

Henceforth the twin concepts of deterrence and training and treatment of the offender were seen to provide the framework within which the penal system could develop and grow to meet the needs of society and the prisoners. The Prison Act of 1898

17. Fox, p. 51.
18. Fox, p. 53.
19. Report from the Departmental Committee on Prisons, c. 7702, 1895.
20. Fox, p. 54.

placed more power in the hands of the Prison Commission to determine the details of policy,[1] and this trend has been followed in more recent legislation, as we shall see.

2 1898–1948

After the Act of 1898, as Sir Lionel Fox says, "the legislative way was now wide open to the realisation of a prison system in which deterrence and reform should be primary and concurrent objects".[2] Du Cane retired and his place was taken by Ruggles-Brise, and during his period as chairman of the Prison Commission steady progress was made in implementing the Gladstone Committee's views, and a number of important innovations took place, such as the introduction of borstal training, some attempt at classification of prisoners, and changes in details of the prison régime. Nevertheless, by 1921, when Ruggles-Brise retired, the system was once again subjected to fierce and well-informed criticism, and had become rigid and remote and unnecessarily harsh.[3]

The Hobhouse/Brockway report of the Prison System Enquiry Committee in 1922 concluded that "making every allowance for the slow and cautious development by the Commissioners of certain recommendations of the Gladstone Committee, the principles and effects of their régime were scarcely distinguishable from those of the du Cane régime".[4]

A fresh impetus towards reform came with the appointment of Sir Alexander Paterson to be one of the Prison Commissioners (he was never chairman). Maurice Waller took the place of Ruggles-Brise as chairman. Paterson came in from outside the prison service, indeed from outside the Home Office, but he had long been interested in youth problems.[5] He immediately set to work to implement his own basic philosophy, which was that prison was a place where a man was sent *as* a punishment and not *for* punishment, and that the emphasis should be on training the prisoner to make him more fit to live a law-abiding life upon release.[6] Many changes were made in

1. Fox, p. 58.
2. Fox, p. 61.
3. Fox, p. 61.
4. Fox, p. 62. See *English Prisons Today: Being The Report of the Prison System Enquiry Committee*. Edited by Stephen Hobhouse and A. Fenner Brockway, 1922.
5. Fox, p. 67.
6. *Paterson on Prisons*, ed. S. K. Ruck, 1951, is a collection of Paterson's papers.

the next twenty-five years so as to breathe life into the honoured formulae of the Gladstone Report, and revitalise our prison and borstal systems.[7] But Paterson's main influence was undoubtedly on a personal level. He inspired and led in a way which is given to few men, and his name must rank high in the list of penal reformers and administrators. Sir Lionel Fox continued where Paterson left off, and saw the system through the difficult post-war period.[8]

3 1948 TO THE PRESENT DAY

Space does not allow us to explore all the ways in which Paterson touched the penal system and coloured it. By 1938 the time had come to incorporate some of the changes, and others recommended in various committee reports, into legislation.[9] A bold new Criminal Justice Bill was prepared and introduced in the House of Commons by Sir Samuel Hoare (later Lord Templewood). World War II prevented this Bill from becoming law, and a fresh start was made again in 1947, culminating in the Criminal Justice Act 1948.

This Act may be said to have achieved changes in three main directions:[10]

1. It strengthened and further extended the powers of courts to keep out of prison persons for whom this was not a suitable or necessary solution. This applies particularly to young offenders under twenty-one and to persons suffering from mental disorder;

2. It provided new methods of dealing with persistent offenders. Both preventive detention and corrective training were introduced by the Act of 1948, though the former had a lineage going back to the Prevention of Crimes Act 1908;

3. It established (except for persistent offenders) the single sentence of imprisonment in place of the nineteenth-century system of penal servitude, imprisonment with

---

7. Fox, p. 67.
8. A. W. Peterson, "Sir Lionel Fox's Work in the Prison Commission", in *Studies in Penology* dedicated to the memory of Sir Lionel Fox, Ed. M. Lopez-Rey and C. Germain, 1964, pp. 184 *et seq.*
9. For an interesting account of the discussion about this Bill, see A. G. Rose, *The Struggle for Penal Reform*, 1961.
10. This analysis follows that in the Home Office pamphlet, *Prisons and Borstals (England and Wales)*, 4th Edn. 1960, p. 3, para. 7.

hard labour, and the triple division of imprisonment without hard labour.

The Act also limited the use of corporal punishment to offences connected with prison, viz. grave assaults on prison officers and mutiny.

The third point above deserves comment, if only to quote Sir Lionel Fox's celebrated phrase:

". . . in one historic handful of words the Act of 1948 abolished penal servitude, hard labour and the triple division of imprisonment, and so established, almost by inadvertence, the single sentence of undifferentiated imprisonment—the 'peine unique' of classic criminological controversy. . . ."[11]

Because it was necessary to insert in 3, above, an exception for persistent offenders, Sir Lionel Fox's claim that the 1948 Act established at last one single sentence of imprisonment is not wholly acceptable. But since the Criminal Justice Act 1967 abolished the two special sentences for persistent offenders, viz. preventive detention and corrective training, and substituted the extended sentence idea, which does not involve any special prison régime, we have at last reached the point anticipated in Sir Lionel Fox's comment. Indeed, a modern critic might well maintain that the single undifferentiated sentence of imprisonment results in too many different types of offender serving different kinds of sentence and with different needs, being received in prison and being herded together in large undifferentiated and non-specialised establishments.

Between 1948 and 1967 various developments occurred which must be noted. In 1952 the Prison Act consolidated and replaced the previous statute law governing prisons, and once more allowed the Home Secretary to make Rules thereunder governing the details of prison administration.[12] The Prison Rules, which had been revised in 1949, were once again revised and substantially trimmed and simplified. More now depends on the directions of the Secretary of State, often embodied in departmental Standing Orders and administrative circulars. The result is in the theory to allow much flexibility and room

---

11. Fox, p. 4.
12. Lord GODDARD once commented that the way that the Prison Commissioners and the Home Office had by regulations abolished all distinctions between the different kinds of sentence prior to the 1948 Act had always seemed to him to be "a pretty strong example of what perhaps might be described as administrative law making": Lord GODDARD, "The Working of the Court of Criminal Appeal" (1952), 2 *Jo.S.P.T.L.*, No. 1, p. 6.

for adaptation, but in practice it makes a prisoner's status and rights insecure, to say the least. Thus the prisoner may now be reclassified and shunted here and there for what may be purely reasons of administrative expediency. In practice, humane considerations are just as likely to govern such moves, however. For example, the rules about accumulated visits allow a prisoner in a prison remote from his home to save up his entitlement to visits until he can be moved to a prison more convenient for his visitors.

The next big step in the history of imprisonment came in the Criminal Justice Act 1961.[13] This Act came near to abolishing prison for offenders aged under twenty-one within the inter-mediate range of sentence (six months to three years) by making borstal sentences the only kind of custody which could be ordered within that range. It altered the law governing deten-tion centre sentences, and provided that when there were sufficient detention centres available throughout the country, imprisonment for up to six months for young offenders could be abolished by an Order of the Secretary of State. It has not yet proved possible to take this step, and it seems unlikely that we shall get rid of short terms of imprisonment for young offenders for the time being. Suitably qualified persistent offenders may still be sent to prison for eighteen months or more.

Finally we come to the Criminal Justice Act 1967.[14] This was a landmark just as great as the Act of 1948, according to the then Home Secretary, and some hailed it as revolutionary. It is true that various novel and interesting innovations were made, including, for the first time in Britain, the introduction of the suspended sentence, and parole. It is possible that the Act is a watershed, so that we should speak of a new period beginning with the bringing into effect of its provisions, most of which were made effective in 1968. It is too early to say whether this is a correct view. Another viewpoint is that the Act, apart from the innovations mentioned, was a hotch potch of procedural and penal reforms with few claims to be regarded as a turning-point.

---

13. See review by the author (March 1962), 25 *M.L.R.* No. 2, p. 209.
14. See articles by the author, "Le 'Criminal Justice Act' anglais de 1967 et le sort des délinquants" (1969), *Revue de Science criminelle et de Droit pénal comparé*, No. 3, pp. 623 *et seq.*; "Zwanzig Jahre Strafrechts-reform in England und Wales" (1968), 84 *Schweizerische Zeitschrift für Strafrecht*, No. 1, pp. 1 *et seq.*

CHAPTER 4

The Law Relating to Imprisonment

We shall be dealing elsewhere with the special rules relating to prisoners and such subjects as discipline, work, food, remission of sentence, etc. It is, however, convenient to deal separately in this chapter with general questions concerning the legal basis of imprisonment, and a number of special rules not dealt with elsewhere.

IMPRISONMENT AS A PUNISHMENT

In the past, several different kinds of imprisonment were authorised.[1] There was firstly, penal servitude, introduced by the Penal Servitude Acts of 1853 and 1857, and intended as a substitute for transportation. A sentence of penal servitude had to be a minimum of three years, and release was on licence. The sentence of penal servitude was abolished by the Criminal Justice Act 1948, and ordinary imprisonment was substituted.[2] Secondly, there was ordinary imprisonment. In the past, this kind of imprisonment was itself subdivided into categories, called Divisions of imprisonment, with different rights and obligations attendant upon each. Before 1948 there were three Divisions of imprisonment without hard labour, provided for by the Act of 1898. There was also the sentence of imprisonment with hard labour. It eventually became unnecessary for courts when sentencing offenders to have power to order a sentence of imprisonment without hard labour to be served in the First, Second or Third Division, since the differences were so slight, and in any case courts often "found it difficult to refrain from passing sentences 'with hard labour' even when in later years this form of sentence had ceased to have any signifi-

---

1. See generally, Lionel Fox, *The English Prison and Borstal Systems*, 1952, pp. 44–45, 58–59.
2. Criminal Justice Act 1948, s. 1.

cance".[3] The Gladstone Committee had recommended that the First Class Hard Labour of the previous law should be abolished, but had retained "the shadow of hard labour", viz. that courts should still be empowered to sentence prisoners to hard labour. As Sir Lionel Fox put it, the Act of 1948, in abolishing penal servitude, hard labour and the triple division of imprisonment "established, almost by inadvertence, the single sentence of undifferentiated imprisonment—the 'peine unique' of classic criminological controversy".[4] But when this happened it was no more than a recognition by the law of an already existing situation, says Fox. For by 1948 there was in effect only one kind of imprisonment, and the differentiations of the past had ceased to have any importance.

However, the Act of 1948 did provide two new kinds of sentence for recidivist offenders, viz. corrective training and preventive detention. (See Chapter 14: Recidivist prisoners.) But the Criminal Justice Act 1967 abolished these, and the extended sentence which it introduced in their place cannot really be regarded as involving a special kind of imprisonment to be served under a special régime different from that applicable to ordinary prisoners. It is now more true than it was in 1948 to say that there is only one kind of imprisonment known to the English law. There are one or two minor exceptions to this rule. As we shall see, there may be detention in police cells for very short periods of time, counted in days. Remand prisoners have special rights, as do convicted prisoners who have appealed, prisoners committed or attached for contempt of court, and prisoners convicted of sedition, seditious conspiracy or seditious libel.[5]

MAXIMUM AND MINIMUM TERMS

The abolition of the distinction between felony and misdemeanour effected by the Criminal Law Act 1967 necessitated fresh provisions for dealing with offences for which no penalty was specified by law. Section 7 of the Criminal Law Act 1967 provides that:

---

3. Fox, p. 59.
4. Fox, p. 4.
5. Unconvicted prisoners: Prison Rules 1964, rr. 3(2), 20(1), 21(1), 26(2), 28(5), 34(1), 62; appellants: *ibid.*, rr. 57–61; prisoners committed or attached for contempt: *ibid.*, r. 63; prisoners convicted of sedition, etc.: *ibid.*, r. 64.

"(1) Where a person is convicted on indictment of an offence against any enactment and is for that offence liable to be sentenced to imprisonment but the sentence is not by any enactment either limited to a specified term or expressed to extend to imprisonment for life, the person so convicted shall be liable to imprisonment for not more than two years."

This takes care of those rare cases of relatively minor statutory offences (previously felonies) for which no maximum penalty was provided by the statute which created them, and also limits the maximum punishment for statutory misdemeanours not otherwise provided for to two years imprisonment.[6]

Where an offence is a common law offence as distinct from a statutory one, no maximum penalty is provided by law,[7] but the courts have held that the penalty must not be inordinate,[8] and in the case of conspiracy the sentence ought not to be greater than that which could have been imposed for the substantive offence save in exceptional cases.[9] In the case of attempted crimes, a person convicted on indictment shall not be sentenced to imprisonment for a longer term than to which he could have been sentenced for the completed offence. The same applies to the amount of fines for attempts: they should not exceed the maximum for the complete crime.[10]

A magistrates' court shall not impose imprisonment for less that five days.[11] A magistrates' court having power to impose imprisonment on any person may instead order him to be detained for any period not exceeding four days in police cells or a similar place certified by the Home Secretary to be suitable for the purpose.[12] A woman or girl shall not be detained in any such place except under the supervision of women.[13] This latter provision results in some women being committed to prison for very short terms, of less than five days. A magistrates' court may also in some circumstances order detention of a person convicted of an offence with the precincts of the court-house or

---

6. Criminal Law Revision Committee, Seventh Report, Felonies and Misdemeanours, Cmnd. 2659, May 1965, p. 18, para. 65.
7. *R.* v. *Castro* (1880), 5 Q.B.D. 490, 509.
8. *R.* v. *Morris*, [1951] 1 K.B. 394; [1950] 2 All E.R. 965; *R.* v. *Bryan* (1951), 35 Cr.App.R. 121; *R.* v. *Higgins*, [1952] 1 K.B. 7; [1951] 2 All E.R. 758.
9. *Verrier* v. *Director of Public Prosecutions*, [1967] 2 A.C. 195; [1966] 3 All E.R. 568.
10. Criminal Law Act 1967, s. 7 (2).
11. Magistrates' Courts Act 1952, s. 107.
12. *Ibid.*, s. 109(1).
13. *Ibid.*, s. 109(3).

at any police station for the rest of the day on which the order is made (up to 8 o'clock in the evening).[14]

A person who is in default in paying a sum due to be paid following a summary conviction may be ordered by a magistrates' court to be detained for the night "unless the sum adjudged to be paid by the conviction is sooner paid".[15]

The position with regard to remand in custody is that wherever a magistrates' court has power to remand any person, the court may remand him in custody,[16] and where such a person is brought before the court after remand, the court may further remand him.[17] If the remand in custody is for a period not exceeding three clear days, the magistrates may commit him to the custody of a constable.[18] Persons remanded in custody to prison are the subject of special rules and enjoy certain privileges not accorded to convicted prisoners.

CONCURRENT AND CONSECUTIVE SENTENCES

Where a prisoner is convicted of several offences on different counts of the same indictment or on different indictments at the same assizes or quarter sessions, the court as a general rule has power to direct that the sentences shall run consecutively or concurrently.[19] This power may be exercised even though the aggregate of the punishments may exceed the total allowed by law for one offence. Thus in the case of the spy *Blake*,[20] a sentence of forty-two years made up of three consecutive sentences of fourteen years was upheld on appeal although taken together the sentences passed came to more than the maximum penalty permitted for any one of the offences charged.

It is possible to pass sentence on a person who has already been convicted on another charge and sentenced to imprisonment in such a way as to take effect upon the expiration of the imprisonment to which the person has previously been sentenced.[1] But the courts have limited this in various ways.

Thus a probation order may not be made to take effect after

---

14. Magistrates' Courts Act 1952, s. 110.
15. *Ibid.*, s. 111.
16. *Ibid.*, s. 105.
17. *Ibid.*, s. 105(2).
18. *Ibid.*, s. 105(5).
19. Archbold, *Criminal Pleading, Evidence and Practice*, 37th edn., 1969, para. 637.
20. *R.* v. *Blake*, [1962] 2 Q.B. 377; [1961] 3 All E.R. 125.
1. *R.* v. *Wilkes* (1770), 19 State Tr. 1075, 1132. See also Criminal Law Act 1827, s. 10, applicable to felonies.

the termination of a sentence of imprisonment.[2] It has been held that it was improper to pass a sentence of imprisonment to run consecutively to a sentence of corrective training[3] or preventive detention.[4] Consecutive sentences of borstal training should never be ordered.[5] A sentence of fourteen years' imprisonment consecutive to a life sentence has been held improper,[6] though in another case, where the life sentence was passed on someone already sentenced to 14 years, it was held that it made no practical difference whether the life sentence was made consecutive or concurrent, though the former was undesirable.[7] Ordinarily two consecutive sentences should not be passed for two offences which arise from one and the same act.[8] Usually the English courts will exercise their discretion to order that the sentences shall run concurrently.

The judge ought to make his intention clear on this matter.[9] A suspended sentence which is ordered to take effect should not normally be made concurrent with a sentence for another offence. Nor should it be made consecutive to an extended sentence, as this may create difficulties in administration.

COMMENCEMENT OF SENTENCE

The general rule is that a sentence takes effect from the beginning of the day on which it is imposed, unless the court otherwise directs.[10] But this would operate unjustly where the prisoner has been in custody for a period pending trial, having been committed for trial in custody or remanded after arraignment or where he has been committed under ss. 28 or 29 of the Magistrates' Courts Act 1952 or with a view to a mental health order being made. So it has been provided that the length of any term of imprisonment imposed by the sentence of any

---

2. *R. v. Evans*, [1958] 3 All E.R. 673.
3. *R. v. Talbot*, [1953] 1 Q.B. 613; [1953] 1 All E.R. 340; *R. v. Hedgecock* (1957), 41 Cr.App.Rep. 136; *R. v. Astle* (1960), 44 Cr.App.R. 231.
4. *R. v. Robson*, [1962] Crim.L.R. 490. Cf. *R. v. Nurse* (1960), 45 Cr.App.Rep. 40. A practical solution was suggested, viz. to pass a longer sentence concurrent with the existing sentence, in which case the two sentences would merge.
5. *R. v. Beamon*, [1948] 1 All E.R. 947.
6. *R. v. Foy*, [1962] 2 All E.R. 246.
7. *R. v. Jones*, [1961] 3 All E.R. 668.
8. *R. v. Hussain*, [1962] Crim.L.R. 712. But see *R. v. Cowburn*, [1959] Crim.L.R. 590; *R. v. Newton* (1958), *Times*, 15 October.
9. *Re Hastings*, [1958] 1 All E.R. 707; *Practice Direction*, (1962) 46 Cr.App. Rep. 119. See also *R. v. Anthony*, [1962] Crim.L.R. 259.
10. Criminal Justice Administration Act 1962, s. 17(1).

court shall be treated as reduced by any period spent in custody before sentence in the above mentioned circumstances.[11]

A similar problem arises where a convicted person sentenced to imprisonment appeals. Section 29 of the Criminal Appeal Act 1968 provides that the time during which an appellant is in custody pending the determination of his appeal shall be reckoned as part of the term of any sentence to which he is for the time being subject.[12] But the Court of Appeal may make a direction to the contrary, and where such a direction is given they must give their reasons. They cannot make any such direction where the case is one in which leave of appeal has been granted, or a certificate given by the trial judge or the case is a reference from the Home Secretary.[13]

The section also provides that the term of any sentence passed by the Court of Appeal begins to run from the same time as it would have begun to run if it had been passed in the original proceedings, unless the Court otherwise directs.[14] If the appellant is admitted to bail pending the appeal (under s. 19) the time spent on bail is to be disregarded when computing the term of the sentence.[15] There are special provisions dealing with the position with regard to the computation of the sentence in the case where there is ordered to be a retrial.[16]

TERMINATION OF SENTENCE

The Prison Department must exercise great care to discharge an offender sentenced to imprisonment on or before the date when his term ends. In calculating this, the word "month" used in any sentence of imprisonment is construed to mean calendar month,[17] and a prisoner who is due to be discharged on a Sunday, Christmas Day or Good Friday, must be discharged the day before. There is power to discharge a prisoner temporarily on account of ill health where it is undesirable to detain him in prison.[18] But this power is subject to the odd requirement: "such condition of health being due in whole or

---

11. *Ibid.*, s. 17(2).
12. Criminal Appeal Act 1968, s. 29(1).
13. *Ibid.*, s. 29(2).
14. *Ibid.*, s. 29(4).
15. *Ibid.*, s. 29(3).
16. *Ibid.*, s. 8(4) and Sched. 2.
17. Prison Act 1952, s. 24(1).
18. *Ibid.*, s. 28.

in part to the prisoner's own conduct in prison". The order of temporary discharge may contain conditions. Time spent by a prisoner under sentence in the free community under an order of temporary discharge does not count towards the prisoner's sentence as time served.[19]

TESTING THE LEGALITY OF A PRISONER'S DETENTION OR TREATMENT IN PRISON

It has been decided that a prisoner's remedy against his conviction and sentence lies in appeal to the Court of Appeal (Criminal Division)[20] and that his remedy in regard to any alleged breach of prison rules lies in complaint to the visiting magistrates and not in a civil action against the Home Office.[1]

The courts do not allow a convicted prisoner to use the *habeas corpus* procedure in order to appeal from his conviction, but there may be circumstances where it is appropriate to apply for such a writ, as where he claims he has been held unlawfully. A prisoner may not normally make an application for a writ of *habeas corpus* in person. He must usually have a lawyer to represent him.[2] It used to be thought that successive applications might be made to different judges where the previous application was unsuccessful. But the rule is now clarified, largely as a result of the attempts by the prisoner Hastings to have the matter of the legality of his detention considered by successive courts. He applied first to the Queen's Bench Division,[3] then to a differently constituted court of the same Division,[4] then to a Divisional Court of the Chancery Division.[5] It was held in these cases that an applicant for a writ of *habeas corpus* in a criminal cause or matter, who has been heard once by a Divisional Court of the Queen's Bench Division, cannot be heard again, on a renewed application on the same evidence and the same grounds, by another Divisional Court of the same Division, since the decision of the Divisional Court under the Judicature Acts is equivalent to the decision of all the judges of

---

19. *Ibid.*, s. 28(4).
20. *Re Hastings* No. 2, [1959] 1 Q.B. 358; [1958] 3 All E.R. 625; *Ex p. Hinds*, [1961] 1 All E.R. 707.
1. *Hinds* v. *Home Office*, (1962), *The Times*, 17 January, leave to appeal to the House of Lords refused, (1962), *The Times*, 8 March.
2. *Re Wring, Re Cook*, [1960] 1 All E.R. 536 *n.*
3. *Re Hastings*, [1958] 1 All E.R. 707.
4. *Re Hastings* (No. 2), [1958] 1 Q.B. 358.
5. *Re Hastings* (No. 3), [1959] Ch. 368; [1959] 1 All E.R. 698.

the Queen's Bench Division. Nor could the application be heard again on a renewed application made on the same evidence and the same grounds, by a Divisional Court of the Chancery Division, and the Court of Appeal held that no appeal against this decision lay to the Court of Appeal, for the same reason as they had earlier declined to entertain an appeal from the decision in the Queen's Bench Division, viz. that they were debarred from hearing appeals in any criminal cause or matter.[6]

The position of a person wishing to challenge the refusal of *habeas corpus* application has now been regulated by statute. Section 15 of the Administration of Justice Act 1960 provides that an unsuccessful applicant in a civil matter may appeal as of right to the Court of Appeal and thence, with leave, to the House of Lords. An unsuccessful applicant in a criminal matter may now appeal, with leave of either the Divisional Court or the House of Lords, direct to the House of Lords. It is also provided that no application for *habeas corpus* shall be made on the same grounds to the same court or judge or any other court or judge unless fresh evidence is adduced. The result is to confirm the findings in the Hastings cases but to provide the right of appeal with leave. Hastings was never able to test the original decision not to allow his application for the writ of *habeas corpus* on its merits. It may be some comfort to him to know that this may now be done where the necessary leave is given.

Another prisoner who made legal history was Alfred Hinds. In 1960 Hinds had applied for a writ of *habeas corpus* in the Queen's Bench Division on the ground that he did not have a fair trial in 1953 and that he had a right of appeal to the Court of Criminal Appeal on a point of law but that appeal had never been heard. The Divisional Court held[7] that the applicant's complaint was not a ground for *habeas corpus* but for application to the Court of Criminal Appeal for the point of law to be heard. The applicant had applied for leave to appeal on a number of grounds, some being points of fact alone or mixed law and fact. The whole matter came before the Court of Criminal Appeal in May 1954 and the applicant was represented by counsel, and his application for leave to appeal was refused. The court did not adjourn any part of it to be treated

6. *Re Hastings* (No. 3), [1959] 1 All E.R. 698.
7. *Ex p. Hinds*, [1961] 1 All E.R. 707.

as an appeal on a point of law alone, from which the Divisional Court now concluded that the court must have been of the opinion that no point of law alone was involved, or, if there was, that it was a point of no substance, which the court felt they could deal with and dismiss without adjourning for the prosecution to be present. In these circumstances the Divisional Court was satisfied that the present complaint by the applicant was without foundation, and refused the application for *habeas corpus*. The decision was upheld in the House of Lords.

In 1962 Hinds sought to sue the Home Office for an alleged breach of the prison rules, but it was decided that the proper course was for him to bring his complaint to the attention of the visiting justices. There was provision for prisoners to bring civil actions in certain circumstances, but this was not appropriate here. The judge dismissed the appeal from the decision of the master striking out the statement of claim as being frivolous and vexatious, and the Court of Appeal upheld the judge's decision.[8]

Hinds later succeeded in a civil action for libel against a senior police officer in respect of newspaper articles in which it was alleged that he had committed the offence of shopbreaking for which he was sentenced to twelve years' preventive detention.[9] This decision gave rise to serious misgivings concerning the degree to which successful criminal prosecutions could be challenged in later civil actions, where the rules of evidence and the burden of proof were not the same. The matter was considered by the Law Reform Committee, in its Fifteenth Report, and it was recommended that the Rule in *Hollington* v. *Hewthorn*, which prevented the giving in evidence on a civil trial of the fact of a previous conviction relating to the same circumstances, should be abolished and a special rule be enacted for actions of defamation.[10]

These recommendations were implemented in the Civil Evidence Act 1968. Henceforth a conviction of a criminal offence before a court of competent jurisdiction in the United Kingdom would be admissible in subsequent civil proceedings (whether or not between the same parties) to show that the person concerned was guilty of the conduct constituting the

---

8. *Hinds* v. *Home Office;* (1962), *Times*, March 8.
9. *Hinds* v. *Sparks,* [1964] Crim.L.R. 717.
10. Law Reform Committee, Fifteenth Report (The Rule in *Hollington* v. *Hewthorn*), Cmnd. 3391, (September 1967).

offence, and he should be taken to have committed that offence unless the contrary is proved. A special rule applies to civil actions for defamation: here the fact that a person stands convicted of an offence which is the subject of the action "shall be conclusive proof that he committed that offence". This means that the door to re-litigation of criminal convictions in the civil courts opened in the Hinds case has now been firmly closed. For, as the Law Reform Committee said, "it can only undermine public confidence in the administration of criminal justice if civil courts in actions between private individuals can be forced to re-try the issue of guilt, which has already been determined by a criminal court, and reach a different conclusion".[11]

A prisoner may however sue the Home Office for damages for negligence in respect of injuries sustained from an attack by a fellow prisoner,[12] but he may find it difficult to succeed. It has been said that

"the mere fact that the plaintiff, while in prison, was attacked and injured by a fellow prisoner does not entitle him to succeed against the Government Department responsible for the management of the prison, that is to say, the Home Office. He must show that the injury which he sustained was due to some breach of duty on the part of those responsible for the management of the prison."[13]

Under the Prison Rules a prisoner may be allowed to pursue his ordinary civil remedies against other persons while in custody, and may be given facilities for doing so.[14] The Home Office may also be sued for damage to property done by prisoners while escaping.[15]

ARRANGING FOR A SURETY OR PAYMENT, TO SECURE RELEASE

A person detained in prison in default of finding a surety, or of payment of a sum of money, may communicate with, and be visited at any reasonable time on a week-day by, any relative or friend to arrange for a surety or payment in order to secure his release from prison.[16]

---

11. Law Reform Committee, Fifteenth Report, p. 13, para. 29.
12. *Ellis* v. *The Home Office*, [1953] 2 Q.B. 135; [1953] 2 All E.R. 149.
13. *Ibid.*, *per* JENKINS, L.J., at p. 145.
14. Prison Rules 1964, r. 37(1).
15. *Dorset Yacht Co., Ltd.* v. *Home Office*, [1969] 2 All E.R. 564; *Greenwell* v. *Prison Commissioners* (1951), 101 L.Jo. 486.
16. Prison Rules 1964, r. 36.

PROTECTING THE PRISONER

A prisoner shall not be subjected to any painful tests applied by the medical officer of a prison "for the purpose of detecting malingering or for any other purpose" except with the permission of a Prison Commissioner or the Visiting Committee or board of visitors of the institution.[17] The Prison Act also governs the certification by an inspector of cells as suitable accommodation for the confinement of prisoners.[18] In every prison special cells have to be provided for the temporary confinement of refractory or violent prisoners.[19]

PROVIDING NEW PRISONS, CLOSING OLD PRISONS, ETC.

The Prison Act authorises the Secretary of State to "alter enlarge or rebuild any prison and build new prisons",[20] and to provide new prisons "by declaring to be a prison any building or part of a building built for the purpose or vested in him or under his control".[1] Land may be acquired for the purpose of altering enlarging or rebuilding a prison or for establishing a new prison, "or for any other purpose connected with the management of a prison (including the provision of accommodation for officers or servants employed in a prison)."[2] The procedure for acquiring land is laid down.[3] The Secretary of State may close any prison, subject to certain conditions being observed.[4]

---

17. Prison Act 1952, s. 17.
18. *Ibid.*, s. 14.
19. *Ibid.*, s. 14(6).
20. *Ibid.*, s. 33(1).
1. *Ibid.*, s. 33(2).
2. *Ibid.*, s. 36(1).
3. *Ibid.*, s. 36(2), (3).
4. *Ibid.*, s. 37.

CHAPTER 5

The Use the Courts make of Prison

Prison is used by the courts for a variety of purposes, as follows:

I. Pending Trial for safe custody of the prisoner;

II. Pending Sentence for investigation and report;

III. Under Sentence

(*a*) as a means of coercion or punishment for failure to pay a debt, a fine, or for contempt of court;

(*b*) as a means of punishment for crime.[1]

I. PENDING TRIAL

Large numbers of accused persons are remanded in custody pending trial, and detained in prison (38,274 persons in 1968). Of these more than 50 per cent do not eventually return to prison under sentence. The proportion remanded in custody but not returned to prison has been rising in recent years, from approximately 40 per cent. to the present figure of over 50 per cent. The actual number of persons remanded in custody but not subsequently received in prison under sentence now exceeds 19,000 persons annually, which is as high as the previous very high level obtaining in the years 1913–1914, which was reduced to almost half by 1955.

Considerable concern has been expressed about this situation, and one direction in which a solution has been sought is in measures designed to expand the use of bail. The bail provisions of the Criminal Justice Act 1967 are meant to prevent magistrates from remanding in custody unnecessarily. They preclude

---

1. Much of this Chapter is based on an earlier contribution by the author, printed in *Sociological Studies in the British Penal Services*, 1965, ed. Paul Halmos, entitled "The Use the Courts Make of Prison", pp. 49 *et seq*. Some of the figures have been up-dated. The figures are mainly drawn from the Prison Department Statistical Tables, published annually.

the use of remands in custody where the courts are dealing with offences punishable with not more than six months' imprisonment, subject to certain exceptions.

These exceptions still give the courts considerable discretion about the use of bail, for they cover a multitude of cases. These include:

1. Where the accused has been previously sentenced to imprisonment;
2. Where he has been previously bailed, and has failed, on that occasion, to comply with the condition of his recognisances;
3. Where the offence charged is alleged to have been commited whilst on bail;
4. Where it is necessary to detain him to establish his identity or address;
5. Where he has no fixed abode or is ordinarily resident outside the United Kingdom;
6. Where the offence charged involves an assault on or threat of violence to another person, or having or possessing a firearm, an imitation firearm, an explosive or an offensive weapon, or indecent conduct with or towards a person under sixteen;
7. Where he is likely to commit an offence if granted bail;
8. Where it is necessary for his own protection.

In addition, courts which are dealing with offences punishable with more than six months' imprisonment have unlimited discretion as to the granting of bail.

Where the magistrates have a choice whether to grant bail or not, a right of appeal is conferred on the defendant from their refusal of bail, and the magistrates must give their reasons for refusing bail in writing to the unrepresented defendant, or his legal representative has the right to ask for reasons. There was always a right to appeal to a High Court judge against refusal of bail, but the position of the defendant is now greatly improved. Bail may now be granted subject to conditions, and the police are given a new power to arrest a person who is suspected of being likely to break any condition on which he was admitted to bail.

How effective the new provisions have been in reducing the use of remands in custody it is difficult to say at this stage, but the Home Office is keeping the matter under review. More information is certainly needed concerning bail practice in Britain. It is possible that the use of a simple inquiry procedure involving checks on employment, residence and family status, such as has been developed in the United States by the bail studies, supported by the Vera Foundation, might help. The result might well be to persuade the courts that they are remanding in custody unnecessarily.[2]

II. PENDING SENTENCE

Large numbers of convicted persons are remanded in custody pending sentence, usually in order that further information may be obtained about them—for social enquiries and medical and psychiatric reports. In recent years the use of custody for this purpose has grown considerably. In 1967 a record number of 11,061 persons were remanded in custody for investigation as to their state of mind. A large number of these remands are dealt with in the London remand prisons, Brixton (in 1967 Brixton dealt with 3,318), Holloway and Wormwood Scrubs (in 1960 they supplied between them 59 per cent. of these reports).[3] Also the remand centres spend much of their time preparing reports for the courts.

In many cases the remand will not be for a medical report but for further information to be obtained. There are no precise figures for the number of social enquiry reports, but if one deducts the number of medical reports from the total remanded in custody after conviction over 10,000 cases remain where the report was of a non-medical kind.

In nearly half the cases where a remand is made pending sentence, the eventual sentence chosen is not prison. There has been a slight tendency for the proportion not subsequently returning to prison under sentence to fall in recent years.

III. UNDER SENTENCE

1 CIVIL PRISONERS

These fall into three categories:

(*a*) Those imprisoned for commercial debts;

---

2. See Michael Zander, "Bail—A Re-appraisal", [1967] Crim.L.R. 25, 100, and 128.
3. Report of the Prison Commissioners, 1960, Cmnd. 1467, p. 72.

(*b*) Those imprisoned in default of payment of a fine;
(*c*) Those committed for contempt otherwise than by non-
payment of money under a court order.

(a) Imprisonment for debt

In 1968 the total number of prisoners received into prison
for non-payment of debt via either the High Court, the County
Courts or the magistrates' courts was 6,984. The Prison Department has been concerned at the striking rise in the numbers
of civil prisoners in recent years,[4] especially in 1962, 1963 and
1964, which is largely accounted for by imprisonment for debt.
These are mainly for commercial debts. Figures for non-payment of maintenance, rates and taxes have not risen.

For many years there has been growing pressure for the abolition of imprisonment for civil debt. In a letter to *The Times*
in August 1960 Lord Justice DANCKWERTS remarked that "there
is a real case for the abolition of imprisonment for the non-
payment of debt".[5] The whole question of the procedure for the
enforcement of civil obligations was referred to the Payne Committee, whose Report is summarised below, so far as it concerns
the penal system.

Report of the Payne Committee.—This Committee, appointed in
March 1965, reported in February 1969,[6] and among their
many recommendations were that imprisonment for debt should
be abolished, though there were some members of the Committee (including the chairman) who could not agree to the abolition
of imprisonment as a sanction against maintenance defaulters.

It is not necessary for our purposes to examine in detail the
present machinery for the enforcement of debts and the many
radical changes proposed by the Payne Committee. We are
solely concerned with the use of imprisonment as a sanction
for non-payment of debts. Here the Committee's view is
emphatically stated thus:

"Whilst imprisonment and the threat of imprisonment have
undoubtedly caused extreme hardship to countless inadequate
debtors and their families . . . it has succeeded in extracting
money from judgment debtors who under the present system

---

4. Report of the Prison Commissioners, 1959, Cmnd. 1117, p. 54.
5. *The Times*, 22 August 1960.
6. Report of the Committee on the Enforcement of Judgment Debts, Cmnd. 3909,
February 1969.

might otherwise have evaded payment, and as we recommend the abolition of the sanction we must show that a system of debt collection can be operated satisfactorily without it. In our opinion not only can adequate substitutes for the judgment summons procedure be introduced but a much improved and more effective system of debt enforcement can be established."[7]

It is only right, as the Payne Committee point out, that "citizens ought to repay legally binding debts". But "the legal machinery must be efficient, capable of reaching out to all the assets of a debtor and yet sensitive both to the needs and social circumstances of debtors and the rights of the creditors".[8]

The Committee recommend, among other reforms, that the attachment of earnings should be introduced for the enforcement of civil debts generally. It is presently available for the enforcement of maintenance orders and the payment of fines. In addition to this a new enforcement system is proposed which the Committee consider is essential because the present system "is not only unplanned and untidy on paper but also does not work satisfactorily in practice".[9] A new Enforcement Office would operate an integrated system of enforcement.[10] This office should be empowered to enforce its orders by using the contempt procedure in the County Court preceded by a penal notice served personally on the defendant.

On the subject of imprisonment for debt the Committee reached a unanimous conclusion that committal to prison under the Debtors Act 1869, an Act passed just over one hundred years ago, is "an outdated, often unjust and inappropriate method of enforcement", and should be abolished.[11] They were not unanimous about the question of imprisonment for maintenance defaulters. The Committee were all concerned that their findings on this subject "should result in positive action and that the abolition of imprisonment for civil debt should take place without further avoidable delay".[12]

Among the reasons given by the Committee for their recommendations are the following:

    1. A high proportion of those imprisoned are for one reason or another inadequate;

---

7. Cmnd. 3909, p. 86, para. 307.
8. *Ibid.*, p. 12, para. 46.
9. *Ibid.*, p. 87, para. 313.
10. *Ibid.*, p. 88, para. 316.
11. *Ibid.*, p. 246, para. 955.
12. *Ibid.*, p. 247, para. 956.

2. The hardship which is caused to imprisoned debtors and their families is out of all proportion to the debt which gives rise to the imprisonment;

3. Imprisonment is uneconomic: more than 50 per cent. of debtors in prison are there for default in payment of sums under £20;

4. The vast structure of credit trading does not depend on the threat of or the use of imprisonment;

5. In many other countries alternative methods of enforcement are used effectively, and imprisonment for debt is virtually unknown;

6. Previous English committees of inquiry had been unanimous in advocating the abolition if imprisonment for debt.[13]

Imprisoned debtors.—There is some evidence, which the Committee received, to the effect that imprisoned debtors are men of low mental calibre, who were feckless about their affairs, overwhelmed by the burden of their debts, and generally unresponsive. The Committee summarise the evidence thus:

> "the vast majority of debtors who are actually received in prison under orders of the county courts are inadequate, unfortunate, feckless or irresponsible persons; they are, for the most part, not dishonest and do not therefore require punishment."[14]

This is not to say there are no persistent and dishonest debtors with means who are plausible and "work the system". The Committee suggest various ways in which the system might be strengthened to prevent the persistent dishonest debtor taking advantage of it.

The number of debtors imprisoned under orders of the County Court rose sharply from 1958 onwards to a peak of nearly 8,000 in 1962, but has declined since to 3,329 in 1967. Even so, "the cost to the community of maintaining in prison this body of persons at a time when pressure on prison space and staff is so heavy" is considerable.[15] Moreover, "a further argument against imprisonment, and one of real public interest" is the heavy burden of expense falling on the public by the whole judgement summons procedure.[16]

---

13. Cmnd. 3909, pp. 246–260.
14. *Ibid.*, p. 252, para 982.
15. *Ibid.*, p. 256, para. 994.
16. *Ibid.*, p. 257, para. 1000.

Maintenance Defaulters.—There remain the maintenance defaulters who are imprisoned. Three members of the Payne Committee, including the chairman, wished to retain imprisonment as a final sanction in the case of non-payment of maintenance orders; this would include orders made in favour of a wife or a dependant, and affiliation orders. This view has the support of the Magistrates' Association and the Justice' Clerks' Society, as well as the judges of the Divorce Division.[17] This minority on the Committee assert that imprisonment for non-payment of maintenance is necessary, for

> "By no other expeditious means can the wife extract money from the man who moves from job to job to defeat attachment of earnings, or from the wealthy man who has ample funds and lives well but has his flat, his motor car and his investments in the name of his second wife or his mistress."[18]

Six members of the Committee were prepared to abolish imprisonment for the enforcement of maintenance orders and affiliation orders forthwith, taking the view that imprisonment should only be imposed as a punishment for crime and should have no place in the enforcement procedures of the civil law.[19]

When comparing ordinary civil debtors with maintenance defaulters the main difference found by researchers (and borne out by experience) lies in the difference in attitude towards the debts. Maintenance defaulters were more often deliberately and stubbornly refusing to pay for the maintenance of their wives and families. From this the six Committee members conclude that "many maintenance defaulters are just as inadequate and socially incompetent as civil debtors although their inability to cope with reality takes a different form".[20] No sharp distinction can be drawn between civil debtors and defaulters. Perhaps the most forceful argument is the one based on administrative expediency. Under the proposed new enforcement procedure, it is argued that the position of defaulters should be the same as that of debtors:

> "either they have the means to pay or they have not. If they have the means the maintenance order will not be flouted because the machinery of extraction will be exercised to the full. If they lack

---

17. Cmnd. 3909, section 2, pp. 261–278, paras. 1008–1087.
18. *Ibid.*, p. 269, para. 1043.
19. *Ibid.*, section 3, pp. 279–287, paras. 1088–1100.
20. *Ibid.*, p. 281, para. 1092.

the means to pay, they are not wilfully or culpably refusing to pay. From the community's point of interest, imprisoning maintenance defaulters is futile."[1]

These arguments are finely balanced, and while experience suggests there is much to be said in favour of the view of the minority of three, the view of the six commends itself as more forward-looking and practically sound in light of the new procedure proposed. If this could be made effective, few would wish to see imprisonment of defaulters retained. Even the minority of three would be prepared to see it go.

Two further minority views are expressed in regard to the imprisonment of maintenance defaulters. Both Mr. John Shufflebotham and Professor Wheatcroft take the rather cynical but realistic view that whatever system "there will always be some fraudulent debtors who obtain credit knowing they are unlikely to have the means to pay". While they concur fully in the Committee's unanimous recommendation to abolish imprisonment for civil debt, they would not be surprised if the new system turned out to be no more effective in terms of debt recovery than the old one. The remedy lies with those who choose to extend credit to take much more care. This argument does not apply to the position of maintenance defaulters, consequently these two members of the Committee join forces with the minority of three to support the retention of imprisonment for maintenance defaulters, at least until the State makes better provision for the deserted wife and child, or the new system for enforcement of civil debts has been in operation for some years, and has been found to work efficiently.[2] In another minority report, Mr. Registrar Bryson appears to agree that there is not the same urgency about the abolition of imprisonment for maintenance defaulters, and he would be content if first priority were given to the abolition of imprisonment for civil debtors.[3]

One reflection may be permitted about the proposals of the Payne Committee. Granted that the new procedure using the resources of the Enforcement Office will be more likely to lead to the efficient collection of money owing, whether under a civil debt or maintenance order, what should concern us is how

---

1. Cmnd. 3909, p. 284, para. 1096.
2. *Ibid.*, section 4, pp. 287, 288, paras. 1101–1104.
3. *Ibid.*, section 5, p. 289, paras. 1105–1108.

many debtors and defaulters will have to be dealt with under the contempt procedure. The Payne Committee seem to think this procedure would rarely be employed but we may say that if they were wrong in their estimate and the numbers were considerable, we should be in no better position under the new arrangements from the point of view of receptions into prison than under the present system. Let us hope that this would not be the experience.

Not much information exists concerning the imprisonment of civil debtors. Paul de Berker has found that in many cases "permanent debt seems to be a way of family life", and argues that in all cases the debt "was a facet of a much more generalised picture of social difficulty such as marginal employment, general incompetence in financial planning and the like".[4] Pauline Morris has said that "the régime for civil prisoners can only be described as custodial". She argues that they should be regarded as socially handicapped persons, which means that their imprisonment would be avoided wherever possible.[5] The proposals of the Payne Committee would certainly be a great step in that direction, though it has not been without its critics.[6] The Government introduced in November 1969 a Bill designed to implement the main proposals of the Payne Committee but without the provision of an Enforcement Office.

(b) Non-payment of fine

This accounts for a substantial number of committals annually (13,115 in 1967). Again this is a figure which has increased rapidly in recent years. In 1962 it was double what it was in 1953. It now approaches the very high figure prevailing between 1914 and 1935 which was reduced by legislation designed to ensure that a proper enquiry was made as to means before sending a person to prison for non-payment of a fine.[7] It is possible that the improved machinery for the collection of fines through the attachment of earnings, introduced by the Criminal Justice Act 1967, will help reduce these figures. (See Chapter 20: Fines.)

---

4. Paul de Berker, "Impressions of Civil Debtors in Prison"(July 1965), 5 *B.J.C.*, No. 3, pp. 310–314.
5. Pauline Morris, "Debtor's Prison Still Exists", 1 *New Society*, No. 9, 29 November 1962. See also Pauline Morris, *Prisoners and Their Families*, 1965.
6. Tom Hadden, "In Prison for Debt", *New Society*, 20 February 1969.
7. *Sociological Studies in the British Penal Services*, 1965, ed. Paul Halmos, pp. 56–57.

(c) **Contempt**

There has been some increase in committals under this head, due possibly to the activities of nuclear disarmers and other political demonstrators, but the total numbers are small in comparison with those previously mentioned (some 200–300). Since 1960 there has been a right of appeal from any order of a court punishing for contempt of court.[8]

The total contribution that all these civil prisoners makes to the prison population is not very great, as they are imprisoned for such a short time. It is in fact, as Sir Lionel Fox put it, "a trifling proportion".[9] In 1962 no more than 4 per cent. of the total male prisoners and just over 5 per cent. of females were imprisoned for debt or as fine defaulters. In 1967 civil prisoners constituted 1·3 per cent. of the average population of our prisons. But the work involved in processing them in and out of the prison system is considerable and occupies time and energies which could be more profitably spent in other directions.

PRISONERS UNDER SENTENCE FOR CRIME

The overwhelming majority of prisoners come to prison under sentence and without the option of a fine. In 1962 of the total *receptions* into prison, 67 per cent. of males and 64 per cent. of females, were received under sentence.

The prison population has risen sharply since the Second World War. Whereas pre-war it stood at about 10,000–11,000, it has exceeded 30,000 in recent years. In 1967 the average population of all prison service establishments (prisons, borstals, detention centres and remand centres) was 35,009, compared with 33,086 in 1966. This high figure is in part due to an increase in receptions, in part due to a tendency towards longer sentences, and in part due to the increased proportion of offenders who committed serious offences (the increased number committing indictable offences). The Prison Department and the Home Office statisticians have tried to explain the total rise in the prison population in their Reports of 1955 and 1956.[10]

---

8. Administration of Justice Act 1960, s. 13.
9. Fox, p. 112.
10. Report of the Prison Commissioners, 1955, Cmnd. 10, November 1956, p. 46, Home Office, Criminal Statistics, 1956, Cmnd. 286, p. xxiii.

Lord Gardiner put it neatly in the House of Lords debate on 15 July 1964 when he said, commenting on the large numbers sleeping three in a cell, "broadly speaking it is true to say that, wherever one finds three in a cell, one would have been there before the war, the second is there because of the increase in crime, and the third is there because of the increase in sentence".[11]

Some criminologists have detected a shift away from short sentences and a rise in the number and proportion of sentences of intermediate length.[12] Whereas in 1938 95 per cent. of males were sentenced for not more than 12 months, in the years 1953–1962 the proportions have been of the order of 82–83 per cent. under 12 months and 14 per cent. over 12 months and up to three years, leaving about 2½ per cent. of the total as sentences of more than three years. In 1967 5·5 per cent. received sentences of imprisonment of three years or more. It still remains a remarkable feature of the English penal system that so few sentences are passed of more than three years. But far too many still get ridiculously short sentences.

At the other end of the scale, the trend in the use of long-term sentences has been examined by the Radzinowicz Sub-committee, and its Report contains some useful statistical analysis.[13] If one takes a long-term prisoner as one serving a term of imprisonment (or in the past of preventive detention) of over four years, as the Sub-committee did, one finds that on 15 October 1967 approximately 14 per cent. of male adult prisoners were serving long terms. However, what is really more interesting is the number and proportion serving *very* long terms, and Table B of the Sub-committee's Report showed that the number of men received into prison on a sentence of ten years or more (including life) had not increased greatly, and had remained a fairly constant proportion of total receptions, at least until 1966. In that year there was a considerable increase, but the Sub-committee said "it is not yet clear if any new trend is appearing".[14] However, "a quite different picture" emerges if one takes the use made by the courts of determinate

---

11. House of Lords Debates, Vol. 260, col. 250, 15 July 1964.
12. See discussion in *Sociological Studies in the British Penal Services*, 1965, ed. Paul Halmos, pp. 61–66.
13. Home Office, *The Régime for Long-term Prisoners in Conditions of Maximum Security*, 1968, pp. 4–6 and Appendix B.
14. *Ibid.*, p. 5, note to Table B.

sentences of fourteen years and over.[15] Here in the years 1956–1960 an average of only three prisoners a year were received. In the years 1961–1966 an average of about ten prisoners a year were received with such sentences. Added to these are the increasing number of life prisoners received annually, especially since the abolition of capital punishment. In 1968 ninety-one life sentences were imposed[16] whereas in 1958 there were only thirty-two.[17] Some of these will undoubtedly have to be detained for very long periods indeed. Many of these prisoners are regarded as high security risks.(See Chapter 7: Safe Custody and the Security Problem.) Of the 138 male prisoners included in the first list of Category A security risk prisoners, early in 1967, analysis showed that only five were serving a total period of imprisonment of less than ten years.[18] One of the problems facing the Prison Department is how to accommodate the increasing number of really long-term prisoners who are difficult and dangerous to manage. The Sub-committee figures show nearly 400 male adult prisoners serving sentences of ten years or over, and nearly 500 life prisoners or Her Majesty's pleasure prisoners. There would appear to be a population of just under 1,000 male adult prisoners to be catered for with long or indeterminate sentences.

Effect of Length of Sentence on Prison Population.—There are several ways in which one can demonstrate the relation between the length of sentence and the population of the prisons at any one time. One is simply to compare the proportion of receptions in any single year with the daily average population of the institutions. This point will be understood more easily if one takes the metaphor of the cafeteria. The pressure in seating in a cafeteria depends not only on how many enter and use it but on how long they occupy their seats at the tables. So it is with prisoners and cell accommodation. There is no direct relationship between the number of receptions and the daily average population. This would be so only if all prisoners were sentenced to the same term. It follows that one can make an estimate of the trend in sentences from studying the relationship

---

15. *Ibid.*, p. 4, para. 15.
16. Home Office, Criminal Statistics (England and Wales) 1968, Cmnd. 4098, July 1969, p. 184.
17. Home Office, Criminal Statistics (England and Wales) 1958, Cmnd. 803, July 1959, p. 40.
18. P. 7 of the Radzinowicz Sub-committee's Report.

D

Receptions male and female 1967

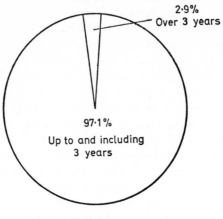

2·9%
Over 3 years

97·1%
Up to and including
3 years

DIAGRAM A

between the rate of receptions and the daily average population. If the average length of sentence remains steady, any rise in the number of receptions will be accompanied by a similar rise in the daily average population. If the latter rises more swiftly than the former, the only conclusion must be that the average length of sentence has increased, unless, since 1968, parole is making for a dramatic reduction in prison population;

Average population male and female 1967

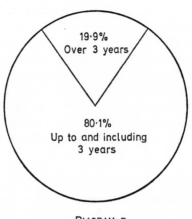

19·9%
Over 3 years

80·1%
Up to and including
3 years

DIAGRAM B

Receptions male 1967

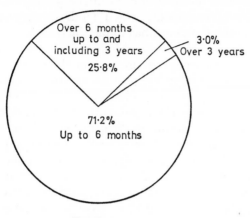

Over 6 months up to and including 3 years
25·8%

3·0%
Over 3 years

71·2%
Up to 6 months

DIAGRAM C

we doubt that it is in fact having more than a marginal effect. At one time graphs published by the Home Office showed an apparent divergence in the two curves for receptions and daily average population,[19] but since this was corrected in 1960, after a statistical error was detected, it would appear that the two curves have moved fairly parallel with one another, at least

Average population male 1967

20·2%
Over 3 years

55·4%
6 months to 3 years

24·4%
Up to 6 months

DIAGRAM D

19. See, for example, the Home Office pamphlet, *Prisons and Borstals (England and Wales)*, 4th Edn., 1960, p. 5.

since 1950.[20] However, close examination reveals that the daily average population has in fact been rising more sharply than the number of receptions, which tends to suggest that the average length of sentence has in fact increased.

The precise explanation for this increase is hard to find, however. It does not necessarily mean that the courts are passing longer sentences than in the past for the same kind of offence. The increase could be due to an increase in the seriousness of offences as well as in the criminality of the offenders, and in addition there is the decline in the use of short sentences. Courts are very reluctant these days to send a person to prison, and when they do so, often it is only as a last resort and for a substantial period. It seems also to be a fact that more of the prisoners received into prison have previous proved offences recorded against them, and more have previously experienced institutional sentences. At least so far as male prisoners are concerned, the composition of the prison population is deteriorating in quality. This might explain the tendency towards longer terms of imprisonment.[1]

It is of some interest to compare the proportion of receptions with the daily average population sentenced to various terms. Diagrams A and B show the position with regard to male and female prisoners, Diagrams D and E are limited to male prisoners. What one sees in both cases, but more dramatically in the case of male prisoners, is the very high proportion of receptions which are for short terms of imprisonment (three years and under) and the disproportionate share of the prison accommodation which has to be devoted to the provision for long-term prisoners. Five-sixths of the adult male prisoners are not serving more than three years. "The central problem of the prison administration", as the author has pointed out,[2] "is to devise a satisfactory régime for the vast number of prisoners sentenced to terms not exceeding three years, the majority of whom are recidivists with previous institutional experience".

---

20. Home Office, Report of the Prison Commissioners, 1960, Cmnd. 1467, August 1961, p. 3.
1. The matter is discussed in *Sociological Studies in the British Penal Services*, 1965, pp. 60–67.
2. *Ibid.*, p. 66.

CHAPTER 6

Types of Prison and the Classification of Prisoners

TYPES OF PRISON

A sophisticated penal system requires the development of different kinds of institution for different purposes. Prisons should be classified according to the régime provided and the different types of prisoner for whom they are intended.

The classification of prisons in the English penal system has tended to follow certain historical facts as well as serving certain functional purposes. Until recently, there were three main types of institution:

1. Local prisons;
2. Central prisons;
3. Regional training prisons.

This reflected on the one hand the need for prisons to serve a court catchment area, and to receive in that area all prisoners remanded in custody pending trial, and many who had been sentenced to serve short terms of imprisonment only. On the other hand, there was the need to provide a régime for really long-term prisoners in secure conditions but with more privileges than ordinary prisoners enjoyed. The former were the local prisons, the latter the central prisons. (The historical origin of the latter lies in the convict prison of the nineteenth century). In between the local prison and the central prison there developed in modern times the concept of the regional training prison, where selected prisoners could be given more vocational and industrial training and a fuller working week than was possible in the local prisons. The attempt to provide a special régime for those sentenced to corrective training, after the 1948 Act, eventually merged in the more general effort to provide training for all prisoners who might benefit from it. This development eroded the significance of corrective training, but of course, there were always too few places where such training could be made a reality. Wakefield and Maidstone prisons were good examples of regional training prisons. Each of these prisons was, historically speaking, the scene of an experimental régime of its own.[1] but eventually the system incorporated the experiment, and generalised the experience, as so often happens, and the "training" prison was the result. After 1948 several new training prisons were opened, at Sudbury and Portland, for men, and at Askham Grange for women. Broadly speaking, the difference between a central prison and a training prison was the length of the term to which the prisoners had been sentenced. The regional training prisons took prisoners with sentences of more than one year but less than five years, while the central prisons took prisoners sentenced to five years or more for "ordinary class" prisoners (those who had served a previous sentence) and three years or more for "star class" prisoners (those who had not served a previous sentence).[2]

It has now been found possible to adopt new and simpler descriptions of the various types of prisons for male adult prisoners. In April 1969 it was decided that in future these prisons will be known as

1. Local prisons
2. Short-term training prisons
3. Medium-term training prisons
4. Long-term training prisons

or by combinations of the above expressions.[3] There is still a differentiation according to the length of sentence; broadly speaking this is as follows:

Short-term imprisonment—up to and including 18 months.
Medium-term imprisonment—18 months up to but excluding 4 years (Stars), and 5 years (Ordinaries).
Long-term imprisonment—4 years and over (Stars), 5 years and over (Ordinaries).

The local prison remains as the "maid-of-all-work" of the Prison Department, with the duty to receive all prisoners from

---

1. Fox, p. 69, says "the first steps in establishing what has become known as the Wakefield system were recorded in 1923". See also pp. 101 and 277.
2. Royal Commission on the Penal System in England and Wales, Written Evidence, Vol. I, p. 43.
3. Information supplied by the Home Office.

the courts on remand and under sentence, and it provides the initial assembly and distribution point for the whole prison system, with the exception of the persons under 21 who are dealt with in the Remand Centres.

Some of the local prisons used to be called "special" local prisons, since they provided short-term training in open conditions for selected prisoners, whereas most local prisons were necessarily closed institutions and had rather poor training facilities. These "special" local prisons, like Eastchurch on the Isle of Sheppey, will henceforth be known as short- and medium-term training prisons.

In the local prisons, the prisoners are classified according to whether they are untried or not, this being necessary because of the special privileges accorded to untried prisoners, and the need to prepare reports about them for the courts, and for several other reasons.

Sentenced prisoners are classified under the Prison Rules and Standing Orders after their receptions interview has taken place. They will then be allocated to one of the closed or open training prisons, according to their security category, length of sentence, and their training and social welfare needs, or they will be kept in the local prison to serve their term.

"The broad principle is that as many prisoners as possible should be removed as early as possible from the local prisons to some other prison", says the Home Office pamphlet, *The Sentence of the Court*. The pamphlet continues:

> "Ideally, all prisoners other than those serving very short sentences should go from their local prison to an allocation centre where their needs could be carefully studied before a decision was reached on the prison to which they should be transferred. But the present pressure of numbers prevents this except in the case of those with sentences of three (in the case of prison recidivists generally five) years or over, for whom there is an allocation centre in each region. . . . Allocation of other prisoners is dealt with at the local prisons. . . ."[4]

The number of prisons of different types at present is as follows:[5]

Local prisons   24   (including Risley Remand Centre)

---

4. Home Office, *The Sentence of the Court*, 2nd Edn., 1969, pp. 40–41, para. 145.
5. Figures derived from information supplied by the Home Office.

Short-term training ..	..	22 ⎫	Many prisons serve
Medium-term training	..	24 ⎬	more than one of these
Long-term training ..	..	18 ⎭	purposes
Open institutions ..	..	14	(including 3 fenced)
Closed institutions ..	..	44	(including Grendon Psychiatric Prison)

It should be understood that all the local prisons are closed, and fourteen of the training prisons, out of thirty-four, are open, which is a fairly high proportion. Six of the local prisons also serve as *Remand Centres, i.e.* special institutions for receiving from the courts young persons under the age of 21, who are either remanded in custody pending trial or pending sentence, often for the purpose of obtaining medical and other reports. Some prisons contain special units, usually housed in separate wings or buildings, and many have particular features of their own programme which are unique. There is also one Remand Centre which is purpose built (at Risley) and the Psychiatric Prison at Grendon.

The development of the *Open Prisons* is a chapter in the history of the English prison system which deserves special mention.[6] Open borstal institutions had existed since 1930, when Lowdham Grange in Nottinghamshire was built, largely with the help of borstal boys, as an open institution. Then in 1936 Wakefield Prison began to use a camp called New Hall Camp, nine miles from the prison, for the accommodation of selected prisoners. After World War II, Leyhill Prison, in Gloucestershire, was developed as an open prison, and used for certain categories of long-term prisoners. There are now so many open institutions that it is impossible to describe them in detail. The main feature is usually that there is no wall, though three are now fenced, and no locked doors, though dormitory exits are usually barred at night.

The men are under a considerable temptation to run away, but they know that if they do so they will probably be recaptured and have to serve the rest of their time in a closed prison. There is usually a fairly full programme of work and leisure-time activities, and efforts are frequently made to involve the local

---

6. See Fox, pp. 69 and 100. A. Leitch, "The Open Prison", 2 *B.J.D.*, p. 25. (1951–1952); T. E. James, "Open Prisons and Borstals", [1955] Crim.L.R. 170; Lionel Fox, *International Review of Criminal Policy*, No. 2, July 1952, pp. 1–11.

population in various ways in the life of the institution, and to involve the prisoners in certain aspects of the life of the community. The risks of escapes is obviously higher from an open institution than from a closed establishment, but the likelihood of further serious offences being committed by escaping prisoners in the vicinity of an open institution is not very great. Dangerous prisoners are not selected for open conditions, and those who do escape wish to get as far away as possible in the shortest time. They may steal some clothes or money or a vehicle, however. Sex offenders and prisoners with a propensity to violence are not normally selected for an open prison, nor are long-term persistent offenders and those prisoners who are considered to be bad escape risks.[7] An open prison (at Ashwell) has been used since 1962 for recidivist prisoners (ordinaries) and this experiment proved so successful that it has been extended to other open institutions.[8] Mr. Butler once described the open institution as one of the really distinctive features of the English penal system.[9] Of course, they exist in other countries, too, but the completely open institution may perhaps be described as the most significant single contribution which the English penal system has made to the development of penal theory.

THE CLASSIFICATION OF PRISONERS

To some extent, the different ways in which prisoners are classified has been anticipated in the discussion of the different types of prison, since the one is necessarily and inextricably involved in the other.

Apart from the security classification into four categories of security risk, which is discussed elsewhere (see Chapter 7: Safe Custody and the Security Problem), prisoners are classified into different groups along the following lines:

1. Male and female prisoners;
2. Civil and criminal prisoners;
3. Remand and sentenced prisoners;
4. Adult and young prisoners (under 21);
5. Stars and ordinaries.

---

7. Home Office, *The Sentence of the Court*, 2nd Edn., 1969, p. 42, para. 150.
8. Report of the Prison Commissioners, 1962, Cmnd. 2030, June 1963, pp. 14–15; Prison Department Report, 1963, Cmnd. 2381, June 1964, p. 15.
9. House of Commons Debates, Vol. 594, col. 508, 31 October 1958.

The Prison Rules require that "prisoners shall be classified, in accordance with any directions of the Secretary of State, having regard to their age, temperament and record and with a view to maintaining good order and facilitating training and, in the case of convicted prisoners, of furthering the purpose of their training and treatment as provided by Rule 1 of these Rules".[10]

The separation of the sexes is required by the Prison Act of 1952, s. 15, as well as by the Prison Rules, 1964, r. 9.

The Prison Rules also require unconvicted prisoners to be "kept out of contact with convicted prisoners as far as this can reasonably be done",[11] and confer certain privileges upon such prisoners with regard to wearing their own clothes, being supplied with food at their own expense or that of friends, visits and correspondence. Civil prisoners enjoy similar privileges to an unconvicted prisoner but only with respect to clothing and correspondence.

The Rules also state that nothing in them "shall require a prisoner to be deprived unduly of the society of other persons".[12] They are thus clearly predicated upon association of prisoners in the prison community subject to safeguards, a far cry from the old "solitary confinement" of the early nineteenth century.

In the past the Prison Rules expressly provided for the separate classification of prisoners under 21 years of age in a Young Prisoners' Class. There is now no Rule to this effect, but the same result is reached under Prison Standing Orders. These are the basic administrative code issued by the Home Office for the guidance of governors and those in charge of institutions.

A prisoner placed in the young prisoners' class may at any time be removed from it, if he is regarded as unsuitable for that class, and may be reclassified as an adult prisoner. "Removal from the young prisoners' class may be ordered because the prisoner is thought to be a disruptive influence or because it is considered that he is of sufficient maturity to be accommodated with adult prisoners".[13]

The classification of adult prisoners into "Star Class" and "Ordinaries" was also previously enjoined by the Prison Rules, but is now done under the Standing Orders. The Star Class is

---

10. Prison Rules 1964, r. 3(1).　　　　11. *Ibid.*, r. 3(2).
12. *Ibid.*, r. 3(3).
13. Home Office, *The Sentence of the Court*, 2nd Edn., 1969, pp. 36–37, para. 132.

basically reserved for prisoners with no previous prison experience. This often includes persons with long experience of crime and of custodial institutions for young offenders, such as approved schools, detention centres and borstal institutions, and therefore does not necessarily mean prisoners lacking criminal sophistication, though no doubt that was the original idea and is still the basic consideration. Ordinaries are those who have been in prison before.

As early as 1956 we find evidence that the Prison Commissioners regarded the classification between "Star Class" prisoners and Ordinaries as unsatisfactory. Already "Stars" were being mixed with "trainable ordinaries", and there had been what is described as a considerable blurring of the edges of traditional classification. A Working Party had been set up to examine the position.[14] The Home Office in 1966 stated the principles governing classification thus:

> "in principle, the aim is to allocate all prisoners, save those serving very short terms, on the basis not only of length of sentence and previous prison experience but also of other factors such as aptitude for particular work or vocational training; psychiatric requirements; need for special security or suitability for open conditions; social and personality problems. It is also the aim to allocate prisoners as far as possible to establishments in the region from which each comes. . . . Heavy pressure on prison accommodation restricts the extent to which these aims can be achieved, and over-crowding in local prisons impedes the development of sophisticated and precise observation and allocation processes."[15]

The fact is that classification of prisoners and the use to which prisons are put fall victim to the demands of expediency, and pressure on the system, which forces the adoption of solutions which are convenient rather than ideal. There is little room for a sophisticated classification and allocation procedure in a system which is at its wit's end to cope with the day-to-day realities of the situation. While lip-service may be paid to the need to study and reflect on the prisoner's needs and capabilities and so on, there are only so many possible places to which he can be sent once the security classification is decided. Indeed, the basic administrative set-up for a proper classification and allocation procedure does not really exist.

---

14. Report of the Prison Commissioners, 1956, Cmnd. 322, p. 24, para. 3, (December 1957).
15. Estimates Committee, Eleventh Report, Minutes of Evidence, p. 2.

PRISON PROVISION SINCE 1946

The story of prisons since 1946 has been one of adaptation and response to enormous pressures generated by the rising population. Between 1946 and 1955 no less than thirty new establishments were brought into service, though none of them were purpose built. They were either old prisons brought back into service or service camps which were adapted for prison use.

Mr. Butler's White Paper of February 1959 announced a massive new building programme and admitted that "the present buildings stand as a monumental denial of the principles to which we are committed".[16] No new prison had been opened since 1912 until Everthorpe in 1958, and we are saddled with a great many nineteenth-century "fortress-type" prisons, which are too solid to scrap, and too old to modernise satisfactorily.

One constant complaint of penal reformers concerns the absence of sanitary provision in cells, which necessitates the unpleasant ritual of "slopping-out" by prisoners each morning in common recesses. It has always been maintained that English prisoners would not respect the sanitary facilities even if they were provided, and would break them or block them. The example is cited of Pentonville, which was originally plumbed for separate cell sanitation, but this had to be removed. Why it is possible to provide W.C.s in cells in other countries such as the U.S. and Canada and not in Britain is a puzzle, but there may be a technical explanation in the pressure flush system of those countries as contrasted with the English system of gravity flushes. In any event, the solution to this vexed problem seems likely to be sought nowadays in two quite different directions: firstly, the provision of dormitory accommodation with access to a common bathroom and toilet area, serving a dormitory of a dozen to twenty beds, and, secondly, the electronic unlocking of particular cells on remote control, when prisoners seek to visit the toilet. It is to be hoped that experience with these solutions will eventually enable all prisoners to have the right to enjoy these minimum standards of decency in their daily living arrangements. The same might be said for provision of adequate bath facilities, necessitated by rising standards of living which are reflected quite naturally in the needs and expectations of the prison population.

---

16. Home Office, *Penal Practice in a Changing Society*, February 1959, p. 14.

Everthorpe, near Hull, planned as a secure prison, and opened in 1958, was converted immediately to borstal use. Blundeston (Suffolk) houses long-term prisoners. Albany (Isle of Wight) is the latest secure prison to be completed, and was opened in early 1967. It is built to the Blundeston design, but with some modifications and improvements such as the installation of electronic locking and unlocking of cells in one wing which enables prisoners to make use of sanitary facilities on the landings at night and thus obviates the need for "slopping-out". Also additional security provisions are now being added, since the Mountbatten Report.

The 1967 Prison Department Report speaks of a regional system of classification centres for long-term prisoners being established at Birmingham, Bristol, Liverpool and Wandsworth. For the time being, however, as Wandsworth was not yet equipped to deal with all the long-term prisoners received in the south-east region, Wormwood Scrubs continued to assist in this process, classifying star prisoners serving more than three but less than ten years. "Local prisons were given the task of classifying short-term prisoners", and "prison officers were trained for this work", says the Report, "and found great satisfaction in this useful development of their skills".[17]

Some reclassification of prisons was involved in these developments. Thus in 1967 Wandsworth and Pentonville, which previously had comparable tasks, were given distinctive roles. Wandsworth takes all prison recidivists sentenced in the London Area to terms exceeding twelve months and Pentonville takes those given sentences of twelve months or less.[18]

NEW PRISONS IN THE CURRENT PROGRAMME

In 1969 a new industrial prison was opened at Coldingley, near Bisley, Surrey, providing productive industrial work for 300 prisoners. Two new prisons are to be built which will provide additional accommodation for Class A security risks:

Long Lartin, Worcestershire, likely to be opened in 1970.

Full Sutton, Yorkshire, likely to be opened in 1972 or 1973. Two more new closed prisons are expected to be completed by the end of 1970 (and another three by 1972 or 1973) to accom-

---

17. Prison Department Report, 1967, p. 6, para. 8.
18. *Ibid.*, p. 6, para. 9.

modate Class B prisoners. It is also hoped that three new closed prisons will be completed in the next five years (and a start made on three more) to accommodate Class C prisoners. One of the above will be the former Ministry of Defence camp at Wartling, near Bexhill.[19]

There is also an extensive development programme for young offenders:

1. The new closed borstal at Onley (opened at the end of 1968) has enabled the borstals at Reading and Portsmouth to be closed, and these establishments have reverted to prison use;

2. In 1970, funds permitting, a start will be made on Glen Parva, Leicester, where it is proposed to develop a complex of young offenders' establishments comprising a training borstal, a borstal allocation centre and a remand centre;

3. Plans are being considered for the replacement of the Wormwood Scrubs allocation centre by a new establishment and for the provision of additional remand accommodation.[20]

With regard to female offenders there has been a major revision of policy. The women's prison at Holloway is to be rebuilt on the same site (see Chapter 16: Female Prisoners) and will be used largely as a medical and diagnostic facility.

PRISON DESIGN

There are two features of prison architecture which deserve mention:

(*i*) *The break away from the traditional tiered block with landings.*—Prisons traditionally have been designed on the basis of a three-or four-tier wing, built radially from a centre where a good view can be obtained of what is going on in each wing. These involve open landings which are noisy, but the layout contributes to ease of observation and management. Although the design for Everthorpe is disappointing, with a lot of money spent on a high wall, and no cell sanitation system, there is much pride in the design for the new prisons, Blundeston in particular. An

19. Rt. Hon. James Callaghan, House of Commons Debates, Vol. 773, cols. 660–661, 14 November 1968.
20. *Ibid.*, cols. 661–662.

entirely new design has been developed, getting away from the old open halls with landings, and allowing for small groups to be organised within the prison on a small-section basis. Also there are no high walls, but there are two security barriers, (1) an eight-foot concrete wall for privacy and (2) a chain-link fence topped with barbed wire. Originally twelve feet in height, this has since been strengthened and raised in height to a twenty-foot fence. An ordinary office block forms part of the perimeter, through which access is gained to the prison, instead of via the usual formidable gateway.[1]

The modern blocks are not entirely satisfactory from the point of view of ease of management of prisoners, however, neither is the telegraph pole system of a central corridor with wings branching off at right angles, which has been used at Onley borstal. The three floors of a modern prison block are approached by one narrow stairway, and it is difficult for a single officer to keep observation. They do have the advantage of providing dormitory accommodation for some prisoners, and breaking up the prisoners into groups of up to ten in a corridor facilitates the surviving applications of the Norwich system (see Chapter 10: The Prison Community), and allows an officer to be allocated to have special responsibility for getting to know one group of up to ten prisoners, which system is successfully used in Blundeston.

In the existing buildings there have been considerable improvements, both in the living accommodation and in the workshops and educational and recreational facilities. A lot of money has been spent on sanitation, especially since Peter Wildeblood's account of Wormwood Scrubs,[2] and pastel shades of paint and bright colours have largely replaced the traditional green, cream and chocolate colours.

(ii) *The development of a new type of prison cell without bars was announced in February* 1959.[3]—This is actually smaller than the traditional cell, which was thirteen feet by seven feet by nine feet, and the bars are built into the window frame which incorporates manganese steel bars. There is a table built into the

---

1. The Report of the Prison Commissioners for 1959, Cmnd. 1117, August 1960. pp. 116–117 contains a description of the plans for Blundeston prison.
2. Peter Wildeblood, *A Way of Life*, 1956. For pictures of the Wormwood Scrubs outside lavatories, old and new, see Report of the Prison Commissioners for 1958, Cmnd. 825, p. 91.
3. *The Times*, 11 February 1959.

wall, and the general impression is of more space. There is still no W.C. provided to avoid the daily "slopping-out" procedure which is the bane of prison reformers.

The Prison Department may shortly be turning towards use of the enclosed courtyard with access to the prison only via an administrative block built into one of the four walls, a design familiar to the American federal correctional institutions, such as Danbury, Connecticut.[4] Old-fashioned prison windows may eventually be replaced by the modern kind which provide more light and air. Faced with the necessity of keeping in service some of the nineteenth-century "fortress" prisons, it has been decided to re-allocate some resources to improving and modernising these and bringing them up to more acceptable standards. There is a Penal Institutions Joint Development Group which supervises the preparation of plans for new prisons, consisting of representatives of the Home Office and the Ministry of Works and Buildings.[5]

Much thought has been given by some writers to the relation between prison architecture and design and prison programmes.[6] But while it may be true that what is possible in the way of programme is to some extent limited by the physical set-up, it is also true, as Paterson insisted, that it is through men, not through buildings or regulations, that reform in the spirit of our prison and borstal systems is to be achieved.

There is also evidence of a lack of communication between the architects and planners and those who actually have to work in the institutions concerning the practical needs of operating these places. Thus new workshops are built without an adequate power supply, and buildings are provided which can be climbed by using the new style square barred windows. There is undoubtedly a great deal of room for improvement in the kind of provision made by those whose business it is to supply the prison system's needs for new buildings.

---

4. Paul W. Tappan, *Crime, Justice and Correction*, 1960, has some illustrations.
5. See Memorandum 20, Appendices to the Minutes of Evidence, Estimates Committee Eleventh Report, Session 1966–1967. See also Memorandum 19, "The Prison Building Programme", and Memorandum 15 on "The Emergency Building Programme".
6. Leslie Fairweather, "Prison Architecture in England", 1 *B.J.C.*, p. 357, 1960. John Madge, "Building for Prisoners", *New Society*, No. 22, pp. 12–14, 28 February 1963.

CHAPTER 7

Safe Custody and the Security Problem

CONFLICTING GOALS OF PRISON ADMINISTRATION

Reference has already been made to the different goals which inspire those in charge of custodial institutions, as contrasted with the goals of sentences. The twin goals of penal administrators were identified as (1) Safe Custody, and (2) Training and Treatment.

The problem of safe custody is not simply that of devising a setting which is physically secure in order to prevent escapes, though this is the aspect of the matter which has received so much attention recently. Safe custody has at last four different meanings in the custodial setting:

1. Prevention of escapes (which we will call the security problem);
2. Prevention of physical attacks by prisoners on each other or on prison staff;
3. Prevention of contamination of prisoners, by segregation or physical isolation;
4. Generally, the problem of control or discipline.

Although the first of these aspects of safe custody, the prevention of escapes, has given rise to most concern, the other aspects of the matter deserve attention. How far should steps be taken to make escape physically impossible? How far should prisoners be protected from each other? In what circumstances should certain prisoners be isolated from the general prison community in their own interests? How much indiscipline can be tolerated in the prison community? Posed in this way, the questions are seen not to involve any absolutes but to be questions of degree to which qualified answers must be given.

One reason for this is that the other goal of penal administrators, Training and Treatment, requires that every effort should be made to make the experience of being imprisoned a positive one, from which the prisoner can derive benefit in terms of his attitudes and personality. It has been said by a former Governor of a maximum security prison that there is no necessary conflict between security and treatment. The measures which are considered necessary for safe custody can be used constructively to show the prisoner the kind of problem he presents to others, and to enable him to learn from experience so that he can progressively be trusted. But not everyone, even in the prison service, would agree about this, and there is certainly a tension between these different goals which tend to pull in opposite directions. The low morale of the prison service today probably stems largely from confusion about these goals and a failure to appreciate how any synthesis can occur.

The main difficulty with regard to most prisoners is that when they come into prison their lives are already in a state of disarray. The Prison Rules state that the object should be "to encourage and assist them to lead a good and useful life". What does this mean? In many cases the most that can be hoped for is that they should become less criminal and lead better and more useful lives—again it is a question of degree, and too much should not be expected in the way of complete success with such unhopeful material

The problem of control or discipline is bound up with the smooth running of any community, and figures strongly in the Prison Rules. Thus Rule 2, concerning the Maintenance of Order and Discipline, requires that:

1. Order and discipline shall be maintained with firmness, but with no more restriction than is required for safe custody and well-ordered community life;

2. Officers shall seek to influence prisoners through their own example and leadership, and to enlist their willing co-operation;

3. At all times the treatment of prisoners shall be such as to encourage their self-respect and a sense of personal responsibility, but a prisoner shall not be employed in any disciplinary capacity.

The question which frequently poses itself in the day-to-day running of penal institutions is how much disturbance and deviant behaviour can be tolerated or suffered within the context of what is supposed to be a "well-ordered community life". It is vital to provide opportunities for prisoners to express themselves and find out about their own weaknesses and limitations and the nature of their relations with others. A large part of Training and Treatment consists of developing self-reliance and self-knowledge among prisoners as well as self-control. This is not an easy task in a community of persons with pretty mixed-up lives, living very closely together, and with a poorly developed sense of responsibility and acceptance of each other's shortcomings.

That it is possible at all to run a prison community peaceably (not to say peacefully) must be regarded as a remarkable tribute to the gifts of tolerance and human understanding and the skills of prison staff at every level. The problems of safe custody, security, and control are never far from the surface, and it is within the context of these pressures or demands that rehabilitative effort must find its place.

THE SECURITY PROBLEM AND THE MOUNTBATTEN REPORT

Following the dramatic escape of the spy George Blake from Wormwood Scrubs Prison, an inquiry was set up in 1966 under the Earl of Mountbatten to look into the whole question of escapes and prison security. The inquiry was later extended to include other escapes including that of Frank Mitchell from Dartmoor. The Report found clear weaknesses in physical security and in prison administration, both at the local level and at the head office.[1] Earl Mountbatten and his team of investigators concluded that there was no really secure prison in Britain, though bold and imaginative plans existed for a new security prison at Albany, on the Isle of Wight, close to Parkhurst, and these were commended.

> "For several years", the Report says, "not enough care has been taken to reduce unnecessary escapes from the old prisons. Much can be done towards this without imposing a harsh and inhumane régime . . . the modern policy of humane liberal treatment aimed at rehabilitating prisoners rather than merely exacting punishment is right and . . . escapes should be prevented by far better perimeter security."[2]

1. Home Office, Report of the Inquiry into Prison Escapes and Security, Cmnd. 3175, December 1966.
2. *Ibid.*, p. 4, para. 14.

A new classification of prisoners into four categories, based on the security risk, was proposed, and has been adopted.[3] These categories are:

Category A Those whose escape would be highly dangerous to the public or the police or to the security of the state.

Category B Those who need less secure conditions but for whom escape must be made very difficult.

Category C Those who cannot be trusted in open conditions but who do not have the ability or resources to make a determined escape attempt.

Category D Those who can be trusted in open conditions.

The Report recommends that proper machinery should be set up to ensure that prisoners are allocated to the correct category. The overcrowding of prisons is described as a serious risk to security, and the reception of more prisoners with very long fixed sentences has added to the strain.[4] New security devices should be introduced, and the staff should be trained in these matters.[5]

The existence inside prisons of a number of hostels (there were eleven) from which prisoners went out to work in the day in the free community was regarded as a serious security risk. Such hostels provided a ready means of communication for potential escapers with the outside world. They should be removed from prison premises, and located in suitable premises outside the institutions. The closing of the hostels did not involve any condemnation of the policy of easing the transition to outside life for the prisoners by this means. The Mountbatten Report expressly recognised the importance of the hostel schemes in this connection.[6]

SEQUEL TO THE MOUNTBATTEN REPORT

Following the Mountbatten Report, large sums of money (some £2 million) were spent on re-equipping and reorganising the prisons from the point of view of security. Not only were locks improved, walls were mounted with barbed wire, fences raised in height or newly provided and lit by searchlights, dog

---

3. Cmnd. 3175, p. 4, para. 15.
4. *Ibid.*, pp. 54–55, paras. 205–207.
5. *Ibid.*, p. 5, para. 18.
6. *Ibid.*, pp. 81–82, paras. 303–306.

patrols were introduced by day and by night and there were constant checks made on the perimeter. In some places, television scanning of walls, corridors and other vulnerable places was introduced, and already in some places has been discontinued. Uniformed prison staff were supplied with "walkie-talkie" radio equipment. About 140 prisoners were classified as Category A prisoners, and detained in very restrictive conditions at Durham, Leicester and Parkhurst prisons. There was initially a sharp fall in evening classes of an educational and recreational kind. The number of prison escapes was, however, substantially reduced, as may be seen from the following figures:

ESCAPES FROM CLOSED PRISONS AND REMAND CENTRES[7]

1961	1962	1963	1964	1965	1966	1967	1968
114	56	71	93	79	85	23	21

TOTAL NUMBER OF ESCAPES AND RECAPTURES[8]
(England and Wales)

Year					Escapes	Recapture
1965 ..	..	..	..	..	404	396
1966 ..	..	..	..	..	376	370
1967 ..	..	..	..	..	240	233
1968 ..	..	..	..	..	243	236
1969 to 30th June	..		··	..	140	121

THE RADZINOWICZ REPORT

In 1967 the Home Secretary asked the Advisory Council on the Penal System "to consider the régime for long-term prisoners detained in conditions of maximum security, and to make recommendations". A sub-committee of the Advisory Council, presided over by Professor Leon Radzinowicz, prepared the report, which was accepted by the majority of the Council.[9]

There were several questions which the Sub-Committee considered:

1. Concentration or dispersal of high security risk prisoners;
2. The question of arming prison staff.

---

7. Home Office, "People in Prison", Cmnd. 4214, November 1969, p. 80; The Mountbatten Report, Cmnd. 3175, December 1966, p. 55.
8. House of Commons Debates, Written Answers, 25 July 1969. Vol. 787 col. 529.
9. Home Office, *The Régime for Long-term Prisoners in Conditions of Maximum Security*, Report of the Advisory Council on the Penal System, 1968.

I CONCENTRATION OR DISPERSAL OF HIGH
SECURITY RISKS

The Report begins by showing the proportion of prisoners
with very long-term sentences (here defined as determinate
sentences of 14 years and over) who have been received into
prison in recent years. The problem is accentuated by the
increased number of prisoners with life sentences among the
receptions, especially since the abolition of capital punishment.
There are also the persistent offenders who "spend long periods
in prison punctuated by only brief spells of liberty".[10]

The conditions in which the fifty or sixty Class A prisoners
were held in the maximum security units at Durham, Leicester
and Parkhurst, are described as "a temporary and most undesirable expedient. The physical limitations of the building
preclude any major improvement in the conditions".[11] It is
hardly surprising that there have been several disturbances at
each of these centres in the last few years.[12] A stern line was
taken by the Home Office about such disturbances, and at the
same time steps have been taken to alleviate the conditions in
which these men have to live and work so far as possible.[13]

A Press Association reporter who has been allowed to visit the
security wings twice has commented that "conditions are vastly
improved compared with those when the wings were first
opened. . . . There is more space, more interesting work, better
facilities inside the cells and out. Within the walls supervision
is less close because of better security arrangements."[14]

But the same observer expressed his doubts, which he shared
with some of the prison staff as well as with the prisoners,
"whether mentally they can survive the confined conditions
they are in, seeing the same few faces day after day". Since this
comment was made, the conditions for visitors to the security
wings have been tightened up, following the recommendations
of the Advisory Council,[15] and no one pretends that the condi-

---

10. Cmnd. 3175, p. 6, para. 17.
11. *Ibid.*, p. 7, para. 19.
12. Durham, *The Times*, 11 February 1967, 20 December 1968; Leicester, *The
    Times*, 11 December 1968; Parkhurst, *The Times*, 28 August 1968.
13. *The Times*, 9 April 1968, "Callaghan warns gaol rebels". *The Times*, 13 April
    1968, " 'Evil men' among rebel prisoners. Lord Stonham replies."
14. *The Times*, 27 July 1968, "Survival in security gaols", by Alfred Browne, Press
    Association reporter.
15. *The Times*, 25 June 1969, House of Lords Debates, 24 June 1969, Vol. 303,
    col. 138 (Lord Stonham).

tions are ideal or such that ought to be tolerated for very long.

"The conditions in these blocks", said the Mountbatten Report, "are such as no country with a record of civilised behaviour ought to tolerate any longer than is absolutely essential as a stop-gap measure. . . . A purpose built prison is required at the earliest possible date."[16]

The argument in favour of concentrating the high security risks in one place was that in this way, by providing perimeter security, the régime inside the walls could be made more relaxed and humane. The Mountbatten Report approved the plan for a new small maximum security prison which it was planned to build at Alvington, on the Isle of Wight,[17] but the Radzinowicz Sub-committee came down firmly in favour of a policy of limited dispersal of security-risk prisoners to three or four long-term prisons.[18] This solution was suggested by the experience of the American prison systems, in particular that of the U.S. Federal Bureau of Prisons, which had closed Alcatraz and abandoned the policy of concentration. They found that the majority of the inmates settled down satisfactorily in their new environment, and the behaviour of some of the more difficult prisoners actually improved. We are told that, while a small proportion of dangerous and disruptive prisoners remained, the general régime of the other institutions was not jeopardised.

The Radzinowicz Sub-committee recommend the creation of small segregation units within the larger prisons,[19] while contemplating a general increase in the security of long-term prisons, by way of strengthening perimeter security, the erection of observation towers, patrols, etc.

The Sub-committee report also makes recommendations about the type of régime to be provided for long-term prisoners, improvements in the personal facilities of prisoners, the work situation, and educational and other activities, and contact with the outside world. It is in the latter connection that the suggestion is made for conjugal visits to be permitted as an experiment.[20] This has been rejected by the Home Office as unsuitable in the conditions existing in the present closed prisons. Instead, the Home Secretary has announced that he

16. Cmnd. 3175, p. 56, para. 212.
17. *Ibid.*, p. 58, para. 215.
18. *Ibid.*, section IV, pp. 13–17; pp. 25–27, paras. 62–67.
19. *Ibid.*, p. 17, para. 42; pp. 63–64, paras. 163–167.
20. *Ibid.*, Section XII, pp. 53–56.

proposes to extend the home leave system.[1] At present this applies to prisoners serving five years and certain prisoners serving between two and five years during the last four months of their sentence. The details of the new scheme have yet to be announced, but it is likely to allow additional short periods of week-end leave for long-term prisoners, especially in the last year of their sentence, and provide for a gradual development of the home leave arrangements.

Other recommendations

The Radzinowicz Report included other recommendations:
1. There is need to gather as much information as possible about a prisoner and his associates, before deciding upon his security classification;
2. There is need for the prison authorities to review such security classification regularly;[2]
3. There should be more research into the existence and nature of what is referred to as deterioration among prisoners serving very long sentences;[3]
4. There should be another committee to study the treatment of psychopaths and the relation between the prison system and the special hospitals.[4]

2 THE QUESTION OF ARMING PRISON STAFF

The Radzinowicz Sub-committee divided on the question whether it would be right to arm prison officers and station them in towers on the perimeter, as a protection against an armed rescue or insurrection. The Advisory Council was also divided (one might almost say they were at sixes and sevens, since that is the way they split).

The majority view of the Sub-committee supported by six members of the Advisory Council, started from the generally accepted fact that rescue or assistance from the outside is the real danger today. Curiously none of the countries visited by the Radzinowicz Sub-committee had any experience of this. The possibility of organised outside help cannot be discounted whenever a member of a gang of professional lawbreakers is

---

1. House of Commons Debates, 14 November 1968, Vol. 773, col. 663.
2. Cmnd. 3175, p. 11, para. 30.
3. *Ibid.*, Recommendations (xxxv), p. 82.
4. *Ibid.*, Recommendations (xliii), p. 83.

held in custody serving a long sentence. The proceeds of a large
and successful robbery might enable members of such a gang
to command quite considerable resources.[5]

The ideal would be to equip officers in towers with some form
of non-lethal weapon. No such weapon is currently available.
So the Sub-committee favoured arming the guards, to provide a powerful deterrent: "no other deterrent would be as
powerful, and nothing would do as much to convince both
prisoners and staff that escape attempts would fail as the
presence in the tower of alert guards equipped with firearms."[6]
There would be no question of arming officers inside the prison,
or of keeping firearms or ammunition inside the prison. There
would be no separate group of men manning the towers.
Prison officers would be liable to a tour of duty of perhaps
three months on observation in the towers, just as officers are
liable to other supervisory duties at present. When on such
duty they would be equipped with a rifle or pistol in the use of
which they would be trained. Their instructions would be to
use this weapon only if it was clear that a determined attempt
was being made to breach the security of the prison, and if
sufficient prison officers could not be deployed in time to
prevent the escape.[7]

The alternatives are spelled out, including

"continued restrictions on the daily and yearly existence of these
prisoners of a kind that many liberal minded people might well
feel even more repugnant than the possible use of firearms. . ."

"In the present situation we regard the arming of officers in
the observation towers of a small number of closed prisons as
an essential, though regrettable, part of the security of a prison
which aims to provide for long-term prisoners a liberal and
humane régime."[8]

A Note of Reservation signed by one member of the Sub-
committee (Dr. Peter Scott) was supported by seven members
of the Advisory Council.[9] Dr. Scott's view was that arming
prison guards in order to man the perimeter would be counter-
productive. The Mountbatten Report after careful consideration had recommended against this. One of the three very

5. Cmnd. 3175, p. 22, para. 56.
6. *Ibid.*, p. 23, para. 59.
7. *Ibid.*, pp. 23–24, para. 60.
8. *Ibid.*, p. 24, para. 61.
9. *Ibid.*, pp. 84–86.

senior police officials who gave evidence was strongly against the use of guns in prison defence. So were some prison governors. Evidence from other countries where there was a much more general use of firearms was not convincing because of the different circumstances. Prison officers might not wish to be armed since this would detract from their increasingly therapeutic function. In fact their Association later emphatically rejected the use of firearms and the Police Review also condemned the proposal. The danger of an arms race between authority and the criminal must be considered.

Dr. Scott analyses the 140 or so cases in Class A, about which the Sub-committee had received information. He points out that there are several groups:

1. The frankly psychiatric group, and sex offenders (overlapping but not identical);
2. The spies;
3. The so-called professional criminals.

"The evidence shows that in general this group is uneducated and unskilled and as disorganized in their personal and social lives as is the common small-scale criminal, yet capable of extremes of ruthless impulsive violence. Only a very few of them (for instance the great train robbers) have belonged to criminal groups which would have the resources and capacity to organize determined rescue . . . and none has in fact been achieved since security has been improved. It is this tiny group within a group and the spies, which have brought us to the point of using guns."[10]

A further point made by Dr. Scott is that in general (but with recognisable exceptions) the better organised the criminal group, the less likely will they, and their prisoner colleagues, be to commit wanton violence. (These well-organised criminals are unlikely to be primarily killers, though we may make them so if we oppose them with guns.)[11]

Acceptance and implementation of the Radzinowicz Report

The Home Office have accepted the recommendations of the Radzinowicz Report relating to dispersal of high security risk prisoners. Six prisons are to be converted to take such prisoners. Gartree, Hull and Albany will be added to Durham, Leicester

---

10. Cmnd. 3175, p. 85, para. 6.
11. *Ibid.*, p. 85, para. 7.

and Parkhurst in the next few years, and eventually two new prisons, Long Lartin, Worcs. (1970) and Full Sutton, Yorkshire (1972/1973) will be added. That will give a range of secure prisons, and, as the Home Secretary put it, "this will help . . . to break down the anti-hero complex which some of them (maximum security prisoners) seem to have, when they pick themselves out, public attention is focused on them, and they become the aristocrats of the prison system".[12]

At the same time, the Home Secretary announced that after considering the arguments very carefully, he rejected the Advisory Council's recommendation that armed security guards should be used at the dispersal prisons to prevent escapes. He said he was reinforced in this decision by the attitude of the prison officers. There has been very little discussion of this part of the Home Secretary's decision.

The Prison Officers' Association, as the Home Secretary admitted, was in favour of concentration, and *The Times* reported that the new policy was likely to bring the Home Office into conflict with the local authorities in the areas where the prisons are situated, as well as with the Prison Officers' Association. *The Times* also mentioned that "prison workers are concerned that the plan may take years to implement and mean that the unsatisfactory conditions in existing security blocks at Parkhurst, Durham and Leicester will continue".[13] The Mountbatten Report and the Advisory Council Report had condemned the conditions in these places.

Mr. Castell, of the Prison Officers' Association, has described the Home Office's acceptance of the Radzinowicz recommendations in preference to the Mountbatten view as a mistake, and says that the Radzinowicz Committee went beyond its terms of reference which was simply to recommend a suitable régime for a prison built for this purpose.[14] The decision has caused dismay in the prison service, it is said. The point about the terms of reference is hardly correct, since the Advisory Council was simply asked "to consider the regime for long-term prisoners detained in conditions of maximum security, and to make recommendations". They were not precluded from

---

12. House of Commons Debates, 14 November 1968, Vol. 773, cols. 658–660.
13. *The Times*, 30 July 1968.
14. Fred Castell, "Prisons—Has the Home Office Blundered?", *Police*, October 1968.

recommending that the conditions should not involve the concentration of such prisoners in one place but dispersal. However,
it might have been thought that this matter was already
decided by the acceptance of the Mountbatten Report.

Only time will show whether the one Report or the other
was more correct in its analysis of the situation and the remedies
proposed.[15] While there are some who believe that the remedy
of dispersal was correct but should have been more radically
embraced, others continue to suspect that in the end we may be
driven to the solution of concentration. The thought of having
in one institution the train robbers, the Kray brothers and their
associates, and the Richardson gang, should provide a caution-
ary argument in favour of the present policy of limited dispersal.
The latest administrative moves inside the head office of the
Prison Department show that security is now regarded as of
great importance.[16] The Mountbatten Report recommended
the creation of the post of Inspector-General of Prisons, which
has now been reinforced by the appointment of two Assistant
Directors as inspectors, and the Controller (Operations) will
also have a senior official charged with special responsibility
for security.

DISCIPLINE IN PRISON

A basic requirement of the prison community is order, and
this can only be maintained at times by the use of disciplinary
measures. To be effective such measures may either be imposed
from above with crushing authority, in which case they might
just as well be characterised by arbitrariness and vindictiveness
as by justice and fairplay; alternatively they may be imposed
by procedures which are manifestly fair, and accepted as such
by the inmates. They may also serve a subsidiary purpose as
part of the training process. In practice prison discipline shares
all these characteristics in varying degree.

In the English penal system, as we have seen, the Rules
require that "order and discipline shall be maintained with
firmness, but with no more restriction than is required for safe
custody and well-ordered community life". Moreover "at all

---

15. For discussion, see Hugh J. Klare, "Prisons Since The Mountbatten Report",
    New Society, 31 August 1967; "Prisoners in Maximum Security", *New Society*,
    4 April 1968.
16. See Chapter 8: Prison Staff, sub-title 5, Headquarters Staff, and Home Office
    announcement of 4 July 1969.

times" (and this must include the time when he is being disciplined) "the treatment of prisoners shall be such as to encourage their self-respect and a sense of personal responsibility".[17]

Discipline is the responsibility of the staff, and this cannot be shared with prisoners: "a prisoner shall not be employed in any disciplinary capacity", say the Rules.[18] An officer in dealing with a prisoner "shall not use force unnecessarily",[19] and when the application of force to the prisoner is necessary, one would expect the same rule to apply as in the case of civil population acting in self-defence, that the force used was reasonable. But the prison rule is narrower than this; it simply states that "no more force than is necessary shall be used".[20] The prison officer's own disciplinary code makes it an offence to use unnecessary force. Moreover, "no officer shall act deliberately in a manner calculated to provoke a prisoner".[1]

The English prison officers carry staves (concealed in a special pocket) for use only when essential and in self-defence, but no fire-arms or tear-gas or the like are held in prisons. In the past, at Dartmoor, officers supervising outside working parties carried carbines, but this practice ceased in the last twenty years.[2]

One measure of a prison system is the number of disciplinary offences in relation to the total prison population. Fox says that prior to World War II the average number of prisoners punished over a ten-year period was 4·5 per cent. of the population. Since the war, the figure has increased to 8 per cent. (mentioned by Fox in 1952). Corporal punishment as a prison disciplinary measure was abolished by the Criminal Justice Act 1967.[3] In recent years few awards of corporal punishment had been made, and these had rarely been confirmed.

The measures available in order to control prisoners include removal from association (under Rule 43), temporary confinement (under Rule 45), and restraints (which are physical devices such as loose canvas jackets, body belts, handcuffs, ankle straps, and confinement in special cells) (under Rule 46).

---

17. Prison Rules 1964, r. 2.   18. *Ibid.*, r. 2(3).
19. *Ibid.*, r. 44(1).
20. *Ibid.*
1. *Ibid.*, r. 44(2).
2. Fox, p. 159. The Radzinowicz Sub-committee Report, 1968, p. 23, para. 59.
3. Criminal Justice Act 1967, s. 65.

These may be used only for short periods on the governor's authority. For example, with regard to removal from association the governor may arrange for this to be done, where it appears desirable for the maintenance of good order or discipline or in the prisoner's own interests, but a prisoner shall not be removed from association for a period of more than 24 hours without the authority of a member of the visiting committee or board of visitors, or of the Secretary of State. An authority so given shall be for a period not exceeding one month, but is renewable.[4] Likewise with regard to placing a prisoner under restraint, the governor's power is severely limited, and after 24 hours the written authority of a member of the visiting committee or board of visitors or someone acting on behalf of the Secretary of State is required. Restraints are not to be used as a means of punishment, and the temporary confinement of a prisoner in a special cell when he is violent or refractory is likewise not to be used as a punishment.[5]

Punishment may be ordered for offences against discipline (twenty-one offences are listed in Rule 47) after a charge has been properly laid and inquired into by the Governor. The penalties are divided into those which the governor may award, and those which require some other authority. Governor's awards include caution, forfeiture or postponement or privileges, not exceeding 28 days, exclusion from associated work and stoppage of earnings, not exceeding 14 days, cellular confinement and restricted diet, not exceeding three days, forfeiture of remission of sentence, not exceeding 14 days, and various other losses of privilege.

Graver offences cannot be dealt with by the governor, unless he dismisses the charge upon investigation, but must be referred to the visiting committee or board of visitors.[6]

Each local prison has a visiting committee of magistrates appointed annually by the local quarter sessions or borough sessions. Other prisons such as training prisons and borstal institutions, have boards of visitors appointed by the Secretary of State from suitable local people, including a proportion of magistrates.[7]

---

4. Prison Rules 1964, r. 43(2).
5. *Ibid.*, r. 46.
6. *Ibid.*, r. 51(1).
7. Fox, p. 85.

The disciplinary function of the visiting committee or board of visitors concerns the grave offences against prison discipline, such as escapes or attempted escapes, assaulting an officer, and gross personal violence to anyone not an officer, also any serious or repeated offence against discipline. There is also a category of especially grave offences such as mutiny or incitement to mutiny, and doing gross personal violence to an officer. The range of punishments for grave offences includes, in addition to caution, forfeiture or postponement of privileges, exclusion from associated work, stoppage of earnings, cellular confinement, for not more than 56 days, restricted diet (not exceeding 15 days) and forfeiture of remission of sentence, not exceeding 180 days. Especially grave offences may lead to an award of more than 180 days forfeiture of remission, and in the past, male prisoners could be ordered to undergo corporal punishment. The latter order needed the confirmation of the Secretary of State.

The Prison Department Annual Reports contain information about the number of offences and punishments awarded in the different kinds of establishments. This shows annual averages per head of the average population for each kind of institution. In 1967 there were as follows:

Institutions for Males			*Females*
Open prisons	0·7	.. ..	0·6
Closed prisons	0·9	.. ..	1·3
Open borstals	0·8	.. ..	—
Closed borstals	1·6	.. ..	4·4
Open detention centres (Senior)	0·4 ⎫		
Closed detention centres (Senior)	2·3 ⎬		3·4
Detention Centres (Junior)	2·0 ⎭		

There was a disturbing outbreak of violence against prison officers in 1961 but special steps were taken to remove violent prisoners to a separate wing at Brixton Prison, where they were placed under intensive supervision. These measures appear to have effectively prevented repetition of this trend.[8]

The most frequently used punishments in 1967 were stoppage

8. Prison Commission Report, 1960, Cmnd. 1467, August 1961, p. 15; *The Times*, leading article "Trouble-makers in Prison", 12 May 1961. But the recent trouble at Parkhurst prison, 24 October 1969, shows that the problem is a recurring one.

or reduction of earnings and forfeiture or postponement of privileges (over 8,000 awards each). Next came forfeiture or remission and exclusion from associated work (over 5,000 awards each) and cellular confinement (nearly 5,000 awards). Restricted diet was ordered in nearly 4,000 cases out of a total of 11,642 inmates punished. (These various punishments may have been frequently combined in any particular case.)

SEGREGATION UNDER RULE 43

From time to time prisoners have to be segregated from the main prison population for their own protection. This is frequently done at the prisoner's request, and may be sought for several reasons, such as the expected arrival in the prison of an old enemy, or the suspicion of being guilty of "grassing" to the police or the prison authorities. From October 1964 a special wing was set aside at Manchester prison for prisoners from all parts of the country who ask to be segregated from other prisoners under Rule 43. This arrangement is intended primarily for prisoners serving sentences of nine months or over who have been under Rule 43 continuously for their own protection for a period of at least three months and for whom there seems to be no prospect of an early return to ordinary prison conditions. Exceptionally it may be used for other cases. The idea is to provide a more positive and constructive régime for these prisoners, while at the same time maintaining their segregation.[9] These "segregation" prisoners were eventually transferred to Shepton Mallet.[10]

DIET AND RESTRICTED DIET

At one time there were two kinds of restricted diet (Nos. 1 & 2) one being a more severe restriction than the other, but the Departmental Committee to Review Punishments in Prisons, etc. recommended that the more severe No. 2 diet should be abolished[11] and this has been done for both prisons and borstals. No restricted diet is now used in women's establishments, and this is likely to be dropped for male prisoners very soon.

One might add here that Rule 21 requires that food provided

---

9. Prison Department Report 1964, Cmnd. 2708, July 1965, p. 13.
10. Prison Department Report 1966, Cmnd. 3408, October 1967, p. 8.
11. Report of a Committee to Review Punishment in Prisons, Borstal Institutions, Approved Schools and Remand Homes, Parts I & II, Cmd. 8256, June 1951.

for prisoners shall be "wholesome, nutritious, well-prepared and served, reasonably varied and sufficient in quantity". No convicted prisoner is allowed to have any other food than that which is ordinarily provided, but unconvicted prisoners may be supplied with food at their own expense or that of their friends. No convicted prisoner shall be given less food than is ordinarily provided except under an award of restricted diet or upon the medical officer's recommendation.[12] As always where institutional cooking is involved, the quality of food varies considerably from one institution to another. (Bread from the bakery at Wormwood Scrubs and other prisons is of high quality.) From time to time serious complaints are made about food served in prisons,[13] but these have never been substantiated. The worst feature is no doubt the long gap between supper and breakfast, and the stodginess of the meals and the high carbohydrate content of the menu. Also the complete absence of alcohol must be a severe deprivation for some prisoners.

COMPLAINTS BY PRISONERS; GENERAL SUPERVISION

The duties of members of visiting committees or boards of visitors go beyond the purely disciplinary function, and extend to a general oversight of the management of the prisons and borstals. They must meet regularly as a committee or board, but in addition the local prisons must be visited at least once a week by some member of the visiting committee, and similar visits must be arranged between meetings of a board of visitors, by at least one of its members. Every prisoner has a right to be interviewed by a member of the committee or board "out of the sight and hearing of the officers" of the institution. A member of the committee or board also has access to the records of the prison. Each committee or board presents an annual report to the Prison Department. The Magistrates' Association has arranged for members of visiting committees or boards of visitors to keep in touch, through a Prisons and Borstals Committee, and also by means of an Annual Conference.[14]

Visiting committees or boards of visitors may be called upon to "inquire into and report upon any matter into which the

---

12. Prison Rules 1964, r. 21(3).
13. See the 1962 Report of the Prison Reform Council, "Inside Story".
14. Fox. p. 86.

E

Secretary of State asks them to inquire".[15] They have some-times been used in this way to make investigations into allega-tions by prisoners. For example, in the case of the Reading Borstal Inquiry, members of the Board of Visitors conducted the investigation which found there was some substance in the allegations of irregular behaviour by certain officers, and the Home Secretary accepted the recommendation that Reading should cease to combine the functions of a borstal recall centre and a corrective centre. The recall centre has now been trans-ferred to Onley borstal, and Reading has reverted to prison use.[16]

An alternative procedure has been to set up an internal inquiry, presided over by senior members of the Prison Depart-ment head office staff. This was done in 1969 in respect of the allegations of brutality made in a Sunday newspaper in a letter signed by 120 prisoners from Parkhurst prison. The prison officers were very apprehensive of the danger of such inquiries and threatened to boycott the investigation, but in the event the Parkhurst officers were cleared.[17]

The same internal procedure was used to investigate com-plaints of brutality at the Risley Remand Centre; concern had been expressed at the large number of suicides at the Centre since it opened, but the Prison Department found nothing to justify suggestions that conditions at Risley were such as to drive anybody to commit suicide.[18]

It is a question whether the public anxiety and concern is satisfactorily resolved by the setting-up of these internal and private inquiries. No report of the investigation is made to the public, and we are left almost completely in the dark and have to accept on trust that the Home Office have dealt with and interpreted the findings in an appropriate manner.

Although it may be doubtful how effective the right to com-plain to a member of the visiting committee really is as a pro-tection for the prisoner, since the Parliamentary Commissioner Act 1967, an alternative avenue has been open to him. It has become possible for a prisoner's complaint to be scrutinised by

15. Prison Rules 1964, r. 94(2).
16. House of Commons Debates, Written Answers, Vol. 760, col. 129, 7 March 1968.
17. *The Times*, 17 March 1969, 18 March 1969; House of Commons Debates, Vol. 780, col. 729, 20 March 1969; *The Times*, 21 March 1969; *The Times*, 7 June 1969.
18. *The Times*, 10 April 1969.

the Parliamentary Commissioner for Administration (the Ombudsman) if it is passed on to him by a Member of Parliament. The Annual Reports of the Parliamentary Commissioner provide evidence of the kind of problems which have so far attracted attention. The 1968 Annual Report gives details of the complaint by a prisoner that the Home Office and an assistant governor had refused to allow him to correspond with certain persons, including writing to a marriage bureau, and corresponding with a mother and daughter and two young ladies. Although there was evidence of some maladministration in the two latter respects, it was found that there was nothing seriously wrong and what was wrong had been put right.[19] The 1967 Annual Report gives details of a prisoner's complaint that he was refused permission to institute legal proceedings against his wife or to investigate an alleged confession by her that she was responsible for frauds for which he was convicted. Here the Parliamentary Commissioner found no evidence of maladministration, since it is not the practice of the Home Office to allow prisoners to attempt to bring a private prosecution either against witnesses at the trial or against persons otherwise connected with the case.[20]

While it may be of great consequence to prisoners to have the right to have their complains investigated by the Ombudsman, it is apparently causing a great deal of time to be spent investigating these matters within the Home Office.

---

19. Second Report of the Parliamentary Commissioner for Administration, Session 1968–1969. Annual Report for 1968. H.C. 129, 18 February 1969, Case No. C.445/68, pp. 47–48.
20. Fourth Report of the Parliamentary Commissioner for Administration, Session 1967–1968. Annual Report for 1967. H.C. 134, 28 February 1968, Case No. C. 709/67, pp. 23–24.

CHAPTER 8

Prison Staff

Prison staff may be considered under six heads:

1. The Governor grade;
2. The Uniformed staff;
3. The Professional staff;
4. The Technical Training staff;
5. The Headquarters staff.
6. The Administration staff;

I THE GOVERNOR GRADE

A unified service?

As the Wynn Parry Committee pointed out, the prison service, although it is technically part of the civil service, is really *sui generis*, in that there is no really comparable work inside or outside the civil service.[1] Moreover, certain characteristics of the service distinguish it from other public services, though in this respect it is not unique.[2] The nature of the tasks involved, the hours of work, the often unattractive atmosphere, and the sometimes unpleasant nature of the duties to be performed, the element of danger, the inconvenience of the situation of prisons and the quarters provided, all these combine to make the service what it is. The prison service is not a unified service,[3] like the police, where all entrants go through the ranks (though it must be admitted that in recent years the schemes for accelerated promotion of promising young police officers have tended to erode this distinction). This means that for the prison service entry to the Governor grade has hitherto been largely from outside the service, directly to the rank of Assistant Governor, from the universities and other walks of life. There

---

1. Report of the Committee on Remuneration and Conditions of Service of Certain Grades in the Prison Services, Cmnd. 544, October 1958, p. 6, para. 7.
2. *Ibid.*, p. 6, para. 8.
3. *Ibid.*, pp. 6–8, paras. 10–14.

has also been developed a system of recruitment to the Governor grade from within the prison service, by promotion of chief officers and the like, or by annual competition limited to serving members of the prison officer class, *i.e.* the uniformed staff. In this way many uniformed officers have been given the opportunity to qualify for training and acceptance in the Governor grade.

Recruitment of graduates direct to the Governor grade has been disappointing in terms of numbers in recent years. In the four years before 1966 only thirteen graduates were recruited, and in 1966 there were no recruits at all straight from the universities.

Details of recruitment to the Governor class during a recent five-year period are as follows:

	Limited competition (prison officers only)	*Promotion (chief Officers)*	*Open competition (open to those in and outside the Service)* *	*Total*	*Total from prison officer class*
1964	5	1	16 (0)	22	6 (27%)
1965	6	1	19 (4)	26	11 (42%)
1966	10	1	15 (1)	26	12 (46%)
1967	10	1	39 (4)	50	15 (30%)
1968	13	2	39 (7)	54	22 (41%)

*Figures in brackets are serving members of the Prison Officer class.
Source: Home Office Press Notice, 27 February 1969.

Recruitment to the Governor grade

The Wynn Parry Committee recommended that the recruitment of persons to the Governor grade should continue to be by open competition, which means taking persons from outside the prison service with no previous prison experience.[4] There is considerable support for this view among prison governors,[5] and prison reformers like Hugh Klare have also expressed approval of the system of going outside the prison service for recruits to the Governor grade.[6] But the Prison Officers'

---

4. Cmnd. 544, p. 8, para. 13.
5. Memorandum by the Prison Governors' Branch of the Society of Civil Servants, Estimates Committee, Eleventh Report, p. 67.
6. Hugh J. Klare, *Anatomy of Prison*, 1960 p. 46.

Association has, not unnaturally, always wanted a closed service, with promotion only from within the ranks.

In February 1969 the Home Secretary announced that he had appointed a Working Party to examine what changes were required to ensure that future vacancies in the Prison Governor class would normally be filled by promotion from within the prison service.[7] It seems to be the Home Office view that it would be to the advantage of the prison service if this were the situation with regard to recruitment to the Governor grade. At the present time the majority of the candidates have come from outside the service. Out of a present total of 426 posts in the governor grade, only about one-third (151) are currently filled by persons who have served as prison officers. The intention appears to be to move towards what is described as a one-tier system of appointment and promotion in the prison service. The Working Party, consisting of senior officials of the Home Office and representatives of the prison governors and the uniformed prison staff, is to recommend what changes are needed to secure this goal over a period of time. It is said that the prison governors are likely to insist on some kind of special entry system for graduates, and others, similar to that now operated by the police.[8]

So the question of principle appears to have been resolved, and whatever doubts might be felt about the wisdom of this move are largely irrelevant. The task must be to ensure that the prison service can itself provide persons of sufficient calibre. This can only be done by improving the entry standard and providing extensive opportunities for training within the service. Promising candidates should be sent for university training in much the same way as happens in the police service. Great ingenuity will be required to meet the needs of the prison service at a time of increasing pressures on all sides.

Training of the Governor grade

Training of the Governor grade takes place at the Prison Staff College at Wakefield, and normally lasts eight months. University courses have also been attended by governors, to

---

7. House of Commons Debates, Written Answers, 27 February 1969.
8. Home Office Press Notice, 27 February 1969. See also Hugh J. Klare, "Recruitment of Prison Governors" (October 1969), 9 *B.J.C.*, No. 4, pp. 394–396.

acquire knowledge in such subjects as group counselling methods and management techniques. Refresher courses and specialist courses of various kinds are provided from time to time. Many of these were interrupted by the crisis over escapes in 1966, but have now been resumed. It is intended that refresher training should be decentralised, with the Staff College providing support.[9]

The role of the Assistant Governor

Upon entry into the prison service in the Governor grade, the appointee serves initially in the capacity of Assistant Governor. In the English prison and borstal service a somewhat unique and distinctive role has been developed for the Assistant Governor. This originated in the borstal institutions, where the "house-master" was responsible not only for the administration of each house but "for the personal training of the inmates in it".[10] In the prisons too, Assistant Governors who are placed in charge of a wing are expected to get to know the inmates personally and carry out what in other connections would be called social case-work. It is true that the role of an Assistant Governor in charge of a large wing at a security prison is not really comparable with that of the borstal house-master, but there is certainly in the smaller institutions a close parallel.

As far as borstal institutions are concerned it has been accepted by the Advisory Council that the role of the Assistant Governor should continue and that the main social case-work function should still be entrusted to him.[11] It followed that he should be specially trained for such duties. It has now been decided that there should be no real basic differences between the basic training of prison and borstal Assistant governors.[12]

While there is much to be said in favour of the encouragement of these developments, and the Assistant Governor may be regarded as a key person in the rehabilitative work of English penal institutions, whose role has been the subject of favourable

9. Estimates Committee, Eleventh Report, p. xxvii.
10. Borstal Rules 1964, r. 4.
11. Home Office, The Organisation of After-Care, Report of the Advisory Council on the Treatment of Offenders, pp. 26–28, paras. 91–95.
12. Estimates Committee, Eleventh Report, Minutes of Evidence, p. 66.

overseas comment,[13] there is a certain ambivalence about the Assistant Governor's position in a situation where professional social workers have now been introduced into penal institutions as full-time staff, and when the demands of security and administration weigh so heavily. It has been said that "the history of this grade has been a troubled one and the role has not yet been properly defined".[14] Is the Assistant Governor to be regarded primarily as a treatment agent, or is he a manager of the treatment which is provided by others?

The role of the Governor

As Sir Lionel Fox said, somewhat mixing his metaphors, "in any type of penal establishment the Governor is the keystone of the arch. Within his own prison, he is in much the same position as the captain of a ship—supreme in an isolated community, responsible for the efficiency and welfare of his crew as well as for the safe arrival of his passengers at their journey's end".[15] Nothing more determines the shape and direction of a prison's programme than the character and personality of the Governor. Unfortunately, due to the frequency of movement by posting to another prison, plans introduced by one Governor barely have time to mature before he is removed from the scene, and unless the foundations have been very securely laid they are unlikely to survive under his successor.

It is this very personal characteristic of the English prison system (including borstals and detention centres) which is possibly the most distinguishing feature of the system in the period since 1922. Its emergence is clearly the result of the policy pursued by Paterson in the years between the wars, and continued by his successors in the period since 1946. Solid benefits have accrued from what to some more orderly minds may appear to be little more than the encouragement of eccentricity. Perhaps it is the excessive mobility of staff in the Governor grade which is a better target for our criticism than the freedom to innovate. Few can seriously maintain that the strength and

---

13. John P. Conrad, "The Assistant Governor in the English Prison" (June 1961), 10 *B.J.D.*, No. 4, pp. 245–261.
14. Estimates Committee, Eleventh Report, Minutes of Evidence, p. 66. See also Royal Commission on the Penal System in England and Wales, Written Evidence, Vol. III, pp. 42–43, 56–58.
15. Fox, p. 87.

morale of the service is improved thereby. Unnecessary strains are imposed on the Governor staff and their families, as well as on those who serve under them and have to learn to adjust to the new governor and his personal "style" of administration. Prison officers in the uniformed grades are also subject to frequent posting to different institutions.

Another source of uneasiness is the relation of the Governor with head office. This has never been more acute than at the present time, as the evidence of the Governors to the Estimates Committee revealed.[16] Partly this is because the rapid growth of the prison service as a whole has necessarily increased the size and complexity of the head office set-up; partly this is because of the lack of any clear definition of the status of the professional heads of the prison service in relation to those administrative grade civil servants who have held key positions; partly it is due to the excessive centralisation of the administration.

Whatever the reasons, the merger of the Prison Commission with the Home Office in 1963[17] did little to restore the confidence of the professionals within the prison service, and the Mountbatten Report showed that there were many weaknesses in the head office organisation at that time. These were not all cured by the appointment of an Inspector General of Prisons as the professional head of the prison service, as recommended by the Report. The whole organisation of the head office needed to be reviewed, and such a review was carried out by a team of outside management consultants, assisted by official organisation and methods experts. Their recommendations led to the wholesale reorganisation of head office staff recently announced. (For further discussion see below, 5, The Headquarters Staff.)

2 THE UNIFORMED STAFF

Recruitment of the uniformed staff

Recruitment of uniformed staff is usually done by advertisement followed by interview and enrolment in the local prison for four weeks on a temporary basis, after which the recruits are sent for a two-month period of residential training, either at Wakefield or Leyhill. After completion of this training, they

16. Estimates Committee, Eleventh Report, p. 66, para. 13.
17. For an account of the Prison Commission, see below, 5, The Headquarters Staff.

serve a probationary period of one year before being accepted into the prison service as established civil servants.[18]

Although initial recruitment is done on a local basis, an extensive and expensive advertising campaign has been conducted nationally, as well as locally. There is no basic educational qualification required apart from "normal school-leaving standards" but selection standards are said to be quite high. Of over 9,000 men who applied for training as prison officers in 1967, just over 1,000 were found to be suitable, and passed through all the stages of their training successfully. The recruiting arrangements for female prison staff are managed differently from those for the male staff. Each female institution engages its own staff, who are then sent for training if found to be suitable.

Training of the uniformed staff

The Imperial Training School for prison officers, established at Wakefield in the 1930s, reopened in new buildings in 1946, and was used until the end of 1958 for training prison staff. In 1958 the training of prison officers was transferred to temporary premises at Wakefield, and training also took place at Leyhill in Gloucestershire. In September 1968 a new phase of prison officer training began with the opening of completely new buildings at Wakefield, costing nearly half a million pounds, and including lecture and demonstration rooms, a gymnasium, administration block, and recreation and living accommodation for some 170 prison officers.[19]

The training is necessarily concentrated heavily on the duties of prison officers with respect to the reception and safe custody of prisoners, their supervision at work and during recreation, escort duties, and so on. Increasing attention is given to the new roles of prison officers as treatment agents, and the problems posed by these new responsibilities. There is also a good deal of in-service training after the initial training is complete, specialist and refresher courses are arranged, and there are many opportunities for prison officers to attend education and training courses outside the institutions in universities and other extra-mural settings.

---

18. See the promotion literature printed at Maidstone Prison with such titles as "A new job, a brighter future" (Men) and "If you enjoy helping others, join me in the modern Prison Service" (Women). Also Central Youth Employment Executive, Choice of Careers pamphlet, New Series, No. 76, 1956.
19. Home Office Press Notice, 13 September 1968.

Nevertheless, despite all the efforts and facilities mentioned above, the recruitment position of the uniformed staff can hardly be described as satisfactory. There is a very high wastage of staff by resignation from the prison service and retirement. The result is that in 1964 582 men were recruited but the net gain to the ranks of male prison officers in the basic grade was only 235. In 1965 438 men were recruited but the net gain to the ranks of male prison officers in the basic grade was only 13.[20] This situation may be compared with that which prevailed in the police service at the time of the Royal Commission Report.[1] The recruitment position has improved a little since these gloomy figures were supplied to the Estimates Committee. In 1966 761 men were recruited and the net gain was 420. In 1967 1046 men were recruited and the net gain was 710.[2]

Promotion of the uniformed staff

One of the reasons for the high wastage in prison officers may well be the poor prospects for promotion. Both the Wynn Parry Committee and the Mountbatten Committee, as well as the Estimates Committee in 1952, commented on the length of time it took for a basic grade officer to reach the rank of Principal Officer (an average of 18–19 years).[3] The proposals made by the Prison Officers' Association for a new grade of Senior Chief Officer were rejected by the Wynn Parry Committee,[4] but the Mountbatten Committee recommended,[5] and it has since been agreed, that a new grade of senior prison officer should be created, between prison officer and principal officer, "to enable principal and chief officers to concentrate more on supervisory duties and to give them a better promotion structure".[6] A review of the structure of the senior ranks was also recommended.[7]

In the last few years the demands on the prison service have increased, with the opening of so many new institutions, the

20. Estimates Committee, Eleventh Report, p. xxi.
1. Royal Commission on the Police 1962, Interim Report, Cmnd. 1222, November 1960; Ben Whitaker, *The Police*, 1964, Chapter 5.
2. Prison Department Report, 1966, Cmnd. 3408, October 1967, p. 5, para. 11; Prison Department Report, 1967, Cmnd. 3774, October 1968, p. 3, para. 16; see also H.C. Debates, 14 November 1968, Vol. 773, col. 668.
3. Wynn Parry Report, p. 8, para. 15. Mountbatten Report, p. 61, para. 224.
4. Wynn Parry Report, p. 11, para. 22.
5. Mountbatten Report, p. 61, para. 226.
6. H.C. Debates, 14 November 1968, Vol. 773, col. 668.
7. Mountbatten Report, para. 228.

rise in the number of prisoners of all types, and the development
of new tasks and roles for the uniformed staff. Serious staff
shortages exist, in so far as one can judge the position in terms
of the decline in the prisoner–staff ratio, and the amount of
overtime worked.[8] The latter may not be a very reliable gauge,
however, since the rather low basic rates of pay have forced
officers to seek overtime and escort duties in order to supplement their meagre earnings. The prisoner–staff ratio improved
slightly in 1967.[9] The introduction of a new scheme of working
for officers (the V-Scheme) involving a 40-hour 5-day week in
place of the 84-hour twelve-day fortnight (plus overtime) has
added to the problem of shortage of staff. It has been said that
400 new officers would be needed to work the V-Scheme without
overtime,[10] while the Prison Officers' Association have mentioned a current shortage of 1,000 to 1,500 officers.[11] The Home
Secretary said in 1967 that over the next three years, allowing
for normal wastage, it would be necessary to recruit 3,800
officers, in order to cope with new establishments, new security
duties, and to take into account the effect of the V-Scheme.[12]
As the Estimates Committee pointed out, if the necessary staff
are not in fact obtained, these new developments will mean
longer hours for the prison officer.[13]

The role of the modern prison officer

The Wynn Parry Committee and the Estimates Committee
both commented on the changing role of the prison officer. He
is "being encouraged (and to a certain extent trained) to adopt
a much more positive, rehabilitative role, in conjunction with
the specialists . . . this type of officer will be the backbone of the
future service", said the Estimates Committee.[14]

When all allowance is made for the activities of the Governor
grade and the services of the professional and technical staff,
it is the uniformed prison officer who is most frequently in contact with the prisoner throughout his stay in custody, and has

---

8. Estimates Committee, Eleventh Report, Minutes of Evidence, Appendix 3, p.
   432.
9. Prison Department Report, 1967, Cmnd. 3774, October 1968, p. 37, para. 21.
10. Estimates Committee Eleventh Report, p. xx.
11. Estimates Committee, Eleventh Report, Minutes of Evidence, p. 85.
12. H.C. Debates (1966–1967), Vol. 741, c. 838. See also Estimates Committee,
    Eleventh Report, p. xx.
13. Estimates Committee, Eleventh Report, p. xxi.
14. Estimates Committee, Eleventh Report, p. xxi.

the best opportunities to observe his attitudes and behaviour. Less mobile than the other prison staff, his work brings him into daily contact with the prisoner for long periods on a very personal level.

It is now accepted that the prison officer is no longer simply a guard or warder or turnkey. (The phrase "prison warder" was abolished in 1919 and the broad arrow of convict uniform disappeared, though cartoonists and press commentators appear not to have caught up with this change.) The prison officer is no longer simply concerned with locking and unlocking doors, counts and security checks, and escorts. The Norwich system, which eventually became widely adopted in the prisons, encouraged and expected the uniformed prison officer to perform a much more positive role, to get to know each member of a group of prisoners assigned to him, and to write reports and make recommendations, and participate in decision-making about him. (See Chapter 10: The Prison Community.)

In 1963 the Prison Officers' Association submitted to the Home Office a remarkable memorandum on "The Role of the Modern Prison Officer", which made a strong plea for recognition of this changing situation and the new demands being made on the prison officer:

> "It is the Prison Officer who because of this personal and constant contact, knows the man better than the Governor, better even than the Welfare Officer and it would thus appear logical that he is the man who should be mainly concerned with rehabilitation work. Many Prison Officers have a deep concern over the way the present prison system is going and in addition to an awakening interest there is an increasing awareness that something needs to be done urgently if current criminal trends are to be reversed—in other words the time is ripe for them to enter this rehabilitative field."[15]

If this new and changing role is accepted, it follows that there must be better opportunities for training, that a higher standard of entry should be set, and that conditions of work and pay should be improved. The Prison Officers' Association case was not purely altruistic, but nevertheless it made a lot of sense. Unfortunately, too little has yet been done to recognise the changes that have taken place in the role of the prison officer,

---

15. Royal Commission on the Penal System in England and Wales, Written Evidence, Vol. III, p. 97. *The Times*, 1 November 1963.

and to reflect the value of his contribution, both actual and potential. The Mountbatten Report and its consequences have thrown the emphasis back on the negative side of his responsibilities, and a more security-conscious staff now finds the adoption of the therapeutic role more difficult than previously. At the same time, the prison officer is not often highly regarded by prisoners, who consider that the kind of person who is willing to become a "screw" for a career must be a very strange kind of sub-human type, nor does the job have much status with the general public.

A sociological observation might be added to what has already been said about the role of the prison officer. He is expected to represent and express certain values and attitudes which are more usually associated with middle-class ethos, yet he frequently has his own roots firmly in the working class, in terms of educational and social background. Thus he is caught in a conflict situation in yet one more respect. Not infrequently one may suspect that it is more comfortable and easier for him to temporise rather than resolve such a conflict. If all classes and social groups shared the same value system and ethos, or shared it to the same degree, this particular form of conflict would not occur. Yet of its presence there can be little doubt.

Escorts

There has been some discussion about three further aspects of the work of uniformed staff. The first is the question whether it might be possible to recruit a separate escort service for the purpose of relieving prison officers of their duty to provide escorts for prisoners to and from the courts. This duty takes away from the local prisons, remand centres, and many other institutions large numbers of staff in any working day. The Estimates Committee considered the matter, and recommended that "a feasibility study should be carried out" to see whether an alternative arrangement could be developed. If the results were hopeful, a pilot scheme should be introduced in one region.[16]

The same recommendation had been made by the earlier Estimates Committee fifteen years previously.[17] They thought

16. Estimates Committee, Eleventh Report, pp. xxvii–xxviii.
17. Estimates Committee, Seventh Report. Session 1951–1952, Prisons, H.C. 236, July 1952, Recommendation (8), p. xxiii.

that a separate escort staff of ex-prison officers or pensioners from the armed forces might be employed. The prison staff view is that the escort of prisoners is a difficult and sometimes dangerous task requiring considerable vigilance and physical fitness on the part of the escort. Recent experience of the "springing" of prisoners while on the way to court suggests that it would be foolish to expect retired persons to perform this kind of duty unaccompanied.

A cadet service?

The second suggestion made to the 1966–1967 Estimates Committee was for the formation of a cadet service, like the police, to encourage young men to enter the prison service. The Estimates Committee were attracted by the idea, but reluctantly accepted the view that this would not be appropriate in the case of prisons, where a certain degree of maturity was required in the performance of the job.[18]

Quarters

The question of the living accommodation for prison staff, especially of the uniformed grade, is a difficult one. There can be little doubt that in some of the older prisons living conditions for staff have been deplorable. The Wynn Parry Committee commented that the living and working conditions of many officers could only be described as "Dickensian".[19] Since then, a great deal of money has been spent on improving officers' accommodation, but the Estimates Committee found that more discontent in the prison service is generated around the provision of quarters than almost anything else. When it is realised that normally quarters are provided for up to 80 per cent. of basic grade prison officers, and that in the more inaccessible institutions this rises to 100 per cent., it will be seen that the importance of the subject cannot be under-estimated, and it is undoubtedly a factor in recruiting.[20]

Many prisons now have pleasant and attractive housing estates attached to the prison where married staff may live

---

18. Estimates Committee, Eleventh Report, pp. xxvii–xxviii.
19. Report, Cmnd. 544, p. 20, para. 52.
20. Estimates Committee, Eleventh Report, pp. xxiv–xxv, paras. 64–68. See also Prison Officers' Association Memorandum on Quarters, Appendix 16, p. 452.

with their families. There is the question whether it would be better to disperse the living quarters so as to provide less in-group pressures and encourage more mixing with the ordinary community. But, like the police, the prison service tends to be socially isolated and turns to its own members for support in leisure as well as at work. This is not to discount the almost heroic efforts of some staff to integrate with the local community. Prison governors and their wives often resemble the local squire and his lady in this respect, and a great deal of devoted community service is offered in the cause of good public relations.

3 THE PROFESSIONAL STAFF

When we speak of the professional staff in relation to the prison service, the term encompasses, in addition to the staff of the prison medical service, chaplains, psychologists, educational organisers, prison welfare officers and other social workers. The governor grade staff together with the medical officers and chaplains used to fall into a special category of "superior staff" whose appointment was a matter for the Secretary of State,[1] but this is no longer true today. The rapid growth of the prison psychological service in recent years, the appointment of trained social workers as prison welfare officers, and the general expansion of educational activity, as well as the introduction of research workers, has increased the number of professionally trained personnel working inside the prisons considerably. Their relations towards each other and to the other members of the prison community, in particular the uniformed staff, are not always easy and harmonious ones, and yet a great deal of the success of an institution in its rehabilitative efforts necessarily depends upon the degree to which the professional staff are accepted not only by the prisoners but by each other and by other members of the prison staff. It is clear that jealousies are likely to arise and misunderstandings occur, where there is insufficiently clear definition of the different roles and responsibilities of each member of the prison community. American

---

1. This was the case under the Prisons Act, 1877 (see Fox, p. 87). But since the Prison Act 1952 the only statutory requirement is that "every prison shall have a governor, a chaplain and a medical officer and such other officers as may be necessary": s. 7(1).

experts in penology have underlined the need for care in this connection.[2]

A former Principal of the Staff College at Wakefield, Mr. David Hewlings, has said that in the College the specialist is taught in the course of his training to be a supporter of staff and a trainer of staff himself:

"The specialist is a resource man in the organisation, not a man who works as a virtuoso behind closed doors on an individual treatment problem. He goes out and gets involved with the staff and helps them with their problems."

In the past, says Mr. Hewlings, the prison service has not used its specialists in this way.

"That has resulted in roles being unspecified and in lack of understanding or communication with the staff and lack of support for dealing with the new specialisms. This has, inevitably, reduced the status of the prison officer in his own eyes."[3]

One wonders to what extent these statements of the ideal and the desirable do not need some qualification to take into account the current realities of the situation.

The prison medical service

The medical care of prisoners together with the general oversight of all matters relating to their physical and mental health is the responsibility of the Medical Officer. In 1967 there were eighty-one full-time medical officers and eighty-five part-time officers in post in prison service establishments. There are a number of senior posts with supervisory duties (called principal and senior medical officers) and at the head office there is a Director of Prison Medical Services supported by a principal and a senior medical officer. On one view, there is no shortage of medical officers,[4] though on the other hand there is clearly considerable pressure at certain times and places on the present staff to cope with their numerous responsibilities, and the Working Party in 1964 were satisfied that there was serious undermanning.[5] Broadly speaking, these responsibilities may be defined as:

---

2. Richard R. Korn and Lloyd McCorkle, *Criminology and Penology*, 1959, pp. 488 *et seq.* Don C. Gibbons, *Changing the Lawbreaker*, 1965, chapter 4.
3. Estimates Committee, Eleventh Report, Minutes of Evidence, p. 307, para. 2192.
4. Estimates Committee, Eleventh Report, p. xxxvi.
5. Home Office, *The Organisation of the Prison Medical Service*, 1964, p. 3.

1. Care of the physically sick;
2. Psychiatric work;
3. Reports to court;
4. Supervision of the general health and hygiene of establishments.

Some of the larger penal institutions have more elaborate medical facilities including fully equipped surgical theatres. It is surprising how many prisoners have urgent medical needs.

Nursing is done by trained male hospital officers in the men's prisons, and in the women's prisons and girls' borstals nursing is carried out by state registered nurses (S.R.N.s) assisted by state enrolled assistant nurses and hospital orderlies. They are under the control and general supervision of a nursing matron-in-chief at head office. There is also a staff of qualified pharmacists employed at the larger establishments, and visiting physiotherapists and one senior occupational therapist. Dental work is usually carried out by visiting dentists. Specialist services are supplied by the National Health Service, and inmates suffering from severe illnesses may be transferred to National Health Service hospitals for treatment.

A degree of regionalisation of the prison medical service is being developed by organising a chain of thirteen "group hospitals" in the four different regions to provide for the more effective use of the facilities and the staff.[6] It is planned to spend up to £4 million on these developments. The Estimates Committee accepted that in the long term this would be the most effective method of providing efficient and economical prison medical services. A pilot study to see how the new scheme works was launched in the north-west.

On the psychiatric side, the major development has been the opening of Grendon in September 1962 as a secure prison hospital with 300 beds. The Director of Prison Medical Services has described the four primary tasks of Grendon as follows:

1. The investigation and treatment of mental disorders generally recognised as responsive to treatment in suitable cases, other than those suitable to be dealt with under statutory hospital orders;
2. The investigation of offenders whose offences in themselves suggest mental morbidity;

---

6. Estimates Committee, Eleventh Report, Minutes of Evidence, Appendix 18, p. 472.

3. An exploration of the problems of psychopathy;
4. Research.[7]

A fuller account of the work of Grendon and its place in the treatment of mental disorder in prisons will be given later. (See Chapter 15: Mentally Disordered Offenders.)

One of the criticisms made of the prison medical service in the past has been the fact that so few of the prison medical doctors have had psychiatric training. The Report of the Working Party on the Organisation of the Prison Medical Service, 1964, made a number of recommendations designed to strengthen the service, particularly in this direction. At the time of the Report, out of 140 doctors in the Prison Medical Service, forty-one had previous psychiatric hospital experience, and of those, eleven possessed the Diploma in Psychological Medicine. The need to provide more medical reports for the courts and to use the available resources fully and intelligently suggests that there is room for much improvement. The Working Party suggested that arrangements should be made for joint appointments of doctors to serve part-time in the prison service and part-time in a psychiatric hospital or clinic outside the forensic field, and possibly also in a teaching post. This would attract young doctors by making possible ready interchange between working in prison service establishments and in the National Health Service. It was also recommended that a number of specialist posts both at the consultant level and the junior level should be created at suitable establishments. The first three of these joint consultants in forensic psychiatry took up their posts in 1967. Eventually it is hoped that all reports on the state of mind of accused persons will be made by doctors trained and specialising in forensic psychiatry (recommendation 6 of the Working Party). Contacts with the National Health Service have been improved, and several prison medical officers have spent a period at Broadmoor on secondment.

While there are said to be no difficulties in recruiting doctors for the prison medical service, where the salaries compare favourably with the National Health Service, real difficulties occur over the recruitment of psychiatric social workers. But that is part of a wider problem of shortage of persons in that category.

---

7. Estimates Committee, Eleventh Report, Minutes of Evidence, Memorandum on Prison Medical and Psychological Services, pp. 137–141, at p. 139.

One solution to the problem of providing adequate diagnostic facilities for courts dealing with persons accused of crime might be to develop more forensic psychiatry clinics on the lines of the clinic which has been organised so successfully in Glasgow. Other countries have provided the courts with impressive diagnostic facilities, outside the penal institutions themselves, which may be used on an ambulatory or short-term commitment basis, *e.g.* New Jersey's Diagnostic Centre at Menlo Park, Baltimore's Court Clinic linked for so long with the name of Manfred S. Guttmacher. It is time we pressed for similar out-patient facilities in the United Kingdom. To some extent, one might argue that the Remand Centre is supplying this need. (See Part V, Offenders Under Twenty-one: Chapter 21, Prison). But for adult offenders this provides no answer.

The prison psychological service

This is a much newer branch of prison work, which has developed within living memory. In 1967 there were thirty-four full-time psychologists and one part-time, assisted by about twenty psychological testers, and under the over-all direction of the Chief Psychologist at head office. The original function of the psychologists was to assist in the allocation of inmates and the provision of reports to the courts. Their function now extends beyond classification and diagnosis, and includes treatment, staff training and consultation, and research.

The psychologist interviews persons in custody and gives them personality, intelligence and aptitude tests. The work has been described thus:

> "His report aims in general to assess an inmate's intellectual powers and educational level, his maturity and social competence, his attitude and likely response to training or treatment, his attitude to his criminality, his emotional stability and his attitude to, and his relationship with, his family. The psychologist then draws attention to any special problems emerging from his assessment and makes any special recommendations he considers appropriate. Such reports are of value to governors and medical officers. . . ."[8]

Where psychological testers are available, they administer routine group tests which are used, for example, to identify inmates of low intelligence, who may need to be investigated

---

8. Estimates Committee, Eleventh Report, Minutes of Evidence, p. 140.

further, and to indicate vocational aptitude and training potential, especially in borstal institutions.

Beyond classification and diagnosis stretch an unlimited number of further tasks many of which have been developed by psychologists themselves as part of their contribution to the programme in institutions. They take part in the treatment of inmates in the psychiatric treatment units. They contribute to the planning of training and treatment programmes at all levels, and assist in the training of staff.

> "The psychologist's role is particularly important in helping to start group work programmes. He acts as adviser, participating in meetings of group leaders to discuss their inter-action with inmates and to examine the implications of group work for the management of the establishment."[9]

In this way they have made a tremendously important contribution to the prison training programme in recent years. In addition they have contributed significantly to the body of criminological knowledge about offenders through extensive research both individually and collectively.

As regards recruitment, the Chief Psychologist has said that "we have never managed to fill all the vacancies we have got. There is a very, very great shortage of psychologists throughout the country. . . . "[10] They are only appointed to sixteen prisons, and operate in thirty-one others on a sort of visiting basis.[11]

The chaplain

Each prison has either a full-time or a part-time Church of England chaplain, a Roman Catholic priest, a Methodist minister, and other denominations are provided for as necessary.[12] In 1966 there were 35 Church of England chaplains full time, and 74 part time, and 5 Roman Catholic priests full time and 88 part time, and their work is supervised by a Chaplain-General of Prisons and an Assistant Chaplain-General. There are also 15 Church Army officers, male and female.

It will be seen that, as Sir Lionel Fox put it, "the duties of the Chaplain in the majority of establishments are performed by local clergymen appointed on a part-time basis at a remunera-

9. Estimates Committee, Eleventh Report, Minutes of Evidence, p. 140.
10. *Ibid.*, p. 157.
11. *Ibid.*, p. 158.
12. *Ibid.*, p. 57.

tion appropriate to the size of the prison".[13] At the larger establishments where a full-time post is necessary, the policy is to appoint chaplains for a seven-year period, and not usually to retain them longer, it being the view that "a man who spends too many years in the highly specialised, difficult and often discouraging work of a penal establishment tends to lose that spiritual zest, that freshness of touch which is essential in what must always be uphill work, however rewarding".[14]

One might comment that to a greater or lesser degree this might well be true of others in the prison service whose "many years in the highly specialised, difficult and often discouraging work" cannot be relieved by a return to pastoral duties in the free community. This is not to doubt the wisdom of the above-stated policy concerning the chaplains or in any way to devalue their work. The point is that we ought to make it easier for others (apart from the prisoners) to escape from time to time and take a different role in the life of the free community. Study leave may be the answer for the governor grade, but no prizes are offered for any other solutions.

The chaplain often engages in social work, and in this respect his work overlaps with that of the prison welfare officer as well as the Assistant Governor, prison visitor, the other professional staff and indeed the Governor himself. He must be sensitive to the need to develop co-operation with the professional services and not seek to carve out for himself a spiritual empire in whose domain he is paramount. For this is likely to create tension and discord and a diminution in the total effectiveness of the prison as a therapeutic community.

The prison welfare officer

The Maxwell Report on after-care of prisoners in 1953[15] recommended the appointment of full-time Prison Welfare Officers at local prisons, who should be persons trained and experienced in social case-work, who would operate inside the prisons but in close liaison with the organisations concerned with after-care outside the prisons, at that time mainly the Discharged Prisoners' Aid Societies. After a pilot scheme intro-

---

13. Fox, p. 90.
14. *Ibid.*, p. 90.
15. Report of the Committee on Discharged Prisoners' Aid Societies, Cmd. 8879, June 1953.

duced in four prisons showed the value of these "Maxwell workers", as they were once known, progressively the number of Prison Welfare Officers was stepped up, and their role was confirmed by the Report on The Organisation of After-Care, 1963,[16] but changes were made in the method of their appointment. Originally they were appointed by the National Association of Discharged Prisoners' Aid Societies (N.A.D.P.A.S.), but the 1963 Report recommended that appointment should be by the Home Secretary and supervision should be by the probation inspectorate.[17] Eventually a different solution was adopted and it was arranged to incorporate the prison welfare officers into the reorganised probation and after-care service, and to staff the prison welfare service by secondment from the probation and after-care service.[18] Secondment is for a fixed period of not less than two years (normally of three to five years). The inspection of prison welfare officers' work became the responsibility of the probation and after-care inspectorate of the Home Office.

The duties of the Prison Welfare Officer have been officially described as follows:

"While in a prison welfare post the seconded officer is a member of the prison team with particular responsibility for helping the prisoner in his relationship with individuals and organisations outside the prison; and the officer advises and assists in any immediate problems which may arise during the sentence. He makes plans for the after-care of prisoners who will be subject to statutory after-care, or who wish to have the benefit of voluntary after-care.[19] He is a member of the prison's home leave board which . . . considers applications by prisoners for five days' home leave towards the end of their sentence. . . . The prison governor retains general responsibility for the service provided by the seconded officers. . . . The seconded officer has, however, at all times a right of access to his local senior or principal probation officer on any professional matter. . . ."[20]

---

16. Home Office, Report of the Advisory Council on the Treatment of Offenders, The Organisation of After-Care, 1963.
17. *Ibid.*, p. 24, para. 82.
18. Home Office, Report on the Work of the Probation and After-Care Department, 1962–1965, Cmnd. 3107, October 1966, pp. 35–38, paras. 100–107. See also Estimates Committee, Eleventh Report, Minutes of Evidence. Memorandum on Prison Welfare and After-Care, pp. 180 *et seq.*
19. The distinction between voluntary and compulsory (statutory) after-care is explained in Chapter 11: Release.
20. Report of the Probation and After-Care Department, Cmnd. 3107, October 1966, pp. 36–37.

Many problems faced the trained social worker injected into prison but not a member of the prison service, especially in the early days when the whole idea was new. It was often said that the greatest need for social work was with the staff themselves, but gradually the prison welfare service has come to be accepted as performing a vital function in the correctional continuum (from reception, through training to release and supervision in the free community). The Prison Welfare Officer provides a link with the outside, and while he or she is frequently over-worked and often engaged in trivial matters of detailed admin-istration, there can be little doubt that to have members of the probation and after-care service spending part of their careers seconded to the prisons can only enure for the benefit of both the prison and probation services by drawing them more closely together.

The number of officers appointed rose very rapidly between 1953 and 1968. By 1967 there were 143 prison welfare officers and an authorised establishment of 180. Research is being done on the role of social work in prisons.[1]

The education staff

The history of education in the penal system goes back a long way. In the nineteenth century, and even before that, the moral and educational instruction of prisoners was considered im-portant. Books were allowed to certain prisoners as a privilege, and prison chaplains gave elementary instruction in the "three R's", as well as religious instruction.[2] As long ago as 1896 there was a Report of a Departmental Committee on the education of prisoners.[3] In 1922, as Sir Lionel Fox says, "a start was made with organising an adult education scheme throughout the local prisons", in co-operation with the Adult Education Com-mittee of the Board of Education.[4] This scheme was based on voluntary teachers, and at each prison an Educational Adviser was appointed, drawn from the ranks of professors, headmasters and educational administrators. This system remained in being

---

1. Report on the Work of the Prison Department, 1967, Cmnd. 3774, October 1968, p. 9.
2. Fox, pp. 43 and 50.
3. Report of the Departmental Committee on the Education and Moral Instruc-tion of Prisoners in Local and Convict Prisons (Prisoners' Education Com-mittee) Cd. 8154, 1896; Minutes of Evidence, Cd. 8155.
4. Fox, pp. 68, 69.

until World War II and was replaced after 1946 by the present system. Building on earlier experience in Durham prison since 1945, and acting on the recommendations of an Advisory Committee,[5] the Prison Commission developed a strong arrangement with the educational services which has endured to this day. A Director of Education and Welfare was appointed in the Prison Commission in January 1947.

The prime responsibility for the education of inmates rests on local education authorities, who are empowered under the Education Acts to provide education in prisons, borstals and detention centres. These authorities have appointed tutor organizers (whole-time or part-time according to the size of the establishment) to devise educational programmes and enrol suitable teachers for the various classes. The cost of this service, which annually amounts to around half a million pounds, is reimbursed to the authorities by the Home Office.[6]

The justifications for this involvement of the local authorities in prison education are the desirability of maintaining links between the education of free persons and the education of inmates, and the lack of any specific separate educational techniques which are appropriate to inmates. "If there were special educational techniques which were effective in turning inmates away from crime there might be a case for a separate educational service in prisons, borstals etc."[7]

The local authorities' proposals for class programmes are submitted to the Home Office for approval, and there is now at head office a Chief Education Officer who acts as the Department's representative in dealing with the authorities and with the Inspectorate of the Department of Education and Science. One of H.M. Inspectors of Education has a specific responsibility in this matter, and other H.M.I.s make visits to penal institutions in their own localities.

In July 1965 there were forty-two full-time tutor-organisers, eight half-time tutor-organisers, forty part-time tutor-organisers, and one educational psychologist. The half-time appointments are a recent development, whereby the appointment is shared with a local education authority Technical College or College of Further Education, an arrangement which has

5. Fox, pp. 68, 69.
6. Royal Commission on the Penal System in England and Wales, Written Evidence, Vol. 1, p. 67, Memorandum on Education in Prisons.
7. *Ibid.*, p. 67.

several advantages.[8] Further developments include the use of tutors from the W.E.A. and Extra-Mural Departments of the Universities.

Like the chaplains, tutor-organisers play an important role in the prison programme, but it is thought desirable that they should "keep fully in touch with the many current developments in education", and, until recently, the policy was to appoint them for a period of not longer than seven years. This policy has now been reversed and they may now stay indefinitely as prison educators.

Much of the work is done in evening classes, daytime education, apart from physical education and group counselling, being largely confined to young offenders' establishments.[9] But in some prisons there are classes in business subjects, and there are classes for adult illiterates during working hours. There are also correspondence courses available for inmates. Some inmates even attend courses at local colleges of technology where their educational needs require it.[10]

Physical education is organised separately from the other forms of education, under the guidance of an Organiser of Physical Education, and his assistant at head office. There are five physical education specialists seconded by local authorities, otherwise the instructional staff consists of physical education instructors who are members of the prison officer grades who have received training in physical education. A great deal of zeal and enthusiasm goes into these activities, which is no doubt communicated to the inmates to a certain degree. Substantial improvements in the physical health, alertness and general physical performance of inmates, especially the young offenders, has been a feature of this work. Such activities as weight-lifting have recently become very popular even among long-term prisoners. One of the common observations about offenders is how many of them, especially the young offenders, have poor physique and general health.

4 THE TECHNICAL TRAINING STAFF

These include the civilian instructors, numbering about 460,

---

8. Royal Commission on the Penal System in England and Wales, Written Evidence, Vol. I, p. 131.
9. *Ibid.*, p. 66.
10. *Ibid.*, p. 68.

who are not prison officers but belong to the general civil service grades, and who are employed to supervise and instruct prisoners in the workshops and prison industries. These tasks are facilitated by the employment of 540 prison officers as trade instructors (for which a special allowance is paid).

Considerable changes are being made in the quality of the training a prisoner receives. A firm of consultants has been engaged to train a team of specialist trainers in instruction at shop floor level. Great efforts are being made to improve the industrial set-up. (See Chapter 9: A Prisoner's Work and Earnings.) There are thirty-three industrial managers in charge of the work programme; they are to be found in the larger establishments and many of them cover smaller prisons in the area.[11] There is also an administration officer who looks after the commercial side of the job. Above these there are six regional industrial officers, under the general control of the Director of Industries and Stores. There are also a few senior technical officers in the field and at head office. Recent developments include the appointment of a chief production engineer (1965) and a marketing manager (1968) both of whom had previous experience in industry.[12]

Those familiar with prison conditions will testify to the well-known fact that some of the civilian instructors possess considerable powers of influencing prisoners, not only in relation to their trade or vocational training, but also in terms of their general adjustment and rehabilitation. Perhaps it is on account of their pride and dedication to their job, perhaps because they are not perceived by prisoners in the same way as "screws", perhaps they are often endowed with rugged independence and strong character—whatever may be the reasons, there is abundant evidence of their being able to make a considerable contribution to the prisoner's training and treatment.

One of the sources of complaint in the past, that the industrial manager was not properly consulted about questions of the placement of prisoners in shops, has to some extent been recognised and dealt with. Following the recommendations of the Advisory Council on Work for Prisoners, "a particular point has now been made of encouraging prison governors to bring the many sides in prison together", so that now "indus-

---

11. Estimates Committee, Eleventh Report, Minutes of Evidence, p. 213.
12. *Ibid.*, p. 206. See also H.C. Debates, 14 November 1968, Vol. 733, col. 666.

trial managers are brought properly into the allocation of prisoners".[13]

5 THE HEADQUARTERS STAFF

The Prison Commission

Prior to the Prisons Act of 1877, local prisons were an essentially local service administered under the supervision of the local justices. The convict prisons were directly under the Home Office control and inspection. When it was decided to bring all the prisons under the central administration, the device of establishing a statutory board of commissioners was adopted. This was quite common in the latter part of the nineteenth century as a governmental device for the provision of public services.[14] The Act of 1877 established a Prisons Board as a body corporate, with a common seal, and power to hold land. The Prison Commissioners could not exceed five in number, but they were usually assisted by a number of other officials, eventually numbering about ten, all of them civil servants. There was a Chairman, Deputy Chairman and Secretary of the Board.[15] A rather precarious balance of power was maintained in the membership of the Board between administrative grade civil servants and professional prison staff.

The Home Office had for many years regarded the Prison Commission as anomalous, and desired to bring its work within the normal departmental framework of the Home Office. It was variously described as "something of a curiosity"[16] and "a vestigial anachronism",[17] and the Criminal Justice Bills of 1939 and 1947 sought to abolish the Commission, but the clause was deleted. The Act of 1948 conferred new responsibilities upon the Prison Commission, for developing the detention centres and remand centres. An administrative reorganisation made the Prison Commission directly responsible to the Secretary of State, instead of, as hitherto, via the Criminal Division of the Home Office.[18]

---

13. Estimates Committee, Eleventh Report, Minutes of Evidence, p. 214.
14. Cf. the Metropolitan Water Board, the Metropolitan Police Commission, the Local Government Board.
15. Fox, pp. 79–80.
16. Fox, p. 79.
17. Estimates Committee, Eleventh Report, quoted by Hugh Fraser, H.C. Debates, 14 November 1968, Vol. 773, col. 643.
18. Fox, p. 80.

The Home Office finally succeeded in procuring the abolition of the Prison Commission in the Criminal Justice Act of 1961, but not without considerable opposition being expressed. The House of Commons at first voted against the move, and *The Times* published a leading article regretting the proposal, and several letters appeared in its correspondence columns. But in the end the Home Office view prevailed, and the Prison Commission was finally laid to rest in 1963 by statutory instrument.[36]

It is worth considering the alleged advantages of the Prison Commission set-up. The Prison Commissioners, it was said, had become known to the public, in a way which is not normally permitted for professional civil servants, as the persons responsible for penal institutions. They had a direct personal relationship with the staff of the institutions, and had established for themselves a degree of independence from the Home Office. At the same time, the Home Secretary was answerable to Parliament for their activities, and was constitutionally responsible for the care and custody of the prisoners. It was not really tolerable for a body to establish a degree of independence from the Home Office and its Ministers and senior advisers. When the Prison Commission was abolished, an undertaking was given that the senior prison administrators would be just as accessible as previously not only to the prison staff but to the interested members of the general public. Certain changes in the internal organisation of the work of the Prison Department followed at this time, including the creation of a Chief Director of Prison Administration in addition to the Director of Prison Administration and the Director of Borstal Administration.

Recently two members of the House of Commons Estimates Committee suggested that there was a strong case for going back to an autonomous body responsible to the Home Secretary, like the Prison Commission, for running the prison service. One of them, Hugh Fraser, M.P., said:

> "This is a huge province managerially, administratively, economically, medically, and penologically, which needs at its head, not a faceless civil servant, however admirable or devoted he be, but a person of the calibre of Paterson whom the public, the Prison Service, and indeed, the prisoners themselves, can trust."[20]

---

19. Prison Commissioners Dissolution Order 1963, S.I. 1963, No. 597 made under the Criminal Justice Act 1961, s. 24.
20. H.C. Debates, 14 November 1968, Vol. 773, col. 644.

The Home Secretary asked what would be the position concerning accountability in terms of custody and treatment of prisoners, "matters on which the Home Secretary is rightfully challenged in this House, and for which he has a direct responsibility".[1] The answer given was that it would be the same as with the former Prison Commissioners, who were responsible to the Home Secretary. There would be no problems in this respect. The other member, Mr. Gresham Cooke, argued that an autonomous body under the Home Office would be "in tune with the times", and would give the head of the department rather more power and prestige than he has at the moment. He could be given a grant and instructions to go ahead and apply the best methods which are used abroad.[2]

It was already recognised that the whole organisation of the Prison Department needed looking at with a view to a comprehensive overhaul. This was necessitated both by the growing volume and complexity of the work and by the need to provide an integrated service in which the professional civil servants and the professional prison staff might each share, contributing according to their different skills and experience. A firm of independent management consultants was brought in to examine the situation in co-operation with organisation and methods experts from within the civil service,[3] and their report has led to certain changes.

Prison department reorganisation

In February 1969 the first step in a major reorganisation of the top management of the prison service in England and Wales was announced.[4] The Chairman of the Prisons Board, a senior civil servant, became the full-time Director-General, and the Prisons Board itself, previously consisting of thirteen members, was reduced to five members together with the Director-General, who will be the chairman. These five members are as follows:

Controller (Administration);
Controller (Operations);

---

1. H.C. Debates, 14 November 1968, Vol. 773, col. 645.
2. *Ibid.*, col. 652.
3. *Ibid.*, col. 655 (Rt. Hon. James Callaghan).
4. Home Office Press Notice, 11 February 1969. *The Times*, 12 February 1969, press report and leading article.

Controller (Planning and Development);
Inspector General;
Director of Prison Medical Services.

Subject to the general supervision of the Permanent Under-Secretary of State and the directions of Ministers, all members of the Board share collectively in the formulation of major policy developments and decisions.

In July 1969 a number of further appointments were made of senior staff in the Prison Department below Board level, and to the key posts as regional directors in the four regional head-quarters which are being developed, viz. the North, the Midlands, the South-west and the South-east.[5]

Manchester, Birmingham, Bristol, and a site near London will provide the base for each of the regional headquarters, which will eventually comprise some thirty staff, headed by a Regional Director, a Deputy Director (Operations) and a Deputy Director (Administration).[6]

It has been suggested that the new arrangements will provide a brighter prospect for someone who wishes to make his career in the prison service. Until now the highest posts were reserved for the professional civil servants, and the top prison administrators were always subordinate to the top civil servants. Now that the structure has been changed the way is open right to the top for every prison officer:

"This will not mean the exclusion of Civil Service administrators, who will work in the prison service for what may be indefinite time if they are particularly interested and fitted for the duties . . . but it will mean that in future the service will be run by people who have spent either a full career or at any rate a considerable time in prison work."[7]

These changes are to be welcomed but it is too early to gauge their precise significance. They may serve to reduce the mis-

---

5. There is now an Assistant Controller (Personnel) working under the Controller (Operations) and charged with the duty of providing liaison between the Prison Department and the Establishment Department of the Home Office in relation to senior appointments. There is also a senior official carrying special responsibility, under the Controller (Operations) for security problems. There are two senior officials to assist the Inspector-General as inspectors of the prison service, and two senior officials to assist the Controller (Administration), while three of the Assistant Directors presently serving at headquarters remain in their present appointments, dealing respectively with staff training, women and girls, and borstal release.

6. Home Office Press Notice, 4 July 1969.

7. *The Times*, leading article, 12 February 1969.

understandings and friction between head office administrators and prison staff, and encourage a more imaginative and professional approach to the task. But it would not be wise to assume that they can end the tension between head office staff and persons in the field. The regionalisation of the administration will serve to cut down the amount of paper work at present dealt with directly at head office. But there is always the danger that the administrative complications will outweigh the benefits.

The close parallel between the recent reorganisation of the Prison Department under a Board of five members and the old Prison Commission should not be allowed to obscure important differences. Now there is a more clear division between the various areas of responsibility, and the solution adopted appears to be better adapted to the needs both of planning and developing a professional service and at the same time of representing strongly the element of public accountability. The Controller (Administration) and the Inspector General will have much to do in the latter connection, while the Controller (Operations) and the Controller (Planning and Development), respectively, can get on with the detailed day-to-day administration and with long-term planning. As for the faceless civil servant argument, we may perhaps express the hope that these important officials will in time make themselves known both to those in the field and to the less well-informed public outside the prison service itself. Only in this way can the needs of present-day administration be married with the genuine interest and desire of the public at large to be involved. Indeed, in the long run, the whole future policy of the penal system depends on what the public is willing to tolerate in the way of policies and provide in the way of resources.

6 THE ADMINISTRATION STAFF

Each penal institution has its own administrative needs which are provided by members of the civil service executive class known as Administration Officers assisted by clerical officers, and other staff. In the old days the officer in charge of the administrative side of a prison was known as the Steward[8] but he is now called the Administration Officer. A great deal of detailed work of a clerical, accounting and store-keeping nature

8. Fox, p. 93.

is required in order to enable establishments catering for hundreds of persons to run smoothly. At the remand prisons and remand centres there is rather more office work in the preparation of reports for courts and the documentation which each prisoner requires.

The administration staff have asked for a clearer definition of their roles and responsibilities and the transfer to them of some of the executive and clerical duties of other grades of prison staff, which they claim would be justified to enable those other staff to concentrate on their prime tasks of custody, training and rehabilitation.[9] It seems that much administration still has to be done by all grades of prison staff and it is not clear how far there could be any substantial redistribution of duties. What is clear, however, is how much the daily functioning of these large institutions depends, as in so many other walks of life, on the conscientious performance of administrative chores by people whose work is often not appreciated sufficiently.

---

9. Royal Commission on the Penal System in England and Wales, Written Evidence, 1967, Vol. III, Memorandum by the Society of Civil Servants on behalf of the Prison Department Outstations Branch. See also G. E. Hart, "The Administration Officer", January 1967, 6 *Prison Service Journal*, No. 22, p. 32.

F

CHAPTER 9

A Prisoner's Work and Earnings

A PRISONER'S WORK

The Prison Rules require a convicted prisoner to work, and permit unconvicted prisoners to work if they wish to do so.[1] It has long been assumed that the provision of regular work forms an important part of the prison training programme. It is frequently said that the inculcation of regular work habits may form one of the most important factors in the rehabilitation of offenders. Yet on the other side it must be realised that "offenders do not come to prison because they have failed as workmen, and the task of the prison is to train the whole man: a prison is not therefore, and should not be, first and foremost a factory".[2]

> "Nevertheless a prisoner's work must always be in some ways the basis of his training. It fills the greater part of his day, and his response to it and to the conditions in which he has to do it may well affect his response to other forms of training. It should therefore be obviously purposeful, efficiently organised, and carried out so far as possible in conditions similar to those in outside workshops. It should at least enable him to acquire habits of regular and orderly industry, and at best give him a trade skill which he can use when he goes out. Above all, there should be enough of it to keep him busy for a whole working day, week in and week out."

This was the Home Office view in 1959. It was admitted at that time that conditions in many of the prisons, especially the local prisons, fell far short of those ideals, though in the central and regional training prisons the situation was much more satisfactory.

The Estimates Committee in 1952 had reported that "the potentialities of prison labour are not being realised to the full",

---

1. Prison Rules, 1964, r. 28(1) and (5).
2. White Paper, Penal Practice in a Changing Society: Aspects of Future Development (England and Wales) Cmnd. 645, February 1959, p. 15, para. 65.

142

and that the procedure laid down for obtaining contracts from government departments for work to be done by prison labour was not working satisfactorily. There was a lack of co-ordination between the various departments concerned, and what was required was a "smooth flow of satisfactory orders". It was recognised, however, that "prisons are not . . . primarily industrial undertakings; such goods as are produced in their workshops are by-products of a process of training and reclamation."[3]

Strenuous efforts have been made in recent years to improve the situation, by re-equipping workshops and reorganising prison industries along modern industrial lines, and by seeking new outlets for prison manufacture. An Advisory Council on the Employment of Prisoners was established in 1960, and has issued three reports.[4] A chief production engineer and a marketing manager have been appointed to the Prison Department (see Chapter 8: Prison Staff) and there have been substantial improvements in the working conditions in prisons.

Many prison workshops are now equipped with up-to-date machinery, some of which has been supplied by outside manufacturers, and the work is organised more on the lines of modern industrial practice. It still remains true, however, that there are serious deficiencies. The local prisons have difficulty in finding work for twenty-five to thirty hours a week, and the nature of much of the work remains dull, repetitive and monotonous such as sewing mailbags and dismantling and salvaging damaged post-office equipment. The training prisons and the borstals manage to provide a fuller working week (up to 40 hours).

The source of much of this work derives from the needs of government departments, though, increasingly, private industry is being drawn in to offer work on a contract basis. The Departmental Committee on the Employment of Prisoners in 1933[5] considered whether it would be desirable and how far it would be possible to have a compulsory system of state use of the products of prison labour, such as they have in some states in

---

3. Select Committee on Estimates, Seventh Report, Session 1951–1952, Prisons H.C. 236, July 1952, pp. xvii–xxi, paras. 28–35.
4. *Work for Prisoners*, 1961; *Work and Vocational Training in Borstals (England and Wales)*, 1962; *The Organisation of Work for Prisoners*, 1964.
5. Departmental Committee on The Employment of Prisoners, Report, Part I, Cmnd. 4462, November 1933.

the U.S.A. This Committee recommended against a compulsory system of state use, but as a result of its Report, a Director of Prison Industries was appointed, and the position improved somewhat. But by 1959 it was clearly unsatisfactory and needed to be looked at afresh. Hence the appointment of the Advisory Council on the Employment of Prisoners. Its Reports of 1961, 1962 and 1964 have clearly been most valuable and have set the direction for the present efforts to improve the work situation.

One problem which has be be faced in this connection is the hoary principle of less eligibility, which Dr. Mannheim so brilliantly explored in his *Dilemma of Penal Reform*, 1939. This originated in relation to the old Poor Law, but was extended to the penal system in the nineteenth century as a means of softening the blow to the older concepts of retribution which the new reform movement had delivered:

> "When deterrence as the chief aim of punishment became increasingly supplemented by the idea of reformation, public opinion, in harmony with many penal reformers, insisted that the new idea of reformation had to be made innocuous, and this process of removing the sting from it was carried out largely by means of an application of the Poor Law principle of less eligibility to the penal problem."[6]

Spelled out in simple terms, this meant that conditions in the prisons should not be made more comfortable or superior to those of the least privileged members of the free community. Prison standards must be slightly below those of the lowliest wage slaves or labourers. Such a harsh principle could hardly be applied inflexibly, and "was sometimes exchanged for . . . the principle of *non-superiority*, *i.e.* the requirement that the condition of the criminal when he paid the penalty for his crime should be at least not superior to that of the lowest classes of the non-criminal population".[7] This old idea, wrote Mannheim in 1939, "still represents the most formidable obstacle in the way of Penal Reform".[8]

This is hardly the case today, but it is obvious that in the improvement of conditions inside the prisons and the provision of work facilities, the Prison Department must tread warily.

---

6. Hermann Mannheim, *The Dilemma of Penal Reform*, 1939, pp. 56–57.
7. *Ibid.*, p. 57.
8. *Ibid.*, p. 59.

Occasionally a somewhat shrill note has been sounded when discussing the problem, as in the 1959 White Paper:

> "The solution of the problems of work in prisons does not rest with the administration alone. Indeed, they will never be solved until society as a whole accepts that prisons do not work in an economic vacuum, and that prisoners are members of the working community, temporarily segregated, and not economic outcasts."[9]

There has been very little opposition to the employment of prisoners stemming from the trade unions. "In the general development of our prison industries we have encountered almost no trade union opposition,"[10] said a Home Office official giving evidence to the Estimates Committee in 1967. Where difficulties have arisen, they have usually been at the local level. Outside work parties employed on casual labouring obviously are vulnerable to fluctuations in the local employment situation, and may have to be withdrawn when local unemployment rises.

It was recently announced that a new national agreement had been reached between the Home Office representatives and the Amalgamated Union of Building Trades Workers whereby at any prison where site construction work was being carried out by prison labour, the union is willing to vet the work of the men, and, if it is approved, to admit them into the union. Similar negotiations are being conducted with other unions, and this is regarded as a big step forward. Union membership will make it easier for a prisoner to find a job on release, by continuing the trade he has followed while in prison.[11]

The economic threat which the employment of a source of cheap labour might seem to pose has been met by charging outside employers the rate for the job. This applies not only to work done outside the prisons by working parties but to the arrangements whereby "firms instal machinery in prison workshops, supply material and in effect hire prisoners as operatives."[12] They pay the Prison Department the appropriate "free" labour rates plus a contribution to overheads. The

---

9. Cmnd. 645, para. 71, p. 17.
10. Estimates Committee, Eleventh Report, Minutes of Evidence, p. 218.
11. Lord Stonham, opening the new education block, Ashwell Prison, 14 April 1969, Home Office Press Notice, *The Times*, 15 April 1969.
12. Estimates Committee, Eleventh Report, Home Office Memorandum on Work for Prisoners, p. 201.

prisoners are paid according to the earnings scheme (see below).

Probably the most important development in the employment of prisoners in recent years has been the use of prisoners
to build new prisons under the direction of qualified staff of
the prison service. The new detention centre at Eastwood Park,
in Gloucestershire, opened in March 1968, was built in this
way, by parties of prisoners brought from neighbouring prisons,
mainly from Bristol and Leyhill prisons. Prison labour accounted
for about 80 per cent. of the work done, and the men worked a
normal five-day, 40-hour week, for which they were paid a
rate higher than the normal under the incentive earnings
scheme (see below). It is estimated that over £100,000 was
saved by the use of direct labour in this way. Many of the
building accessories were manufactured in prison workshops,
including windows and doors, and furniture.[13] Looking ahead,
the Prison Department hopes to make extensive use of prison
labour in the building of other new institutions. Substantial
economies in building costs would result.

A PRISONER'S EARNINGS

Linked with the question of employment for prisoners is the
question of prisoners' pay, or what is better described as earnings, since it amounts to an average of 7s. a week at present
and can hardly be dignified with the word "pay". The system
of earnings was introduced in 1929 at the suggestion of the
Howard League. Small weekly sums could be earned either
on a flat rate basis or on piece rates, which enabled the prisoners to purchase from the canteen various items such as
cigarettes and tobacco, toilet articles, stationery, certain items
of food, and greetings cards. This is still the basis for most
prisoners' reumuneration though the amounts a prisoner can
earn have been slightly improved, and, as has been mentioned
above, in some situations such as where the incentive earnings
scheme applies, prisoners can earn up to £1 or 30s. a week.
Mention should also be made here of the hostels scheme, under
which a prisoner may work in the free community at full wages,
subject to deductions, and may accumulate a certain amount
in savings by the time of his release (see below).

---

13. Lord Stonham, opening Eastwood Park Detention Centre, 13 March 1968,
    Home Office Press Notice.

The possibility of introducing a more realistic wage, "the economic rate for the job", is a matter which has received consideration in recent years. This has been under study by the United Nations, but there are many practical difficulties, to be overcome. In several countries, such as Sweden and Yugoslavia, a prisoner is paid a more adequate wage in return for work done. The matter was discussed in the White Paper of February 1959 where it was said that "this conception of the 'economic rate' cannot provide a general solution of the prison earnings problem until the general level of productivity and efficiency of prison industry approximates much more closely to that of outside industry". There is the wider question whether in the event that the payment of full wages might become possible, it would not be right to consider whether prisoners should "be required to make restitution from their earnings to the victims of their offences".[14]

A major difficulty lies in the poor quality of much of the labour force. The right kind of job to choose for the majority of prisoners is, as the Advisory Committee pointed out, semi-skilled, repetitive machine minding.[15] For many prisoners, the most that can be provided, even today, is "some kind of occupation. . . . You are forced to put them somewhere and you may even have to leave them in their cells and give them something to occupy their hands with".[16] On the other hand, some of the skilled work carried out in certain trades is of a very high standard, for example, in the tailoring shops. At this point we can conveniently summarise the findings of the First Report of the Advisory Council on the Employment of Prisoners:

The Advisory Council's recommendations (1961)

1. The provision of work for prisoners is not intended as part of their punishment, nor simply as a means of keeping them occupied. "Suitable work, if properly organised, is a most valuable part of a prisoner's training."[17] Good work is good training.

2. To provide this it is essential that prison industries be well organised in accordance with modern industrial

14. Cmnd. 645, p. 17.
15. Report of 1961, Work for Prisoners, p. 12, para. 46.
16. Estimates Committee, Eleventh Report, Minutes of Evidence, p. 206.
17. P. 7.

practice[18] and should provide a general experience in modern industrial techniques and conditions.

3. The amount of work provided from outside the Prison Service in England and Wales should be quadrupled. This would be no threat to the non-criminal working population, for the prison population constituted less than one-tenth of 1 per cent. of the total working population.[19]

4. The efficiency of prison industries could be improved by reorganising workshops, by providing job-training for selected prisoners (see below), better incentives, and better consultation with the industrial staff.

5. More attention should be paid to the training of prisoners for work in prisons (job training).

6. Prisoners' earnings should be improved.

7. Local advisory committees on the employment of prisoners should be set up at the larger prisons in industrial areas.

Since that report was published, in 1961, there have been various developments. In the last few years several important steps have been taken to improve the work situation:

1. A new incentive earnings scheme was introduced experimentally in connection with Kirkham prison in Lancashire and the building of the detention centre at Eastwood Park (Gloucs.). About 1,000 prisoners were enabled to earn up to £1 a week and work a normal five-day 40-hour week. This proved so successful that an extension of the scheme was recently announced by the Home Secretary, under which it is hoped to raise the number of prisoners and trainees participating to just short of 3,000. The new pay structure which has been introduced enables some men to earn up to 33s. a week instead of the former £1 maximum. Some borstal trainees are being included in the incentive pay schemes for the first time on an experimental basis.[20]

2. Increased industrial production in prisons now amounts to £6 million worth a year compared with £2

---

18. P. 41.
19. P. 13, para. 54. The proportion stated is 0.06 per cent.
20. Home Office Press Release, 18 September 1969.

million two or three years ago. It is likely to rise very rapidly in the next few years, if the projected rate of development is realised. As many as 14,000 prisoners are now engaged in manufacturing industry.

3. A new factory prison has been opened at Coldingley in Surrey. This is Britain's first prison with an almost entirely industrial régime. The 300 prisoners are selected for their suitability for the work involved. The industries include light engineering and a laundry. Every job has been carefully studied and a job specification worked out in consultation with work study experts. Bonuses are paid for good production achievements.

4. The prison industries are being rationalised and concentrated on six types of industry: metal recovery, carpentry, light engineering, weaving, tailoring and laundering. A start has been made in the North Region, and the Midlands and the South plan to follow suit and concentrate 60 per cent. of the industrial labour in the same six industries.

> "The remaining 40 per cent. will be employed as far as possible in small, but still viable, industries such as printing and concrete moulding. In addition the employment of prisoners on building and maintenance work will continue to expand. This is essential work that also gives prisoners useful training and experience. Other prisoners will continue to be required for work on the prison farms, in the kitchens and on other work essential to the day-to-day running of prisons."[1]

5. With regard to job-training of prisoners, a firm of consultants is training a team of specialist trainers in instruction at shop floor level. With regard to management, it is recognised that "many modern management techniques have their part to play, and it is intended that they should be used as fully and effectively as in the best outside practice. No commercial technique, however, can provide the answers needed to cope fully with the exigencies imposed by a penal situation".[2]

---

1. Estimates Committee, Eleventh Report, Home Office Memorandum on Work for Prisoners, pp. 199 *et. seq.*, at p. 200.
2. *Ibid.*, pp. 200–201.

6. Vocational training, that is, instruction in the skills and knowledge appertaining to a trade or vocation, forms an important part of the prison work programme, especially in borstals, where at one time about 30 per cent. of the boys admitted were given vocational training. The Advisory Council, while endorsing the policy of vocational training in general, recommended that more training in semi-skilled work should be introduced, such as the operation of mechanical plant, scaffolding and steel bending, machine minding, etc.

> "Vocational training courses", the Prison Department has said, "make considerable intellectual demands and the majority of inmates would be quite incapable of meeting these demands and benefiting from the courses. . . . the needs of most, as the Advisory Council recognised, are best served by the development of good class semi-skilled work."[3]

Despite all these significant developments, the Prison Department spokesman giving evidence to the Estimates Committee in March 1967 had to admit that "a fair proportion of the total available prison labour force" was "not properly employed either from the economic point of view or from the point of view of giving them good training and experience".[4]

Thus men are employed on sewing machines for whom there is no equivalent work outside,[5] though it is claimed that experience of using a sewing machine may help a man to get a job as a machine minder, perhaps in a motor car firm.[6] Men are employed on sewing mailbags simply to occupy their time. The difficulties arise in part from the poor quality of the labour force, which has already been described, but they also stem from the rapid rise in the size of the prison population. Attempts to rationalise prison industries are baulked for lack of space and money for new workshops as well as by the rise in the prison population. It has been said that £7,000,000 would be needed for the workshop space required.[7]

---

3. Estimates Committee, Eleventh Report, Home Office Memorandum on Work for Prisoners, p. 202.
4. *Ibid.*, Minutes of Evidence, p. 209.
5. *Ibid.*, p. 210.
6. *Ibid.*, p. 211.
7. *Ibid.*, Minutes of Evidence, pp. 209–10.

As *The Times* put it in a leader in November 1968, headed "Making the Prisons Pay", the development of prison industry has been "a long and painful business" but "the news that prison industries are now operating at a profit for the first time in their history offers good hope for the future". "Money has always stood in the way of creating a modern prison system in Britain but in this field at least there is an answer." The answer is "to organise work realistically and to concentrate on only a few profitable industries" and to seek orders from outside industry.[8]

However rosy a picture one may paint about the innovations now being made in the sphere of prison work and earnings, the blunt fact must be faced that many of these high-minded intentions fall flat on their face when it comes to actual realisation. Shops remain too often idle waiting for work, difficulties may occur over providing the prison staff to work a double shift system, which may in fact lead to the abandonment of the system. One can easily make out a long catalogue of tales of woe and inefficiency. The conclusion must be that much remains to be done in this area to provide the basis for a sound employment situation.

---

8. *The Times*, 25 November 1968.

CHAPTER 10

The Prison Community

As Paul Tappan put it, "only in recent years has there been some effort to interpret the prison in terms of social psychological theory as a complex community with a 'culture' that is in a measure unique, with characteristic processes of individual and social accommodation, and with typical attitudes and values shared by inmates". He goes on to observe that "thus far . . . the analysis of the quality and processes of prison life has been limited in the main to maximum-security institutions of the traditional type".[1]

It was the American sociologist Donald Clemmer who in 1940 first drew attention to this "community" aspect of prison life.[2] Prison, in particular the maximum security institution, is essentially a closed community, and may be likened in some ways to a monastery or a mental hospital. Goffman has vividly described the characteristics of such "total" institutions, where the anti-staff anti-authority attitudes of the inmates may be regarded as forming an inmate sub-culture set up in opposition to the official culture of the staff and the treatment personnel.[3] Not all the inmates share this set of attitudes: there are a few who stand aloof from it and make their own way through their prison term; but for the vast majority, in order to relieve the "pains of imprisonment",[4] the adoption of this inmate sub-culture provides a ready and acceptable means of adaptation and survival.

Whether the inmate sub-culture is developed as a response to the inmate's situation and as an adaptation to custody itself or whether it is something which is brought in to the prison community by the prisoner from outside, and is simply a continuation of attitudes previously acquired, has been a subject of

1. Paul W. Tappan, *Crime, Justice and Correction*, 1960, p. 669.
2. Donald Clemmer, *The Prison Community*, 1940
3. Erving Goffman, *Asylums*, 1961.
4. A term introduced by Gresham Sykes, *Society of Captives*, 1958.

discussion among sociologists. Stanton Wheeler prefers the second view[5] but most writers prefer to assume that the former view is the only explanation for the inmate culture. It seems likely that in fact both these factors contribute to the development of an inmate sub-culture.

The different types of inmate have been identified and classified by Sykes and others, and the matter is not only one of academic observation: prison administrators with considerable practical experience, like Dr. Lloyd McCorkle, have endorsed this approach to the analysis of prison life.[6] In the latter's view it is essential that all those employed within the prison community should be aware of the hidden significance of the prison culture and its likely attempts to corrupt the prison officer through friendship, reciprocity or default.

So it is commonly said that prisons are run with the consent of the inmates, or indirectly by them, and no doubt there is much truth in these assertions.[7] Whether the inmate sub-culture altogether prevents the training and treatment programme from having any effect is a moot point, but there can be little doubt that it reduces the effectiveness of the official efforts towards rehabilitation.

The very human desire to contribute towards the comfort and happiness of one's charges provides an additional pressure working from the staff side in the same direction, for it does not follow that what makes the inmate happy and comfortable contributes to his rehabilitation. Morever, staff may indulge in what some call "easing" behaviour in order to alleviate the boredom and improve the comfort of their own situation. For it must always be remembered that in the institutional situation, staff are in some respects just as much prisoners as the inmates from certain points of view; they are limited to the performance of certain tasks within a defined physical setting, and are committed to this situation in all probability for longer periods of time. Many staff serve a life term in this sense.

It would be wrong to over-estimate the significance of the

5. Stanton Wheeler, "A Study of Prisonization", in *The Sociology of Punishment and Correction*, eds. N. Johnston, L. Savitz and M. E. Wolfgang, 1962, p. 161.
6. R. R. Korn and L. W. McCorkle, *Criminology and Penology*, 1959, pp. 495 *et seq*
7. Terence and P. Morris (with B. Biely), " 'It's the prisoners who run this prison' —a study of Inmate Leadership" (January 1961), 1 *Prison Service Journal*, No. 2, p. 3. Same authors, "The Experience of Imprisonment" (April 1962), 2 *B.J.C.*, No. 4, p. 337. *Pentonville, A Sociological Study of an English Prison*, 1963

inmate sub-culture on the impact of the treatment programme just as it would be absurd to be over-confident about the success of such a programme. The plain truth appears to be that "prisonisation" is least developed among inmates with short sentences, with fairly stable personalities, who maintain positive relationships outside, who are not much integrated into inmate prison groupings, who do not accept the dogmas and codes of the population, and who engage fully in the formal programme of the institution.[8] It is most developed among the recidivists in the prison population who are in any case least likely to be reached by the programme. It is more likely to be powerful in larger institutions than in smaller ones, and in closed institutions rather than in open ones.

The degree to which inmates adhere to the prison sub-culture is also determined in part by the stage they have reached in their period in custody. Sociologists speak of a U-shaped curve of adherence to the prison sub-culture and amenability to the training programme. At the commencement of his term, when he realises the mess he has got himself into, the offender is likely to be more amenable than in the middle period when he rides out his term; and again towards the end of his stay his amenability rises as his anxieties about his release and his future bear in on him and he ceases to rely on the prison culture to carry him through.[9]

COUNSELLING AND THE WELFARE OF PRISONERS

Group counselling

One of the major developments inside prisons and borstals in the years since 1948 has been the development of group counselling. This had its origin in California in the work of Dr. Norman Fenton, first with naval offenders, later with State prisoners in the adult correctional system. An elaborate code of rules and extensive training of staff who took part characterises this system, the essence of which lies in the conduct of informal group discussions at regular intervals among small numbers of inmates led by a member of the discipline or treatment staff.

---

8. Tappan, *Crime, Justice and Correction*, p. 673, quoting from Clemmer, p. 301.
9. Stanton Wheeler, "A Study of Prisonization", in *The Sociology of Punishment and Correction*, eds: N. Johnston, L. Savitz, M. E. Wolfgang, 1962, p. 152. A. Little, "Borstal: a study of inmates' attitudes to the staff and the system". Unpublished Ph.D. thesis, University of London, 1961.

What distinguishes this from the more traditional types of individual and group psychotherapy[10] is that the latter are carried out directly under the aegis of a skilled practitioner, whereas group counselling relies heavily on the services of group leaders who, in any professional sense, are more or less untrained. The fact that they are given instruction on how to lead groups and have opportunities to discuss their experiences with their colleagues in staff meetings, and receive the guidance and advice of psychologists who have taken a very active part in the development of these activities and their supervision, barely detracts from the basic weakness of the endeavour, viz. its inherently amateur character.

No doubt much good work has been done in the direction of relaxing tensions within an institution[11] and giving both inmates and staff opportunities to air their views about each other and about various matters concerning their situation. The ground rules of group counselling forbid the making of personal attacks on someone who is not present, and there are various other prohibitions.[12] That group counselling does little harm may be accepted, but there is little evidence that, apart from the contribution it makes to the general climate of the institution and the improvement of personal relationships between staff and inmate, it does any permanent good. Perhaps this is not the touchstone upon which the matter should be judged, and the very fact that it provides a better setting within which other influences may be brought to bear on the inmate is itself a sufficient justification.

The Norwich experiment

Among the attempts made since 1948 to improve relations inside prison was the Norwich experiment. In 1956 an experiment was started in Norwich prison to see whether certain changes of routine and method, coupled with a fresh approach by staff towards the prisoner, might be worth while in producing a more wholesome and constructive atmosphere in the prison. Prisoners were allowed more freedom in the daytime

---

10. On group psychotherapy in prison, see J. J. Landers, "Group Therapy in H.M. Prison, Wormwood Scrubs", 9 *Howard Journal*, 1957, 328.
11. John P. Conrad, *Crime and Its Correction*, p. 243.
12. Paul de Berker, "Group Counselling in Penal Institutions—The Problem of Communication" (July 1963), 4 *B.J.C.*, No. 1, p. 62.

inside the prison, and the locking and unlocking of doors and the making of counts of prisoners by the prison staff was cut down. The time saved by the officers was to be used by encouraging them to get to know the prisoners. Each officer was assigned a group of prisoners in his wing whom he was expected to get to know. The experiment was so successful that by 1957 it was extended to various other small local prisons, and by 1959 it had spread upwards through the larger institutions. Experts from the Tavistock Clinic were called in to study the effects of the introduction of the system at Bristol prison in 1958. But after that time little more was heard of the "system", and up until the Mountbatten Report the general relaxation of security indicated by the Norwich system had progressed so far that it ceased to command special mention.

Induction units

Another attempt to alleviate "the pains of imprisonment" and save the prisoner from the harsher consequences of prison were the short-lived Induction Units. These were started in Cardiff prison in 1957, a separate wing being set aside to accommodate every prisoner received from the courts, after he had been through the reception procedure. In this unit the man was informed about prison routine and what to expect; instead of being thrown in at the deep end he was taught to swim, so to speak. The staff were to get to know him as an individual, and after two or three weeks he would be classified and allocated to another part of the prison and decisions would be made about his work assignment and so on. Wakefield prison made some experiments with a similar scheme, though in that institution prisoners are received not from the courts but from other prisons.

The hostel scheme

Foremost among the post-1948 developments in the prison system must rank the hostel scheme. This originated in Bristol with long-term prisoners, men selected for the third stage of preventive detention. They went to live in a hostel situated within the prison walls, and from there went out to work in the city during the day, returning to the hostel to sleep at night. They were permitted to remain out until 9.30 p.m. and received home leave from time to time. Their jobs were remunerated by the payment of regular wages, and each week they brought their wage packet back to the hostel and handed it to the hostel officer. He would give them a sum for pocket money and the cost of any fares and lunches, and, after deducting a sum for the cost of their maintenance in the hostel, and, if their families were in receipt of social security benefits, a sum towards that, the balance of the money would be banked on behalf of the prisoner and accumulated pending his release. In this way quite substantial sums of money were saved up by prisoners, before their discharge, which could provide a most valuable cushion to minimise the financial burden in the period between release and the finding of a job. On release quite a few of the men were taken on by the employer who took them in as "hostellers".

The hostel scheme grew rapidly and was extended to sixteen prisons and applied to long-term prisoners other than those serving preventive detention. In many cases, such as in Birmingham, the hostel was situated outside the confines of the prison, but eleven were inside the walls. The Mountbatten Report commented unfavourably on this feature of a scheme the general terms of which were found to be praiseworthy.[13] "I recognise", said Earl Mountbatten, "the importance of the hostel scheme in easing the transition to outside life, . . ." But the hostel inside the walls constituted a security risk—it could be the means for conveying information and assistance from outside the prison to those desirous of escaping. The result was that several hostels were closed: in 1967 the hostels at Cardiff, Chelmsford and Wandsworth were closed on security grounds.[14] The hostel at Lincoln was also closed because of lack of suitable employment in the area.

The Home Office Research Unit has been studying the suitability of various types of prisoner for selection for the hostels scheme, and prisoners' attitudes to the régime.[15] The success of the hostel scheme is difficult to measure. There have clearly been disappointments but this was only to be expected. So far, the general public has not reacted unfavourably to hostellers working in the free community, and substantial sums of money

---

13. Cmnd. 3175, p. 81, para. 304.
14. Prison Department Report, 1967, Cmnd. 3774, October 1968, p. 26.
15. *Ibid.*

have been saved by some prisoners prior to release, varying from £90 to over £200. The A.C.T.O. Report on Preventive Detention recommended that the provision for hostels and half-way houses should be extended. Some voluntary provision has been made for post-release hostels, which will be described later. (See Chapter 11: Release.)

The therapeutic community

In some situations it has been thought right to borrow from the ideas and practice now being applied in the field of mental health and introduce the idea of the therapeutic community. This idea originated during and after the war, in dealing with ex-prisoners of war, and was later applied to neurotics and psychopaths, under the leadership of Dr. Maxwell Jones, at the Belmont Social Rehabilitation Unit, now known as the Henderson Hospital. The basic notion is that the whole community of doctors, nurses and patients is involved in the treatment process, and everything which occurs in that community may be scrutinised in the community meetings and its significance reviewed.

"The essential features of the system in its classical form as applied, for example, at the Henderson Hospital can be summed up as follows: the self-conscious pooling of all the resources of staff and patients alike in furthering treatment, the active involvement of patients in treatment roles; a democratic, egalitarian social structure, a sharing of responsibility and decision-taking, a permissive atmosphere, open communications (with no communications regarded as privileged) and free expression of feelings; the provision of peer-group support to enable the patient to examine his poor relationships with others, to recognise and work through his difficulties with authority, to face up to the social consequences of his behaviour, to accept his need for personality and attitude change."[16]

This is not the place to examine the significance of the therapeutic community method of treatment of psychopaths, and others have written extensively about it. But the notion has been carried over to the field of corrections, and applied to prisoners who need psychiatric treatment, at Grendon Prison hospital, at Herstedvester in Denmark and in the Van der

16. R. L. Morrison, "Individualization and Involvement in Treatment and Prevention", *Frontiers of Criminology*, ed. Klare and Haxby, 1967, p. 93.

Hoeven Clinic Utrecht; to youths at Highfields, New Jersey; to drug addicts at Synanon; and to homeless ex-borstal lads.[17]

One of the difficulties about introducing the therapeutic community idea in the custodial setting lies in the necessity for certain routines and restraints to be accepted where a larger population is involved in the interests of orderly management:

> "Existing correctional institutions cannot all be torn down and replaced with small living units designed for milieu treatment. Instead, rehabilitative ventures will continue to be carried on, in part at least, within existing large facilities. Although some important steps might be taken to transform these places into systems in which the general institutional climate is more conducive to therapy, there are some limits to the extent to which this can be accomplished."[18]

Milieu therapy

The term "milieu treatment" is used in the above passage. R. L. Morrison has distinguished the more traditional efforts directed towards individualisation of treatment and the development of an acceptable training programme (which he calls the programme approach) from the more modern approaches towards "milieu therapy" or "milieu management", the distinguishing features of which are the deliberate and systematic use of the institutional environment in both its physical and social aspects as a therapeutic experience. He accepts that "community therapy in its classical form is perhaps too unrealistic a model for the penal institution which is expected to contain and control its inmates as well as treat them".[19] But he believes that the idea can be adapted to the penal setting without loosing its essential character.

The strategy of involvement

Morrison develops another theme, which may be described as the "strategy of involvement". This means the deliberate utilisation of the patient or inmate in the treatment process, both as an agent (certainly) and (hopefully) as an object of treatment.

While Gibbons views with some reserve the efforts which

---

17. Derek Miller, *Growth to Freedom*, 1964.
18. Don C. Gibbons, *Changing the Lawbreaker*, pp. 170–171.
19. R. L. Morrison, *op. cit.*, p. 93.

have been made to "involve" prisoners in their own or others' treatment,[20] Morrison is less sceptical about the possibilities, and cites Cressey's observations in favour of this approach as well as the deliberations of a conference in California on the subject.[1]

HUMANITARIANISM AND TREATMENT PROGRAMMES

Many of the changes which have been introduced or are advocated for custodial institutions are inspired more by humanitarian considerations than by any view about the contribution these might make to the reform or rehabilitation of the offender. This is not to say that they are not justifiable changes, but simply to observe that we have little or no evidence that these changes contribute in any degree to the rehabilitation process. They do not need to be justified on these grounds since they derive their support from humanitarian principles.

Thus, the frequency of visits and letters, the provision of proper food and decent clothes, permission to have a few personal possessions about one, visits and the vexed question of conjugal visits and relations with the opposite sex, these are all matters where the decision need not be based on the contribution which the item makes or might make towards the reformation of the prisoner. It would hardly seem necessary to make these observations were it not the fact that

> "considerable confusion exists in the public mind (and sometimes even in the thinking of correctional persons) concerning the differences between treatment and humane gestures. The latter are frequently assumed to be rehabilitative or therapeutic as well, although there is little reason to suppose that such activities do have rehabilitative consequences."[2]

Adjuncts to treatment

Another distinction made by Gibbons concerns those items which may be regarded as adjuncts of the training programme, but which are not the core of treatment itself. For example, in order to enable the treatment of prisoners to take place, a prime

---

20. Don C. Gibbons, *op. cit.*, pp. 172 *et seq.* He cites the history of the Intensive Treatment Program at Chino prison, California, which was only a partial success.
1. D. R. Cressey, "Theoretical foundations for using criminals in the rehabilitation of criminals", *The Future of Imprisonment in a Free Society*, 1965. "Experiment in Culture Expansion (1963), *N.I.M.H.*
2. Don C. Gibbons, *op. cit.*, p. 130.

requirement is effective classification. Also the provision of suitable educational and vocational training opportunities may be justified both on humanitarian grounds and also because they provide the setting in which it is possible to begin treatment.

"None of these are treatment *per se*, for none of them deal directly with some therapy problem presented by the inmate. For example, vocational training may contribute to the eventual rehabilitation of an offender who is subjected to such a program, insofar as that experience provides the prisoner with good work habits and vocational skills. But it is likely to have some impact only when it is accompanied by some kind of direct resocialization experience in which the inmate is led to modify his negative attitudes towards work."[3]

The distinction between adjuncts to treatment and treatment itself may be regarded as somewhat artificial and academic. In practice, as those concerned know very well, any modification of negative attitudes which occurs may be the result of any one or a combination of experiences during custody. Indeed they may not be related to custodial experiences at all.

Prison visitors

There is a long-standing tradition of lay interest in what goes on in the prisons in England and Wales, and visits from lay persons determined to find out and to help wherever possible. This goes back to John Howard and Elizabeth Fry. There are echoes of it in the Report of the Gladstone Committee (1895) which records the good work done by lady visitors to female prisoners, and recommends that outside helpers could be brought in to supplement the work of the prison staff under proper rules and regulations.[4]

A Lady Visitors' Association was set up in 1901, but visitors to men did not get going until 1922. In 1924 the National Association of Prison Visitors was founded, and collaborated closely with the Lady Visitors' Association until 1944, when the two were merged.

In 1965 there were 688 members of this association organised in forty-four branches. They visit men and women in H.M. prisons in England and Wales but do not at present visit borstal

3. *Ibid.*, p. 135.
4. Fox, p. 205.

institutions or detention centres. Prison visitors see inmates alone usually in the evenings, and at week-ends, mainly in their cells. Each visitor normally sees four to six inmates, and most visitors see each inmate once a week or once a fortnight, in general over the whole period of sentence. They may thus see an inmate regularly over a period of several years.

Prison visitors are carefully screened before being appointed by the Home Office. There is an interview with the Prison Governor and the chaplain, who then make recommendations to the Prison Department. If approved, the prison visitor receives a letter appointing him for one year. There is an annual review which may or may not lead to reappointment. Occasionally the voluntary services of a prison visitor have to be terminated, which is done with as much tact as possible.

Prisoners are allocated to prison visitors by the reception board at the prison. Men usually visit male prisoners and women female prisoners, but there are instances where women visitors are employed to visit young men. As Sir Lionel Fox says, "it has been found that well-chosen women may have a most helpful influence on young prisoners".[5]

The voluntary prison visitor should not be confused with the Visiting Committee, members of which are chosen by the local bench of magistrates and serve a rather different purpose, (see Discipline: Chapter 7 above).

It should be noted, moreover, that coming into the prison but not part of the prison service itself there are a number of voluntary social workers. For example, the allocation centre for borstal boys at Wormwood Scrubs uses the services of a small band of part-time women social workers who come in weekly and see the boys and help in the allocation and teaching activities.[6]

The value of the prison visitor should not be assessed solely in terms of the contribution made towards rehabilitation of the prisoner. Nor is his work on the welfare side so important now that there are prison welfare officers. His contribution lies more in being concerned in an unofficial capacity as a fellow human being with the prisoner as another human being temporarily incarcerated. The prison visitor provides for the prisoner a link with the outside world, which, in terms of the prisoner's friends

---

5. Fox, p. 208.
6. Estimates Committee, Eleventh Report, Minutes of Evidence, p. 29.

and family, has frequently rejected him and turned its back on him. The visitor may help with restoring family relationships, maintaining the prisoner's self-confidence, hearing his grouses and exploring possible injustices, he may ensure that the after-care arrangements are running smoothly, and keep in touch with the prisoner after release.

There is clearly an area of overlap between some of these activities and those of after-care associates or voluntary auxiliaries. It has been suggested that the prison visitor is an anachronism in the modern penal system because of the changing role of the prison staff, the increased 'association' of prisoners during lecture hours, and the improvement in the prison welfare and after-care services. But the official view is that there are important functions still remaining for the voluntary unofficial visitor. Perhaps at the very lowest, prison visitors act as adjuncts of the system, helping to relieve the harsher features of imprisonment for the friendless and blunting the edges of officialism. They assist in providing the setting wherein other reformative influences may begin to take effect. At the very highest, their contribution to reformation of prisoners is intangible and impossible to assess.

CHAPTER 11

Release

A number of truisms have been uttered about the difficulties facing the prisoner on release. Thus the Home Office pamphlet in 1950 began its chapter on After-Care of Prisoners with these words:

> "It has been said that a prisoner's real punishment begins when he is discharged; and, again, that the true test of a prison system is what happens to a man when he comes out."

Sir Lionel Fox added that while it is the easiest thing in the world to imprison a man, it is not so easy to release him in a satisfactory manner.[1] This chapter will be concerned with the problems surrounding the release of prisoners, and their supervision and help under what may be termed the after-care arrangements.

THE AIM

The aim of the system in regard to release ought to be to carry out this operation at the best possible moment from the point of view of the prisoner's rehabilitation and the prevention of further crime, and in the best possible manner, in other words, to make the transition from the prison community to the free community as smooth and painless as possible, by giving the prisoner financial and material assistance and psychological instruction and guidance, and by offering or imposing some degree of continuing supervision where this is desirable. Help may be needed in obtaining (and keeping) employment, in obtaining accommodation, in re-establishing his position in the family, in settling various debts incurred while he was in custody or prior thereto, and in countless other directions.

---

1. Fox, pp. 72–73.

THE HISTORY OF AFTER-CARE

With more limited objects in view, during the nineteenth and twentieth centuries a network of voluntary associations, known as prisoners' aid societies, was developed, coupled with a degree of official provision under the authority of various statutes. At first these efforts were concentrated on material aid on discharge. Statutes of 1776, 1779 and 1824 provided that certain offenders might receive financial aid on discharge, and the visiting justices should make recommendations. Side by side with this were developed the efforts of the voluntary societies. In 1862 the partnership between the official provision of after-care and the voluntary societies began, which has endured until the present day. The Discharged Prisoners' Aid Act, 1862, enabled the visiting justices to give recognition to a Discharged Prisoners' Aid Society and pay them a sum of money not exceeding £2, to be used for the benefit of any discharged prisoner. Earlier limitations on the prisoners who qualified for aid were no longer continued, and the principle was accepted that all discharged prisoners were eligible for assistance. It by no means followed, of course, that all received such assistance. Hinde says of the earlier provisions, "how far these . . . were in fact put into effect is not known".[2] When in 1877 the prisons were "nationalised", to use his phrase, and similar provision was made for aid on discharge, there are records of the sums disbursed, from which it seems that the justices used their powers very sparingly, and there were considerable variations from place to place.

The Prison Commissioners now took a hand in the matter and laid down rules for the guidance of the local societies, for under the Act of 1877 they were to be the authority which ordered the money to be paid. They were to act on the recommendation of the Visiting Committee. The money now came out of a Parliamentary vote and not from local funds.

In 1878 a Central Committee of Discharged Prisoners' Aid Societies was established with the object of improving and extending the voluntary administration of the grants. But by 1895 the position was profoundly unsatisfactory, and the Gladstone Committee made certain criticisms and recommendations, which led to an inquiry by the Prison Commissioners. The

---

2. R. S. E. Hinde, *The British Penal System* 1773–1950, p. 212.

report of this inquiry led to a new scheme, but this was not a success and was dropped in 1913.

A new rate of financial subvention from public funds to the voluntary societies was adopted, which continued, with variations, until 1948.

Meanwhile, special arrangements had been made for long-term prisoners (convicts) discharged from the central convict prisons like Dartmoor and Parkhurst, and for borstal inmates and female prisoners. In 1911 a new organisation was established called the Central Association for the Aid of Discharged Convicts. Winston Churchill had proposed this in 1910 when he was Home Secretary. It was necessary because the local aid societies were not really appropriate for dealing with the discharged convict. The same realisation had motivated the founding of the Borstal Association in 1908 to deal with the needs of male borstal inmates on discharge. It was not until 1928 that the Aylesbury Association was established to deal with the after-care of women and girls.

By 1918, as Hinde puts it, "there was a widespread desire on the part of various societies for some change in central organisation which would strengthen its executive function".[3] The result was the setting up of the Central Discharged Prisoners' Aid Society, with the aim of promoting the co-ordination of efforts of the various societies.

RECONSTRUCTION PRIOR TO WORLD WAR II

Several efforts were made to reorganise the system of after-care provision in the nineteen-thirties. A Departmental Committee produced a Report (the Salmon Report) in 1935,[4] but its proposals for reorganising the work of the societies were unacceptable to the societies, which rejected the recommendations in a Conference in July 1935, and set up their own inquiry. The result, the Whitbread Report of 1936, recommended certain changes, one of which, the establishment of the National Association of Discharged Prisoners' Aid Societies, provided for a stronger central organisation in place of the old Central Discharged Prisoners' Aid Society. In 1937 NADPAS, as the new association became known, was formally constituted.

---

3. Hinde, p. 219.

Amalgamation of some of the smaller societies into larger groups also took place.[4]

The Criminal Justice Act 1948 made new demands in connection with after-care. It became necessary to set up the Central After-Care Association in 1949 to provide for the supervision and after-care of those prisoners who were released on licence and under compulsory after-care, by virtue of the Act. These included borstal inmates, prisoners sentenced to corrective training and preventive detention, persons released after being sentenced to life imprisonment, and persons under 21 released from sentences exceeding three months (Young Prisoners or Y.P.s for short). There was thus created one central organisation in place of the three bodies hitherto occupying this part of the field, the Borstal Association, the Central Association for the Aid of Discharged Convicts, and the Aylesbury Association. Three separate Divisions within the C.A.C.A. reflected the main areas of the work: the Men's Division, the Women's and Girls' Division, and the Borstal Division. The closest cooperation with the work of NADPAS and the local aid societies was intended, and to this end, the same person was made General Secretary of NADPAS and Director of the C.A.C.A. From 1949 it became the responsibility of probation officers to act as local associates of the C.A.C.A. The Criminal Justice Act 1948 expressly recognised that after-care was a proper function of the probation service. But the C.A.C.A. did employ after-care officers of its own in London and other large cities. There was some criticism of the qualifications and training of the staff so appointed.[5]

The Maxwell Committee

In 1952 a Departmental Committee on Discharged Prisoners' Aid Societies looked at the whole question again, reviewing the functions and finance of the local aid societies and NADPAS.[6]

---

4. There is a convenient short history of prison and borstal after-care in Appendix B of the Report on The Organisation of After-Care, 1963.
5. Pauline Morris, *Prison After-Care: charity or public responsibility?* Fabian Research Series 218, November 1960, p. 5.
6. Report of the Committee on Discharged Prisoners' Aid Societies, Cmnd. 8879, June 1953.

It made several recommendations. Firstly the local societies should concentrate less on purely material aid on discharge and should develop and deepen after-care work. Secondly prison welfare officers should be appointed at local prisons as full-time social workers, from amongst people with suitable training and experience.

These prison welfare officers would operate in close liaison with the existing Welfare Officers of the voluntary societies, who would operate outside the prisons and carry out home visits. After a pilot scheme in four of the larger local prisons had demonstrated the value of the arrangement, prison welfare officers were rapidly appointed to other prisons. Several large prisons have two or three, and some four, prison welfare officers. The total number of posts is now 200. (See Chapter 8: Prison Staff, above, subtitle 3, Professional Staff.)

The ACTO Report of 1958.

The next stage in the extremely tangled history of after-care came when the Advisory Council on the Treatment of Offenders issued its Report entitled "The After-Care and Supervision of Discharged Prisoners" in October 1958. This dealt with two matters:

(*i*) *The provisions of the Prison Act* 1952, s. 29.—This required certain discharged prisoners to report their addresses to the C.A.C.A., who then passed them on to Scotland Yard and the local police. About 3,000 prisoners per annum were subject to this requirement, which had proved ineffective and unsatisfactory. It was recommended that the requirement to report the address in this way should be abolished. This was done by the Criminal Justice Act 1961, s. 21.[7]

(*ii*) *The extension of compulsory after-care.*—The Advisory Council recommended a gradual extension of the categories of prisoner who should be subjected to compulsory after-care, rejecting alternative proposals to the effect that the selection of those persons who should be subject to statutory after-care should be left to the sentencing court or that the decision should be left to a case committee prior to the prisoner's release or to the prisoner's own choice. Several new categories of statutory

---

7. By the same Act, after-care was introduced for detention centres.

after-care were proposed, and legislation was in fact passed to enable these recommendations to be implemented. But in the main these recommendations were never brought into effect, being overtaken by subsequent developments.

Sir Lionel Fox wrote in 1952 that

> "it may be . . . that the time is ripe for a radical reassessment both of the nature of 'aid-on-discharge' and of the relative responsibilities of the State and of private benevolence in providing and administering it. It may also be that in any such reassessment emphasis will be shifted from the economic to the psychological problems, from 'aid-on-discharge' to 'after-care'."[8]

The ACTO Report on the Organisation of After-Care

It was as a result of a further report on after-care emanating from the Advisory Council in 1963 that the radical reorganisation took place.[9] This report stemmed from a reference to them by the Home Secretary, in April 1961, of the whole question of the future of after-care. The Report, consisting of 87 pages, represents a comprehensive review and recommends a radical reorganisation (though not radical enough for three of its members, who published a memorandum of dissent).

As the Committee observed, in its review of the complicated history,

> "three main trends in the development may be observed:
> One has been the humanitarian concern for all ex-prisoners, whatever the nature or length of their sentence; another the idea that for recidivist prisoners a period of supervision on licence at the end of a long sentence may be beneficial. Yet another has been the growth of specialised systems of after-care of a positive kind for particular classes of offender."[10]

The Committee laid down five principles which should govern after-care provisions. These, it said, had emerged from the practical experience of the past hundred years and were of great importance to the future development of after-care.

---

8. Fox, p. 256.
9. There has been several unofficial studies made of the after-care situation and attempts to formulate reform proposals. Pauline Morris's Fabian pamphlet, 1960, see note 5, was followed by the Report of the Pakenham-Thompson Committee, "Problems of the Ex-Prisoner", National Council of Social Service, 1961.
10. Fox, p. 3.

Broadly speaking, they accepted the concept of after-care as a skilled rehabilitation service integrated with the work of the penal institutions as an essential part of the rehabilitative process. They saw the need to amalgamate the compulsory and voluntary after-care into a common service, employing professional social workers on after-care, both in penal institutions and in the community. With this end in view, they recommended that the probation service should be expanded and reorganised to undertake both compulsory and voluntary after-care in the community. Some members of this service might specialise on after-care work. (It should be observed that all prison welfare officers are now probation officers seconded for that purpose to work inside penal institutions.)

A considerable expansion of voluntary effort was foreseen as essential in order to enable the probation and after-care service to carry out these new responsibilities. Voluntary workers would be trained as after-care auxiliaries (see below: subtitle, The Role of Voluntary Effort in After-care).

Social workers in prison, the ACTO Committee thought, should be appointed by the Home Secretary, but inspection would be by the probation inspectorate. This suggestion was not accepted but, instead, it was found preferable to adopt an arrangement whereby most of the existing prison welfare officers became probation officers and to staff the prison welfare service by probation officers seconded for that purpose.[11]

Inside the Home Office the transitional arrangements were worked out by a special after-care planning unit in 1963 and 1964, which eventually was incorporated into the new probation and after-care department.[12]

A considerable expansion in the provision of hostels for discharged offenders was also called for, and here too, as well as in providing after-care auxiliaries, new scope was offered for the efforts of the various religious bodies and voluntary organisations in the local community. Under the National Association for the Care and Resettlement of Offenders (NACRO) which was established in 1966 in order to promote and encourage these efforts, the provision of voluntary hostels and other arrangements for ex-prisoners has been

---

11. Report on the Work of the Probation and After-Care Department 1962-1965, Cmnd. 3107, October 1966, p. 36, para. 101.
12. *Ibid.*, p. 32, para. 92.

steadily increased. Already in 1965 there were about 800 groups or organisations providing voluntary hostels and homes and similar services, associated with each other in a federation (the Voluntary Hostels Conference). A Directory of Prison After-Care Projects showed what a great variety of provision had been made including specialised hostels and the Norman House kind of half-way homes for homeless men. Since then, the need for special hostels for alcoholics and drug addicts has increased and so has the provision.

The families of offenders need attention both during the prison sentence and afterwards. The Women's Royal Voluntary Service (W.R.V.S.) has provided in some cases for a home visit to an offender's family when he has been before the courts. The ACTO Report recommended that the needs of offenders' families should be included within the ambit of after-care. For further discussion of hostels or half-way houses, and the provision made for the families of offenders see below (The Role of Voluntary Effort in After-Care).

The organisation of after-care in the big cities had previously involved the employment of C.A.C.A. officers as after-care agents, instead of probation officers. While the ACTO Committee did not dissent from the view of the Morison Committee that there should be no general movement towards specialisation at present, it recognised that specialisation in after-care work would become desirable in the larger centres of population. The result has been that a special unit has been set up as a central after-care office. This refers to area probation officers persons who have settled addresses: the homeless men and women who stay in inner London after release from prison are however cared for by officers stationed at the central office. Similar arrangements involving a degree of specialisation in after-care work have been introduced in Birmingham and Liverpool, and in other large provincial centres. Apart from these special cases

> "In places where the volume of after-care work does not justify a separate office, it is sometimes being done by one officer who specialises in it; but often the better plan is found to be for each probation officer to take a share of after-care work, usually on the geographical basis on which the rest of the work is organised."[13]

---

13. Cmnd. 3107, p. 17, para. 45.

After-care arrangements for borstal institutions, detention centres and approved schools

Discussion of the 1963 ACTO Report on the Organisation of After-Care would not be complete without some reference to its impact on the arrangements for borstals, detention centres and approved schools.

With regard to borstal institutions, the after-care arrangements do not differ from the general scheme. But inside the institutions themselves, the ACTO Report accepted that the main social case-work functions should remain in the hands of the house-masters and house-mistresses, where it already belonged. But it was recommended that their recruitment and training should be revised with these extended duties in mind. "Then", we are told "specialist social workers would not be needed in borstals." But it was admitted that there were arguments on the other side, and even that "specialist social workers may be necessary, at any rate as a temporary measure".[14] Moreover, the case for the employment of specialist social workers is stronger with regard to the girl's borstals.[15]

The arrangements whereby borstal reception centres employ social workers, both professional and voluntary, have no bearing on this matter, as they are concerned mainly with home visits, and the preparation of reports with a view to classification and allocation to suitable training institutions and with immediate "first-aid" problems.

Detention centres.—These are included in the general scheme. The ACTO Committee reported that social workers had already been appointed to work in detention centres, but it was recommended that arrangements for social casework in detention centres should be kept flexible. As the probation and after-care service now provides supervision for youths released from detention centres, it is suggested that early involvement of the probation officer with the youth he will be supervising may be helpful. "The probation officer, who may be supervising a youth before his detention and after his release, may help by visiting the youth at the detention centre or by keeping in touch with his family."[16]

Approved Schools.—The approved schools were unique in that

---

14. ACTO Report, 1963, p. 27, para. 93.
15. *Ibid.*, p. 28, para. 95.
16. *Ibid.*, p. 28, para. 96.

many of them provided after-care supervision through the agency of approved schools welfare officers. In 1962, the ACTO Report says, approved school welfare officers undertook the after-care of 52 per cent. of boys placed out from approved schools, and the probation service only 29 per cent. The local authority child-care service looked after most of the remainder (15 per cent. of boys). For girls after-care was provided from the probation service (65 per cent.) and the local authority child-care service (22 per cent.).

The arrangements for the appointment of approved school welfare officers originated during World War II, and by 1962 there were forty-nine such officers each of whom was responsible for the after-care of boys from a number of different schools, discharged into a particular area. These arrangements were not universal and hardly ideal, and the system was not extended to girls because of the comparatively small numbers in any one area.

The Ingleby Committee had recommended in 1960 that the approved school welfare service should be allowed to run down gradually, and be replaced by probation and the local child care authorities. The traditional concept that the managers of an approved school remained responsible for the resettlement of the child after he leaves the school should be retained.

The ACTO Report of 1963 endorsed these views, and recommended that approved school welfare officers should have an opportunity to enter the probation service, and receive training where necessary.

The strong case for the continuation of the approved school welfare service was not regarded as convincing, for various reasons, by the Advisory Council and it was recommended that a date should be set for the service to be wound up.[17]

THE QUALITY OF AFTER-CARE

Several things need saying about the nature of the after-care operation and the quality of the service which is needed. First, many prisoners are homeless, and have few if any personal relationships with family or with any other persons. Strenuous efforts are now being made to provide hostels for homeless ex-prisoners, but it may be doubted whether there is sufficient

---

17. ACTO Report, 1963, pp. 56–57, paras. 197–199.

G

provision and whether what is available is always in the right place at the right time. Many male prisoners are or have become feckless inadequate persons with little idea how to look after themselves, to manage on a small budget, or to deal with essential day-to-day matters like the purchase of clothes, personal laundry and so on. For these, a supportive environment is helpful if not essential.

Secondly, many ex-prisoners have an extremely poor work record. It is not simply a question of finding a job but of keeping it. They may be poor time-keepers, lack persistence in effort, and easily drop out of the labour market. We have seen, in the section on Prison Work and Earnings, that many are capable of semi-skilled jobs of a repetitive nature like machine-minding, and efforts are now being made to train them in this direction. The vocational training in various skilled trades is less likely to lead to employment opportunities, and may have been over-emphasised in the past, no doubt in many cases for the best of reasons. This was partly due to the enthusiasm of the training instructors, partly due to the policy of the prison administration in this matter.

Family problems may already exist in the life of the ex-prisoners, or they may become acute on his release when he finds a rival installed in his wife's affection if not in the home. Suspicion about such "goings on", aroused sometimes by information contained in letters or acquired otherwise, is a frequent source of anxiety to the prisoner during his term, and may often lead to escapes. Prisoners are often failures in many different directions, as well as in crime; in work, in home making and as spouses. All these areas are the proper concern of after-care.

There is also the prevention of further crime. This involves the after-care official being sensitive to the dangers of his charge getting into bad company, and where release is on licence, the delicate question when to ask for his recall. It demands a mature judgment and considerable experience to know how to handle such matters. Herein lies much of the skill and responsibility of the after-care officer. Too many failures will certainly damage the image of the system, yet it would be unrealistic to expect complete success in the form of total abstinence from further crime on the part of many offenders. The borstal figures for recidivism show that after one failure many ex-borstal inmates settle down and do well, and probation figures point in the same direction. Where the further offence is an isolated lapse and not in itself too serious or damaging from the public point of view, it may be right to be tolerant and forgiving. The real trouble stems from sensational crimes committed by ex-prisoners.

THE ROLE OF VOLUNTARY EFFORT IN AFTER-CARE

Important developments have taken place in the provision and organisation of voluntary service in connection with after-care in the last ten years. It is not easy to chronicle these developments reliably. The activities of New Bridge, Apex, the Circle Trust, the work of the Blackfriars Settlement, which runs an elaborate and well-considered scheme employing volunteers, the various groups of prisoners' wives, the organisation which arranges fidelity guarantees for prospective employees who are ex-prisoners, these are just a few of the most important developments.

The ACTO Report on the Organisation of After-Care said that much valuable work was being done and that attention should be paid to the need to recruit and train auxiliaries. The dangers of inappropriate selection or incautious use of auxiliaries must be recognised:

"this is not work for inexperienced amateurs. It requires a warm heart but also a clear head, compassion combined with insight, lack of illusion, and preparedness for disappointment."[18]

There are clearly limitations to what can be undertaken and what can be achieved in this connection. Research by Lacey in 1963 revealed how little was in fact achieved and how few contacts with ex-prisoners endured for any length of time.[19]

More recently, a research study sponsored by NACRO relating to "Helping Prisoners' Families" showed that considerable resistance existed on the part of many probation officers to the use of volunteers:

"probation officers are uneasy about the ways in which work done by volunteers may overlap with their own."[20]

18. ACTO Report 1963, p. 37, para. 132.
19. Albert W. Lacey, "The role of voluntary effort in the after-care of offenders", unpublished Ph.D. thesis, University of London, 1963. See also Lacey's article "The Citizen and Aftercare" (1963), 11 *Howard Journal*, No. 2, p. 194.
20. *NACRO* Papers and Reprints No. 3, "Helping Prisoners' Families", November 1968, p. 11.

There is some feeling that the right kind of volunteers are not available, that their use will be too troublesome to the probation officers and will involve additional work. One Principal Probation Officer is quoted as saying that his staff:

> "think volunteers are more trouble than they are worth, this is because they wrongly imagine that the function of the volunteer ought to be to save the probation officer time, in fact to be a probation officer substitute; they do not realise that the work of a volunteer should complement that of the probation officer, and so *extend* the service being offered to the client."[1]

The training of probation officers has not hitherto sufficiently stressed the possible uses of voluntary helpers.

Another category of help is that of the voluntary organisations such as the W.R.V.S. The NACRO study contains an excellent assessment of the possibilities and problems here. It also reviews the sources of official aid and assistance of a financial and material nature, through probation service funds, the Department of Health and Social Security, etc.

Prisoners' wives groups

These are a feature of the contemporary after-care scene which cannot be overlooked. The NACRO Report mentions that twenty-one groups were known to exist at the time of that study. These groups are of two kinds. Most are *local* groups, consisting of wives of men resident in an area who may be imprisoned anywhere. Some are on the other hand *contact* groups which meet in premises near a particular prison and are attended by wives visiting their husbands. Outside London the groups have close links with the probation service, but in the London area, where the Circle Trust organises the four groups, they have received no assistance or encouragement from the Probation Service.

Some of these groups are run entirely by volunteers, but most are run on some kind of partnership basis, with probation officers and volunteers sharing the responsibility. Once again, as with the use of volunteers as auxiliaries, opinions differ about the value of the activities.

The prisoners' wives service

This is a different kind of activity which functions in the

---

1. *Ibid.*, p. 13.

Inner London area, and is accredited to the Inner London Probation Service. A part-time probation officer acts as liaison officer between the service and the Prisoners' Wives Service, and two part-time administrative staff man the office. Its function is to respond to requests to visit prisoners' families, most of which emanate from probation and prison welfare officers.

HOMELESS DISCHARGED PRISONERS: THE WORKING PARTY REPORT, 1966

Mention has been made of the development of hostels or half-way houses for ex-prisoners, such as Norman House. A scheme to provide a limited amount of financial assistance from Government funds has been introduced by the Home Office, following an Interim Report of Lady Reading's Working Party on the Place of Voluntary Service in After-Care. This Committee has since issued two most important and valuable reports. The first concerns Residential Provision for Homeless Discharged Offenders (1966).

The Working Party found that there were only twenty hostels in being, providing 242 places, including four hostels (38 places) for young offenders. This number was quite insufficient to cope with the need. Moreover, there was insufficient variety in the range of clients provided for:

> "existing voluntary effort in this field, which is mainly in the form of "Half-way houses", is not only insufficient quantitatively but is unable to cater for more than a limited category of homeless offenders. The large numbers of offenders who present the more difficult personal problems can be accommodated only to a very limited extent and may often be excluded."[2]

The Committee classify offenders according to their dependency needs, as indicated by various criteria, such as homelessness, inability to keep a job, difficulties over companionship, and in accepting help when it is offered, and specific disabilities. There are, in their view, three groups, those with low dependency, high dependency and intermediate dependency. The provision required varies according to the nature and degree of these needs. Some people need only a social club, others need special

---

2. Home Office, Report of the Working Party on the Place of Voluntary Service in After-Care, Residential Provision for Homeless Discharged Offenders, 1966, p. 3, para. 15.

staff and care permanently or for long periods. "It is in the accommodation of those of intermediate dependency that the greatest variety, and intensity of effort will be required." The Committee recommend that provision should include the following:

(a) multi-purpose hostels;
(b) general non-supportive accommodation for single men;
(c) hostels consisting mainly of "bed-sitters";
(d) half-way houses;
(e) hostels for permanent or semi-permanent stay;
(f) proposed hostels administered from prisons;
(g) hostels for young offenders;
(h) specialised hostels for alcoholics;
(i) other specialised hostels;
(j) hostels with special work facilities for extreme inadequates;
(k) specialised hostels for men selected by prison medical officers;
(l) hostels or homes for aged offenders.

The Report contains detailed recommendations concerning the staffing, finance and administration of such hostels, and the use of voluntary helpers. Not the least of their contributions is the clear recognition that hostels may provide an alternative to imprisonment as well as a sequel to it. In sum, the report contains a powerful case for the expansion of hostel provision as an integral part of our crime prevention and social work programme.

THE SECOND REPORT OF THE WORKING PARTY, 1967

This concerned The Place of Voluntary Service in After-Care. It covers much of the ground which has already been described. A number of important recommendations are made, which may be summarised as follows:

1. There should be instituted by the Home Secretary a deliberate programme of information and education designed to inform the public about discharged offenders and mobilise their support in the task of rehabilitation and acceptance of the returning prisoner;

2. There will continue to be an important role for voluntary effort in this area. Volunteers should be described as "associates" when they provide support for considerable periods by a personal relationship and should be called "accredited associates" when they have been appointed by a probation committee.

3. Formal responsibility for recruiting and accrediting associates should rest with probation committees and each appointment should be initially for one year.

4. Probation officers need to be trained in the use of volunteers.

5. Expenses of volunteers and of voluntary organisations, should be met from probation funds, at the discretion of probation committees. In suitable cases the necessary accommodation should be provided.

6. With the consent of the offender, the spouse of every person sentenced to imprisonment should be visited by the probation officer.

7. More provision should be made for a prisoner to receive visits and to write and receive letters.

8. More assistance should be available towards the cost of visits to prison.

9. Prisoners' wives groups should be eligible for a small initial grant and possibly some further assistance from public funds.

10. Grants should be available to housing associations which provide accommodation for offenders and their families in suitable cases.

11. Different levels of grant should be available to hostels according to the dependency needs catered for and the extent to which therapeutic staff are employed.

12. The training needs of hostel staff should be provided for, including pre-service as well as in-service training.

Finally, the Working Party, which held no less than eighty meetings and in the space of two years produced two most valuable reports, asks for the appointment of an independent group of five persons to keep the whole developing field of voluntary service relating to delinquency under review, and for certain other purposes.

CHAPTER 12

Remission, Pardon and Parole

REMISSION

As Sir Lionel Fox remarks, "from the days of transportation and the early penal servitude system, eligibility to earn a remission of part of the sentence by good conduct and industry has been the first and most valuable privilege accorded to prisoners, as the power to forfeit remission has been and remains one of the strongest sanctions against bad conduct".[1]

The old convict sentence of penal servitude carried with it the right to earn a "ticket of leave" which was really a conditional licence under which the prisoner might be recalled to serve the remainder of his term in the event of further offences. The history of the matter is bound up with the system of transportation.

There is also evidence that the hulks which were used earlier to house convicts also operated a system of early release. But it is in connection with the Australian scene that the system of ticket of leave was more fully developed. Transported convicts were either allotted to merchants and farmers as "assigned labour" or were kept in penal colonies to carry out certain public works (later a system of release on probation was developed). Release could be either by conditional pardon, which freed a convict of all restrictions, the only condition being that he should not leave the colony, or it could be on "ticket of leave", which gave the convict far less freedom, and was coupled with a scale of entitlement. Thus a life prisoner might expect to get his ticket of leave in eight years, a fourteen-year man in six years, and a seven-year man in four years. Not all those eligible for ticket leave were granted this privilege. Only one-third of those eligible received it in Van Diemen's Land. Many who received it had not served the minimum period.[2]

When transportation was replaced by penal servitude in

---

1. Lionel Fox, *The English Prison and Borstal Systems*, 1952, p. 165.
2. See A. G. L. Shaw, *Convicts and the Colonies*, 1966, pp. 83, 187, 229, 230. L. L. Robson, *The Convict Settlers of Australia*, 1965, footnote 14 to chapter 5, p. 236.

convict prisons at home, by the Act of 1853, there was considerable public anxiety about the system which included early release by ticket-of-leave. Tobias says:

> "The public did not take kindly to the premature release of criminals in Britain itself. People had not realised that systems of this sort had operated for many years . . . the ticket-of-leave system under the Penal Servitude Acts was the subject of a great public outcry."[3]

Later legislation made it more difficult for convicts to get a licence, and improved the system of supervision after release.

Under the Prison Act of 1898 this privilege of ticket-of-leave was extended from penal servitude to ordinary imprisonment, with this important difference; that the person granted remission of part of his prison term was not under licence and liable to recall to serve the remainder of the term. The amount of remission on a sentence of penal servitude was one-quarter of the term in the case of male prisoners and one-third in the case of female prisoners. In the case of a sentence of imprisonment the remission was one-sixth. "During the Second World War, primarily as a measure to reduce the prison population, a flat-rate of one-third for all sentences was introduced."[4] and this rate was continued after the war under the Prison Rules of 1949 and 1964. There were two kinds of limitation however, relating to the length of sentence and the kind of sentence. As to the length of sentence, a prisoner must be serving a sentence of more than one month to be eligible for remission, and no sentence can be reduced to less than 31 days. As to kind of sentence there were certain limitations and special provisions relating to prisoners serving special sentences.[5]

This modern remission of one-third of a prisoner's term is said in the Rules to be based "on the ground of his industry and good conduct", but in practice it is only forfeited for bad behaviour, so that "it is perhaps hardly correct to speak of a prisoner 'earning' his remission".[6] As we have seen when discussing prison discipline, forfeiture of remission is a frequent form of disciplinary award or punishment, and may represent

---

3. J. J. Tobias, *Crime and Industrial Society in the 19th Century*, 1967, p. 213.
4. Fox, *op. cit.*, p. 165.
5. Prison Rules 1964, r. 5. Remission does not apply to sentences of imprisonment for life, nor to sentences for sedition except in certain circumstances, *i.e.* in respect of any period during which the prisoner works as if he were an ordinary convicted prisoner: r. 5(4).   6. Fox, *op. cit.*, p. 166.

a substantial punishment imposed on the authority of a visiting committee or a board of visitors. (See Chapter 7: Safe Custody and the Security Problem.)

Borstal training has always been a special case with regard to remission. From the very beginning, the régime envisaged some part of the term served in custody, and another part served on licence and subject to recall. There have been variations in the minimum and maximum periods of custody and the period spent on licence. (See Chapter 21: Borstal Training.)

After 1948 the new sentences of corrective training and preventive detention carried with them a system of release on licence, the eligibility for licence being after two-thirds of the term served in the case of a sentence of corrective training, and two-thirds or five-sixths in the case of preventive detention (after the ACTO Report on Preventive Detention this also became two-thirds for everyone sentenced to that kind of term).

It will be seen therefore that there is nothing sacrosanct about the period of remission. This has varied in the history of the matter according to the length of term and the type of term, as well as the sex of the prisoner. Where parole is given to a prisoner sentenced to the newly introduced extended sentence, this involves the prisoner being under licence until the end of the extended term, whereas an ordinary prisoner paroled is under licence to the end of two-thirds of the term, at which point the normal remission would have taken effect. The same applied to a young prisoner serving eighteen months or more who is given parole.

PARDON

The prerogative of pardon is used to release a number of prisoners on various grounds. Free pardons may be on technical grounds such as the failure to comply with some legal requirement, and substantial grounds, such as mistaken identity. Conditional pardons involving remission of part of the term are given to prisoners also on technical grounds or grounds of substance, and also on compassionate grounds. Details of the exercise of the prerogative power are given annually in the Criminal Statistics (England and Wales). A summary of ten years' experienced is contained in the following table:[7]

---

7. A similar table appears on p. 29 of the JUSTICE Report "Home Office Reviews of Criminal Convictions", 1968. The source of these figures is the annual Home Office Criminal Statistics (England and Wales).

TABLE SHOWING THE USE OF THE PREROGATIVE
1959 – 1968

	Free Pardon		Remission		Remission
	Substance	Technicality	Substance	Technicality	Compassionate grounds etc.
1959	3	2	18	11	104
1960	22	2	28	13	142
1961	18	3	15	4	173
1962	22	8	16	7	132
1963	37	3	25	11	204
1964	107	22	19	9	138
1965	125	4	15	18	127
1966	209	3	11	12	168
1967	88	2	21	28	233
1968	381	10	18	69	248

Note: 1. These figures include summary convictions.
    2. There is also the Home Office power to refer a case to the Court of Appeal (Criminal Division) under the Criminal Appeal Act 1907, s. 19, which was used twenty times in the ten-year period; see now the Criminal Appeal Act 1968, s. 17.

JUSTICE issued a Report in 1968 entitled Home Office Reviews of Criminal Convictions, which examined the adequacy and effectiveness of the present procedure whereby the Home Office investigates and reviews alleged wrong convictions. It observed that:

"The overriding factor governing the exercise of the powers available to the Home Secretary is a proper concern to avoid even the appearance of interfering with the independence of the judiciary. Home Secretaries have accordingly taken a very restricted view of the proper scope for executive intervention—a matter which has been dealt with before a competent court is not normally considered to be reviewable."[8]

The consequence is that many petitions are received from prisoners which cannot be entertained. Moreover, at the stage of executive review the onus of proof is effectively reversed: "the Home Secretary will not grant a pardon unless the petitioner can establish his innocence beyond reasonable doubt", although where the petitioner establishes that a serious doubt

---

8. P. 7, para. 12.

exists as to his guilt he may be granted some remission of his sentence, or be released on licence if the sentence is appropriate. "Remission is more commonly granted however in respect of matters arising during the currency of the sentence, such as ill-health, or as a reward for assistance to the police or prison authorities."[9]

The JUSTICE Report makes certain recommendations designed to improve the Home Office procedure for investigating petitions.[10] Initial sifting and selection of petitions justifying further investigation should remain with the Home Office as at present, but where it is felt that further investigation is justified, one of a panel of senior barristers and solicitors should be asked to look at the papers, and direct any further factual inquiries and make a report to the Home Secretary, who would normally act on it. Where the further investigations did not resolve the complaint, "a hearing should be held before a commissioner with high authority with full powers to examine witnesses and call for documents in a search for the truth". The commissioner's report would be final, and would recommend either the rejection of the complaint or the grant of a pardon.

The JUSTICE Report also recommended improvements in the arrangements for informing a convicted person of his legal rights and that legal advice should be made available to the petitioners in the presentation and submission of petitions seeking to challenge the correctness of their convictions on the grounds of their innocence.

These recommendations have received some support,[11] but so far the official response has been negative. Clearly there are difficult issues involved in improving the machinery for challenging decisions of trial courts other than by way of appeal, but it is to be hoped that the reasonable and carefully reasoned proposals made by JUSTICE will in due course be implemented.

PAROLE

For many years penal reformers have wished that there could be more flexibility about the date of release of prisoners. This demand stems in part from a growing recognition of

---

9. *Ibid.*
10. See summary of recommendations, pp. 27–28.
11. Editorial comment, [1969] Crim.L.R. pp. 181–182.

discrepancies in the length of prison sentences imposed by the courts. In part it derives support from the notion that a prisoner some time during his sentence reaches a stage of maximum adjustment, and after this his further detention may lead to a decline or deterioration. The growing interest in the problems of release and rehabilitation has increased the pressure for maximising the opportunities for reform by enabling the prisoner's release to take place at the right moment.

The difficulties surrounding this notion are manifold. There is the relation of the time served to the nature of the offence and the length of the original term, there is the difficulty of knowing when the right moment has come, and the danger of subjecting the public to the risk of repetition of the offence, or the commission of other offences by the prisoner on release.

The White Paper on The Adult Offender announced the Government's intention of introducing a parole system, which has now been carried into effect in the Criminal Justice Act 1967. It said that

> "a considerable number of long-term prisoners reach a recognizable peak in their training at which they may respond to generous treatment, but after which, if kept in prison, they may go downhill. To give such prisoners the opportunity of supervised freedom at the right moment may be decisive in securing their return to decent citizenship."[12]

Clearly, everything depends upon the determination of what is "the right moment" for parole, and the correctness of the view stated concerning the "recognisable peak" during a long-term prisoner's sentence. The White Paper accepts that "release on licence would be limited to those who were likely to respond to generous treatment *and who were not regarded as a risk to the public*" (italics supplied).[13] It is clear from this that parole will not automatically be granted to those who may well be ready for it, where the danger to the public may suggest caution. Experience so far with the parole scheme suggests that extreme caution is being exercised in the early stages, and rightly so, since unfortunate lapses during the inception of the scheme could well prejudice the success of the venture, which depends to a large extent on the public's acquiescence if not their active support.

---

12. Home Office, The Adult Offender, Cmnd. 2852, December 1965, p. 4, para. 5.
13. *Ibid.*, p. 4, para. 6.

The parole scheme

Parole was one of the innovations introduced by the Criminal Justice Act 1967. The parole provisions came into effect on 1 April 1968.

Who is eligible?

Parole is theoretically available to the following categories of prisoner:

(*i*) *Persons serving a sentence of imprisonment of definite duration, who have served not less than one-third of their term or 12 months thereof whichever is the longer* (*s.* 60.)—Thus a prisoner with a 9-year sentence would be eligible after serving 3 years; a prisoner with a 6-year sentence after serving 2 years; a prisoner with a 3-year sentence after serving 12 months; a prisoner with a sentence of 2 years after serving 12 months. Some prisoners with sentences of between 18 months and 2 years would be eligible after serving 12 months. (This would be less than two-thirds of the term, when they would normally be released anyway.)

(*ii*) *Life Prisoners* (*s.* 61).

What is parole?

Release on parole is release on licence and under supervision of a probation officer until the normal date of release (of two-thirds of the sentence) is reached. Any prisoner under licence may be recalled by the Home Secretary on the recommendation of the Parole Board, or without consulting the Board in an emergency: s. 62(1) and (2). There is a right for a prisoner recalled in this way under 62(1) to make written representations and the matter must then be referred to the Parole Board. Prisoners recalled under the emergency power must have their cases referred to the Parole Board.

Two categories of prisoner will be on parole for longer periods:

    1. Those serving extended terms, s. 60(3) (a);

    2. Young prisoners serving 18 months or more, s. 60(3) (b). These prisoners if paroled will remain under licence to the end of their sentences.

The Parole Board

The Parole Board is a board of some twenty members together with Lord Hunt as chairman, set up under the Act, by s. 59 and Sched. 2. Its membership includes judges, psychiatrists, a retired police officer, persons with knowledge and experience of the supervision of after-care of discharged prisoners and experts in criminology. They are expected to meet five days a month, and are paid a fee and expenses. They have to make an annual report to the Home Office which will be laid before Parliament. The first such report was published in June 1969.

The selection process

(*i*) *Local review committees.*—The selection begins at the prisons where the prisoner is held. Local review committees have been established to review the cases. These consist of the prison governor, a member of the board of visitors or visiting committee (probably a magistrate), a senior probation officer and an independent person. A prisoner may submit evidence in writing to the committee and is also interviewed by one member, other than the governor.

(*ii*) *Home Office.*—The case is then referred with a recommendation to the Home Office. It is here that at first most of the cases were foundering, according to newspaper reports. Only a relatively small number were passed on by the Home Office to the Parole Board.

The Home Secretary announced on 25 June 1968 that all prisoners recommended for parole by local review committees would in future have their cases considered by the Parole Board, regardless of whether or not the Home Office agreed with the recommendation. Under the earlier arrangement local recommendations were referred to the Board only after the Home Office had considered them and agreed that there was a *prima facie* case for parole. 559 cases had been refused at this stage. However, in forwarding cases to the Board the Home Office will give its own opinion, and it reserves its veto, referred to under (iv) below.[14]

(*iii*) *The parole board.*—This Board makes recommendations to the Home Office. At first they sat in two panels, one under Lord Hunt, the other under a High Court Judge. It has now been decided to work experimentally in three panels.

(*iv*) *Home Office veto.*—The Home Office does not have to parole a prisoner whom the Board has recommended—

---

14. House of Commons Debates, Written Answers Vol. 767, cols. 62–63, 25 June 1968 (Rt. Hon. James Callaghan). Home Office Press Notice, 25 June 1968. Additionally, some cases are referred which the local review committee has not deemed suitable, in special circumstances.

although in the normal course, it will accept the Parole Board's recommendation. On the other hand, no parole can be granted which is not recommended by the Parole Board.

Conditions may be attached to licences, and the Parole Board has the duty to advise the Home Secretary with regard to such matters, including the variation or cancellation of such conditions.

There is a provision that the Board may request one of its members to interview the prisoner if in any particular case the Board thinks it necessary.

There is no right to be legally represented, and no right of appeal. Prisoners are notified in writing but the Governor of the prison has discretion how to convey the results of the parole application to the prisoner.

The working of the parole scheme

By 30 September 1969 the Parole Board had recommended 2,500 prisoners for release. Ninety-one of these had been recalled.[15] The first Report of the Parole Board describes the way in which the Board has approached its task, and shows the tremendous efforts which were made to cope with the initial case load, so as to ensure that all those eligible for parole consideration had been considered by 1 April 1968 when the scheme came into effect.

> "The work of this initial phase led to 350 prisoners being recommended for release on or about 1st April, 1968. Subsequent consideration of deferred cases, and reconsideration of those put back for an early review, brought the total of positive recommendations to 406, which represented 8·5 per cent. of the 4,764 prisoners eligible for parole on 1st April 1968, or three-quarters of the 541 'backlog' cases actually referred to the Board."[16]

As the Board itself admits, it was only a small percentage of eligible prisoners who were granted parole, and the parole periods were often very short, since many prisoners had already served nearly two-thirds of their sentences by 1 April 1968. In the circumstances, it was no surprise that there should have been a great deal of unfavourable comment in the press about the parole scheme. One Sunday paper produced the headline

---

15. Home Office, "People in Prison", November 1969, Cmnd. 4214, p. 48, para 115.
16. Report of the Parole Board, H.C. 290, 17 June 1969, p. 14, para. 30.

"Great Parole produces a tiny, ailing mouse".[17] There was inevitably a good deal of cynicism and disappointment among prisoners.

In 1969 it was forecast there would be over 7,000 "eligible" cases to be considered,[18] including some cases up for further review and cases of life sentence prisoners which now come before the Board.[19] The average weekly case load is now rising to seventy cases.

The Board resolved "to proceed with caution in the early stages".[20] They can hardly be criticised for doing so, since the whole future of the scheme might have been jeopardised by some disastrous failures in the first few months. Disappointment of many prisoners, hopes was perhaps inevitable since "despite the note of caution struck in Parliament, the introduction of parole had stimulated the hope that it might spell liberty for large numbers of prisoners and relieve some of the burden of the congested prisons".[1]

What was not anticipated was that so many prisoners would refuse to be considered for parole. To avoid misunderstanding, a signed and witnessed statement is taken from each prisoner refusing parole consideration to the effect that he understands his action. There is no compulsion, and if a Local Review Committee is satisfied that an inmate does not wish to be considered they will not review his case. Up to 31 December 1968, 8·5 per cent. of prisoners eligible for parole had exercised their right to decline to be considered (910 cases out of 10,695).[2] This is about the same proportion as have been granted parole. It has happened that a prisoner has refused even to sign a statement witnessing his refusal to be considered.

The proportion refusing to be considered for parole varies from prison to prison according to the type of establishment, and the Parole Board admits that the percentage is a high percentage but says "it is perhaps understandable at the early stages in the evolution of the parole system."[3] A number of

---

17. *Sunday Times*, 24 March 1968.
18. Report of the Parole Board, p. 15, para. 33.
19. It was announced in February 1968 that prisoners serving life terms would be eligible for parole after they have served seven years of their sentence. *The Times*, 16 February 1968.
20. P. 13, para. 26.
1. *Ibid.*
2. P. 19, para. 46.
3. P. 19, para. 46.

different reasons are given by prisoners for setting their faces against parole. These include the wish not to be under any control or supervision on their release, the fear of failure on parole leading to their being made to serve a longer term, and preference for consideration for the hostel schemes. Many prisoners denied parole are already being considered for placement in prison hostels and have been given a date.

The relationship between parole and the sentencing courts is carefully spelled out, and the Report states clearly that the Board does not act as a court of appeal.[4] The Court of Appeal for its part has recognised the existence of the parole system and the eligibility of certain appellants for parole consideration.[5] But Lord PARKER has made it plain that this does not enable it to shirk its own task by "putting it on to the Parole Board".[6] Each must accept its own role and discharge its separate responsibilities. Morever, the Board thinks there is no sign of an increase in sentences in order to offset or minimise the effect of the parole system, and agrees with Lord PARKER that it would be quite wrong if this were to happen.[7]

The experience of many prisons has been that of the cases recommended by local review committees for parole few have been successful. This must be more likely in recidivist prisons like Blundeston, but it was surprising to discover it in closed raining prisons like Maidstone. On the other hand, one would expect open prisons to have a higher rate of selection.

The Parole Board Report has a most informative and interesting section on the problems of selection, which conveys the gist of the Board's thinking on the criteria for assessing cases. As it says at the beginning of the Report, "rehabilitation requires a guided return to the responsibilities of living in the free community. It is in this context that a parole system appears logical and necessary".[8]

---

4. P. 25, para. 65.
5. See *R.* v. *Langan,* (1968), *The Times,* 7 October. *R.* v. *Eaton,* (1968), 53 Cr. App. Rep. 118.
6. Parole Board Report, p. 9, para. 7.
7. *Ibid.,* p. 10, para. 8.
8. *Ibid.,* p. 8, para. 4.

CHAPTER 13

The Results of Prison Custody
(and Other Measures)

Following the description of the system of custodial "training and treatment" in prison it is a fair question to inquire what are the results of prison custody. We can reply by saying that we have a certain amount of information concerning recidivism and the success and failure rates of particular classes of offender. But one is bound to admit that the information available is still rather crude and unsatisfactory, and a great deal more work is needed to assess accurately the effectiveness of the penal system. A recent American study suggests the complexity of the task;[1] although a mammoth and most sophisticated research effort was involved, the findings have not been without their critics.

Moreover, such research as there has been has mainly been concerned with the effects of the sentence on the offender in terms of recidivism, and as Roger Hood has pointed out:

"There are no substantial research results that throw any light on the effectiveness of penalties in deterring potential offenders. Nor is there any research into the extent to which the courts successfully effect their broader social functions of reinforcing social values and allaying public fear of crime."[2]

Such wider considerations belong more appropriately in the realm of sentencing research, and we may here properly limit the discussion to a consideration of the effect of the custodial treatment on the offender himself. However, even when the inquiry is so limited, there are difficulties in knowing what measures to take, and in interpreting the results. The most usual measure is the crude reconviction figures, studied in relation to a single form of treatment considered in isolation from its alternatives. A number of studies have taken this

1. Daniel Glaser, *The Effectiveness of a Prison and Parole System*, 1964.
2. R. Hood, "Research on the Effectiveness of Punishments and Treatments", Council of Europe, *Collected Studies in Criminological Research*, 1967, p. 74.

criterion. It is now recognised, however, that more sophisticated comparisons are required between the results of alternative treatments. It is of little assistance to know that the results of one form of sentence such as prison are that 80 per cent. of first offenders do not return (see below) unless we know what would have been the position had the alternatives of fine or probation or suspended sentence been employed. The Streatfeild Report called for such comparative information.[3]

Some results of research are conveniently summarised in the Home Office handbook for sentencers, *The Sentence of the Court*.[4] In general terms, one might say that first offenders have the lowest reconviction rates in all treatments, that reconviction rates tend to increase as the number of previous convictions increases, that on the whole older offenders have lower reconviction rates than younger ones. In other words, the result is to demonstrate the obvious.

One can now go further than these studies, and say that certain offenders with certain characteristics are more likely to succeed if given one kind of sentence rather than another. But such researches tell us more about the best way of handling the offender than about the penal measure which is chosen, and its effectiveness. An examination of the evidence may possibly lead us to conclude that we are mistaken in expecting to be able to judge the success of a régime by its results.

I BARE RECONVICTION FIGURES

The Home Office statistics contain tables of reconviction figures for different categories of offender dealt with in the penal system, and the official publications describing the penal system tend to rely on these figures in assessing the success of the different kinds of régime. But it is admitted that there are many extraneous factors at work, and that such a statistical count leaves much to be desired:

"While any system must stand to be judged by its results, it does not yet seem possible to frame any statistical criterion of the effectiveness of a prison system; there are over any given period too many extraneous factors, such as variations in social and economic conditions, in legislation, in statistical presentation, or in

3. Report of the Interdepartmental Committee on the Business of the Criminal Courts, Cmnd. 1289, February 1961, pp. 80–81, para 277.
4. Home Office, *The Sentence of the Court*, 2nd Edn., 1969.

the practice of the police and the courts. Nor are the effects of a sentence of imprisonment on those who suffer it entirely susceptible of statistical assessment; only an extensive social research could show, of any group of persons released who have not returned to prison, whether they were 'reformed', or 'deterred', or would have been unlikely to revert to crime in any case; or of any group of those who do return, whether they were in fact better or worse human beings, more or less likely to revert to crime, as a result of their imprisonment."[5]

The figures are presented in the official pamphlet from which the above quotation is taken, "without attempt to draw from them deductions as to the efficacy of the present system", as follows:[6]

1. Of offenders received under a first sentence of imprisonment of not more than two years for a finger-printable offence,[7] the figures show that, up to 1950, about three-quarters of these prisoners had not returned to prison for a further offence.

2. Of star prisoners discharged since 1949 from a sentence of imprisonment of any length, well over 80 per cent. had not returned to prison by the end of 1958.

3. Of ordinary prisoners discharged from central prisons, 44 per cent. were reconvicted and returned to prison within two years of discharge.

4. Of ordinary prisoners discharged from open prisons during 1954, 1955 and 1956, 15 per cent. had been reconvicted and returned to prison by the end of 1958.

5. Of ordinary prisoners discharged from medium security and closed prisons in those years, 26 per cent. had been reconvicted and returned to prison in the same period.

The crude reconviction rates for borstal training appear at first sight to be very discouraging in relation to the period since World War II. Since 1945 the success rate, judged in terms of the number of boys reconvicted within a period of three years of discharge, has declined from 60 to 40 per cent. and the borstal system has been pronounced a failure in several quarters.[8]

---

5. Prisons and Borstals; Statement of Policy and Practice in the Administration of Prisons and Borstal Institutions in England and Wales, 4th Edn., 1960, p. 20, para. 29.
6. *Ibid.*, pp. 20–21.
7. An indictable offence or a serious non-indictable offence.
8. See, for example, A. N. Little "Penal Theory, Penal Reform and Borstal Practice" (January 1963), 3 *B.J.C.* 257.

There may be a number of different factors which should be taken into account to explain these figures, such as the rise in the number of committals, resulting in increased pressure on the system, and the decline in the quality of persons who are committed, but the figures themselves are also open to a number of different interpretations. Thus the 1962 report of the Prison Department says that of those who had been at risk from one to five years in 1962, having been released between 1957 and 1961, and taking the end of 1962 as the base line, only 47 per cent. had been reconvicted and returned to custody.[9] Of those reconvicted there is evidence that at least one-third had become completely stabilised personalities. In other words, many apparent failures were in fact modified or complete successes. The view is frequently expressed that one should not look too unfavourably on a single lapse on the part of an ex-borstal inmate. Two-fifths of those who lapse will not do so again.[10] Dr. Gibbens has shown that recovery from criminal habits is for many boys a slow and difficult business.[11]

Other figures quoted about borstal reconvictions throw doubt on the claims that between 60 and 70 per cent. recidivate. Thus the 1965 Prison Department Report says:

"Study of the subsequent records of boys discharged from borstals in each of the years 1959 to 1962 shows that, three years after the end of the year of discharge, a consistent proportion (32 per cent.) had not been reconvicted. An additional 23 per cent. of those discharged in each year had been reconvicted only once."[12]

2 FOLLOW-UP STUDIES

The traditional method used by criminologists to assess the effects of custodial measures is the follow-up study, by which the subsequent careers of a sample of offenders are traced and analysed. The Gluecks have adopted this method in a number of American studies,[13] and it has been practised in the United Kingdom with regard to several groups of offenders.

The American studies have, with the exception of Glaser's recent study, tended to contradict the usual claims made by

---

9. Cmnd. 2030, June 1963, p. 38.
10. *Ibid.*
11. Prison Department Report, 1965, p. 26.
12. *Ibid.*
13. Sheldon and Eleanor Glueck, 500 *Criminal Careers*, 1930; *Later Criminal Careers*, 1937.

prison administrators and others, that in the majority of cases their methods succeed in that the offenders imprisoned do not return. Glaser was concerned to investigate the alternative myth, that two-thirds of those leaving prison do return after committing fresh crimes. The converse is nearer the truth of the American prisons, as it is of those in the United Kingdom.

Glaser's study shows the desirability of adopting much finer distinctions with regard to the criteria of success or failure of penal methods. Cases of clear reformation, he believed, should be distinguished from cases of "marginal reformation". He used the following basis for making this differentiation:

> "Persistence in the pursuit of legitimate occupations and avoid-ance of clearly delinquent or criminal associates were taken as indexes of clear reformation. The marginal reformation category comprised all cases who were not declared violators, despite the failure to meet these two criteria of clear reformation."[14]

With regard to failure, a similar twofold classification was adopted, discriminating between clear recidivism and marginal failure. In this way, with the aid of case histories, a valuable picture is drawn of the complexity of the problem.

Donald West has drawn attention to the problem of inter-preting crime-free interludes in the records of criminals. He found that, in relation to his sample, out of fifty-nine men who showed an apparent gap in their criminal records, only thirty-five (60 per cent.) could be said to have had a genuinely crime-free interlude.[15] At least two-fifths of those studied had not genuinely ceased to follow their criminal careers, but had simply succeeded in evading detection and prosecution.[16]

3 DIFFERENT TYPES OF OFFENCE

Another level on which recidivism can be studied is in relation to different types of offence. At one time it was thought that such studies were of little value because of the frequency with which offenders mix their offences. Thus the Cambridge study of sexual offences found that many sexual offenders also committed property crimes.[17] This is a difficulty acknowledged

---

14. Daniel Glaser, *The Effectiveness of a Prison and Parole System*, 1964, p. 54.
15. D. J. West, *The Habitual Prisoner*, 1963, p. 40.
16. *Ibid.*, p. 50.
17. *Sexual Offences:* A Report of the Cambridge Department of Criminal Science, 1957.

by Glaser: "One barrier to classification of criminals by offence", he says, "is the frequency with which they mix their offences. . . . Nevertheless, most criminals are committed to prison for only one type of offence, and others can be classified by that offence which the law has treated most seriously."[18] Glaser's conclusion is supported by other research.

The British researches have concentrated so far on crimes of violence, and sexual offences, though there are some studies of taking and driving away a motor vehicle.[19]

4 DIFFERENT KINDS OF OFFENDER

The above type of study soon slides over into a study of different offender types, and it is possible that these two kinds of study are inseparable. Much can be learned about shop-lifters, serious motoring offenders, white collar criminals, and so on, but here we are soon engaged in a discussion of the etiology of the crimes as well as the prognosis for the offender.

5 DIFFERENT TYPES OF DISPOSITION

If it is difficult satisfactorily to study the success of our custodial and non-custodial measures with different types of offence and offender, it is equally difficult to approach the matter from the other end, as it were, and study the different types of disposition. There have been elaborate studies of measures such as probation,[20] and the Home Office Research Unit's study of that subject in depth is still going on, and has already resulted in several reports being published. On the custodial side, preventive detention for persistent offenders was intensively studied,[1] and there was a certain amount of discussion about corrective training prior to its abolition.

A few comparative studies of different methods of disposition have been carried out, but their results must be interpreted with caution, as Dr. Nigel Walker has observed.[2] With regard to borstal training, compared with the use of imprisonment for

---

18. *Op. cit.*, p. 42.
19. F. H. McClintock and Evelyn Gibson, *Robbery in London*, 1961. F. H. McClintock, *Crimes of Violence*, 1963. *Sexual Offences:* A Report of the Cambridge Department of Criminal Science, 1957.
20. *The Results of Probation*, A Report of the Cambridge Department of Criminal Science, 1958.
1. W. H. Hammond and Edna Chayen, *Persistent Criminals*, 1963.
2. Nigel Walker, *Crime and Punishment in Britain*, 2nd Edn., 1968, pp. 248–250.

young offenders under twenty-one, Sir George Benson showed that there appeared to be very little difference in the results of either disposition when comparing carefully matched groups of offenders sentenced to either measure. Sir George also found no overall differences in the results of borstal training compared with detention centres.[3]

Wilkins has compared the reconviction rates of offenders placed on probation by a court using probation in a large proportion of cases with offenders from another court having a more normal distribution of probation. He found that overall the proportion reconvicted at both courts was the same.[4] Walker comments that Wilkins neither destroys faith in probation nor enhances it. Although he suggested that "a larger proportion of offenders who are now sent to prison or borstal could be put on probation without any change in the reconviction rate as a whole", in fact what he did was "to cast doubt on the assertion that if probation were applied wholesale to males over 17 in place of fines, prison and borstal, the reconviction rates would be markedly less".[5]

Another comparative method which has been developed by the Home Office Research Unit is to compare the expected rates of reconviction of selected categories of offender with the actual rates, a technique which has been exploited in the California penal system by the use of what are known as "base expectancy scores". The Annex to the Home Office pamphlet *The Sentence of the Court* gives some results of such comparative studies. The method of comparison is explained thus:

"The expected number of reconvictions (within a certain period) for a particular class of offender—irrespective of the type of sentence—is calculated mainly on the basis of age, current offence and previous convictions. For the sake of simplicity the expected number is taken as 100. The figures shown in the tables are the ratios of actual reconvictions (from the date of sentence or from the date of release from custody, whichever is the later) to expected reconvictions and they are referred to as indices of effectiveness. Thus figures below 100 indicate fewer reconvictions than expected, while figures above 100 indicate more."[6]

3. Sir George Benson, "Prediction Methods and Young Prisoners" (January 1959), 9 *B.J.D.*, 192 *et seq.* For further comment, see Part V, Offenders Under Twenty-One: Chapter 21: Prison.
4. L. T. Wilkins, "A Small Comparative Study of the Results of Probation" (1958), 8 *B.J.D.*, 201.
5. *Op cit.*, p. 251.
6. *The Sentence of the Court*, 2nd Edn., pp. 69–70.

One of the tables given in the Annex (Table 5) is reproduced below, with the permission of the controller of Her Majesty's Stationery Office:

FIRST AND RECIDIVIST OFFENDERS

Indices showing results of sentences compared with expectation
(100 = Expected rate of reconviction within five years except where otherwise stated)

	Under 17		17 to under 21		21 to under 30		30 and over	
	1st Offenders	*Offenders with previous offences*	*1st Offenders*	*Offenders with previous offences*	*1st Offenders*	*Offenders with previous offences*	*1st Offenders*	*Offenders with previous offences*
Discharge	89	100	89	98	109	90	133	104
Fine	75	83	75	94	63	99	84	65
Probation	118	101	122	101	153	115	(150)	121
Approved School	138	102	—	—	—	—	—	—
Borstal training	—	101	}	95	—	—	—	—
Detention Centre	—	106	} 150	110	—	—	—	—
Attendance Centre	—	119	}	—	—	—	—	—
Imprisonment	—	—	—	106*	146†	111*	(91†)	104*
Corrective Training	—	—	—	—	—	104*	—	—

* The calculation was based on a *three year* follow-up and it was necessary to exclude sentences of over three years.

† Excluding six sentences of three years or longer.

Notes: (1) Round brackets indicate very small numbers of offenders.

(2) The number of juvenile first offenders committed to institutions other than approved schools was too small to provide a satisfactory result; similarly in the 17 to under 21 age group the results had to be combined into one figure for "institutional treatments". (Of the group, the borstal result was the best, being about average in effectiveness.)

The comments made on the above table may be summarised as follows:

1. Fines are the most successful methods of dealing with both first offenders and recidivists.

2. Probation scores well, and produces relatively better results when used for offenders with previous convictions than when used for first offenders, although at best the results were only about equal to expectation.

3. Approved school results were also better for offenders with previous offences.

4. Imprisonment results were better for offenders with previous convictions than for first offenders, except

among those aged 30 or over, but with regard to the latter, too much reliance should not be placed on these figures.

5. In relation to particular offences, probation appeared to be more successful for offenders convicted of breaking and entering than for those convicted of larceny, while fines were especially successful with the latter. Fraud offenders, particularly those placed on probation, were among the least "successful groups of adult offenders.

The Home Office asks us to treat the results of this research with a good deal of reserve, for it is recognised that "to study reconviction rates is . . . to assess the effectiveness of sentences from one point of view only". Moreover, these studies do not allow for factors concerning the offenders' social circumstances so that the assessment is necessarily incomplete.[7]

Interchangeability of penal measures

Before leaving the subject of the comparison of different measures, we must deal with one assertion which is frequently made today, as a result of the kind of research which has been described above, viz. that it makes very little difference which penal measure is selected, since the results will be similar whatever is done to the offender. This is what Walker means when he speaks of "the interchangeability of penal measures".

One possible answer to this is to point to the chance that offenders may have been imperfectly selected for the different kinds of measures to such an extent that the mistaken choices mask the true effect of the treatments in question. Wilkins seems to subscribe to this possible explanation, which is also mentioned by Hood, but Walker maintains that "while the hypothesis of mis-classification is an encouraging one, and suggests interesting lines of research, it is not yet the most probable one. The evidence in favour of it is very scanty".[8] Walker seems to prefer the view that penal measures are for most offenders interchangeable. Hood describes this assumption as follows: "That at present treatments are more or less equally irrelevant."[9]

---

7. Home Office, The Sentence of the Court, 2nd Edn., pp. 72–73.
8. Nigel Walker, *Crime and Punishment in Britain*, 2nd Edn., 1968, p. 257.
9. R. Hood, "Research on the Effectiveness of Punishments and Treatments", Council of Europe, *Collected Studies in Criminological Research*, 1967, p. 83.

The significance of high or low success rates

Much of the anger and indeed the anguish over success and failure rates in relation to offenders and the penal or other measures taken about them stems from the assumption that a high success rate means success, and a low success rate means failure. We have already noted, in connection with borstal training, the view of those concerned with borstal after-care that the figures have been misinterpreted, and are in fact more favourable than is generally assumed. Now we can note the interesting suggestion sometimes made by those experienced in dealing with offenders, that too high a success rate shows that you are not taking enough risks (i.e. in the use of probation or parole) and when the rate comes down to about 50 or to 60 per cent. success (or even 40 per cent.) this is a better working basis. We should not expect more than two out of three who are subjected to any particular penal measure to benefit by it and be reformed characters.

Another interesting thought is that in discussing this matter, without reference to the quality of the after-care arrangements or the nature of the offender's situation on release from custody, we are speaking as if the penal system worked in a vacuum. Of course this is patent nonsense, for we cannot properly speak of the success of a penal measure in isolation from the offender's total situation, including his home and family surroundings, his employment situation, and the community in which he lives and the degree to which he shares or is influenced by its norms. Viewed thus, any talk of the success of a penal measure seems slightly unrealistic.[10]

---

10. On the whole subject, see the author's article, "Evaluating penal methods", 1966, 18 *International Social Science Journal*, No. 2, pp. 162 *et seq.*

PART III

Special Classes of Offender

There are three classes of adult offender which require separate discussion:

1. Recidivist prisoners;
2. Mentally disordered offenders;
3. Female offenders.

A fourth class, young prisoners, will be dealt with in Part V, concerned with Offenders Under Twenty-one.

CHAPTER 14

Recidivist Prisoners

As we have seen, the Criminal Justice Act 1948 introduced two new kinds of sentence for dealing with recidivist prisoners, Corrective Training and Preventive Detention. These were to replace the former sentence of preventive detention for habitual criminals, which was a failure. The Criminal Justice Act 1967 has now in turn replaced Corrective Training and Preventive Detention, which were also failures, with the new provisions concerning the Extended Sentence. It seems that whatever we do about recidivism is characterised, like the subject itself, by lack of success. As Sir Lionel Fox remarks:

> "throughout this century the penal systems of Europe and America have sought, with little enough success hitherto, the answers to many questions arising from that central problem of penal law, the habitual criminal."[1]

THE SIZE AND NATURE OF THE PROBLEM

It is usually accepted that in England and Wales 80 per cent. of prisoners coming to prison for the first time never return. Of the remaining 20 per cent. a substantial proportion return very often and spend long periods of their lives in custody.[2] Few of these recidivist prisoners attract long terms or the special sentences with which we are here concerned. They remain a majority of the prison population and, as we have said elsewhere: "the central problem of the prison administration is to devise a satisfactory régime for the vast numbers of prisoners sentenced to terms not exceeding three years, the majority of whom are recidivists with previous institutional experience".[3]

---

1. Fox, p. 297.
2. *Ibid.*, pp. 278–279, 297.
3. J. E. Hall Williams, "The Use the Courts Make of Prison", *Sociological Studies in the British Penal Services*, 1965, ed. P. Halmos, p. 66. See also C. Blackler, "Primary Recidivism in Adult Men: Differences between Men on First and Second Prison Sentence" (April 1968), 8 *B.J.C.*, No. 2, p. 130.

Our concern here is for the small portion of the recidivist prisoner population which is subjected to a special sentence.

CORRECTIVE TRAINING

This was intended for persistent offenders aged over 21 who needed training of a corrective character for a substantial period of time. The courts decided how long a period was necessary, within statutory limits of not less than two and not more than four years. The Court of Criminal Appeal decided that normally the prisoner should not be over thirty years of age and that the sentence should virtually be three years.[4] But in 1962 they changed their view on the desirable length of term to two years.[5]

The trouble with corrective training was that as more and more star and ordinary prisoners were selected as suitable for training in the regional training prisons, it became difficult to distinguish the programme provided for corrective training, especially since it often took place in the same regional training prisons. The two main differences in the end were: (1) a person sentenced to corrective training had a prior claim to be selected for a training prison; (2) he was obliged to undergo supervision after release (compulsory or statutory after-care). The courts realised that it made very little difference to the prisoner to be sentenced to corrective training, and the use of the sentence rapidly declined. The Advisory Council never pronounced on this subject as they did on preventive detention, but its abolition was accepted almost without demur,[6] when it was announced in the White Paper on The Adult Offender in December 1965,[7] and implemented in the Criminal Justice Act 1967. This is how the White Paper put it:

"10. Corrective training was introduced by the Criminal Justice Act, 1948. Courts are empowered to pass a sentence of between two and four years' corrective training on an offender of 21 or more whose offence and record show that he needs "training of a corrective character with a view to his reformation and the prevention of crime". This provision is generally agreed to be

---

4. *R. v. Grant*, [1951] 1 K.B. 500; [1951] 1 All E.R. 28.
5. *Practice Note* [1962] 1 All E.R. 671. *Sub nom. Practice Direction*, [1962] 1 W.L.R. 402.
6. A. E. Bottoms argued against its being regarded as a failure: [1965] Crim.L.R. 582 & 650; [1966] Crim.L.R. 155. But see J. D. McClean [1964] Crim. L.R. 745: "Corrective Training—Decline and Fall".
7. Cmnd. 2852, December 1965.

now inappropriate. Today all suitable prisoners, whatever their sentence, are given training. The number of sentences of corrective training has fallen steadily to about 200 a year. There are at present only some 260 men and women serving such sentences.

11. It is proposed that the special sentence of corrective training should be abolished."

The abolition was effected by s. 37(1) of the Criminal Justice Act 1967. No special measure dealing with the young adult recidivist has been put in its place, though at one time Lord PARKER, C.J., did remark that he would personally favour some kind of indeterminate sentence being applied to a higher age group than the present borstal age group, which presumably means those up to the age of 25 or 30.[8]

PREVENTIVE DETENTION

Like corrective training, preventive detention was provided for by the Criminal Justice Act 1948, but, unlike corrective training its history goes back further, to the Prevention of Crime Act 1908. That Act provided what came to be known as a double-track system, involving a recidivist prisoner in a separate sentence of preventive detention tacked on to the sentence for the current offence.[9] The Act of 1948 substituted a single sentence of preventive detention, to be fixed by the court of trial, of between five and fourteen years' imprisonment, provided the prisoner was suitably qualified by reason of age and previous convictions. He had to be over thirty years of age and have had at least three previous convictions for serious offences, of which at least two resulted in imprisonment, borstal or corrective training. The new provisions were recommended by the Departmental Committee on Persistent Offenders in 1932.[10]

The Court of Criminal Appeal influenced the development of preventive detention through its decisions on sentence appeals. It immediately ruled that sentences of preventive detention should normally be seven or eight years,[11] and in

---

8. House of Lords Debates, 1 May 1961, Vol. 230, col. 1103. See also *J.P.J. & L.Gov't.Rev.*, 7 December 1963; *The Times*, 10 December 1963.
9. See Norval Morris, *The Habitual Criminal*, 1951.
10. Cmd. 4090, 1932.
11. *R.* v. *Sedgwick*, [1950] 2 All E.R. 397. See T. E. James, "The Persistent Offender", [1954] Crim.L.R. 889; Glanville Williams, "The Courts and Persistent Offenders", [1963] Crim.L.R. 730.

H

1962 decided that normally such sentences should not be imposed unless a person was nearing 40, and should be regarded as a last resort.[12] In many cases, sentences of preventive detention were set aside where the circumstances involved trivial offences, where there was evidence that the offender had made an effort to reform and had a long offence-free period prior to the current offence, where an employer or hostel was willing to take him, and so on. Sentences of ordinary imprisonment or even probation were substituted.[13]

Research on preventive detention showed that of those eligible only a few were selected for preventive detention, and that there was little to distinguish those who were selected from those who were not. Many were minor property offenders with many previous convictions who were more of a nuisance than a menace. The more dangerous criminals tended to receive long sentences of ordinary imprisonment.[14] Dr. West's research shows conclusively that the majority of preventive detainees were "of the passive inadequate type, feckless and ineffective in every sphere, who regard the commission of crime as a means of escaping immediate difficulties rather than a part of a deliberately anti-social way of life. Very few of them are of the seriously violent or aggressive type of personality".[15] Dr. Hammond's research showed that, apart from the very small group of offenders who commit offences of violence against the person or sexual offences, there were broadly three types of offender sentenced to preventive detention:

1. Housebreakers who are generally professional criminals in their 30s or 40s;
2. A group of fairly serious larceny or fraud offenders who manage to make away with large sums of money;
3. Petty persistent thieves or false pretence offenders of the socially inadequate type already referred to in connection with Dr. West's research.

Hammond argued that no single form of sentence could deal satisfactorily with such a varied collection of types of offence and offender. The conclusion seemed inescapable that preven-

---

12. *Practice Note*, [1962] 1 All E.R. 671.
13. D. A. Thomas, "Theories of Punishment in the Court of Criminal Appeal" (September 1964), 27 *M.L.R.* 546, at pp. 553–554.
14. W. H. Hammond and Edna Chayen, *Persistent Criminals*, 1963.
15. D. J. West, *The Habitual Prisoner*, 1963, p. 8.

tive detention should be abolished. It was a source of resentment and bitterness among prisoners, and had a very poor success rate, as might have been expected.

The Advisory Council examined the arguments in favour of retaining preventive detention very fully, and considered carefully the need to provide for public protection[16] They believed

"if preventive detention were abolished and nothing were put in its place the general deterrent effect of the penal system would not be weakened to any significant extent."[17]

However, they did not leave the matter where the logic of their argument had rested.[18] In view of the difficulty which the courts had experienced in upholding long sentences other than preventive detention on persistent offenders whose offences consisted of minor property offenders, because of the tariff principle of punishment which normally applied, the Committee recommended that extended terms of imprisonment should be provided for, where the maximum sentence for the offence was not sufficient, thus enabling the courts to pass a sentence of up to ten years' imprisonment in certain circumstances.

THE EXTENDED SENTENCE

The ACTO recommendation of 1963 was followed in the White Paper on The Adult Offender, 1965, which also accepted that preventive detention should be abolished.[19] The proposal was here more fully spelled out, and the necessary preconditions were indicated. It was now proposed that when the courts have before them a person who has committed an offence and in addition is shown to be a persistent offender, they should have power to impose a longer sentence than they would have imposed had they been sentencing him only for the crime for which he has been convicted.[20]

The new provisions have been enacted in s. 37 of the Criminal Justice Act 1967. As before, to be qualified for such a sentence, a persistent offender must have been convicted on

---

16. Home Office, *Preventive Detention*, 1963.
17. *Ibid.*, p. 23, para. 58.
18. For critical comment on the ACTO Report, see Hermann Mannheim and D. A. Thomas (October 1963), 4 *B.J.C.*, No. 2, pp. 181–191.
19. Cmnd. 2852.
20. *Ibid.*, p. 5, para. 14.

indictment of an offence punishable with a term of two years' imprisonment or more. In addition the following conditions must be satisfied:

(*a*) The offence must have been committed within three years of a previous conviction of an offence similarly punishable or of his final release from prison after serving a sentence of imprisonment, etc., passed on such a conviction;

(*b*) The offender must have been convicted on indictment on at least three previous occasions since he attained the age of 21 of offences punishable on indictment with imprisonment for a term of two years or more; *and*

(*c*) (i) the total length of the sentences of imprisonment, etc., to which he was sentenced on those occasions was not less than five years

(ii) *and* either one of them was preventive detention *or* at least two of them were imprisonment or corrective training *and* of those sentences *either* one was imprisonment for a term of three years or more in respect of one offence *or* two were sentences of imprisonment each for a term of two years or more in respect of one offence.

The court may then impose an extended term of imprisonment, where it is satisfied, by reason of the prisoner's previous conduct and of the likelihood of his committing further offences, that it is expedient to protect the public from him for a substantial time.

The extended term which may be imposed may exceed the maximum term authorised for the offence apart from this section, where the maximum so authorised is less than ten years, but there is this limitation on the power conferred:

1. The term shall not exceed ten years if the maximum so authorised is less than ten years;

or

2. The term shall not exceed five years if the maximum so authorised is less than five years.

The court shall issue an "extended sentence certificate" where an extended term is imposed on an offender under s. 37.

The qualifying conditions

These are rather more elaborate than those which previously applied to preventive detention. The basic requirement of an offence punishable on indictment with two years' imprisonment or more remains the same. There is no lower age limit of 30. Three previous convictions are required, but these must be since the age of 21, not 17 years, as before. There is a new requirement of previous sentences totalling five years' imprisonment at least, and instead of at least two of the three previous convictions being borstal training, imprisonment or preventive detention, it is now required that one of them should be preventive detention or at least two of them imprisonment for substantial periods (either one term of at least three years or two of two years or more). A new requirement is (*a*) above, that the offence now in question must have been committed within three years of a previous conviction of an offence similarly punishable or, where prison ensued, within three years of final release from prison. In other words, a man who has gone straight for three years need not fear an extended term.

Length of term

There has already been a House of Lords decision on the meaning of these provisions, concerning the length of term permitted. This was *Director of Public Prosecutions* v. *Ottewell* in 1968.[1] The respondent had pleaded guilty to two counts of assault occasioning actual bodily harm and was sentenced to two years and two years imprisonment to run consecutively. The trial judge also directed that these sentences be an extended term under the Criminal Justice Act 1948 and issued a certificate. On appeal the Court of Appeal (Criminal Division) dismissed the appeal against the length of sentence, but set aside the extended sentence certificate, holding that an extended term of imprisonment under the section meant a term extended beyond the maximum for the particular offence.

The House of Lords allowed the Crown's appeal, holding that, provided the requirements of s. 37 were complied with, a court had power to impose an extended term of imprisonment although the extended term did not exceed the maximum term for the offence.

---

1. [1968] 3 All E.R. 153.

Lord Reid explained that "the difficulty in interpreting this section is caused by the fact that there is no definition nor explanation of what is meant by an extended term". Three possible answers had been suggested:

1. Extended beyond the term which the judge would otherwise have imposed;
2. Extended beyond the maximum term otherwise authorised by the law;
3. Extended beyond the normal sentence for that type of crime.

Only the first two were in Lord Reid's view possible solutions. The Court of Appeal preferred the second solution, on the ground that the courts already possessed the power to lengthen a sentence "for the express purpose of protecting the public" within the maximum allowed by the law. But the House of Lords points out that there were serious limitations to the exercise of that power, and regarded s. 37 as freeing the courts from those limitations.

> "It was regarded as improper to extend a sentence of imprisonment beyond a term which bore some relation to the gravity of the last offence . . . section 37(2) is designed to remove that limitation and to authorise an extended term, not as punishment for the last offence nor as additional punishment for previous offences, but for the purpose stated in the section, *i.e.* the protection of the public from the persistent offender for a substantial time."[2]

Lord DONOVAN took a similar view.

It may be respectfully suggested that this decision does not accord with our understanding of the intention behind the recommendations of the ACTO Report and the White Paper of 1965. Moreover, it seems to require us to read the words of s.37(3) authorising the extended term to "exceed the maximum term authorised for the offence apart from this section", so as to be permissive rather than explanatory or definitional. These points require elaboration.

The ACTO Report on Preventive Detention states that

> "where a person aged 21 years or over is convicted on indictment of an offence punishable with imprisonment for a term of *five years or more*, and the court is satisfied, having regard to his antecedents and to the need to protect the public, that it is

---

2. Pp. 156–157.

necessary to impose a longer term of imprisonment than is *at present permitted* for the offence in question, the court should be empowered to pass a sentence of up to ten years' imprisonment. Such a provision would, of course, in no way affect the court's power to impose a longer sentence than ten years' imprisonment *where this was already permitted by law.*" (italics supplied)[3]

In this passage, the last phrase of the last sentence speaks of sentences "permitted by law" and this throws light on the meaning of the words "at present permitted" in the previous sentence. The reference to offences punishable with imprisonment for a term of *five years or more* being the ones where extended terms might be provided also suggests that the Committee were thinking in terms of the maximum punishments.

When we come to the White Paper of 1965, as previously mentioned, the proposal is spelled out in more detail, and the precise words used were quoted above. There are now two limbs to the new power:

"(*a*) we propose to empower the Courts to sentence a persistent offender to up to 10 years' imprisonment where *the ordinary maximum term* for the offence is five years or more and not more than ten years; and

(*b*) to up to five years' imprisonment where *the ordinary maximum term* is two years or more and not more than five years." (italics supplied)

In both cases the phrase used is "the ordinary maximum term". The paragraph ends with the sentence: "Where the ordinary maximum term exceeds 10 years, there will be no greater maximum for the persistent offender."

The Explanatory and Financial Memorandum which accompanied the Criminal Justice Bill when it was introduced in the House of Commons,[4] says that clauses 20 and 21 (together with other clauses) "give effect to the proposals on persistent offenders" and for licencing of prisoners put forward in the White Paper. More specifically, clause 20 "empowers the courts, when dealing with a persistent offender with a specified minimum record, to impose for the protection of the public an extended sentence of imprisonment which may within limits *exceed the normal maximum for the offence.*" Once again, the thinking appears to relate to a "maximum for the offence" but this is prefixed by the word "normal". Did this

3. P. 25, para. 63.
4. 29 November 1966.

signify a change of intention? It is submitted that when we turn to the words of the section and read three times in s. 37(3) the phrase "maximum so authorised", referring to an earlier reference to "the maximum term authorised for the offence apart from this section", the meaning becomes clear. The section refers to the maximum allowed by the law, which is the same as that which is implied when we say that an offence is "punishable" with so many years' imprisonment.

It was argued in support of the Crown's view in *Ottewell* that to interpret the section in the way suggested was necessary in the light of the provisions concerning release on licence (s. 60). Lord Reid did not think that this was a valid argument, and yet at the end of his speech when he returns to the question, he does not really deal with the matter satisfactorily. All he said was that "we were informed that this (section 60(3)) is now the only provision authorising release on licence". The purpose of the extended term certificate, he explains, is "to bring section 60(3) of the Act into operation so that the Secretary of State may, instead of granting remission of part of the sentence, direct that the prisoner be released on licence subject to conditions".

The argument based on the desirability of ensuring that persistent offenders should be released on licence is more fully discussed in Lord DONOVAN's speech. He discusses the history of statutory after-care provisions, which required that certain prisoners should be released on licence and subject to supervision.

These were repealed by the Criminal Justice Act 1961, but s. 20 of that Act and Part I of Sched. 3 made certain other provisions designed to ensure that supervision of certain categories of prisoner and discharge on licence was continued. The Secretary of State was to bring these provisions into effect by means of an order. This was never done, so that "at present the only way for a judge to ensure some supervision after a person's release is to pass an extended term of imprisonment under the Act of 1967 which then brings into effect the release on licence provisions to be found in section 60". From this, Lord DONOVAN goes on to conclude that "it would seem a little incongruous that a sentence exceeding the statutory maximum should have to be passed by the judge in order to procure that effect."

With respect, the incongruity surely lies in the conclusion

that because a judge desires to ensure that a persistent offender is under supervision on release, this is a reason for interpreting the applicability of the extended term more widely than Parliament intended, or the ACTO Committee and the White Paper anticipated. The Act is not speaking of "extended supervision" on release but of "extended term of imprisonment", and it seems odd to regard the release position under section 60 as a guide to the meaning of s. 37. That is not to say that it might not be wise to provide for the extended supervision of the persistent offenders under compulsory after-care. The Home Secretary still has power to do this if he pleases.

The reader may wonder why so much space has been devoted to such a problem. One reason may well reveal itself in the degree to which the courts impose extended terms under the *Ottewell* decision, and the danger that this will provide yet another source of pressure on the hard-pressed prison system, with offenders coming into prison for longer terms than they would otherwise. We should not make it too easy for courts to lengthen sentences. They need little enough stimulation in that direction, as all history shows. If the extended terms were more likely to protect the public from the menaces rather than the nuisances among offenders, there might be more justification for these developments. One is bound to say that it is profoundly disappointing that the ACTO Committee did not accept the logic of its own analysis and rest content with abolishing preventive detention, leaving the courts to develop in their own ways an appropriate response to the danger to the public represented by serious and persistent crime.[5]

THE RÉGIME FOR RECIDIVIST PRISONERS

The problem of providing a régime for the recidivist prisoner is not the same as that of providing for security risks or long-term prisoners, previously discussed. Many persistent offenders are received into prison for short terms, and for terms of intermediate duration. Apart from the extended term, there is now no separate sentence available for dealing with the persistent offender, and even those sentenced to an extended term are not the subject of any special or separate régime.

---

5. For an interesting point of view see Nigel Walker, "The Habitual Criminal: An Administrative Problem" (Autumn 1963), *Public Administration*, 265 *et seq.*

Under preventive detention, prisoners were subject to a number of special rules concerning the stages of their sentence and the privileges to which they were entitled, and rules governing release on licence and recall. These provided for a sentence of preventive detention to be served in two stages, the first stage in a local prison under conditions similar to those for ordinary imprisonment and the second stage in a prison or part of a prison specially set aside for prisoners serving sentences of preventive detention. Here the prisoner should be eligible for additional or extended facilities and privileges. Between one and two years would be spent in the first stage after which the prisoner would be transferred to the second stage. He could be returned to the first stage on the grounds of misconduct or in the interests of good order. Release on licence was possible after serving two-thirds of the sentence, though until 1963 there was a third stage which had to be reached before qualifying for one-third remission, and many prisoners only received one-sixth. The decisions about release were made on the recommendations of a Preventive Detention Advisory Board. This provided the only indeterminate element in the system of preventive detention and it proved so unsatisfactory that the ACTO Report of 1963 recommended its abolition, which was effected by administrative action prior to the eventual abolition of preventive detention under the Criminal Justice Act 1967.

It is still of some interest to record the régime developed for preventive detention. This is well described in the ACTO Report. Some time during the first stage the prisoner was removed from the local prison to the allocation centre at Wandsworth Prison. Here he was examined and eventually allocated to one of the central prisons set aside for preventive detention. These were Parkhurst, Nottingham and Chelmsford, and a separate section at Eastchurch Prison for the older men. Nottingham was for men thought capable of responding to constructive training in skilled work and Chelmsford for a slightly lower class of that category. Both prisons provided certain training facilities. Parkhurst was for men requiring conditions of maximum security. Blundeston also received some preventive detention prisoners. Women sentenced to preventive detention, because they were so few in number, were accommodated in the same wing of Holloway Prison as women serving long sentences of imprisonment.

In these prisons during the second stage the prisoner enjoyed certain amenities and privileges which were not available to the ordinary prisoner. This was in accordance with the recommendations of the Departmental Committee on Persistent Offenders of 1932. Thus payment for work done was at a higher rate, there were additional facilities for the cultivation of garden allotments and for spare-time activities of the handicrafts kind. Additional letters and visits were allowed. But even so, as the ACTO Report admitted:

"While prisoners in the second stage of preventive detention do in certain respects have a somewhat easier life than if they had been sentenced to a term of ordinary imprisonment, their conditions are basically the same as those confined in a central or regional training prison and have the same limitations."[6]

Moreover, as conditions in the local prisons improved the contrast between the first and second stages of preventive detention became less marked, so that in the end there was little to distinguish preventive detention from ordinary imprisonment, save the release on licence and the hostel scheme. Sir Lionel Fox in 1952 had recognised that the provision of a régime appropriate to habitual criminals detained for very long periods had come to require "no more than the application to the particular case of the general principles of the system".[7]

The release on licence remained the most distinctive feature of preventive detention. This was to the care and supervision of the Central After-Care Association, where, as we have seen, there was a Men's, Women and Girls', and Borstal Division.

These arrangements were sometimes described as a positive licence, presumably because they required something positive by the prisoner in the way of employment and honest living, otherwise he was liable to return to the prison to complete his term.

The resemblance between the régime devised for preventive detention and earlier régimes for convict prisoners, in particular the Irish system developed by Sir Walter Crofton, did not pass unnoticed by that shrewd observer Sir Lionel Fox.[8] One is tempted to remark that there is nothing new in penology.

---

6. P. 11, para. 29.
7. Fox, p. 305.
8. *Ibid.*, p. 45.

The rules governing the third stage permitted prisoners "to live in conditions of modified security designed to form a transition from prison life to freedom", as and when suitable arrangements could be made. This was the cue for the development of the hostel system, and the ACTO Report describes the provision made:

> "In November 1953 there was established at Bristol, within the walls of the local prison, a hut furnished as a hostel for men in the third stage, where they live as much as possible in the conditions of a working men's hostel, and are not subject to prison discipline. Similar accommodation has also been available since 1957 in a separate wing at Nottingham. . . . The prisoners normally stay in the hostel for about six months, until they are released on licence. Work is found for them in the neighbourhood, where they attend and draw their wages as ordinary employees. Deductions from their wages are made to cover board and lodgings and any expense incurred in maintaining their dependants, and an allowance varying between ten shillings and thirty shillings a week is made to them for necessary expenses and recreation; the balance of wages is put to compulsory savings. These prisoners are allowed a good deal of freedom in the evenings and at weekends and some local families have been good enough to welcome them into their homes."[9]

Herein lies the origin of the hostel scheme previously described (see Chapter 10: The Prison Community). As we have seen, the hostel scheme was eventually extended to cater for certain other long-term prisoners. A development which was originally confined to preventive detention has been universalised. It seems that it is one of the basic laws of penology that developments originating as limited experiments, confined to a particular class or group of inmate, become generalised and incorporated into the very fabric of the system as a whole. The borstal system has provided the stimulus for similar generalisations.

SOCIAL DEFENCE AND THE DANGEROUS OFFENDER

One characteristic of the social defence movement in penology, which has been so strongly supported in certain European countries, is the development of the concept of dangerousness as a criterion for deciding how offenders should be dealt with, and the provision of special measures of preventive detention or

---

9. Home Office, Report on Preventive Detention, 1963, p. 15, para. 38.

segregation for the offenders who were designated as dangerous.

The attempt to arrive at a satisfactory definition of social dangerousness has been fraught with difficulty, and we have seen that the English approach to this matter was that an accumulation of convictions of a certain degree of seriousness gave courts certain additional powers in sentencing offenders, and still confers the power to impose an extended sentence in certain circumstances.

There has been some revival of interest in the problem of defining the dangerous offender in recent years.[10] This is because the decision whether to release on parole or on licence from a prison or a medical institution frequently turns on an estimate of the kind of danger to the community which the offender represents. Also the security classification of prisoners depends on an estimate of the offender's social dangerousness.

Professor Edwards has suggested that the degree of harm that the offender is likely to commit must be balanced with the degree of risk of a further offence:

> "Balancing then these inter-related considerations of risk and harm, it may be said that where, notwithstanding the high degree of risk that may be involved in, say, releasing an offender on probation or parole, the degree of harm that is likely to be occasioned is within the tolerable limits acceptable to society then a calculated risk involving a lesser degree of restraint is permissible. On the other hand, where the degree of harm of which the individual is capable is judged to be of a serious and heinous character then, notwithstanding the low degree of risk that may be involved, on balance a negative approach to the offender's conditional liberty is fully justified."[11]

Such considerations may well enter into the minds of those charged with the duty of advising on parole. But it is submitted that they provide little more than the basic framework for decision-making. The most difficult task is to know when to take a calculated risk, not with those who do not threaten great harm if they offend again, but with those who do. The release of murderers may be taken as the extreme case.

---

10. Several papers in the CIBA Foundation Symposium, *The Mentally Abnormal Offender*, ed. A. V. S. de Reuck and R. Porter, 1968, deal with the concept of dangerousness. They also discuss the treatment of the mentally disordered offender.

11. J. Ll. J. Edwards, "Social Defence and Control of the Dangerous Offender" (1968), 21 *Current Legal Problems*, 23 *et seq.*, at p. 38.

Professor Edwards recognises the difficulties in reaching a satisfactory definition of dangerous offenders, and refers to the attempts already made to formulate categories of dangerous offenders in the Model Sentencing Act prepared by the Advisory Council of Judges of the National Council on Crime and Delinquency, and in the Model Penal Code, prepared by the American Law Institute. He seems to subscribe to the view that it would be possible to draw up a list of categories of offender who could be regarded as dangerous. He would include not only violent offenders with a propensity towards criminal activity, whether due to a severe personality disorder or not, but organised or syndicated crime or racketeering, and trafficking in narcotics. He also appears to favour the inclusion of sexual offences involving molesting young children "where the propensity is high and the harm is seen to be in the violation of the unprotectable".[12]

Immediately, we are in very deep water. The precise definition of each of these categories, and whether or not they are the right ones, could lead to prolonged discussion, and different views might legitimately be held about several aspects of the matter. Professor Edwards seems to recognise this when he comes to discuss the suggestion that there is no reason to stop at offences involving harm to the person. He asks whether offences against property ought to be included, and seems to suggest that certain serious forms of property crime, such as arson, robbery, burglary and fraud "at once suggest themselves for possible inclusion in any exhaustive list of dangerous forms of conduct".[13]

But Professor Edwards seems to have some reservations about basing any categories of "dangerous" offences on traditional legal definitions alone. He has even graver doubts about the wisdom of a psychiatric definition, and in the end seems prepared to settle for nothing more dramatic than a common review tribunal for deciding on release, whether of mental patients or prisoners.[14]

Professor Norval Morris covers much the same ground, reviewing all the different legal approaches, and concluding that so far "none of these techniques has effectively brought us to grips with the variety of classifications we must have for

---

12. P. 40.
13. P. 45.
14. P. 51.

dangerous offenders if our criminal justice system is to become socially protective".[15] He maintains that

"To take power over the lives of others on predictions as to their future criminality—particularly as to the likelihood that they will inflict physical injury on others—is no light assumption of competence."[16]

He would prefer to reject increased power over an offender based on predictions as to his dangerousness. But he believes that some discriminations about dangerousness are essential to rational decision-making. This leads him to a discussion of the danger of psychiatric predictions of dangerousness which are not backed by prediction tables but based on individual clinical judgment. The use of base expectancy rates is a further development of prediction methods, which Professor Norval Morris rates highly. (See Chapter 13: The Results of Prison Custody (and Other Measures.)

He concludes that "such an approach to predicting dangerousness does not of course define the types of criminal behaviour which are and are not 'dangerous'—the *types of risk* which the community should and should not have to bear".

"But adequate prediction does lead us to the central policy issue after this definition. What *degree of risk* should the community bear in relation to the countervailing values of individual freedom?"[17]

Until the psychiatrists have contributed much more in the way of hard statistical data about the subsequent behaviour of offenders, it would not be proper, in Professor Norval Morris's view, to structure any sentencing or paroling process around psychiatric predictions of dangerousness, and he would resist the proposals contained in the Model Penal Code and the Model Sentencing Act on the ground that they are based upon false assumptions of knowledge.[18]

The third contribution to the current discussion comes from Professor Leon Radzinowicz.[19] This is more of a historical and factual survey than a theoretical discussion of questions of

---

15. Norval Morris, "Psychiatry and the Dangerous Criminal" (1968), 41 *Southern California Law Review*, No. 3, pp. 514 *et seq.*, at p. 531.
16. P. 532.
17. Pp. 535–536.
18. P. 536.
19. Leon Radzinowicz, "The Dangerous Offender", The Fourth Frank Newsam Memorial Lecture, 1968, *The Police Journal*, September 1968.

social dangerousness, but there is some interesting material concerning early nineteenth-century proposals for dealing more effectively with habitual criminals, such as those of Matthew Davenport Hill and Colonel T. B. L. Baker.[20] There is also some discussion of the search for ways to control the persistent criminal which took place on the continent of Europe under the influence of the positive school of criminology. Their proposals were hotly debated in international penological discussions.

Professor Radzinowicz does not reveal his own solution, though he doubts the wisdom of the latest English attempt to deal with the persistent offender, viz. the extended sentence. He says "it is doubtful whether it will get to the root of the problem. Where the offence itself justifies prolonged detention, the maximum sentence is, in most cases, already long enough".[1] While Professor Radzinowicz does not want to minimise the problem of persistent crime, he does not wish to exaggerate it either, and is "all for keeping cool" about it. But he believes that "the search for more effective approaches to the treatment of those whose offences are associated with severe mental illness or abnormality must be continued. . . . Some may need mental hospitals rather than prisons. But again no easy way out is in sight."[2]

To conclude this discussion, we may say that we share the doubts about the wisdom of defining categories of social dangerousness in connection with crime, and support the desire for better predictive information. Until this is available, it would not be wise to base social policies on more arbitrary grounds. The social danger of defining social dangerousness for the purpose of classifying and disposing of offenders must be recognised. It is all too easy to think we have solved a problem by developing a new category or definition. By this means, we may simply be creating more danger for society in the long run.

20. P. 27.
1. P. 30.
2. Pp. 34–35.

CHAPTER 15

Mentally Disordered Offences

The Mental Health Act 1959 provided a new legal classification together with a framework for handling mentally disordered persons in the ordinary mental hospitals and in the special hospitals.[1] This divided mentally disordered persons into four main groups:

1. The mentally ill;
2. The severely subnormal;
3. The subnormal;
4. The psychopathic.

No legal definition is provided for the different forms of mental illness (category 1) which it is left to the medical profession to identify. Subnormality (category 3) and severe subnormality (category 2) are defined, and these together cover most of the ground of the old description of mental deficiency, the Mental Deficiency Acts of 1913 to 1938 being now replaced. Psychopathic disorder (category 4) is defined to mean:

"a persistent disorder or disability of mind (whether or not including subnormality of intelligence) which results in abnormally aggressive or seriously irresponsible conduct on the part of the patient, and requires or is susceptible to medical treatment" [s. 4(4).]

The medical categories of mental illness include:

1. Organic brain disease;
2. Psychopathic disorders of functional origin;
3. Neurotic disorders;
4. Psychopathy.

PRISONERS AND MENTAL DISORDER

A very small proportion of prisoners are found to be suffering from mental disorder on reception. Dr. Norwood East, formerly

1. See 23 *M.L.R.*, No. 4, p. 410, July 1960, for a discussion of the Mental Health Act 1959, by T. C. N. Gibbens and the author; Henry R. Rollin, *The Mentally Abnormal Offender and the Law*, 1969. See also S. F. McCabe, H. R. Rollin and W. D. Walker, "The Offender and the Mental Health Act" (October 1964) 4 *Medicine, Science and the Law*, No. 4, pp. 231–244.

in charge of prison medical services, pointed this out in 1928,[2] and more recently Dr. Nigel Walker observed that in 1961 the proportion of adults and young offenders dealt with as being mentally abnormal represented only 0·65 per cent. of all those found guilty by the courts.[3] American experience is similar.[4] Powers exist to transfer the prisoner so found to an ordinary mental hospital or to one of the special hospitals, even though he has been sentenced to imprisonment.[5] He may also be transferred to the psychiatric prison hospital at Grendon, Bucks. Courts may remand accused persons in custody for a medical report, and certain alternative powers are available to the courts for dealing with mentally disordered offenders. These we must now examine in detail.

POWERS OF COURTS TO DEAL WITH MENTALLY DISORDERED OFFENDERS

(a) Remand for investigation and report

Every year a large number of prisoners are received on remand for the purposes of carrying out a mental investigation and preparing a report for the guidance of the sentencing court. The power of the magistrates' courts to make such remands derives from the Magistrates' Courts Act 1952, s. 26, which replaced the provisions of the Criminal Justice Act 1948 in the matter. Section 26 of the 1952 Act has in turn been amended by the Mental Health Act 1959.[6] The power of the higher courts to remand for medical inquiries derives from their general powers to order remands.

There has been a massive growth in the use of prisons in order to obtain medical reports about offenders prior to sentence, as may be seen from the fact that in 1953 5,218 cases were remanded to prison for mental observation and report, whereas in 1967 the figure was 11,061, more than double. Recent prison reports have referred to the growth of remands

---

2. W. Norwood East, "Heredity and Crime" (1928–1929), 20 *The Eugenics Review* 169.
3. Nigel Walker, *Crime and Punishment in Britain*, 2nd Ed.n, 1968, p. 282.
4. See Walter Reckless, Criminal Behaviour, 1940, p. 205; E. H. Sutherland, *Principles of Criminology*, 6th Edn., 1960, p. 121; Paul W. Tappan, *Crime, Justice and Correction*, 1960, p. 118.
5. Mental Health Act 1959, s. 72.
6. 7th Sched.

of this nature. A large proportion of these remands are dealt with at Brixton prison (3,318 in 1967) and at Holloway and Wormwood Scrubs. Medical officers also volunteer reports on persons whose condition appears to call for such action even though the remand has not been expressly for this purpose. In 1967 there were 1,095 additional persons on whom reports were thus submitted for the consideration of trial courts. One might add that a very much smaller number of persons are remanded for a report on the physical state of their health (585 in 1967).[7]

It by no means follows, of course, that as a result of the reports received the courts make their dispositions in all these cases on account of mental disorder. The power to make a hospital order (see **(b)** below) under the Mental Health Act 1959 was exercised in just over 10 per cent. of the cases remanded (1,273 in 1967). The courts also made 628 probation orders under s. 4 of the Criminal Justice Act 1948, *i.e.* with a condition of attendance or residence at a hospital or clinic for mental treatment (see **(f)** below). These various orders require some discussion.

(b) Hospital orders

Under the Mental Health Act 1959, s. 60, a court of assize or quarter sessions is given power to make a hospital order (or a guardianship order) where a person has been convicted before it of an offence other than one for which the sentence is fixed by law, provided that certain conditions are satisfied. Magistrates' courts may also make such orders, under similar conditions, under s. 60(2) in the case of a person suffering from mental illness or severe subnormality, without proceeding to a conviction, if they are satisfied that the accused did the act or made the omission charged.

The conditions which have to be complied with for making a hospital order are:

    1. Written or oral evidence of two suitably qualified medical practitioners (for the qualifications see s. 62): s. 60(1)(a);

---

7. See Report of the Prison Department, 1967, Cmnd. 3774. Also J. E. Hall Williams, "The Use the Courts Make of Prison", *Sociological Studies in the British Penal Services*, 1965 ed. by Paul Halmos, pp. 52–53.

   2. The court must be satisfied on the above evidence that
     (i) the offender is suffering from mental illness, psychopathic disorder, subnormality or severe subnormality, and
    (ii) the mental disorder is of a nature or degree which warrants the detention of the patient in a hospital for medical treatment, or the reception of the patient into guardianship under the Act;
   3. The court is of the opinion, having regard to all the circumstances, that this is the most suitable method of disposing of the case: s. 60(1)(b);
   4. The court must be satisfied, in the case of a hospital order, that arrangements have been made for the admission of the offender to a named hospital, and in the case of a guardianship order, that a local health authority or other approved person is willing to receive the offender into guardianship: s. 60(3).

In the case of children and young persons brought before a juvenile court, similar powers are conferred on that court by s. 61, subject to certain modifications.

A Restriction Order.—Under s. 65 a restriction order may be coupled with a hospital order, where it appears to the court, having regard to the nature of the offence, the antecedents of the offender and the risk of his committing further offences if set at large, that it is necessary for the protection of the public to make such an order. A restriction order subjects the offender to certain special restrictions, set out in s. 65, either without limit of time or during such period as may be specified in the order.

Only a higher court can make a restriction order, and the power does not extend to the magistrates' courts, but the magistrates may commit a convicted person over 14 years of age to quarter sessions to be dealt with in respect of the offence, where they consider that a hospital order together with a restriction order should be made(s. 67).

The effect of a restriction order is to limit the power of the patient or his nearest relative to obtain the patient's discharge. Only the Home Secretary shall have power to order the discharge of the patient or grant leave of absence or transfer (s. 65(3)). The Home Secretary may direct that a patient shall cease to be the subject of s. 65 if he is satisfied that the restriction order is no longer required for the protection of the public. He may also discharge the patient absolutely or subject to conditions and he may in the case of a patient who has been conditionally discharged recall the patient by warrant (s. 66).

Some protection is afforded by the provisions governing reference of the case of a patient subject to a restriction order to a Mental Health Review Tribunal for their advice (s. 66(6) and (7)).

Case law on hospital orders.—There have been a number of decided cases, mostly sentence appeals, where the courts have considered the policy in relation to the making of hospital orders. These cases have considered the general effect of making hospital orders with or without restriction orders, and in particular the question of the degree of protection afforded to the public by committal to a mental hospital or prison sentence. The courts have explained that the effect of making a restriction order is not to guarantee the detention of the patient in secure conditions but to control the circumstances in which he may be discharged by transferring the decision to the Home Secretary. They have also said that the judge must use his discretion whether to send the offender to prison or make a hospital order. There are, of course, the special hospitals to which an offender may be committed in suitable cases. The court must not rely on the Home Secretary to exercise his powers to transfer prisoners to mental hospitals or special hospitals but must make a choice itself. In the event of a hospital order being made, the order must state the hospital to which the offender is committed. It will not necessarily be wrong to commit an offender to prison where the safety of the public cannot be secured in any other way.[8] With regard to restriction orders the safer course is to make such an order unlimited in point of time.[9]

(c) Emergency powers

The police possess certain emergency powers to enable them to deal with persons found in a public place and appearing to be suffering from mental disorder and to be in immediate need

---

8. *R.* v. *Morris* [1961] 2 Q.B. 237; [1961] 2 All E.R. 672; *R.* v. *Higginbotham*, [1961] 3 All E.R. 616.
9. *R.* v. *Gardiner*, [1967] 1 All E.R. 895. A Practice Note summarises the effect of these cases and is printed in the law reports.

of care or control.[10] A constable finding such a person may, if he thinks it necessary to do so in the interests of that person or for the protection of other persons, remove that person to a place of safety. This means either residential accommodation provided by a local authority for the purpose, or a mental hospital, nursing home or residential home for mentally disordered persons, or a police station.[11]

There is not much information about the exercise by the police of these emergency powers, or the way in which they

TABLE A

Offenders aged 17 and older who were disposed of in ways reserved for the mentally abnormal in England and Wales in 1961 and 1962

Method of disposal

	1961	1962	1961 and 1962	
(1) Not reported because of abnormality ⎱				
(2) and (3) Reported but not prosecuted ⎬ *Numbers Unknown*				
(3) Conditional discharge after prosecution ⎰				
(4) Transferred from prison to hospital before trial or sentence	17	5	22	*0·5%*
(5) Probation with requirement of treatment as out-patient	374	380	754	*17·8%*
.. .. .. in-patient	392	456	848	*20·0%*
(6) *Guardianship* order under Mental Health Act	16	14	30	*0·7%*
(7) *Hospital* order under Mental Health Act				
without a conviction (*Only a magistrates' court can proceed thus*)	97	52	149	*3·5%*
after conviction, but without restriction order	731	892	1623	*38·4%*
after conviction, and with restriction	150	136	286	*6·7%*
(8) Found *insane on arraignment*	48	36	84	*2·0%*
(9) Found *guilty but insane*	10	9	19	*0·4%*
(10) Found of *diminished responsibility*	36	34	70	*1·7%*
(11) Found guilty of *infanticide*	13	17	30	*0·7%*
(12) Transferred from prison to hospital during sentence	182	140	322	*7·6%*
	2066	2171	4237	*100%*

10. Mental Health Act 1959, s. 136,
11. S. 135(6).

deal with incidents and complaints where mentally disordered persons appear to be involved. Nigel Walker throws a little light on the subject[12] but more research is needed.

Nigel Walker says that "more than half of the prosecuted offenders who are recognised as mentally abnormal are dealt with by means of hospital orders".[13] He gives a table (called Table A) showing the relative importance of the different methods of dealing with mentally abnormal offenders, aged 17 and older. As he points out, this emphasises the relative unimportance, at least so far as numbers are concerned, of the so-called special defences, which include findings of insanity, diminished responsibility, and infanticide. Less than 3 per cent. of the cases were so disposed of.

(d) Findings of insanity or diminished responsibility

Students of the English criminal law will know that *the defence of insanity* may be raised, and this may, if accepted by the jury at a trial on indictment, lead to a special verdict of "Not Guilty by reason of insanity". The result of such a verdict is detention indefinite in one of the special hospitals provided for that purpose. These are Broadmoor, Rampton and Moss Side (see below: Special hospitals).

Since 1957 it has also been possible to raise *the defence of diminished responsibility.*[14] The defence differs from insanity however in being limited to trials for murder and in respect of the result if the defence is accepted. A finding of diminished responsibility leads to a conviction for manslaughter instead of murder (like a finding of provocation) and the court may in sentencing the offender use any of its powers to make orders such as probation or hospital orders or may sentence to imprisonment for any period up to imprisonment for life.

As the table given above reveals, only about 0·4 per cent. of offenders aged 17 and older who are disposed of as mentally abnormal as the result of a criminal offence are dealt with by an insanity finding, and 1·7 per cent. by a finding of diminished responsibility. Taken together these result in approximately

---

12. Nigel Walker, "The Mentally Abnormal Offender in The English Penal System", *Sociological Studies in the British Penal Services* (ed. Paul Halmos), 1965, pp. 133 *et seq.*
13. *Ibid.*, p. 137.
14. Homicide Act 1957, s. 2.

the same proportion of offenders charged with homicide being dealt with by the courts as mentally abnormal since the Act of 1957 introduced diminished responsibility as before the Act.[15]

(e) Findings of unfitness to plead

Frequently the higher courts faced with a mentally disordered offender will reach a finding of unfitness to plead, under the relevant legislation. This has the same effect as a finding of insanity, viz. detention on an indeterminate basis in a special hospital. Walker's figures show that 2 per cent. of those aged 17 and over were disposed of on mental grounds.

Certain problems arise from the fact that where a person is found insane on arraignment or unfit to plead, the substance of the case against him is never investigated at the trial (though of course it will have been explored by the police and the magistrates' courts at an earlier stage). The result may well be that an innocent person may be detained in a special hospital, at least until his innocence is established. Many complaints are made by these patients that they have suffered injustice through never being tried. The Criminal Procedure (Insanity) Act 1964[16] provides a means whereby a trial court can postpone the issue of fitness to plead until it has heard the prosecution evidence. This procedure, where it is employed, should minimise the danger of injustice occurring, though it cannot of course exclude the possibility altogether.

(f) Probation order with condition of medical treatment

Since 1948 it has been possible for magistrates to make a probation order including a condition requiring the probationer to submit to treatment for his mental condition for a specified period of not more than twelve months from the date of the order. Under s. 4 of the Criminal Justice Act 1948, as amended, the court must first be satisfied, on the evidence of a duly qualified medical practitioner, that the mental condition of

---

15. Richard F. Sparks, " 'Diminished Responsibility' in Theory and Practice" (January 1964), 27 *M.L.R.*, No. 1, pp. 9 *et seq.*, says "the total proportion of murderers dealt with by the courts as mentally abnormal—i.e. found insane or dealt with under s. 2—has remained almost unchanged since 1952" (pp. 31–32).
16. See Bernard W. M. Downey, "Criminal Procedure (Insanity) Act, 1964" (January 1965), 28 *M.L.R.*, No. 1, p. 72.

the offender (i) requires and (ii) may be susceptible to treatment but is not such as to justify his detention in hospital in pursuance of a hospital order.[17] The court can only act in this way on the written or oral evidence of a doctor approved under section 28 of the Mental Health Act, which means "approved by a local health authority as having special experience in the diagnosis or treatment of mental disorder". Most prison medical officers have been so approved.[18] In making an order under s. 4, a particular hospital or mental nursing home (other than a specialist hospital) may be specified in the probation order, but the court must first be satisfied that arrangements have been made for the treatment in question.[19]

Probation with a condition under s. 4 of the Criminal Justice Act 1948 has been used fairly extensively for dealing with certain categories of property offender and violent and sex offenders, especially in and around London. According to Walker's figures, nearly 40 per cent. of cases of persons dealt with on mental grounds were disposed of in this way.[20] But Dr. Grünhüt reported that in 1953, out of a total of 30,000 probation orders made, only 700 included a requirement to attend for treatment,[1] and after 1959 the number of cases remanded in custody and dealt with by prison medical officers with a view to a recommendation under s. 4 declined, possibly due to the new powers to make hospital orders under the Mental Health Act 1959.

One of the difficulties about a s. 4 order is that there is no guarantee that the treatment will be completed: the probationer may discharge himself at will from any residential treatment facility or cease to attend for out-patient treatment. This would, of course, constitute a breach of the probation order, but the probationer would remain at liberty until brought before the court for the breach and the doctor cannot himsel recall the patient to hospital if he leaves. On the other hand it is said to be a distinct advantage to the doctor to know that he has the authority of the court behind him, especially in dealing

---

17. The section was amended by the Mental Health Act 1959, 7th Sched., to bring it in line with the provisions of that Act.
18. Estimates Committee, Eleventh Report, Appendices to the Minutes of Evidence, Appendix 6, "Psychiatric Treatment in Prison Service Establishments", p. 438.
19. Home Office, *Sentence of the Court*, 2nd Edn., 1969, para. 196.
20. See his Table A, reprinted above.
1. Max Grünhüt, *Probation and Mental Treatment*, 1963.

with the unstable young offender whose disorder is linked up with disciplinary problems, for whom s. 4 is frequently used. Another difficulty arises from the fact that the period of treatment is limited to twelve months, though the probation order itself may be for up to three years.[2]

THE TREATMENT OF THE MENTALLY DISORDERED OFFENDER

(a) In the special hospitals

There are at present three special hospitals serving England and Wales. A fourth is being planned. They are:

  (i) Broadmoor Hospital, in Berkshire;
  (ii) Rampton Hospital, in Nottinghamshire;
  (iii) Moss Side Hospital, near Liverpool.

They are under the management of the Ministry of Health to whom the functions of the Home Office and the Board of Control in this matter were transferred by the Mental Health Act 1959. By virtue of s. 97 of that Act, the Minister of Health is responsible for providing institutions, to be known as "special hospitals" for "persons subject to detention under the Act, being persons who, in the opinion of the Minister, require treatment under conditions of special security on account of their dangerous, violent or criminal propensities".

The history of these institutions is as follows. Broadmoor was opened in 1863 under the Home Office as a criminal lunatic asylum, taking patients from the old Bethlem Hospital including among others, Daniel McNaughton. Prior to this there were no special hospitals for dealing with the criminal offender who had been found insane. Rampton was opened in 1910 under the Home Office as a criminal lunatic asylum, but transferred to the Board of Control in 1919 and re-opened in 1920 as a state institution for mental defectives with dangerous and violent propensities. Moss Side was opened in 1919 under the Board of Control, for mental defectives, but between 1920 and 1933 was used as an epileptic colony. In 1933 it was re-opened as a state institution for mental defectives. Until 1960 patients could only be received into Broadmoor via the courts or from

---

2. See D. A. Thomas "Sentencing the Mentally Disturbed Offender", [1965] Crim.L.R. 685 *et seq.* for case law on the subject.

the prisons as being of unsound mind, while patients at Rampton and Moss Side could only be received under the Mental Deficiency Acts as being mental defectives. The Mental Health Act 1959 allowed more flexibility in committing and transferring patients to these institutions.

> "The Mental Health Act, 1959, permits patients suffering from any form of mental disorder which is a ground for detention under the Act, and for whose detention legal authority has been obtained, to be admitted to any hospital. . . . The main changes which the Act made in this respect in relation to the special hospitals were to allow the admission or transfer to Broadmoor of patients who have not appeared before a court but who are detained under Part IV of the Act; and to make it possible to allocate or transfer patients freely between the three hospitals, where their treatment so indicates, irrespective of the classification of their mental disorder."[3]

In practice, transfers are not so easily arranged, and Broadmoor has no alternative but to receive and keep most of those committed by the courts or transferred from prison on the grounds of mental illness. Rampton takes the subnormal and the severely subnormal patients, including the older and more dangerous patients. There is also a geographical basis for allocating patients between Rampton and Moss Side. Rampton generally speaking takes patients from the east coast and London, Moss Side taking those from the west coast and Wales. Three-quarters of the patients at Broadmoor are mentally ill, the rest are psychopaths.

The overcrowding in Broadmoor has been described as scandalous, and the Estimates Committee Report on the Special Hospitals were appalled by the conditions they saw when they visited this century-old building. A day room had 35 beds crowded into it, a medical ward was used as an overflow dining-room, and seven beds were placed in a corridor. Staff rooms have had to be turned into accommodation for patients. The position is more acute in the male wards than in the case of female patients. It has been decided to completely rebuild Broadmoor, by stages, on the existing site. There will also be a fourth special hospital, built probably on the site adjacent to the present institution at Moss Side.

---

3. Estimates Committee, Second Report, Session 1967–1968, "The Special Hospitals and the State Hospital", H.C. 31–vii, Minutes of Evidence, p. 2, para. 6.

There is a serious shortage of nursing staff at Broadmoor and
Rampton, but the position is somewhat easier at Moss Side.
Medical and professional staff are always in short supply for
this kind of work, and the general impression is that the day-
to-day administration and treatment of all patients leaves little
or no time for research. Moreover, it seems that the proportion
of aggressive and more active young patients has risen in recent
years, which presents a very serious embarrassment to the
authorities.

The security angle is one which must always be kept prominently in mind in connection with the special hospitals. Their
record with regard to escapes (and in particular, harm to the
public by escaped patients) is not unreasonable. Only three
members of the public actually suffered physical harm from
escaped patients during the twelve years ending in 1966,
though there were 189 patients who escaped.[4]

At any one time there are approximately one thousand
patients in England and Wales subject to restriction orders,
which constitutes some 45 per cent. of the total number of
patients in the special hospitals. The average length of stay
(so far as this means anything) is about ten years for Broadmoor
and Rampton and around seven years for Moss Side. Most
releases are to the care of ordinary N.H.S. mental hospitals,
who then become responsible for the arrangements for eventual
discharge of the patient to the community. This makes it
difficult to obtain reliable follow-up figures or keep track of the
results of treatment in the special hospitals. Non-restricted
discharges are subject to recall within six months but recalls are
relatively few.

A patient or his relative may apply for discharge to a Mental
Health Review Tribunal or, in the case of patients subject to a
restriction order, request the Home Secretary to refer his case
to such a tribunal for advice. A proportion of discharges are
ordered or recommended by these tribunals; these constitute
the majority of discharges from Rampton and Moss Side but
a small minority in the case of Broadmoor.[5]

---

4. In 1952 the Broadmoor Inquiry Committee was appointed "to inquire into the
   adequacy of the security arrangements at Broadmoor and to make recommendations". As a result of this Committee's report, certain improvements
   were made in the security system at Broadmoor. The report emphasised that
   "the security aspect of Broadmoor should never be depreciated".
5. Estimates Committee, Special Hospitals Report, p. xxi, para. 52.

Treatment in a special hospital depends, of course, upon the nature of the mental condition of the patient, but includes the use of drugs as well as electro-convulsive therapy and surgery. There is also a fairly elaborate educational provision and occupational therapy. Workshops provide a fairly full working day for those who can benefit from it. Some work is done outside the perimeter of the hospitals, under supervision. A limited amount of mixing of the sexes is allowed on social occasions. Regular dances are organised at all the hospitals and there are opportunities for mixed meetings of other kinds.

The position of the special hospitals would be greatly relieved if the regional hospital boards would agree to set up special security wings to which some special hospital patients could be transferred, and to which some patients could be admitted who would otherwise gravitate towards a special hospital or prison. The difficulty is that the general trend in N.H.S. psychiatric hospitals has been towards an "open-door" treatment policy. A start has been made by the Sheffield Regional Hospital Board, which has agreed with the Ministry of Health that a self-contained unit housing some thirty patients should be built at Balderton Hospital, Newark, which would have graded security and could then take patients chosen by the superintendents of Rampton and Balderton as being likely to benefit from treatment in such conditions. Some other regional hospital boards have been reviewing the question of medium security units. The Estimates Committee recommended that the Ministry of Health should ask them all to agree in principle to the establishment of units such as that at Balderton. The results of the Balderton project should be made freely available for guidance.

Among the other recommendations of the Estimates Committee were:

1. More research in conjunction with universities;

2. More joint appointments (especially at junior levels) of staff to serve partly in universities and partly in the special hospitals;

3. Management committees might be introduced for the special hospitals. The Scottish special hospital at Carstairs already has a management committee, but the medical superintendent at Broadmoor preferred

working in co-operation with the officials at the Ministry of Health.

(b) Grendon

The psychiatric prison at Grendon, Bucks, is a 300-bed maximum security hospital which opened in September 1962. It owes its establishment to the recommendations of the East–Hubert Report on the Psychological Treatment of Crime in 1939. It is similar to a maximum security prison in that it has an 18-foot wall surrounding it, and a multitude of locks and bars. Searchlights scan the perimeter. But inside, a serious effort has been made to run the institution along the lines of a therapeutic community. (See above, Chapter 10.) It is admitted that "there are great difficulties in developing a therapeutic community in prison". But the authorities believe that "much of the theory and practice evolved in therapeutic communities is applicable in the treatment of offenders".[6]

"It is possible to have maximum security outside and a relaxed permissive atmosphere inside, where men are not shouted at, are treated as individuals and are under minimal supervision."[7]

The selection of cases for Grendon is along the following lines:
1. There is a recommendation from the local or other prison where the prisoner is detained;
2. Selection is by the Director of Prison Medical Services, sometimes after consultation with the medical superintendent, on the basis of the suitability of the prisoner for the kind of facilities and opportunities which Grendon provides.

Dr. Tollington has said:

"In selecting cases for Grendon we stipulate only that they shall be able to fit into a community where there is a minimum of supervision and that they shall volunteer to have treatment. We regard strong motivation as the most important requirement."[8]

The population so far has been largely adult male prisoners with a high degree of neuroticism, but not seriously disordered mentally, and this excludes many prisoners who are psycho-

---

6. H. P. Tollington "Grendon Prison" (January 1966), 6 *B.J.C.*, No. 1, pp. 39 *et seq.*, at p. 43.
7. *Ibid.*, p. 44.
8. *Ibid.*, p. 45.

pathic. The original intention was to provide a special wing for those who were not amenable to treatment, 'for whom reformative measures, however specialised, seemed useless and the severity and hardships of ordinary prison life inappropriate". Whatever may have been the views of Drs. East and Hubert about the role of a psychiatric prison hospital, the fact is that, so far at least, it has not been thought desirable to use Grendon in order to provide a haven for the non-amenable psychopathic offender. The emphasis has been more on the positive side, of treating those amenable to treatment and desirous of receiving it.

It is a little early to judge the results of this effort. What is clear, however, is that not all the places in Grendon have been occupied, while it must be presumed that, out of the total prison population of over 35,000, there are many who could benefit from what Grendon has to offer. Because of shortage of staff, lack of workshop provision or for a combination of rather unsatisfactory reasons, Grendon, having been provided twenty years after it was originally recommended, is still not being fully exploited. The case for a second Grendon, possibly in the north, while it has hardly been recognised in official circles, has been forcibly recommended by the Estimates Committee in 1967.

This Committee was informed that "Grendon has accommodation for approximately 300 prisoners of all ages and both sexes, while the actual population has varied from 150 to 180 (Q.783). The prison is therefore considerably under-used."[9] They concluded that it was "a false economy to allow any part of Grendon to remain closed". Also, they recommended "that the Prison Department should undertake further studies to see if "another Grendon" is or may be required."[10] Their interpretation of the evidence submitted to them was that this was so, yet the Department had "nothing in terms of concrete thinking at the moment for another Grendon".[11]

Patients must have at least six months of their sentence still to run in order to be selected for Grendon. This eliminates those with short terms of imprisonment. The timing of the treatment is important in relation to the stage a prisoner has

---

9. Estimates Committee, Eleventh Report, p. xxxii, para. 95.
10. P. xxxiii, para. 99.
11. Minutes of Evidence, Q. 2917, p. 382.

reached in his sentence. For if he is successfully treated at Grendon and is ready for discharge, there is no power to release him where he still has time to serve, and he must be returned to prison to complete his term. It would be helpful if a successfully treated patient could be released from Grendon even where he still had some time left to serve, but this would obviously raise many questions which are not easily resolved.

(c) Psychiatric treatment in other prison service establishments

It would be quite wrong to assume that only if a prisoner gets sent to Grendon will he have the opportunity to receive psychiatric treatment. A great deal is done in this direction at several prison service establishments where facilities are available, though no central record is kept of how many persons have received psychiatric attention in a given period.[12]

> "Special centres exist for the psychiatric treatment of those whose mental state is not such as to require compulsory detention in a hospital and who are most likely to respond to treatment. These centres are at Wakefield and Wormwood Scrubs for men; at Holloway for women; and at Feltham for borstal boys.... The medical administration of those centres is in the hands of members of the Prison Medical Service but . . . the specialist treatment is for the most part provided by visiting psychotherapists."[13]

In 1965 there were three psychotherapists who visited Wakefield, five who visited Wormwood Scrubs, three who visited Holloway and two who visited Feltham. Visiting psychotherapists were also available at Pentonville and Wandsworth (where special attention is paid to the problem of treating alcoholism) and at Winchester. Psychotherapy may also be undertaken by the medical officer at any other establishment without necessitating the prisoner's transfer to one of the special psychiatric centres. Such treatment is usually of a less specialised character.

No one pretends that the prison service is able to do all that it should in the direction of providing psychiatric treatment for prisoners. Indeed, where sentencing courts are concerned, it is the policy to advise judges not to make recommendations

---

12. Estimates Committee, Eleventh Report, Appendices to the Minutes of Evidence, Appendix 6, p. 438.
13. Royal Commission on the Penal System, Minutes of Evidence, Vol. I, p. 73.

or promises in open court of psychiatric treatment where there is no guarantee that it can be provided, but simply to communicate their wishes to the Prison Department. In this way, false hopes will not be raised in the prisoner.

(d) Transfer from prison to hospital under s. 72

The Mental Health Act 1959, s. 72, confers power on the Secretary of State to transfer prisoners under sentence to a hospital, provided that certain conditions are satisfied. At least two doctors must agree that the prisoner is suffering from mental illness, psychopathic disorder, subnormality or severe subnormality (as the case may be) of a nature or degree which warrants his detention in hospital for medical treatment. There must be a vacancy for him in a special hospital.

One advantage of the use of this power is that the prisoner may be transferred back to prison when treatment is complete or at any time. The Radzinowicz Sub-committee in its Report on Long-term Prisoners, referred to this aspect of the matter, and observed that, in contrast, the offender who is first sent by the court to a special hospital cannot be transferred to prison later.[14] The special hospitals and the prisons share the responsibility for dealing with certain offenders who are to a greater or lesser extent mentally disordered. To some extent they have a common clientele.

"The gravest difficulties for all concerned arise with psychopaths", says the Sub-committee.

> "The shortage of places in special hospitals is one reason why only small numbers of psychopaths are transferred from prison to special hospitals. But a more fundamental reason is the doubt as to which is the right place for psychopathic offenders–special hospitals or prison."[15]

The Report discusses the "very understandable reasons" why few institutions are prepared to receive psychopathic offenders,[16] and the sub-committee on the whole inclined to the view that "most psychopaths, unless manifestly complicated by mental illness or severe sub-normality should initially on

---

14. Home Office, *The Régime for Long-term Prisoners in Conditions of Maximum Security*, Report of the Advisory Council on the Penal System, 1968, p. 68, para. 179.
15. Pp. 68–69, para. 180.
16. P. 69, para. 182.

I

conviction be the responsibility of the prison service and of its improved medical and psychiatric facilities".[17] There was clearly "a need for the urgent provision of additional secure accommodation", both in the hospital and in the prison system for the humane containment of disturbed offenders, and for a flexible and effective system of transfers between institutions.[18] There could be less use by the courts of s. 60 of the Mental Health Act 1969 if more frequent use could be made of power under s. 72 of the Act to transfer prisoners to special hospitals as need arose. The whole complex of questions should be studied as a matter of urgency by an independent committee.

Those who are familiar with the working of the prison service know that although many recommendations for transfer of prisoners under s. 72 are made to head office by prison medical officers, few are in fact acceded to and the prisoners actually transferred. The difficulties referred to by the Radzinowicz sub-committee underline the need for more secure accommodation to be provided outside the prison service, as well as for the provision of a second Grendon within the prison service itself. It may be right to expect the prison service to consume its own psychopathic smoke, but it must be given the facilities for doing so.

(e) Psychiatric prison hospitals abroad

Those who are familiar with prison systems in other countries will be aware of the tremendous international reputations of the psychiatric prison-hospitals at Herstedvester, in Denmark, and the Van der Hoeven Clinic, Utrecht, Holland. This is not the place to dilate on their characteristics and to evaluate them.[19] But with the decline in capital punishment, the increase in the length of sentences, the rise in the proportion of crimes of violence, and the increasingly active and aggressive character of the prison population, there is need to step up our efforts to provide for those who have the misfortune to have a twisted personality or who possess an explosive character. This need becomes daily more urgent, and our failure to provide the

---

17. P. 70, para. 184.
18. P. 70, para. 185.
19. Some account of both institutions mentioned may be found in John P. Conrad, *Crime and its Correction*, 1965, and Eric Stockdale, *The Court and the Offender*, 1967.

resources and staff to study the problems of control of these persons both within and outside the penal system becomes daily more irresponsible and dangerous to the public and damaging to the system itself.

CHAPTER 16

Female Offenders

NUMBER OF OFFENDERS

The most striking fact about female offenders is that there are so few of them in comparison with the number of male offenders. This is a fact which may be observed in all countries, but the proportion of female offenders varies according to the degree of feminine emancipation and the extent of social protection afforded to women in different cultures.

In the United Kingdom in 1968 there were 1,141 males found guilty of indictable offences per 100,000 of the population at risk, compared with 165 females per 100,000.[1] This gives a ratio of male to female of 6·9 : 1·0. The ratio has been going down in recent years. It used to be between 7 and 8 to 1. Only 13·5 per cent. of those found guilty of indictable offences in 1968 were women.[2]

The number of persons actually detained in custody in prisons, borstal institutions and detention centres may be judged from the figures for the daily average population of these institutions, given in the Prison Department reports. In 1967 the daily average population of males was 34,056, compared with 953 females.[3] This gives a proportion of males to females in custody of the Prison Department of 36 : 1. This proportion has risen with the rise in the male population in custody in recent years.

So we can see there is some truth in the assertion that "males are the delinquent sex", and in the corresponding observation that if only we could discover why there are so few women offenders we might be nearer to comprehending what causes

---

1. Home Office, Criminal Statistics, 1968, Cmnd. 4098, July 1969, Appendix II, pp. lvii and lviii.
2. *Ibid.*, p. xiii.
3. Home Office, Report on the work of the Prison Department, 1967, Cmnd. 3774, October 1968, pp. 50–51.

crime. The usual explanation given is that women are still shown much more leniency by the courts, are protected from prosecution more readily, and when convicted are less likely to be given a custodial sentence than men. The kind of crimes committed by females differ to some degree from those committed by males, though property offences such as theft form a large part of the crimes committed by both sexes. The following table gives some idea of the way the different offences are distributed by sex:

PERCENTAGE OF PERSONS FOUND GUILTY OF INDICTABLE
OFFENCES ACCORDING TO TYPE OF OFFENCE[4]

	1968	
	MALE	FEMALE
Larceny..	53·2	82·4
Breaking and Entering	22·8	3·3
Receiving	6·5	4·4
Frauds and False Pretences ..	3·4	3·5
Sexual Offences	2·8	0·1
Violence Against the Person ..	7·8	3·0
Robbery	0·9	0·2
Other Offences	2·6	3·1
Total	100	100

It will be seen that over 90 per cent. of females found guilty of indictable offences are guilty of offences against property. Xenia Field has pointed out that 88 per cent. of women in prison are there for offences against property, and 9 per cent. for offences against the person.[5] The largest proportion of property offences is theft, though there is some fraud and forgery and criminal deception. In a period when crimes of violence are rising, there does not appear to be much change in the distribution of female crime.

Ann Smith concludes that women today face the same family situations as in the past and undergo the same physical and social stresses. "The crimes of women have not varied greatly

4. Home Office, *Criminal Statistics, 1968*, Cmnd. 4098, July 1969, pp. xiii and xiv.
5. Xenia Field, *Under Lock and Key*, A Study of Women in Prison, 1963, p. 16.

over the centuries. . . . Nor is it probable that the ways in which they offend against the law will change radically in the future. Minor forms of dishonesty and antisocial sexual activities, such as prostitution, have always been the typical feminine offences, and are likely to remain so."[6] The measures adopted for dealing with women offenders are likely to change more drastically, for, as we shall see, bold plans have now been made for a new approach towards women in custody.

WOMEN IN PRISON

Various accounts of the experiences of women in prison have been written, both by former prisoners like Joan Henry,[7] Jane Buxton and Margaret Turner[8] and by former governors like Mary Size[9] and Mrs Joanna Kelley,[10] and prison visitors like Mrs. Xenia Field.[11] A full-scale academic study was carried out by Ann D. Smith, and published in 1962.[12] Various researches have been published dealing with selected aspects of the subject, such as the shoplifting and prostitution studies by Professor T. C. N. Gibbens.[13] Professor Gibbens is presently carrying out a more detailed study of women in prison, at Holloway. Dr Moya Woodside published a paper concerning Holloway giving "A Profile of a Prison Population".[14]

In 1967 the Home Office Research Unit published a group of three studies of female offenders, comprising a study of girls aged 16 to 20 years sentenced to borstal or detention centre training in 1963, a study of women offenders in the Metropolitan Police District in March and April 1957, and a description of women in prison on 1 January 1965. The latter is one of the first fruits of the complete index of women prisoners under sentence now being maintained in the Home Office Statistical Branch.[15]

---

6. Ann D. Smith, *Women in Prison*, A Study in Penal Methods, 1962, p. 323.
7. Joan Henry, *Who Lie in Gaol*, 1952.
8. Jane Buxton and Margaret Turner, *Gate Fever*, 1962.
9. Mary Size, *Prisons I Have Known*, 1957.
10. Joanna Kelley, *When the Gates Shut*, 1967.
11. *Op. cit.*
12. *Op. cit.*
13. T. C. N. Gibbens, "Age and Crime" (1965), 24 *Mental Health*, 202.
14. Moya Woodside, "Profile of a Prison Population" (July 1962), 2 *Prison Service Journal*, No. 5, pp. 26 *et seq.*
15. Home Office, Studies in the Causes of Delinquency and the Treatment of Offenders, No. 11, *Studies of Female Offenders*. By Nancy Goodman and Jean Price, 1967; (see review by Sarah McCabe, [1968] Crim.L.R. 207).

THE INSTITUTIONS

There are four prisons for women in England and Wales, the best known being the oldest and largest, Holloway Prison in London. Holloway is a secure prison of the nineteenth century "fortress" type (built between 1839 and 1852) and very forbidding it appears at first sight. With accommodation for 683 prisoners, it now houses under 400. Once inside, the visitor is conscious of a relaxed and friendly atmosphere, the women being allowed to wear their own clothes nowadays instead of the drab prison uniform and ill-fitting shoes which have been so much written about. The reception procedure for new arrivals is no doubt still somewhat traumatic and degrading, but it takes place in pleasant enough surroundings. One-third of the work of Holloway is now concerned with remands, usually for medical and psychiatric reports, and the rest of the prison is divided up according to the different varieties of prisoner. It serves as a local prison for the southern half of England from Birmingham to Southampton. A separate wing houses prisoners under twenty-one, for the rules require the segregation of these prisoners. The borstal recalls are also separately housed, and of course the secure wing houses the long-term prisoners and various highly dangerous prisoners. The rest of the prison population is allotted to different wings according to the degree of criminal sophistication and the degree of association permitted. Those in B Wing are permitted many privileges (including their own radio) and are members of the Cameron Group.[16] There is a separate house for mothers and babies and pregnant women.

Babies are not as a rule born in prison but the expectant mother is removed to a local hospital to have the baby. Thereafter the mother may keep the baby in her care in prison for several months, until it is judged appropriate to make other arrangements. Normally after about nine months the child is removed from the mother, but children over a year old have been housed in Holloway in certain circumstances.

---

16. This is a group of prisoners formed to see what they can do to help others, by means of co-operative projects, and to assist their own rehabilitation; and discussion meetings are held as well as the practical business meetings. It has been assisted by a group of outside "Friends", who later became incorporated as part of the Cameron Group. There is now a Husband and Wife Group meeting fortnightly, and made up of women who are known to have domestic difficulties, their husbands (who come to visit the prison from outside) and a number of married prison officers and their husbands.

Holloway is a closed prison, and is used as a selection centre for the open prison at Askham Grange in Yorkshire and for the medium security closed prison at Styal in Cheshire opened in 1963. Formerly there was a hostel at Holloway but this has now been closed. Following the fire at Hill Hall in Essex, Moor Court in Staffordshire is being used more extensively, and now takes all categories of women prisoner.

Askham Grange, near York, was opened in 1947. It has a carefully balanced domestic training course, and a hostel where 16 women can live who may go out to work in the free community, earning regular wages, under similar conditions to those prevailing in the men's hostels. (See Chapter 11: Release.)

Moor Court, near Burton-on-Trent, opened in 1962, and has a vocational training course in soft furnishing for women with six months to serve.

There is no regular factory situation in Holloway, apart from the seasonal activity of the jam factory, and it is not seen as necessary or desirable to give women prisoners training for semi-skilled jobs as machine minders and the like. In any case, the quality of the population is not thought to call for any tasks other than fairly simple repetitive tasks, such as assembling kits of stationery requisites, placing coloured pencils, rubber and ruler in a plastic case, putting labels on a cardboard carton. Cutting out, sewing and making dolls' dresses, simple overalls and dresses is another area of activity. The senior discipline staff, in evidence to the Royal Commission on the Penal System, expressed the view that:

> "The whole work situation needs reviewing. It would be very satisfactory to have a factory within the grounds, where hard work could reap wages at normal rates, from which deductions could be made for board and lodgings, home commitments, etc., and after a certain allowance of pocket money, some could be saved.[17]

We shall discuss later the present plans for rebuilding and modernising Holloway prison.

Great strides have undoubtedly been made under the last three Governors of Holloway to provide a humane and liberal régime within the confines of these ancient and rather dilapidated premises. One has to be reminded in assessing the situation

---

17. Royal Commission on the Penal System, Written Evidence, Vol. III, p. 73.

that it is the human element which matters most: in Sir Lionel Fox's phrase it is through staff not buildings that this work (of reform must be done. In this case, it is through the quality and leadership of the staff at all levels.

There are now five assistant governors as well as several senior discipline staff at Holloway. There are about 100 officers who wear a pleasant blue uniform. The senior staff (above principal officer) do not wear uniform. There are also a number of male officers employed on the gate, and on security patrols, and a number of technical maintenance staff, who are assisted by a party of male prisoners. There is, of course, a large medical and psychiatric staff, as well as the educational staff, and the part-time teachers and visitors. Indeed, like any modern English prison today, Holloway appears to be besieged by daily visitors who come in to perform or to offer various services. The saddest moment of the day is when at 4.30 or 5.0 those who work full-time take their leave, and the place begins to take on a different air. But even this is not the full picture, for a bustle of evening activity follows for at least a few hours every evening.

THE BORSTAL INSTITUTIONS FOR GIRLS

A somewhat special problem arises with borstal institutions for girls, which in other respects resemble their male counterparts. This is that acute degree of hysteria, perverseness and emotional tantrums which often manifests itself among delinquent women in custody, but especially so in the borstal age group. They are often extremely difficult to handle, it seems, and evidence of this comes from reports of serious outbreaks of indiscipline from time to time. Bullwood Hall, the secure borstal for girls, has been in the news on this account, especially in its early days.

This closed borstal replaced Aylesbury prison which was previously used as a closed borstal. Pleasantly situated on rising ground in Essex, near Southend, the institution was purpose built, and opened in 1962. It has three wings each housing about twenty to thirty girls. They wear their own clothes, and if these are not suitable, a limited budget is available to buy clothes for them. There is a full programme of simple assembly work of plastic products in one workshop, and sewing garments and other items in another workshop, also a laundry and gardeners' party. A pleasant assembly room, a hospital wing, some classrooms and an outside swimming pool complete the facilities. There is a visiting psychotherapist, who also visits Holloway, a part-time medical officer, and three assistant governors, one of whom acts as Deputy Governor. A number of male staff are employed, at the gate and on the maintenance staff. Pre-release girls are housed in a separate quarter, where they can prepare their own light meals, and have a sitting room of their own. Visits to outside church services are permitted and encouraged, and shopping expeditions are arranged. When parents come from long distances to visit inmates, they are sometimes allowed to take the girls out for the afternoon.

The open borstal at East Sutton Park has a homely atmosphere and close links have been developed with the local community.

The pregnant girls and those with babies are sent to Exeter, where there is a closed borstal institution housing about thirty.

Holloway has to deal with borstal recalls. These are usually treated rather more as a psychological problem. A specially experienced person is in charge of these girls, who are asked to face up to the problem what made them behave in this way, and are given certain counselling opportunities.

THE DETENTION CENTRE FOR GIRLS

Moor Court was used for a while from 1962 as a detention centre for girls, but the Advisory Council on the Penal System endorsed the recommendation of its sub-committee on detention centres, and this was that it should be closed as a detention centre and not replaced. Short-term custodial training of the kind given in a detention centre was felt to be unsuitable in principle for girls. Girls of this kind sent to Moor Court would be better dealt with, it was said, non-custodially, or given the longer period of training which borstal provides.[18] A probation hostel might be a suitable place for such girls. There might be rare cases where the only appropriate disposition would be imprisonment. The aim of the Criminal Justice Act 1961, viz. to substitute detention centres for short terms of imprisonment,

18. Home Office, *Detention of Girls in a Detention Centre*, Interim Report of the Advisory Council on the Penal System, November 1968.

could not be realised for girls consistently with the committee's view of the inappropriateness of the detention centre in these cases. Fresh legislation would perhaps be required to make suitable alternative residential provision. There would also be a need for a new borstal for girls in the north of England. The plans for a small specialised borstal attached to a women's prison, with access to all the prison's psychiatric and other facilities, were also approved by the sub-committee, and are likely to be implemented with the rebuilding of Holloway.

FUTURE TREATMENT OF WOMEN OFFENDERS

An important policy statement on the future treatment of women offenders was made by Lord Stonham, Minister of State, Home Office, on 12 April 1969. This followed the Report of the Estimates Sub-committee[19] which made a particular point of the need for a drastic reorganisation of the custodial institutions for women, and insistent public pressure for something to be done.[20] Earlier plans had been to replace Holloway by a new women's prison at Theydon Mount, Essex, but these were dropped in November 1968 because of the small number of women prisoners.[1] It has now been decided to rebuild Holloway itself as a women's prison, eventually clearing the whole site and constructing a new prison complex. A start will be made with a new hospital and an associated range of ancillary buildings and staff quarters. This may possibly be linked with a male remand centre for medical cases and a nurses' training school.

The problem of what to do with our nineteenth-century urban prisons has hitherto defied solution. The attempt to rebuild on the same site poses certain problems. Some ingenious architectural solutions have been suggested, but these are probably out of the question.[2] The stresses and strains of running a maximum security operation of the complexity of Holloway (which holds eight different categories of prisoner)

---

19. Estimates Committee, Eleventh Report, 1967.
20. Renée Short, "Gaol sentences for women are an anachronism", *The Times*, 10 April 1968.
1. *The Times*, 11 November 1968; 17 December 1968.
2. Richard F. Sparks, "Treatment of Offenders", *Forward in Europe*, Council of Europe, April–May 1968, pp. 4 *et seq*, at pp. 8–9, shows photographs of "a British project for a modern urban prison designed to allow the authorities to formulate a realistic rebuilding programme within the limits of existing sites".

side by side with extensive building operations are likely to be severe. The alternative sometimes suggested is to sell the sites for other kinds of property development and move to cheaper more spacious sites outside the central urban areas where these gaols are presently situated. But this appears to pose other kinds of problem, the solutions to which may be equally difficult to find. Lord Stonham claimed in making the announcement of Home Office plans that "by any standards of the prison system the redevelopment proposals at Holloway pose new and challenging problems. In scale alone the project compares with anything so far tackled in the penal field in any country." The progress of these plans will be watched with interest.

A main thrust of the new scheme will be to develop a new policy for women and girls responsive to their needs. "Women offenders are a special case", it is said, "requiring forms of treatment which are not necessarily suitable for men." New forms of non-custodial treatment will no doubt feature prominently, such as compulsory tasks or community work under supervision.

The Magistrates Association had suggested that special rehabilitative centres should be provided for women offenders.[3] The senior discipline staff at Holloway had proposed day attendance centres for women, which they thought would be particularly appropriate for shop-lifters and other petty criminals, and for most first offenders.[4] Lord Stonham said the latter were a possibility but "the small number of women offenders and the greater scatter of them throughout the country might make such centres hard to organise". Something along the lines of the hostel scheme without the necessity of prior prison sentence should be considered. The precise details will be considered by the Advisory Council on the Penal System, in its report on non-custodial and semi-custodial treatments.

---

3. Royal Commission on the Penal System in England and Wales, Written Evidence, Vol. II, p. 22.
4. *Ibid.*, Vol. III, p. 73.

PART IV

Non-Custodial Measures for Dealing with Offenders

CHAPTER 17

Probation

THE HISTORY OF PROBATION

Britain and America share the distinction of originating and developing the ideal of probation, each having played an important part in this matter. In both countries probation developed out of various methods of conditionally suspending punishment of an offender. Traces of such practices are to be found from very early times, but the development of probation linked with suspension of punishment is a nineteeth-century development.

As early as 1820 the Warwickshire Quarter Sessions adopted the expedient in suitable cases of passing sentence of imprisonment for one day upon a youthful offender upon condition that he returned to the care of his parent or master "to be by him more carefully watched and supervised in the future". Twenty years later Matthew Davenport Hill, on his appointment as Recorder of Birmingham (early 1841), introduced the same practice, which he had witnessed in the Warwickshire Sessions as a young lawyer. Hill found suitable persons to act as guardians, and had periodical inquiries made into the conduct of the offenders, and records were kept. But the system lacked any statutory basis.[1]

In 1841 John Augustus, a Boston shoemaker, began to take an interest in offenders, and stood bail for a man charged with being a common drunkard. The defendant was ordered to appear for sentence in three weeks time, and when John Augustus brought him back he satisfied the court the man had made an effort to work and to reform his habits, whereupon a nominal fine of one cent was imposed, plus the payment of costs. For eighteen years, until his death in 1859, John Augustus

---

1. A full account of the development of probation in Britain and the United States of America appears in the United Nations report *Probation and Related Measures*, 1951, pp. 42 *et seq.* See also Cmd. 5122, 1936.

did this sort of thing, extending his work to cover women and children and not only cases of drunkenness. He "bailed on probation" nearly 2,000 cases and achieved a very high proportion of successes.

In 1869 the State of Massachusetts passed a statute providing for the appointment of a state agent to investigate cases of children tried before the courts, to attend such trials and to receive children on probation. But it was not until 1878 that a statute was passed providing general probation. This provided for the appointment of a paid probation officer in the criminal courts of Boston. The U.N. Report on Probation and Related Measures (1951) commented that:

> "It is of no mean significance that this pioneer statute on probation specifically contrasts probation with punishment . . .. Of equal significance is the fact that the statute does not restrict the application of probation to any particular class of offenders (first offenders, young offenders, etc.) or to any particular class of offences, but postulates the likelihood of the individual offender's being reformed without punishment, as the only criterion for the selection of offenders to be released on probation."[2]

Probation was extended to all cities and towns in the state of Massachusetts in 1880 (on a permissive basis) and to the superior courts in Massachusetts in 1898. In 1891 the power of appointment was passed from the municipal authorities to the courts and was made mandatory instead of permissive. Significant developments began to take place in other states towards the end of the nineteenth century, and in the early part of the twentieth century there was a very widespread adoption of probation laws. In 1925 the Federal Court system was provided with a probation service.

Turning back to England, after Hill, the next development was the establishment of the Police Court Missions in 1876 by the Church of England Temperance Society, acting on the suggestion of Frederick Rainer, a Hertfordshire printer. The original aim was to combat alcoholism but the police court missionaries soon concerned themselves with broader questions, and courts frequently assigned them the task of supervising persons placed on probation, who were either released conditionally, on bail given by the missionaries who were charged with their supervision, or they were asked to enter into a

---

2. U.N. Report, p. 31.

recognisance or bond to be of good behaviour. Joan King's book stresses the value of the relationship which developed between the magistrates and the police court missionaries, and in particular, regards the latitude allowed for experiment as important.[3] By 1900 there were 100 men and nineteen women missionaries. The Summary Jurisdiction Act 1879 provided, by s. 16, that courts of summary jurisdiction could discharge a person conditionally subject to his giving security. But it did not recognise probation as such: it merely facilitated it. There was at this time considerable agitation for a probation law similar to the Massachusetts statute of 1878.[4]

In 1887 the Probation of First Offenders Act extended to certain offences other than summary offences the provisions of the Act of 1879, s. 16. Now first offenders convicted of larceny, false pretences or other offences punishable with not more than two years' imprisonment could be dealt with, and the word "probation" was used for the first time in an English statute. Regard was to be had to the youth, character and antecedents of the offender, to the trivial nature of the offence and to any extenuating circumstance. It was not until the Probation of Offenders Act 1907, however, that any adequate legal sanction was provided for breach of probation. This Act inaugurated probation "in the full modern meaning of the term".[5] It consolidated the previous provisions and reinforced them. It enabled courts to appoint paid probation officers. "The contents and scope of the Probation of Offenders Act 1907", it has been said, "were a testimony to the thoroughness with which the pioneers of probation had done their work".[6] This Act laid the foundations of the present day probation service and exercised a far-reaching influence on the development of probation in various parts of the world.[7] The provisions of the Act, though wide in scope, were in general terms, and

"the omission of rigid definitions and controls at this stage was in many ways a good thing, as it allowed for further experiment and development. Lord Samuel, who introduced the Bill, likened it many years later not to the making of a machine but to the planting of a seed with a life of its own, fed by its environment."[8]

3. Joan F. S. King (ed.), *The Probation Service*, 2nd Edn., p. 3 (See now 3rd Edn., 1969, which has been extensively revised.)
4. *Ibid.*, p. 4; U.N. Report, p. 48.   5. U.N. Report, p. 49.
6. Joan F. S. King (ed.), *The Probation Service*, 2nd Edn., p. 8.
7. U.N. Report, p. 110.
8. Joan F. S. King (ed.), *The Probation Service*, 2nd Edn., p. 10.

THE PROBATION OF OFFENDERS ACT 1907

The Act drew a distinction between courts of summary jurisdiction and superior courts, assizes and quarter sessions.[9] For the former it provided three alternatives where the court thought the charge was proved but did not desire to convict the offender:

1. Dismissing the charge;
2. Discharging him conditionally on his entering a recognisance with or without sureties, to be of good behaviour and to come up for conviction and sentence if called on at any time during such period, not exceeding three years, as might be specified in the order;
3. Adding to 2 a condition of being under supervision on probation.

The order of a court requiring the insertion of such conditions in the recognisance constituted a probation order. Other conditions could be inserted in the order. The latter, the superior courts, were empowered to place an offender on probation only after conviction of the offender, and the order required the offender to come up for sentence only. It should be noted here that whereas some countries use a suspended sentence for dealing with offenders, the amount of the sentence being fixed beforehand, this has never been the English practice in connection with probation, though a suspended sentence may now be imposed under the Criminal Justice Act 1967 without probation supervision.

In 1914 the Criminal Justice Administration Act widened the conditions which could be inserted in the recognisance in connection with probation.

In 1925 the Criminal Justice Act implemented the recommendations of the Departmental Committee on the Training, Appointment and Payment of Probation Officers, which had reported in 1922.[10] It made the appointment of probation officers compulsory, and created "probation areas" (either "single" or "combined" areas) out of the petty sessional divisions, each with a probation committee charged with responsibility for the appointment and payment of probation officers; and local committees for each petty sessional division, to

---

9. U.N. Report, p. 111.
10. Cmd. 1601.

supervise their work and receive reports. Details were regulated by Probation Rules made by the Home Secretary. In London the Home Secretary was given special power to undertake all the duties of a probation committee.

It has been said that "taken together, the 1925–26 Acts and Rules represent a comprehensive effort at the legislative level to establish reasonably high and uniform standards as regards working conditions, qualifications and the work itself".[11] But the rate of progress was slow and variable as between different courts.[12] Gradually, in the years between the wars, and more particularly, since World War II, there has been a growing recognition that probation is not simply a measure mainly suitable for children and young persons but that it works well with many adults too. There has also been a movement away from preoccupation with material factors and environment, with the development of interest in and knowledge of the medical and psychological aspects of deviant behaviour.

In October 1934 a Departmental Committee on the Social Services in Courts of Summary Jurisdiction was appointed, which reported in 1936.[13] Its principal recommendations as to the law had to wait to be implemented by the Criminal Justice Act 1948. The purely administrative recommendations were put into effect before this.

THE CRIMINAL JUSTICE ACT 1948

This Act introduced several important changes into the law relating to probation:

1. The power of magistrates' courts to place persons on probation without proceeding to conviction was abolished. The effect of a conviction is minimised by the provision that if the offender satisfactorily completes his probation it shall not count as part of his criminal record. This preserves to some extent the intention of the Act of 1907. The same arrangement applies to absolute and conditional discharge— they do not amount to a conviction, except in the case of a person conditionally discharged and subsequently sentenced for an offence committed during

11. Joan F. S. King (ed.), *The Probation Service*, 2nd Edn., p. 19.
12. *Ibid.*, p. 20.
13. Cmd. 5122.

the conditional period (limited to 12 months under the Act of 1948, up to three years under the Act of 1967).

2. The "rather cumbersome"[14] necessity for entering into a recognisance is abolished but the element of the necessity of the consent of the offender which it imported (a somewhat debatable requirement) was retained by the provision that "if the offender is not less than 14 the court shall not make the probation order unless he has expressed willingness to comply with the requirements thereof" (s. 3(5)). Sureties by other persons willing to give them are still permissible under the Act but may not be required by the court.

3. The previous maximum duration of probation (3 years) is retained, and a minimum duration of one year is introduced (s. 3(1)).

4. Factors to which the court should have regard in relation to making a probation order were listed at length in 1907, but all the 1948 Act says is that the Court "shall have regard to the circumstances, including the nature of the offence and the character of the offender".

5. Conditions of Probation and Supplementary Requirements:

No far-reaching changes were introduced here, there are some innovations. A condition may be imposed that the offender shall undergo treatment for his mental condition (s. 4). A condition of residence is still possible. An offender may be required (in addition to a probation order being imposed) to pay costs and/or damages or compensation (s. 11(2), (3)).

LEGAL CHANGES IN PROBATION SINCE THE ACT OF 1948

The main legal changes in probation since 1948 have been in connection with the reorganisation of after-care, which has become a major and integral part of the probation officer's responsibility, and the few changes in the Criminal Justice Act 1967 concerning the combining of disqualification for motoring

---

14. Joan F. S. King (ed.), *The Probation Service*, 2nd Edn., p. 33.

offences with a probation order (s. 51), and the substitution of conditional discharge for probation (s. 53). It is also no longer essential for a woman or girl to be supervised by a probation officer of the same sex (s. 55).

THE PROBATION SERVICE

The same general pattern of organisation which grew up in the early years of probation has been retained. The probation service is still essentially local in character, but the role of the Home Office has assumed increasing importance. Through inspectors, and by controlling standards of admission and training, a great improvement has been brought about, although there is no room for complacency.

Since 1936 a special division of the Home Office has existed to deal with probation. In 1964 this became the Probation and After-Care Department. In 1949 the Probation Advisory Committee, first appointed in 1922, was reconstituted as the Probation Advisory and Training Board. The Board was reconstituted again on a broader basis as the Advisory Council for Probation and After-Care in October 1962, following the recommendations of the Morison Committee. There is also a separate Recruitment and Training Committee and a new After-Care and Parole Committee. There is a sizeable probation inspectorate which has a wide range of supervision and training functions. The Act of 1948 gave the task of supervising the work of probation officers to "case committees" which were to function in each petty sessional division. This enables the probation officer to keep in touch with his bench. These committees function independently of the probation committee for the whole probation area.

THE PROBATION OFFICER

There has been a gradual transition from reliance on the use of voluntary personnel to a more or less professional service, but there is still a place for voluntary workers in this field, which has been recognized by the various committees which have reported.

The duties of probation officers were defined by the Act of 1948. These include after-care of discharged prisoners. The 5th

Schedule of the Act outlines these duties as follows (in para. 5(5)):

1. To supervise the probationers and other persons placed under their supervision and to advise, assist and befriend them;

2. To inquire, in accordance with any directions of the court, into the circumstances or home surroundings of any person with a view to assisting the court in determining the most suitable method of dealing with his case;

3. To advise, assist and befriend, in such cases and in such manner as may be prescribed, persons who have been released from custody.

   It has been said of this duty to "advise, assist and befriend", that: "Today officers will probably want to reverse their order, since case-work has given them so much insight into the value of befriending and they have come to learn that advice and assistance mean little unless given in the context of a dynamic relationship."[15]

Since 1937 there has been statutory authority for the matrimonial work done by probation officers. The Denning Report and the Royal Commission on Marriage and Divorce led in 1958 to the acceptance of probation officers as the basis of a divorce court welfare service.[16] The probation officer has since come to be regarded very much as the social worker of the courts. In 1961 the Streatfeild Report emphasised the need for more pre-trial inquiries, and this too has generated another growing volume of work for probation officers.[17] The reorganisation of after-care and the introduction of parole have added further to the pressures bearing down on the overworked and underpaid members of the probation service.

THE MORISON COMMITTEE

In 1959 a Departmental Committee was appointed to inquire into all aspects of the probation service in England and Wales

---

15. Joan F. S. King (ed.), *The Probation Service*, 2nd Edn., p. 80.
16. *Ibid.*, p. 111.
17. Report of the Interdepartmental Committee on the Business of the Criminal Courts, Cmnd. 1289, February 1961.

and in Scotland, and into the approved probation hostel system. The Report of this Committee in March 1962 provides a most comprehensive and authoritative review of the development of the probation service and its future role.[18]

The definition of probation

The Morison Committee defined probation as "the submission of an offender while at liberty to a specified period of supervision by a social case-worker who is an officer of the court; during this period the offender remains liable, if not of good conduct, to be otherwise dealt with by the Court".[19] The Committee preferred to define probation in this way rather than as a conditional suspension of punishment, a description which had been adopted in the 1951 United Nations Study, for two reasons:

1. Probation in Britain does not involve (as in some continental systems) an imposition and suspension of sentence on the offender when the probation order is made;
2. Probation in itself embodies a punitive element in the requirement to submit to supervision, and the Committee felt that it was right to stress this disciplinary aspect of probation, since the view that probation was a "let-off" had not yet been wholly dispelled.

The making of a probation order

1. The court which chooses probation must have regard to the circumstances, including the nature of the offence[20] and the character of the offender, and must form the opinion that it is expedient to do so instead of sentencing the offender.[1]
2. The court must explain to the offender in ordinary language the effect of the order and of failure to comply with its requirements or commission of a further offence.[2]

---

18. Report of the Departmental Committee on the Probation Service, Cmnd 1650, March 1962.
19. P. 2, para. 9.
20. The section says it must not be an offence the sentence for which is fixed by law.
1. Criminal Justice Act 1948, s. 3(1).
2. Section 3(5).

3. If the offender is not less than 14 years of age he must express his willingness to comply with all the requirements of the probation order.[3]

4. The common requirements of an order include:
     (i) to be of good behaviour and to lead an industrious life;
    (ii) to notify the probation officer of any change of address;
   (iii) to keep in touch with the probation officer in accordance with such instructions as he may from time to time give;
    (iv) to receive visits from the probation officer, if he so requires, at the offender's home.

5. Additional requirements may be imposed in relation to the following:
     (i) place of residence;[4]
    (ii) attendance for medical treatment;[5]
   (iii) special requirements which may impose precise restrictions on the liberty of action of the probationer, for example, by prohibiting for the time being visits to a particular place or association with a particular person.

6. The court making a probation order shall not include among its requirements the payment by the offender of sums of money by way of damages for injury or compensation for loss,[6] but such an order may be made contemporaneously but separately.[7] There is no power to impose a fine as well as making a probation order,[8] and it is wrong to combine a probation order with a custodial sentence, even where separate courts are involved.[9] But under the Criminal Justice Act 1967 a probation order may be coupled with a disqualification and endorsement for motoring offences.[10] A court which passes a suspended sentence on

---

3. Section 3(5).
4. Section 3(4). A home surroundings report is a pre-requisite here.
5. Section 4.
6. Section 3(3).
7. Section 11(2).
8. *R. v. Parry*, [1951] 1 K.B. 590; [1950] 2 All E.R. 1179.
9. *R. v. Evans*, [1958] 3 All E.R. 673.
10. Criminal Justice Act 1967, s. 51(1).

any person must not make a probation order in respect of another offence of which he is convicted or dealt with by that court.[11]

7. The duration of a probation order may be, and nowadays frequently is, three years. It cannot be for less than one year.

8. The supervising court (that is, the court for the petty sessional division for the time being named in the order as the place where the probationer resides) may, upon application made by a probation officer or the probationer, cancel any requirements of the order or add requirements. This includes extending the duration of the order up to not more than three years where the original order was for less than that period in the first instance.

9. Since 1967, the supervising court, rather than as previously the court by which the probation order was made, may, upon application made either by a probation officer or the probationer, discharge the order. But a court of assize or quarter sessions making a probation order may include a direction that the order shall not be discharged except by the court which made the order.

10. Under the Criminal Justice Act 1967 a conditional discharge may be substituted for a probation order where the court thinks it appropriate.

The value of probation

The Morison Committee emphatically reasserted the value of probation and expressed in most eloquent language the purposes which it serves.[12]

The Committee spelled out the four conditions which must exist in order for there to be an *a priori* case for the use of probation. These are as follows:

1. The circumstances of the offence and the offender's record must not be such as to demand, in the interests of society, that some more severe method be adopted in dealing with the offender;

---

11. Criminal Justice Act 1967, s. 39(2).
12. Cmnd. 1650. See passages summarised in the Home Office pamphlet, *The Probation Service in England and Wales*, under this heading.

2. The risk, if any, to society through setting the offender at liberty must be outweighed by the moral, social and economic arguments for not depriving him of it;
3. The offender must need continuing attention;
4. The offender must be capable of responding to this attention while he is at liberty.

The Committee expressed their conviction that there was a moral case, in a society founded upon respect for human rights, for a system which allows an offender to continue to live and work in the community. Such a system is also desirable on social and economic grounds. But they accepted the need for research into the success of different methods of probation with different types of offender, and in this connection a tremendous amount of important work has been carried out in recent years by the Home Office Research Unit, most of which has been published in research pamphlets.[13]

THE FUTURE OF THE PROBATION SERVICE

In the last few years there has been considerable discussion about the future of the probation service. The impending implementation of the Seebohm Report and the provisions of the Children and Young Persons Act 1969 have raised questions concerning the role of the probation officer in relation to the proposed comprehensive family social service, and in relation to the supervision of delinquent children. These questions have not yet been entirely resolved, but it seems likely that the members of the probation service will continue to see themselves as providing a specialised service for the special needs of offenders, and will remain separately organised and represented through their professional association, The National Association of Probation Officers, rather than merge in the new British Association of Social Workers. No doubt there will be close co-operation between these organisations in many important matters concerning the implementation of the proposed reforms.[14]

---

13. See below, the section on "The Results of Probation".
14. See Robert Bessell, "Probation service troubles", *New Society*, 4 January 1968, pp. 14–15; M. Murch, "Seebohm: A Painful Dilemma for Probation" (March 1969), 15 *Probation*, No. 1, pp. 18–23; Gordon Jones, "The Future of the Probation and After-Care Service" (July 1969), 15 *Probation*, No. 2, pp. 44–51; R. M. Braithwaite, "The Search For a Primary Task" (July 1969), 15 *Probation*, No. 2, pp. 57–60.

PROBATION NOT A ''LET-OFF''

In the past the fact that under the Probation of Offenders Act 1907 probation was mentioned in the same context as dismissal and conditional discharge led to the feeling that probation was a "let-off". Following the recommendations of the 1936 Committee, the Criminal Justice Act 1948 did something to emphasise the difference between discharge and probation by separating them off in different sections, and by requiring courts, before making an order for discharge, to satisfy themselves not only that it is inexpedient to inflict punishment but also that a probation order is inappropriate.

The fact remains that it may be difficult for an offender to regard the offer of probation as anything other than a mild alternative, less severe a sentence than a fine or a custodial sentence. However, in practice many offenders who have had the experience of being put on probation have discovered that it is quite an onerous business, extending as it does for a considerable period (up to three years in duration) and requiring regular reporting and the obligation to account for one's life and activities to an independent person holding a certain degree of power over one because he can take one back to the court as being in breach of probation. Frequently offenders are heard to express a preference for punishment rather than probation, which is eloquent testimony against the notion that probation is a "soft" measure which can be regarded as a "let-off".

RESIDENCE REQUIREMENTS

A requirement as to residence in an approved probation hostel or home may be made, but only if the court has first obtained and considered a home surroundings report.[15] The offender may be required to reside in a specified institution for a specified period of not more than twelve months from the date of the order. The limit of twelve months' residence is thought desirable because "the hostel or home is not intended as a permanent alternative to the probationer's own home".[16]

APPROVED PROBATION HOSTELS AND HOMES

These hostels and homes are for youths and girls over school age but under 21 who need to be removed from their home

---

15. Criminal Justice Act 1948, s. 3(5).
16. Joan F. S. King (ed.), *The Probation Service*, 2nd ed., p. 111.

surroundings and placed in a controlled environment, but otherwise have the potential to respond to normal supervision by a probation officer. The difference between a *probation hostel* and a *probation home* lies in the fact that from a hostel, probationers go out to work daily, and contribute from their wages towards the cost of their maintenance, whereas probationers in approved probation homes initially have full-time training on the premises, though they frequently go out to work towards the end of their period of residence. Hostels normally accommodate 15–25 probationers, and homes are of similar size.

There are some 25 hostels for youths and 12 for girls, providing in all for some 720 residents.[17] The number of homes is much fewer, there being 4 for youths and 3 for girls, providing about 220 places in all. They are maintained out of public funds and run by management committees, under rules laid down by the Home Office and subject to their inspection. Each hostel or home has a liaison probation officer who is appointed by the local probation committee and is responsible for the supervision of the residents as required by their probation orders. The hostel wardens have strictly limited disciplinary powers, and a hostel or home cannot deal with recalcitrant young people who require firm discipline or a long period of residential training.

There are very few probation homes because, in general young offenders who need to be removed from home but who are not suitable for approved probation hostels are likely to benefit more from training in approved schools or borstal institutions.[18]

Leicester had some success with its hostel, which has been written up by its former warden, Mr. Cooks.[19] In the last few years experiments have been made with the combination of the two types of provision.

It has been said that:

"The selection of cases for either of these forms of treatment needs careful consideration, especially in view of the disruptive

17. Home Office, *Report of the Work of the Probation and After-Care Department 1962 to 1965*, Cmnd. 3107, October, p. 66. See also Cmnd. 4233, December 1969, p. 35.
18. Home Office, *The Sentence of the Court*, 2nd Edn., 1969, p. 11.
19. R. A. F. Cooks, *Home Office Approved Probation Hostels*, 1956, pamphlet published by Justice of the Peace, Ltd. See also the pamphlet by J. Spencer and T. Grygier, *The Probation Hostel*, 1952, I.S.T.D.
See also the pamphlet by J. Spencer and T. Grygier, *The Probation Hostel*, 1952, I.S.T.D.

effect an unsuitable case can have upon the treatment of others who may have begun to make progress. Neither homes not hostels are suitable for those who are of exceptionally low intelligence or suffering from severe disturbances, nor should they be used as a 'soft option' where there is reluctance to commit a boy or girl to Borstal or an Approved School. They are inappropriate too, for those who really need a permanent home and do not specially require training. . . . The original aim of hostels and homes was to provide for those needing to be trained in regular habits of life and work, but there has been a tendency in recent years to use them increasingly for cases where there is also pronounced emotional maladjustment."[20]

The second Report of the Morison Committee (Cmnd. 1800), which appeared in August 1962, reaffirmed the value of probation hostels and advocated their improvement and extension.

ENFORCEMENT OF PROBATION ORDERS

A breach of probation is a finable offence, and a magistrates' court dealing with a probationer who has failed to comply with any of the requirements of his probation order may make an attendance centre order where the appropriate requirements are fulfilled. In either of these cases the probation order remains in force. Alternatively, the court may deal with the probationer for the original offence for which the probation order was made. In this case, the probation order is thereby terminated.

Joan King's book observes that:

"Probation officers recognize that people fail to keep the requirements of their orders for a variety of reasons, such as their need for punishment, personal inadequacy or conflict with authority. They have, therefore, a special responsibility for ensuring that the court dealing with the breach is aware of the individual's particular needs. A statement of these needs makes it possible for the court to make an appropriate decision about the subsequent treatment. Probation cannot be said wholly to have failed if it enables the right decision to be taken as regards subsequent treatment and results in the client's willingness to accept such treatment."[1]

---

20. Joan F. S. King (ed.), *The Probation Service*, 2nd Edn., pp. 111, 112.
1. P. 87.

With regard to breach of probation the following comment is made in the same source:

> "Some people are placed on probation at a time when their previous irregular mode of living makes it very unlikely that they will be able to comply with the requirements of the order until they have had time to work through some of their personal difficulties. In such cases a breach of the order is almost bound to occur and the probation officer is then faced with a dilemma from the point of view of his casework relationship with his probationer. If the officer brings him back before the court, the opportunity for further casework help may be lost. If, on the other hand, the breach is ignored, the probationer, knowing that the officer is not carrying out his part of the contract, may feel bewildered and insecure."[2]

THE USE MADE OF PROBATION

About 50,000 persons are put on probation every year. Ninety per cent. of these have been found guilty of indictable offences.

> "The statistics show that although more probation orders are now being made than ever before, the probation of offenders placed on probation has declined. For juvenile offenders the decrease has been a more or less steady one from 51 per cent. in 1938 to 32 per cent. in 1963. For offenders aged 17 and over the proportion fell from 22 per cent. in 1938 to 11 per cent. in 1947, rose to 17 per cent. in 1957 and fell to 13 per cent. by 1963."[3]

This decline in the proportion of offenders placed on probation is probably due in part to the introduction of other methods of non-custodial sentence, such as conditional discharge, and the increasing popularity of the fine. Courts have learned to be more discriminating in selecting offenders who need probation. Another factor is that with the rise in the number of persons convicted, the probation service could hardly have coped with the situation if the same proportion of offenders had been placed on probation as, say, in 1938. There are wide variations in the use of probation in different courts, as several research studies have shown.[4]

---

2. *Ibid.*
3. Royal Commission on The Penal System in England and Wales, Written Evidence, Vol. 1, p. 55.
4. M. Grunhut, *Juvenile Offenders Before the Courts*, 1956; R. G. Hood, *Sentencing in Magistrates' Courts*, 1965.

THE RESULTS OF PROBATION

The Morison Report in its Introduction contains a most useful summary of the research which has been carried out into the results of probation.[5] Until the Home Office Research Unit studies, the most comprehensive attempt to assess the effectiveness of probation was the Cambridge report entitled *The Results of Probation* published in 1958.

> "The Department examined the records of over 9,000 offenders who had been placed on probation for indictable offences by courts in London and Middlesex, and took as the test of effectiveness the satisfactory completion[6] of the probation period and the avoidance of a further offence for three years thereafter. By this test, it was found that success could be claimed for 73·8 per cent. of the adults and 62·4 per cent. of the juveniles studied; that the success rate was higher for women than for men and for the older than the younger probationers; and that, as might be expected, the prospects of success diminished according to the probationer's previous convictions."

The Home Office had earlier reached similar conclusions as the result of a small-scale inquiry. More recently, an elaborate series of research studies has been carried out by the Home Office Research Unit, and several reports of these studies have now been published. An account of this research appears in the Probation and After-Care Department's Reports of October 1966 and 1969.

The probation research project began in 1961, and the aim is to evaluate the results of probation in Great Britain "in a more complete and objective way than had so far been possible ... The general purpose of the research is to study differences in the outcome for different types of offender who have been dealt with in various ways whilst on probation."[7]

After a pilot study carried out in the Middlesex Probation Area, a survey was made of trends and regional comparisons in England and Wales, using probation statistics for 1950 to 1961. Further studies concentrated on eight probation areas, in-

---

5. Cmnd. 1650, p. 6.
6. Joan King's book points out that "for statistical purposes a satisfactory order may be defined as one during which the probationer is not known to have committed any further offence or breach of requirement. There may be little relation between an order that has been successful in this statistical sense and one that is successful from the casework angle". *The Probation Service*, 2nd Edn., p. 99.
7. Cmnd. 3107, p. 72.

volving eighteen probation offices in inner London, and seven large industrial cities;[8] within these areas a more detailed study has been made of male offenders aged 17 and under 21 years who were put on probation in 1964. A typology of treatment methods used in probation has been developed and the different types of personal and social problems experienced by probationers will be related to the types of treatment. "The general purpose of the research . . . is to show whether certain specified forms of treatment are more effective than others in dealing with different types of offender".[9] In addition a prediction study is being carried out in relation to male probationers aged 17 and under 21, drawn from the whole of England and Wales.

> "The purpose of the prediction study is to produce expected reconviction rates for the probationers with various types of problem who are allocated to various types of treatment. Differences between expected and actual reconviction rates can then be regarded as one kind of measure of the effects of treatment."[10]

Among supporting studies which have been undertaken is one into the stresses in the lives of probationers, another on the use of group work in probation, and one on probation hostels, their characteristics, and the boys who are sent there.

THE NATURE OF PROBATION CASE-WORK

There has been much discussion of the problems raised by the attempt to do case-work in the authoritarian setting of probation, where the probation officer remains always to some extent an authority figure responsible to the court, and the client is under some degree of compulsion or pressure rather than seeking help of his own accord, as in many other case-work situations.

This rather special situation was recognised by the Morison Committee, who said it required special skill to overcome the difficulties presented by the situation. Joan King's book does not claim that the probation service "has yet in every respect solved the problem of practising case-work in an authoritarian setting", but the possible benefits of the legal obligations inherent in the probation order are recognised.[11] Some probation

---

8. Birmingham, Coventry, Glasgow, Leeds, Liverpool, Manchester and Sheffield.
9. Cmnd. 3107, p. 73.
10. *Ibid.*, p. 76.
11. Joan F. S. King (ed.), *The Probation Service*, 2nd Edn., p. 78.

officers argue very persuasively that although the probation officer in a sense is there to protect society as well as to help the offender, this double duty is not necessarily an obstacle to effective case-work;[12] indeed it may well "assist him to exert the firm, consistent and benevolent control which some probationers require and many have never experienced".[13]

It seems that the obligations to the court may assist some offenders to recognise that they present a problem in terms of human behaviour and relationships. It has been pointed out in Joan King's book that:

> "since the probation officer deals with clients who are often not aware of having any problem, the casework relationship is not something clients are seeking of their own volition in order to find a solution. Even those who are aware of needing help find this offered to them by someone who represents the very authority with which they may be in conflict."

> "Experience has shown, however, that the probation officer's use of authority in insisting on regular contacts with his probationer may provide an opportunity for stimulating growth and change. . . . The first fact that the probation officer has to face is that he would never see some of his probationers at all but for the element of compulsion in the order and so he would have no chance of establishing any sort of relationship with them."[14]

The actual techniques of probation case-work are not an appropriate subject for description in this book. It is sufficient to note that there are basically two types of interview situation which are used by probation officers, viz. those in which the probation officer visits the probationer in his home and those in which the probationer comes to the office, an exercise known as reporting. "It has been found that a thoughtful combination of reporting and home visiting can be used beneficially in the treatment plan."[15] There is also a good deal of experimental work being done in the direction of running groups for probationers. Sometimes these are attended by successful ex-probationers who discuss their own experience. There has been some

---

12. A. W. Hunt, "Enforcement in Probation Casework" (January 1964), 4 *B.J.C.*, No. 3, pp. 239 *et seq.* F. Felton, "Compulsion and Casework" (March 1967), 13 *Probation*, No. 1, p. 13; Robert Foren and Royston Bailey, *Authority in Social Casework*, 1968.
13. Morison Committee, Report, Cmnd. 1650, p. 23, para. 54.
14. Joan F. S. King (ed.), *The Probation Service*, 2nd Edn., pp. 79 and 92.
15. *Ibid.*, pp. 91–92.

K

attempt to discuss the techniques on a scientific level, and to train probation officers for working with groups, and the Home Office has published a research report on the subject.[16]

---

16. Howard Jones, "Groupwork: Some General Considerations" (November 1965), 11 *Probation*, No. 3, p. 91. D. Bissell, "Group Work in the Probation Setting" (January 1962), 2 *B.J.C.*, No. 3, p. 229. Home Office, Studies in the Causes of Delinquency and the Treatment of Offenders, No. 9, Probation Research, *A Survey of Group Work in the Probation Service*, 1966, (A Home Office Research Unit Report.) This contains a useful survey of the literature, including many contributions in Probation and New Society.

CHAPTER 18

Suspended Sentence

A suspended sentence may be defined as a sentence of imprisonment imposed at the time of conviction but postponed so that it will only be served if a given condition is fulfilled within a given period. This is how the Advisory Council on the Treatment of Offenders defined it in 1952. Various alternative versions of this measure exist in different countries. Sometimes the actual imposition of the sentence is postponed but more generally it is the execution of the sentence which is postponed not its imposition, and it is this version of the suspended sentence which we have to consider here. The sentence is one of imprisonment to take effect upon fulfilment of the prescribed conditions which include a further appearance at a court and conviction of a criminal offence.

One of the major changes introduced by the Criminal Justice Act 1967 was the power conferred on the courts to use the suspended sentence. Previously it had not been thought to be desirable to introduce the suspended sentence in England and Wales, although it is widely used on the Continent of Europe, in North America, as well as in South Africa and Israel.

The matter was considered by the Advisory Council on the Treatment of Offenders in 1952 and again in 1957, and the Council in 1957 adhered to its previously expressed view that "the idea of the suspended sentence was wrong in principle and to a large extent impracticable".[1] The Council's Report on 1952 on the subject was reprinted as Appendix D to the Report of 1957.

It was apparently the late Sir Leo Page who in 1950 proposed that the suspended sentence should be introduced as a new method of treatment. He took the view that probationers did not always appreciate that they would be liable to be punished

---

1. Home Office, Report of the Advisory Council on the Treatment of Offenders, *Alternatives to Short Terms of Imprisonment*, 1957, p. 9, para. 27.

for the offence for which they were put on probation if they should be convicted of a new offence during the probation period. Sir Leo suggested that the suspended sentence would be a more effective deterrent and would be more readily understood by offenders.[2]

An examination of the system in several European countries revealed to the Advisory Council that the essence of the systems adopted in most of these countries was to suspend the execution of the sentence rather than its imposition. Only in Sweden was there a system of deferred sentences which resembled probation and conditional discharge in England and Wales.

> "The Council were informed that the suspended sentence works effectively in the countries about which there is information, but the figures which have been received are not particularly valuable because there is no basis of comparison with the present English system. On a general view the Council are inclined to conclude from the evidence received from foreign countries that their tendency is to develop a system of probation like our own out of the systems of "suspended sentence" with which they started."[3]

In other words, the suspended sentence was a poor alternative to probation. "The Council do not . . . consider that the probation system is in need of strengthening in the sense that it is necessary to add a new form of treatment such as the suspended sentence."[4] The Council were not in favour of the introduction of the suspended sentence either in conjunction with probation or as an alternative sentence standing on its own.

This was the view taken in 1952, and reiterated as we have said in 1957. By 1967 a different view prevailed. A number of influential groups such as the Law Society, the Magistrates' Association, and the Justices' Clerks' Society, recommended the introduction of the suspended sentence in their evidence to the Royal Commission on the Penal System.[5] A number of party political studies came out in favour of the suspended sentence.[6] Mr. Brian Leighton, J.P., mounted a personal campaign of considerable intensity in support of the idea,

2. *Ibid.*, p. 26.
3. *Ibid.*, p. 27.
4. *Ibid.*, p. 28.
5. Royal Commission on the Penal System in England and Wales, Written Evidence, Vol. II, 1967.
6. "Crime knows no boundaries", Conservative Political Centre Pamphlet Number 334, January 1966; "Crime A Challenge to us all", Report of the Labour Party's Study Group, June 1964.

adducing evidence in favour from many European countries and from Israel and South Africa.[7]

One of the main difficulties which had stood in the way of its adoption was the fear that it would lead to injustice if a sentence had to be fixed in advance of the date when it might come into operation. By that time the offender's circumstances might have changed but because of the commission of a further offence by him, the suspended sentence would come into operation automatically and inflexibly. This was a difficulty which was stressed by the Advisory Council in their 1952 Report, where they referred to it as:

> "the problem whether, on fulfilment of the given condition bringing the suspended sentence into operation, the sentence should fall automatically on the offender, or whether the court sentencing for the second offence should have a discretion as [to] the operation of that imposed for the first. If there is to be discretion then the Council think that there is no point in the suspended sentence, as the chances of it having to be served would be no more certain than under the present system. Indeed, in these circumstances the suspended sentence would have a positive disadvantage because it would involve the making of a threat that might never be fulfilled. On the other hand, if the sentence were to operate automatically on the fulfilment of the condition it would be likely to work injustice."[8]

This objection to the suspended sentence was to some extent met by the arrangements proposed and now incorporated in the Criminal Justice Act 1967. Provision is made for the court which eventually has to decide the matter in the light of a subsequent offence either to invoke the suspended sentence or to modify it by substituting a lesser term. This latter alternative is only available if in the opinion of the court it would be unjust "in view of all the circumstances which have arisen since the suspended sentence was passed, including the facts of the subsequent offence".[9] There are two further courses open to the court in these circumstances: (i) they may extend the period of the suspended sentence; (ii) they may decide to make no order with respect to the suspended sentence. The same precondition must be satisfied with regard to these two courses.

---

7. Brian Leighton, J.P., "The Suspended Sentence", *The Magistrate*, August 1965.
8. Appendix D, Home Office Report of the Advisory Council on the Treatment of Offenders, *Alternatives to Short Terms of Imprisonment*, 1957, p. 29, para. 10.
9. Criminal Justice Act 1967, s. 40(1).

THE NATURE OF A SUSPENDED SENTENCE

It is basic to the idea of the suspended sentence under the Criminal Justice Act 1967 that no supervision is provided for the offender. As we have seen, the notion that this could somehow be linked with probation was in the mind of Sir Leo Page when he originally proposed the suspended sentence, and was considered by the Advisory Council in its 1952 Report, and rejected. The Act of 1967 now expressly prohibits the making of a probation order in respect of another offence at the time when a person is being given a suspended sentence.[10]

Also prohibited are the attachment of any conditions to a suspended sentence, such as may be attached to a probation order.

THE POWER TO MAKE A SUSPENDED SENTENCE

There are two kinds of suspended sentence, judged according to the nature of the powers conferred by the Criminal Justice Act 1967.

(a) Mandatory suspended sentence

This applies to all courts passing a sentence of imprisonment of not more than six months, unless the case comes within one of the exemptions listed below.[11] Magistrates' courts are normally limited in their powers to sentences of up to six months, imprisonment so they are particularly affected by this provision.

The exemptions are as follows:[12]

  (*a*) 1. the offences involve acts of violence (an assault on or threat of violence to another person),

  2. or possessing a firearm or explosive or an offensive weapon,

  3. or indecent conduct with or towards a person under sixteen.

  (*b*) 4. the offender is already subject to a probation order or order for conditional discharge, made in respect of that offence or another offence,

---

10. Criminal Justice Act 1967, s. 39(2).
11. Criminal Justice Act 1967, s. 39(3).
12. The numbers do not appear in the statute which uses the lettering shown.

(*c*) 5. the court sentences the offender simultaneously to immediate imprisonment for another offence which sentence the court is not required to suspend,

(*d*) 6. the offender is serving a sentence of imprisonment or borstal training previously passed for another offence or has since the commission of the offence served such a sentence,

(*e*) 7. the offender has at any time previously been sentenced to imprisonment or borstal training for another offence,

8. or has previously been subject to a suspended sentence.

The Secretary of State is given certain powers to provide by order for the modification of these conditions. He may alter the provisions in (*e*) so as to change the reference to "any time" to a period prescribed not being less than three years, and he may also make different provision for different cases under this heading.[13] Furthermore, he has power to extend the application of mandatory suspended sentences to sentences of up to twelve months' imprisonment.[14]

(b) Permissive suspended sentence

Any court passing a sentence of imprisonment for not more than two years may suspend the sentence.[15] This applies to assize courts and quarter sessions as well as to magistrates' courts, with the qualification that magistrates' courts rarely have power to sentence to more than six months' imprisonment, as we have already observed.

The question arises what kind of cases are appropriate for suspended sentence, and there can be no firm answer but we will merely make a few suggestions. It is conceived that cases in which it is desirable to mark the wrongfulness of the behaviour in question, but where it is not desirable to imprison the offender immediately, and where he may be likely to take heed of the warning and not commit further offences, are the most suitable for suspended sentence. Such cases may well include shop-lifters, some serious motoring offenders, and minor offenders against public order or morality.

---

13. Criminal Justice Act 1967, s. 39(4).
14. Criminal Justice Act 1967, s. 39(5).
15. Criminal Justice Act 1967, s. 39(1).

The Court of Appeal has pointed out that a suspended sentence is really a sentence of imprisonment which is not immediately effective. It should not be regarded as a soft option. The courts should approach it in the same way as any other sentence of imprisonment, and the same qualifying conditions apply. This means that they should be satisfied that no other measure is appropriate.[16] Some problems arise in connection with the use of the suspended sentence for persons under the age of 21, which have been described by D. A. Thomas.[17] The Advisory Council in 1952 thought that the suspended sentence could hardly be applied to children and young persons, but that was because of what was thought to be its inflexible nature, for the circumstances of children and young persons "are even more likely than those of adults to change between the original conviction and any fresh conviction".[18] There was also the question of the general policy laid down in the Criminal Justice Act of 1948 which looked on prison with disfavour for persons under 21. This might appear to make it improper to use the suspended sentence for persons under 21.

THE OPERATIONAL PERIOD

A sentence may be suspended for a period of not less than one year or more than three years. This period is known as the "operational period". If during this time the offender commits in Great Britain another offence punishable with imprisonment, the provisions relating to the enforcement of the suspended sentence apply.[19] These provide for the proof of the "violation", and specify the court which is to deal with the suspended sentence.[20]

It will be noticed that the further offence must be punishable with imprisonment. This follows the view taken by the Advisory Council in its 1952 Report that it would not be desirable to regard *any* offence committed within the trial period as sufficient, since this would lead to the "danger that offenders

---

16. *R.* v. *O'Keefe*, [1969] 2 Q.B. 29; [1969] 1 All E.R. 426.
17. D. A. Thomas, "Current Developments in Sentencing—The Criminal Justice Act in Practice", [1969] Crim.L.R. 235, May 1969.
18. Home Office Report of the Advisory Council on the Treatment of Offenders, *Alternatives to Short Terms of Imprisonment*, 1957, Appendix D, p. 30, para. 13.
19. Criminal Justice Act 1967, s. 42.
20. Criminal Justice Act 1967, s. 41.

would be required to undergo their suspended sentence after conviction of offences of a trivial character entirely different from that of the offence for which the suspended sentence was imposed".[1] The Advisory Council considered the proposal to introduce the suspended sentence on the even more limited basis "that the condition on the fulfilment of which the suspended sentence should operate should be the commission during the trial period of a subsequent offence for which a sentence of imprisonment *is actually imposed*".[2]

The second condition which the further offence must satisfy is that it was committed in Great Britain.

There are no other conditions to be complied with under the statute. The Court of Appeal has been developing criteria for the guidance of courts in deciding what to do in the face of a violation of a suspended sentence. So far the decisions indicate that the facts and character of the subsequent offence are clearly appropriate for consideration in deciding whether the suspended sentence should be put into effect. This must be considered in relation to the offender's character and background.[3] It has also been decided that it was wrong in principle, when an order bringing into force a suspended sentence is made, for that sentence to be made concurrent unless there are some very special circumstances.[4]

THE WORKING OF THE SUSPENDED SENTENCE PROVISIONS

The main object of the introduction of the suspended sentence was to reduce the use of imprisonment for short terms. Every year, until now, more than 20,000 offenders have been received into prison for sentences of under six months.[5] It is too early to say exactly what effect the new law is having on reception for short terms. Lord Stonham, when Minister of State, Home Office, said that the results of the first nine months had been encouraging. Some 24,000 offenders had been

---

1. Home Office Report of the Advisory Council, Alternatives to Short Terms of Imprisonment, 1957, Appendix D, p. 26, para. 3.
2. *Ibid.*
3. *R.* v. *Griffiths*, [1969] 2 All E.R. 805; [1969] Crim. L.R. 388; *The Times*, 22 April; see also *R.* v. *Saunders* [1970], *Times*, 17 February; *R.* v. *Moylan*, [1969] 3 All E.R. 814.
4. *R.* v. *Brown*, [1969] Crim.L.R. 20.
5. Mark Carlisle, M.P., House of Commons Debate, 27 April 1967, col. 1957.

given a suspended sentence, and of these only 2,223 had re-appeared before the court, and in 2,042 cases the suspended sentence had been made operative. But he was careful to observe that during this period none of those given suspended sentences had been at risk for the whole of the "operational period".[6] There is some concern lest suspended sentences will lead to the choice of slightly longer terms by the original trial court, many of which will eventually fall to be served. Criminologists and penal reformers are caught arguing both ways here: they want the prison population to be reduced in size, they think short terms of imprisonment are bad in principle, yet they regret the longer terms, which may be imposed only to be suspended, on the ground that many of these will later have to be served.

It has been suggested that there should be power to suspend sentences of imprisonment which are for longer terms than the two years imprisonment which the Criminal Justice Act 1967 provides as the statutory limit.[7] This may well be a matter for consideration in any general review of the working of the suspended sentence. Whether it would also be wise to allow an offender under a suspended sentence to be under supervision is a more moot point.[8] As we have seen, official thinking, reflected in the terms of the statute, is against this.

---

6. *The Times*, 13 March 1969 (Lord Stonham); House of Lords Debates, 5 March 1969.
7. D. A. Thomas, *loc. cit.*, pp. 240–241.
8. *Ibid.*, p. 240.

CHAPTER 19

Absolute and Conditional Disharge, Recognisances and Binding Over

THE MAKING OF AN ORDER FOR ABSOLUTE OR CONDITIONAL DISCHARGE

When a person has been convicted of an offence other than one for which the sentence is fixed by law, and the court is of the opinion, having regard to the circumstances, including the nature of the offence and the character of the offender, that is inexpedient to inflict punishment and that a probation order is not appropriate, the court may make an order discharging him absolutely or subject to a condition.[1]

Where an order for *absolute discharge* is made, the offender is free to go, and the court's decision really amounts to a technical conviction without any penalty. Such an order is suitable where there has been a technical breach of the law without any real fault on the offender's part.[2]

A conditional discharge is subject to a condition that the offender commits no offence during a certain period specified in the court's order. Originally this was for a period not exceeding twelve months, but now, by virtue of the Criminal Justice Act 1967, an order for conditional discharge may be made for a period not exceeding three years.[3] Before making an order for conditional discharge the court must explain to the offender its effect in ordinary language. This is that if he commits another

---

1. Criminal Justice Act 1948, s. 7(1).
2. A recent example was the case of the Methodist minister in Brighton who produced a glass phial containing drugs in the pulpit, to show how easy it was to obtain drugs. He was convicted in January 1967 of being in unauthorised possession of cannabis and given an absolute discharge. It was announced in June 1969 that the Home Secretary had recommended a free pardon "as an act of exceptional clemency".
3. Criminal Justice Act 1948, s. 7(1), as amended by the Criminal Justice Act 1967, s. 52.

offence during the period of conditional discharge he will be liable to be sentenced for the original offence.[4] If he does commit a further offence during the relevant period, and is sentenced in respect of the original offence, the order for conditional discharge ceases to have effect.[5] The same powers extend to the courts in regard to a breach of an order for conditional discharge as apply in respect of a probation order, as regards enforcement. These include the power to issue a summons or warrant directing the offender to appear or be brought before the court in order for the breach to be dealt with.[6]

The court which makes an order for conditional discharge (or a probation order) may allow any person who consents to do so to enter into recognisances for the good behaviour of the offender, if the court thinks it expedient for the purpose of his reformation.[7] The court may also order the offender to pay such damages for injury or compensation for loss as the court thinks reasonable.[8] This is without prejudice to its power of awarding costs against him. In the case of an order made by a court of summary jurisdiction, the damages and compensation together shall not exceed £100 (or such greater sum as shall be allowed in any statute). In the case of an indictable offence, any court convicting an offender may order him to pay compensation not exceeding £400 for any loss or damage to property (other than loss or damage due to an accident arising out of the presence of a motor vehicle on a road).[9]

EFFECTS OF A PROBATION ORDER OR ORDER OF DISCHARGE

Where a person is convicted of an offence and is then placed on probation or discharged absolutely or conditionally the conviction is disregarded for all purposes (including disqualification or disability) except the following:

(i) any right of appeal;
(ii) any plea of autrefois convict;

---

4. Criminal Justice Act 1948, s. 7(3).
5. Criminal Justice Act 1948, s. 7(4).
6. Criminal Justice Act 1948, s. 8.
7. Criminal Justice Act 1948, s. 11(1).
8. Criminal Justice Act 1948, s. 11(2).
9. Forfeiture Act 1870, s. 4, and Magistrates' Courts Act 1952, s. 34, both as amended by the Criminal Law Act 1967, Sched. 2, para. 9.

(iii) revesting or restoration of property in consequence of the conviction;

(iv) the payment of costs.[10]

But where an offender is subsequently sentenced for an offence for which he was placed on probation or conditionally discharged, provided he was not less than 17 years of age at the time of his conviction, the provisions which say that a probation order or a discharge shall be deemed not to be a conviction for any other purpose shall cease to apply to the conviction.[11] This means that in later criminal proceedings this conviction may be counted after all.

DIFFERENCES BETWEEN CONDITIONAL DISCHARGE AND PROBATION

An order for conditional discharge differs from a probation order in that (*a*) it involves no continuing supervision of the offender, and (*b*) only one condition—that the offender shall not commit another offence—may be imposed. It differs from a suspended sentence in that if the offender commits another offence there is no statutory obligation on a court to deal with him for the original offence and there is no predetermined sentence which will then normally be put into effect.[12]

A probation order may be converted into an order of conditional discharge by any court having power to discharge the order upon an application made by the probationer or the probation officer on the ground that the probation order is no longer appropriate.[13] In a case where conditional discharge is substituted for probation, the condition that the offender commits no further offence will last until the expiration of the original probation period.[14]

THE USE THE COURTS MAKE OF THESE POWERS

The Criminal Statistics 1968 reveal that between 4 and 5 per cent. of offenders found guilty of indictable offences at higher courts are conditionally discharged. This is considerably less than the proportion so dealt with in 1950 (upwards of 8 per cent.). In the magistrates' courts the proportion of offenders

---

10. Criminal Justice Act 1948, s. 12(2) and (3).
11. Criminal Justice Act 1948, s. 12(1).
12. *The Sentence of the Court*, para. 9.
13. Criminal Justice Act 1967, s. 53(1).
14. Criminal Justice Act 1967, s. 53(2).

found guilty of indictable offences who are conditionally discharged is considerably higher, though only 1·0 per cent. of persons found guilty of non-indictable offences were so dealt with. (See the table printed below.) No figures are published regularly for the number of conditional discharges where further offences have been committed during the period of the currency of the condition, but some figures for the percentage of discharges where there have been reconvictions are given in *The Sentence of the Court*. These show that, for first offenders, discharges are among the most successful measures, though they are less successful for offenders with previous convictions. In general they were not so successful as fines. (See the comparisons made in the table (Table 5) on p. 198 of Chapter 13, Results of Prison Custody (and Other Measures).) The comment is made that Discharges "seem to have good results, particularly when used for juvenile offenders (for whom the fact of being caught and appearing before the court would often be a sufficient deterrent)".[15]

TABLE SHOWING PROPORTION OF OFFENDERS FOUND GUILTY
OF INDICTABLE OFFENCES WHO WERE CONDITIONALLY
DISCHARGED, 1968

Higher Courts	Percentage
Under 17	5·7
Aged 17 and under 21	5·1
Aged 21 and over	3·5
Magistrates' Courts	
Under 14	29·0
Aged 14 and under 17	20·6
Aged 17 and under 21	10·8
Aged 21 and over	10·7

Source: Home Office, Criminal Statistics 1968, Cmnd. 4098.

RECOGNISANCES AND BINDING OVER

There are several methods available to courts for dealing with offenders by taking from them an undertaking to behave

---

15. *The Sentence of the Court*, p. 73.

in future or requiring them to observe certain conditions. Although they are often lumped together in any discussion and the distinctions between them are blurred, they are in fact legally distinct and different rules apply.

Recognisances are solemn obligations or bonds, entered into before a court or official, under which a person binds himself to the performance of some obligation. The form of recognisance is an acknowledgment of a debt to the Queen, payment of which only becomes due on the non-performance of the obligation. Other persons than the subject of the recognisance may join in the promises as sureties. In the event of failure to carry out those promises, the recognisance may be forfeited or estreated, which means that the court orders that the sums of money mentioned in the bond as payable now become due to the Crown. Recognisances are used for the purpose of bail and securing attendance at the trial, as well as for disposal of offenders at the trial itself, as a sentencing measure.

The power to require a person to enter into recognisances is a common law power as far as misdemeanours are concerned (and since the Criminal Law Act 1967 felonies have been assimilated to misdemeanours). It applies whether the person was tried on indictment or summarily, and may be used in addition to or in lieu of any other punishment, and with or without sureties.[16] The requirement may be either to keep the peace or to be of good behaviour or both. This power may be exercised without sentencing the person convicted to a fine or to imprisonment.[17] Where such a power is exercised of requiring a person to enter into a recognisance the court usually prescribes imprisonment until the recognisances are entered into, and under certain statutes, such a person may, in default of sureties, be imprisoned for not over one year.[18]

When a person is brought back to court for breach of recognisance, the court must be careful to see that the breach is properly proved. It has been said that the breach should be proved with the same particularity as if the allegation were that the prisoner had committed a crime.[19]

A person may also be required to enter into recognisances by

---

16. *R.* v. *Dunn* (1847), 12 Q.B. 1026.
17. Criminal Law Act 1967, s. 7(4).
18. Archbold, para. 665.
19. *R.* v. *McGarry* (1945), 30 Cr.App.Rep. 187.

the magistrates' court even though no offence has been committed, where a complaint has been made. This is usually in the case of a family quarrel. The High Court and courts of assize or quarter sessions possess similar powers at common law to require persons to give sureties for the peace. But there is one important limitation on their powers. The courts may not impose any kind of condition in a recognisance to keep the peace or be of good behaviour, such as a condition to leave the country and not to return for a specified number of years.[20]

Binding over to come up for judgment may be used in all cases, except murder, where such a course is expedient in the interests of justice. The person is required to enter into recognisances with or without sureties to come up for judgment when called upon. Recognisances to keep the peace and be of good behaviour may be simultaneously required of the offender.

It seems that a court binding an offender over to come up for judgment may insert a condition in the recognisance that an offender should leave the country forthwith and not return for a specified period, though such a condition may not be inserted in an order binding over the offender to keep the peace.[1]

Bind overs should not be used as a means of enforcing the payment of debts.[2] The powers of courts of assize and quarter sessions in relation to the forfeiture of recognisances permit them to allow time for the payment of any amounts which become due, in the same way as for fines.[3] Magistrates' courts have similar powers. Between 600 and 700 offenders per annum are required to enter recognisances in respect of indictable offences, and just over 2,500 in respect of summary offences (see the table on p. 285).

BINDING OVER UNDER THE ACT OF 1361

Justices of the Peace have power to bind over persons to keep the peace under the Justices of the Peace Act 1361, but it seems that this power is not to be exercised unless, in the course of the hearing, it emerges that there might be a future breach of the peace.[4] Lord PARKER, in the case which decided this point,

---

20. *R.* v. *McCartan*, [1958] 3 All E.R. 140.
1. *R.* v. *Ayu*, [1958] 3 All E.R. 636, explaining *R.* v. *McCartan*, [1958] 3 All E.R. 140.
2. *R.* v. *Peel*, [1943] 2 All E.R. 99.
3. Criminal Justice Act 1948, s. 14; Magistrates' Courts Act 1952, s. 96.
4. *R.* v *Aubrey-Fletcher, Ex parte Thompson*, [1969] 2 All E.R. 846.

TABLE SHOWING NUMBER OF OFFENDERS FOUND GUILTY
OF INDICTABLE OFFENCES WHO WERE REQUIRED TO ENTER
INTO RECOGNISANCES IN 1968

	Indictable Offences	Non-Indictable Offences
Higher Courts		
Under 14	1	
Aged 14 and under 17 ..	11	
Aged 17 and under 21 ..	79	
Aged 21 and over	121	
	212	
Magistrates' Courts		
Under 14	3	9
Aged 14 and under 17 ..	29	85
Aged 17 and under 21 ..	64	154
Aged 21 and over	337	2304
	433	2552
Total Indictable Offences..	645	

observed that there might be cases where that emerged even
before a defendant had given evidence. But the power is different from that vested in magistrates under s. 91 of the Magistrates' Court Act 1952, for there one first had to have a complaint adjudged to be true; in other words, the case had to be
heard out completely. An order could be made under the 1361
Act at any time during the proceedings, subject to the opportunity being given to the applicant or his advisers to argue
against it. In such a case, as Lord Justice Edmund DAVIES said,
agreeing with Lord PARKER, there need not be proof of the
matters complained of, but an order must not be made capri-
ciously. "There must emerge during the course of the hearing,
which need not be a full hearing, material on which it could be
said that it involved the possibility of a future breach of the
peace."

In another case a woman and her son were bound over after

appearing as prosecution witnesses in a case arising out of a street disturbance in Shropshire. This led to an assurance being given by the Lord Chancellor in reply to a letter from an M.P. that the procedure under which magistrates have the power to bind over *witnesses* to keep the peace will be examined as part of the review of the criminal law. Lord GARDINER said he did not think it would be helpful that only people who were actually summoned should be bound over. The real safeguard was to ensure that no person was bound over without being properly warned what was proposed.[5]

Summary

To sum up the discussion, we may say that there are the following methods of obtaining through the courts undertakings from persons with regard to their future behaviour:

1. Recognisance with or without sureties (Common Law): to keep peace or be of good behaviour or both.
2. Recognisance upon adjudication of a complaint in magistrates' court (M.C.A. 1952, s. 91).
3. Bind-over to come up for judgment.
4. Bind-over to keep the peace under Justices of the Peace Act 1361 (magistrates' court).

There is obviously some uncertainty about the extent of these powers and mistakes can easily occur in attaching inappropriate conditions, etc. In the wrong hands they could become an engine of oppression, and it is good news that they will be reconsidered as part of the general review of the criminal law now taking place.

---

5. *The Times*, 19 February 1969.

CHAPTER 20

Fines, Disqualification, Compensation and Restitution

FINES

THE USE THE COURTS MAKE OF FINES

The fine is a most effective method of dealing with large numbers of offenders. It is particularly suitable for certain classes of offence and offender. The Home Office pamphlet *The Sentence of the Court* says that on the basis of a 1957 sample of first offenders, "fines . . . were followed by fewer reconvictions than any other method of treatment for almost every age group".[1] In further comparison of actual with the expected reconviction rates with regard to the same sample, it was found that

> "Fines were followed by the fewest reconvictions compared with expected numbers for both first offenders and recidivists of almost all age groups."[2]

Fines were particularly effective for larceny. The final conclusion is stated thus:

> "Fines, particularly the heavier ones, appear to be among the most 'successful' penalties for almost all types of offender."[3]

With young offenders there has been a shift of emphasis from probation to fines, comparing the pre-war and post-war period, as Dr. Grünhüt observed.[4] Various possible explanations have been given for this, such as the improved economic circumstances, the greater discrimination in the use of probation on the part of magistrates, and changes in the character of the offences and the offenders. The Cambridge Report on Sexual

---

1. *The Sentence of the Court*, 2nd Edn., 1969, p. 67.
2. P. 71.
3. P. 73.
4. Max Grünhut, *Juvenile Offenders Before the Courts*, 1956.

Offences found that for many categories of sexual offender, the fine is a most effective method of disposition. Among those in their sample not reconvicted, six out of ten had been fined or discharged.[5]

THE POWERS OF COURTS TO IMPOSE FINES

Since 1948 nearly all crimes have become finable.[6] Manslaughter has been finable since 1861, but murder cannot be dealt with other than by the fixed penalty of life imprisonment. At the other end of the scale, there are many offences for which no other penalty than a fine is provided by law. In 1967 fines were imposed on 96 per cent. of offenders found guilty of non-indictable offences, and 51 per cent. of those convicted by magistrates' courts of indictable offences. Of those found guilty in the higher courts, 21 per cent. were fined.[7] Thus it will be seen that the fine is not only the most successful penal measure but also the most popular measure.

The Criminal Law Act 1967 conferred on courts a general power to fine an offender in lieu of or in addition to their other powers of dealing with him, following the recommendation of the Criminal Law Revision Committee.[8] This power is subject to any statutory limitation or existing restrictions with regard to the imposition or amount of the fine. Thus the court is still precluded from imposing a fine where at the same time the court wishes to make a probation order, although there are some who think that there may be occasions where the combination of probation and a fine would be appropriate (including, it seems, some members of the Criminal Law Revision Committee).[9]

The maximum permitted fine has been raised under the Criminal Justice Act 1967 in a wide variety of cases, sometimes by a fourfold increase, sometimes more. This is in order to give the courts ample power with regard to the use of fines, and to reflect the effect of inflation.

There are certain legal rules about the imposition of fines,

---

5. *Sexual Offences:* A Report of the Cambridge Department of Criminal Science, 1957, p. 271.
6. Criminal Justice Act 1948, s. 13.
7. *The Sentence of the Court,* 1969, p. 4, para. 13.
8. Criminal Law Act 1967, s. 7(3); Criminal Law Revision Committee, Seventh Report, Felonies and Misdemeanours, Cmnd. 2659, p. 19, para. 72.
9. Pp. 19–20, para. 73.

and a court which wishes to impose a fine must have regard to certain considerations. Where there is a choice between a fine and other penalties, the court will wish to be satisfied that a fine is in keeping with the circumstances of the offence and the offender's record, and that neither the interests of society nor those of the offender require that he should be detained in custody.

Thus in *R.* v. *Markwick* the Court of Criminal Appeal substituted a sentence of two months' imprisonment for a fine of £500. This had been imposed on a businessman who stole from fellow members of a golf club, in circumstances which placed other members of the club under suspicion. Lord GODDARD said that imprisonment was right because of the essential meanness of the offence, the aura of suspicion cast upon other members, and the risk that a fine might "give persons of means an opportunity of buying themselves out of prison". He stated that "one has to take great care that there should be no suggestion that there is one law for the rich and one for the poor".[10]

The court will also wish to consider the means of the offender when deciding to order the payment of a fine. Under the Criminal Justice Act 1967 a higher court by which a fine is imposed is required to fix the term of imprisonment which the offender is to undergo if he defaults by not paying the sum due. No court may order the immediate committal to prison of a person ordered to pay a fine unless certain circumstances are satisfied:

Either (*a*) in the case of an offence punishable with imprisonment he appears to the court to have sufficient means to pay the sum forthwith;

or (*b*) it appears to the court that he is unlikely to remain long enough at a place of abode in the United Kingdom to enable the sum to be enforced by other methods;

or (*c*) the court making the fine order sentences the offender to immediate imprisonment or detention in a detention centre for that offence, or another offence, or he is already serving a term of imprisonment or detention.[11]

---

10. (1953) 37 Cr.App.Rep. 125.
11. Criminal Justice Act 1967, s. 44(2).

The court imposing a fine may allow time for payment or direct payment by instalments. The court has no power to make other orders such as directing that the accused be held in custody until payment.[12] Nor, as we have seen, may the court combine a fine with a probation order[13] or order for conditional discharge.[14]

MONEY PAYMENT SUPERVISION ORDERS

Under s. 71 of the Magistrates' Courts Act 1952, a magistrate's court dealing with an offence may, when imposing a fine, make an order placing the offender under supervision of a specified person (usually a probation officer), and this order will remain in force as long as the offender remains liable to pay the fine or any part of it, unless it is discharged by the court which made it, or a transfer of fine order is made under s. 72. A transfer of fine order has the effect of making payment of the fine enforceable in some other petty sessional area, where the offender is residing. There is a special provision requiring a magistrates' court which fines a person under 21 not to commit him to prison in default of payment unless he has been placed under supervision or the court is satisfied that such an order would be undesirable or impracticable.

A person subject to a money payment supervision order should not be committed to prison in default without the court first obtaining from the person appointed for his supervision an oral or written report on the offender's conduct and means.

The Morison Committee on the Probation Service considered the position with regard to money payment supervision orders was not entirely satisfactory. They pointed out that such an order was not a substitute for a probation order and should only be used where limited supervision by the probation officer might prevent default of payment.[15]

The court may make an order as to costs and compensation to be paid by the offender, at the same time as making a probation order. The offender may also be assessed with regard to his legal aid contribution. It is hard to see why these monetary

---

12. *R.* v. *Brook*, [1949] 2 K.B. 138; [1949] 1 All E.R. 787.
13. *R.* v. *Parry*, [1951] 1 K.B. 590; [1950] 2 All E.R. 1179.
14. *R.* v. *McClelland*, [1951] 1 All E.R. 557.
15. Report of the Departmental Committee on the Probation Service, Cmnd. 1650, March 1962.

payments may be combined with probation, but not a fine. The theoretical argument is that probation not being a punishment must not be combined with any order which is punitive in intent. This argument begins to wear thin in the light of modern developments in the court's powers. Perhaps there is a case for re-examining the whole question of the combination of orders and penalties. The question might also be considered in connection with suspended sentence (see Chapters 17 and 18: Probation; Suspended Sentences, for the other side of this discussion).

In the case of a young person under 17, there is power to order the parent or guardian to pay the fine instead of the child. In the case of a child under 14 the parent or guardian could be ordered to pay the fine unless the court was satisfied that the parent or guardian could not be found; or had not conduced to the commission of the offence by neglecting to exercise due care of the child or young person. Under the Children and Young Persons Act 1969, fines will not be available as penalties against children under 14, except in homicide, but parents may be ordered to pay compensation (see below: Compensation Orders). Before criminal proceedings are brought against young persons under 17 the police will have to be satisfied that this course is appropriate, and the new law provides them with certain guidance on this subject.

A fine once levied becomes a debt of record to the Crown and is recoverable from the personal representatives of a deceased person if he dies without paying it.[16]

ENFORCEMENT OF FINES

The Criminal Justice Act 1967 contained new provisions for enforcing the payment of fines by way of attachment of earnings, similar to those which had already been introduced for maintenance orders in 1959, provisions which in practice have not been very successful. The difficulty is that it is far too easy for an offender to change his employment and avoid liability. The system is not really efficient, and it has been suggested more than once that a deduction by means of the tax system through P.A.Y.E. and reflecting the fine in the Code Number would be

---

16. *Treasury* v. *Harris,* [1957] 2 Q.B. 516; [1957] 2 All E.R. 455.

preferable. So far, the Inland Revenue have not been persuaded.[17]

It is possible that attachment of earnings in payment of fines may work better than in the case of payment of maintenance orders, because the sums to be paid will be smaller, and there will be less inclination on the part of the offender to avoid payment by moving his job. At the same time, the technical requirements for making an attachment of earnings order (which are the same as those for attachment of earnings in regard to maintenance orders) are such that magistrates' courts may not often wish to be bothered with going through this procedure.

DISQUALIFICATION FROM DRIVING AND ENDORSEMENT OF LICENCE

There are two types of disqualification laid down in the Road Traffic Act 1962 applicable to certain driving offences. These are described as obligatory and discretionary disqualification.

Obligatory disqualification.—For a serious driving offence as defined by Part I of Sched. I of the Act, the court *must* order disqualification of the offender from driving for at least twelve months, and the endorsement of the licence. The only exception is where the court finds special reasons for not applying the sanction. Legal decisions have defined "special reasons" as reasons special to the offence rather than to the offender. Where the conviction is for a drinking offence in connection with driving or attempting to drive, and the offender has been previously convicted within the preceding ten years for any such offence, the mandatory disqualification is for a period of not less than three years.

Discretionary disqualification.—The second group of offences set out in Part II of Sched. I of the 1962 Act involves obligatory endorsement of the offender's licence, unless there are special reasons for not doing so, but the court is not obliged to order disqualification, though it may do so if it thinks fit. This includes exceeding the speed limit and careless driving offences.

The "totting up" arrangement applies to a person who has had his licence endorsed on two separate occasions within the preceding three years for offences within Parts I or II of the schedule and is now convicted again for such an offence. Then

---

17. See Report of the Committee on the Enforcement of Judgment Debts, Cmnd. 3909, February 1969, p. 163, para, 618.

the court must order his disqualification for not less than six months unless there are mitigating circumstances.[18]

In certain circumstances (convictions of driving or attempting to drive under the influence of drink or drugs) the obligatory disqualification is raised to three years where the offender has been previously convicted in the preceding ten years.[19]

A court may also make a disqualification order to last until the offender has passed a driving test. This power must be used additionally to the other powers except where they are permissive and not mandatory.[20]

The purpose of disqualification of driving offenders is to keep them off the road, but as a road safety measure it is not entirely effective and therefore is rather unsatisfactory. It is too easy for persons to get hold of vehicles and drive them after having been disqualified. There is no way of impounding the offender's vehicle, no great difficulty is experienced by a non-vehicle owner in hiring a vehicle if he has a stolen or forged licence, and many offenders (the younger element in particular) find it difficult to resist the temptation to drive, thus committing the more serious offence of driving while disqualified, which almost invariably carries a sentence of imprisonment, as well as the corollary being that these circumstances often mean that the vehicle is being driven while uninsured, which makes a very serious situation for the general public.

A further problem concerns the effect of long disqualification. The Road Traffic Act requires each successive disqualification to be made consecutive to any existing one. The court is then sometimes faced with a person who is a compulsive driver, driving being the only thing he can do really well, and the court is unable "to unravel all the disqualifications and give a young man a chance to do the one thing he can do in life".[21] It has been suggested that power to review a series of disqualifications should be vested in a single tribunal. At present a driver who has been disqualified by several courts has to apply to each of them if he wishes to have his licence restored.[22] In some countries one can apply to a Traffic Commissioner to restore a

---

18. Road Traffic Act 1962, s. 5(3).
19. Road Traffic Act 1962, s. 5(4).
20. Road Traffic Act 1962, s. 5(7).
21. *R.* v. *Johnson*, (1969), *Times*, May 21st.
22. *R.* v. *Shirley*, [1969] 3 All E.R. 678.

driving licence which has been suspended. The time is clearly ripe for Parliament to think again about these matters.

COMPENSATION AND RESTITUTION

COMPENSATION ORDERS

Until the Criminal Law Act 1967 the powers of the courts to require a defendant in a criminal case to pay compensation to the victim of the offence were limited. They were limited in two ways, firstly, as to the type of injury or damage, secondly as to the amount of compensation.

The Criminal Justice Act 1948, s. 11(2), empowered courts to order the payment of reparation by the offender for personal injury to the victim of the offence, but only where the court made a probation order or order for absolute or conditional discharge. In making such an order the higher courts were not limited as to the amount, but magistrates' courts could not make an order for a sum in excess of £100. The phrase used in the section is "such damages for injury or compensation for loss as the court thinks reasonable".

The power was used to a considerable extent in magistrates' courts in conjunction with probation but not so widely in the higher courts. Official figures have been summarised as follows:

> This power is used appreciably by magistrates' courts in cases where probation orders are made. In the ten years 1950–59, 33,458 orders under this section were made; this represented approximately 11·5 per cent. of the cases in which probation orders were made. . . . In the higher courts, orders under section 11(2) are less often made; the figures for the ten years referred to above were 1,184 orders, representing only 2·5 per cent. of the cases in which probation orders were made.[1]

It is pointed out in the White Paper from which this passage is quoted that the power under s. 11(2) is not limited to compensation for personal injury but includes compensation for loss and it is suggested that most of the orders were in fact made in respect of loss of property or damage to it.

Another power existed under the Criminal Law Act 1826 to order the payment of compensation to persons (whether injured or not) who have been active in the apprehension of certain offenders or to the families of persons killed trying to apprehend

---

1. Report of the Working Party on Compensation for Victims of Crimes of Violence, Cmnd. 1406, p. 2, para. 5.

an offender, but this power is rarely used. There were 26 persons who were thus compensated in the years 1950–1959.[2]

Three statutes[3] empowered the courts to order an offender to pay reparation for loss of property (but not for personal injury):

1. The Forfeiture Act 1870, s. 4, and the Magistrates' Courts Act 1952, s. 34, empowered the courts, on the application of any person aggrieved, to order a person convicted of felony to pay compensation not exceeding £100 for any loss of property suffered through, or by means of, the felony.

Since the Criminal Law Act 1967, this power has been extended, as the abolition of felony made it essential to amend it, and the Criminal Law Revision Committee had recommended that extension.[4] The power now conferred by the Criminal Law Act 1967,[5] is wider than the previous power, in the following respects:

(i) it applies to any indictable offence (previously only to persons convicted of felony);

(ii) it applies to damage to property as well as to loss, but does not include loss or damage due to an accident arising out of the presence of a motor vehicle on a road;

(iii) the maximum amount of compensation which may be ordered is raised from £100 to £400.

It is not yet clear how far the enhanced powers given to courts to order compensation will in fact be used.

2. The Criminal Justice Administration Act 1914, s. 14, empowers a magistrates' court to order a person convicted of committing wilful or malicious damage to property of the value of not more than £20 to pay reasonable compensation for the damage.

3. The Riot (Damages) Act 1886 gives a right to claim compensation out of the police rate to persons who suffer loss as a result of damage to, or theft of, their property by rioters.

---

2. *Ibid.*
3. Conveniently summarised in the same White Paper, p. 2.
4. Criminal Law Revision Committee, Seventh Report, Felonies and Misdemeanours, Cmnd. 2659, May 1965, pp. 20–21, para. 78.
5. Criminal Law Act 1967, Sched. 2, para. 9.

This has been invoked occasionally in modern times by persons who have suffered loss as a result of the riotous behaviour of football crowds.

STATE COMPENSATION FOR VICTIMS OF CRIMES
OF VIOLENCE

In the 1950s pressure grew for the state to set up a scheme of compensation for victims of crimes of violence. The original proposal no doubt stemmed from an idea put forward by the late Miss Margery Fry in 1954 for a scheme of compensation by the state, possibly along the lines of the industrial injuries scheme.[6] The matter was raised in Parliament, and in the 1959–1960 session a Private Member's Bill, the Criminal Injuries (Compensation) Bill, was introduced by Mr. R. E. Prentice, M.P., but without success. In February 1959 a Working Party of civil servants was set up by the then Home Secretary (Mr. R. A. Butler) and this Committee reported in June 1961.[7] A number of independent studies were published, including the Report of a Conservative Party Committee, in July 1962,[8] and a Committee of JUSTICE, in April 1962.[9]

A debate in the House of Lords on 5 December 1962 examined the various possibilities, and several speakers preferred the idea of an *ex gratia* payment to the establishment of new legal rights.[10] The Government of New Zealand introduced a statutory scheme of compensation in 1964 and since then several United States jurisdictions have followed suit. In March 1964 a White Paper[11] announced the establishment by the Home Office of a non-statutory scheme, administered by the Victims of Crimes of Violence Compensation Board, a committee of eight experienced lawyers (originally five) together with a lawyer as chairman, who would deal with the applications for compensation and make decisions about the awards.

Since the introduction of this scheme in August 1964, over £4,000,000 of public money has been distributed in com-

---

6. Enid Huws Jones, *Margery Fry, The Essential Amateur*, 1966, chapter XVII.
7. Cmnd. 1406, June 1961. This was a somewhat negative and discouraging Report.
8. *Victims of Violence*. A Report on compensation for injuries through crimes of violence, July 1962, Conservative Political Centre, pamphlet Number 261.
9. *Compensation for Victims of Crimes of Violence*. A Report by JUSTICE, 1962.
10. House of Lords Debates, Vol. 245, col. 245, 5 December 1962.
11. Compensation for Victims of Crimes of Violence, Cmnd. 2323, March 1964.

pensation to victims of crimes of violence; in 1968 the annual figure reached a total of over £1,500,000, and nearly 6,000 cases were dealt with and resolved. Various adjustments have been made to the working of the scheme in the light of experience. Some difficult problems have been encountered, but on the whole the general opinion is one of considerable satisfaction with the operation of the scheme. Nearly 60 per cent. of the awards fall in the £100–£399 bracket, but in many cases awards of thousands of pounds are made, and occasionally an award of £10,000 or more. Police and their dependants have been included in the scheme. There are safeguards against claims of a fraudulent nature, and the amount of an award may be reduced where there was provocation or contributory negligence on the part of the victim. Where the injury was caused by someone who is technically not responsible in the eyes of the law such as an infant or insane person, no awards were possible at first, but the scheme has since been modified to permit awards in such circumstances. Claims arising out of domestic strife and gang warfare are excluded as well as road accidents. The average cost of compensation per case is said to be between £300 and £400.[12] An amended scheme was adopted in May 1969 and is reprinted in the Fifth Report of the work of the Board.[13]

Lawyers who act for the police have expressed some dissatisfaction with the procedure, having encountered certain difficulties over proving their client's claims. The press would like to see the proceedings of the Board given wider publicity, and have urged that provision should be made for reasonable and adequate reporting of the cases which come before the Board.[14]

MAKING THE OFFENDER PAY

One of the anomalies highlighted by the working of this scheme is the discrepancy between the injuries received by the

---

12. See Cyril E. S. Horsford, "The Criminal Injuries Compensation Board: Its Work and Scope", [1966] Crim.L.R. 356 (July 1966); "The Criminal Injuries Compensation Board 1966–1967", [1968] Crim.L.R. 3 (January 1968); "The Criminal Injuries Compensation Board 1967–1968", [1969] Crim.L.R. 3 (January 1969).
13. Criminal Injuries Compensation Board, Fifth Report, Cmnd. 4179, October 1969.
14. *The Times*, 12 November 1968, Letter by Mr. W. G. Ridd.

victim, as reflected in the awards made by the Board, and the penalties imposed by the Courts in punishment of the offender. A recent instance quoted in a legal journal[15] involved a man of 58 who was knocked down by another as he was walking home after spending an evening at a club. He received serious injuries, was in hospital for three months, and received an award of £750 from the Board. His assailant was prosecuted and fined £5. This brings us to the very understandable but slightly different question how to prevent offenders from enjoying the profits of their crime. Assuming they are caught, tried and convicted, the matter depends in the first instance on the courts, who have power to order the payment of fines, and to make compensation orders and orders for restitution and orders as to payment of costs. It may not be possible to secure through these measures that no criminal benefits financially from his crimes. The conventional amounts of fines are small, the use made of the powers to order compensation or restitution limited, and costs of the prosecution are rarely ordered to be paid by a convicted offender. If the offender is given a custodial sentence, the question whether he can be expected to pay something out of his earnings in prison towards the compensation of the victim is hardly a realistic one, as long as the rates of pay inside our penal institutions remain nominal (at present no more than 33*s.* a week for work done as a prisoner). The hostel schemes do provide opportunities for prisoners to work as free men in the outside community at full wages, which are then subject to deductions towards the cost of maintenance of the prisoner and possibly his family, and a small allowance is made towards the cost of meals out and other expenses, and the prisoner is allowed a small amount of pocket money. After all these items are taken into account, there cannot be much room for the setting aside of a weekly sum by way of compensation to the victim. (See Chapter 11: Release.) Particularly in the case of large property crimes, the weekly obligation could be large and onerous unless the prisoner has access to the loot. If he has, then it can be seized and ordered to be returned to its owners. (See Restitution, below.)

The alternative solution which has been canvassed is to have

---

15. *Law Guardian*, No. 42, November 1968, p. 7. J. P. McBrien, "Crime and Punishment—A Case for Concern", *Law Guardian*, No. 48, May 1969, pp. 21 *et seq.*

the convicted offender made the subject of bankruptcy proceedings. If he were adjudged bankrupt on account of his proved inability to pay for the damage or loss suffered by the victim, it is claimed, this would prevent his being able to profit from his crimes since the whole of his financial transactions would become amenable to the intervention of the bankruptcy officials. Thus if he had transferred the property to his wife or other members of his family this could be seized and brought into account to meet the obligations. In this way, a train robber's wife could not be provided for by the offender with any degree of permanence, although she might herself not have committed any offence such as assisting the husband to escape. It appears not to be the practice to institute criminal proceedings against the wife of a criminal where there is no evidence that the wife has taken part in the crime for which the husband has been convicted, even though by continuing to live with the husband after the crime she may have been enjoying the illegal proceeds.[16]

These ideas concerning the use of bankruptcy procedure were mooted in the Committee stage of the Criminal Justice Bill, but were withdrawn.[17] They have been revived in a modest form in the Bow Group pamphlet on "The Treatment of Offenders", but there the suggestion is merely to use the order in bankruptcy against defendants who wilfully refuse to pay fines, and only for sums of over £50 owed to the court.

"The advantage of this is quite simply that the defaulting offender would be subject to all the limitations of bankruptcy, and in an increasingly credit-based society, it might well encourage him to pay the fine. It could be objected that the man who refuses to pay a fine is hardly likely to observe the terms of a bankruptcy order, but this would be noted by the trade protection societies so that he would find it much more difficult to obtain any goods on credit."[18]

---

16. *The Times*, 25 February 1969.
17. A Clause giving the criminal courts power to make a receiving order in certain cases when sentencing an offender was proposed by Dr. Winstanley but defeated. Parliamentary Debates, House of Commons, Standing Committee A, Criminal Justice Bill, Nineteenth Sitting, 22 March 1967, cols. 1133 *et seq*. The Law Society had made certain proposals on the subject to the Royal Commission on the Penal System in July 1965 and in February 1966. The matter was referred by the Home Secretary to the Advisory Council on the Penal System.
18. The Treatment of Offenders, A Bow Group Pamphlet, Conservative Political Centre, Pamphlet Number 388, March 1968.

RESTITUTION ORDERS

(a) Under the Theft Act 1968

Since the Theft Act 1968 the question of restitution of property following conviction for crime may be determined by a new form of summary procedure, where goods have been stolen. There are several prerequisites before the court may exercise its powers under s. 28:

1. Good must have been stolen;
2. A person must have been convicted of an offence with reference to the theft (whether or not the stealing is the gist of his offence);
3. The person must have been convicted by the court which now exercises the power under s. 28;
4. Under s. 28(1) (*b*) and (*c*), the court must only act on the application of the person entitled to recover from the person convicted.

The powers are as follows:

(i) To order anyone having possession or control of the goods to restore them to any person entitled to recover them from him.

As Professor J. C. Smith has observed, this enables the court to order a *bona fide* purchaser to surrender the goods to another with a better title.[19] Unlike the position under the previous law, conviction in no circumstances affects the title to goods, which must be decided according to the rules of the civil law. If courts are unsure about this question of title, it is better not to make an order, but "when the relevant facts do sufficiently appear, an order should generally be made unless there is a real dispute as to the title to the goods".[20]

(ii) To order the person convicted to deliver or transfer to a person who has applied to the court, and is entitled to recover from him, any other goods which represent the goods stolen directly or indirectly (as being the proceeds of any disposal or realisation of the whole or part of them).

(iii) To order that a sum not exceeding the value of the goods stolen shall be paid to a person who has

---

19. J. C. Smith, *The Law of Theft*, 1968, p. 169. See also J. K. Macleod, "Restitution Under Theft Act 1968", [1968] Crim.L.R. 577.
20. J. C. Smith, *op. cit.*, p. 170.

applied to the court, and who, if the goods were in the possession of the person convicted would be entitled to recover them from him, this sum to be paid out of any money which was taken out of the possession of the person convicted on his apprehension.

Again, the same rule applies that the court should only make orders if it is satisfied about the entitlement of the applicant.

Section 28 (4) provides that:

"The court shall not exercise the powers conferred by this section unless in the opinion of the court the relevant facts sufficiently appear from the evidence given at the trial or the available documents, together with admissions made by or on behalf of any person in connection with any proposed exercise of the powers."

Section 28(3) goes further than s. 28(1) in that it confers power on the court, wherever it makes an order under para. (*a*) of s. 28(1), and the goods have to be restored to the owner, to order that the purchaser of the goods or lender of money on the security of them, who has acted in good faith, shall be compensated out of any money of the person convicted which was taken out of his possession on his apprehension. But no more may be ordered to be paid than the amount of the purchase by the applicant or the amount owed to the applicant in respect of the loan.

Orders made under s. 24 may be appealed against to the Court of Appeal, but leave of the court will be necessary, as in the case of an appeal against sentence. The operation of an order for restitution under s. 24 is suspended for twenty-eight days unless the court directs otherwise and the title to the property is not in dispute.

(b) Under the Police (Property) Act 1897

Similar powers are conferred on magistrates' courts by the Police (Property) Act 1897, with the difference that here, after six months has expired from the making of an order, any person's right to bring legal proceedings to recover the property shall cease. Professor Smith has observed that the 1897 Act "may interfere in a rather arbitrary fashion with the rights at civil law, even of persons who are unaware that the proceedings are taking place" and in general he considers that it would be better to use the powers under the Theft Act 1968.[1]

---

1. J. C. Smith, *The Law of Theft*, 1968, p. 171.

PART V

Offenders under Twenty-one

CHAPTER 21

Prison

Both penal reformers and prison administrators have long recognised that prison is not a suitable place for young offenders. This realisation has led to parallel developments: on the one hand, the introduction of several important non-custodial methods for the treatment of offenders under 21, such as probation, attendance centres and the like; on the other hand, the attempt to transform the custodial experiences of the young offender into a theoretically non-punitive and positive régime such as borstal training is intended to provide, or, where punishment is still one of the aims, to link the experience of custody with training in a more hopeful environment. For the very young, imprisonment has been almost entirely superseded by an educational régime in a relatively non-punitive milieu such as is provided by the approved school system. We shall begin by describing the custodial methods used in dealing with offenders under 21, then examine the non-custodial methods.

Since 1908, children under 14 have not been committed to prison as a sentence, though they might be held there on remand.[1] The minimum age of imprisonment as a sentence was raised to 15 in 1948 and to 17 where magistrates' courts were concerned.[2] In 1961 the minimum age for a sentence of imprisonment was raised to 17 for all courts.[3] This change in the law came into effect on 1 August 1963.[4]

The number of sentenced male prisoners under the age of 21 in custody at the end of 1967 was 1,070.[5] Receptions under sentence of imprisonment of persons under 21 years of age totalled 3,493 males and 169 females.[6] In proportion to the

---

1. The Children Act 1908.
2. Criminal Justice Act 1948, s. 17(1).
3. Criminal Justice Act 1961, s. 2(2).
4. Criminal Justice Act 1961, (Commencement No. 2 Order), S.I. 1961 No. 1672, operative 1 August 1963.
5. Prison Department Report, 1967, p. 18.
6. Prison Department, Statistical Tables, 1967, Table C.10, p. 16.

population in the age group, male receptions into prison have been mounting in recent years, having nearly doubled since 1958 in the age-group 16–21, and the situation in the age group 14 and under 16 is no better.

RECEPTIONS INTO PRISON IN RELATION TO THE POPULATION
IN THE AGE GROUP (MALES) PER 100,000
(ENGLAND & WALES)

Year	Aged 14 and under 16	Aged 16 and under 21	Aged 21 and over
1958	57	420	203
1967	97	785	275

Source: Prison Department Statistical Tables, 1967, Table C.2, p. 6.

There has not been a corresponding increase in female receptions in these age groups.

PRISON AS A REMAND OR STAGING POST

Prison is still extensively used for remanding young persons in custody, so that despite the measures adopted to limit the use of imprisonment for young persons as a sentence, many young persons experience imprisonment on remand. In 1967 nearly 11,000 males under 21 and 1,383 females were received in prison other than under sentence.[7] The figures include some young persons between 14 and 17 who are committed to await removal to an approved school, and some who are remanded in custody pending trial but detained in prison because they are too unruly or depraved to be detained in a remand home. The figures for these two categories are as follows:

1967	Male	Female
Committed to await removal to approved school.	234	32
Committed on remand as being so unruly or depraved as to be unsuitable for detention in a remand home.	644	74

Source: Prison Department, Statistical Tables, 1967, Table C.12, p. 18.

7. Prison Department, Statistical Tables, 1967, Table C.11, p. 17.

There are in addition large numbers of young offenders received into prison each year under sentence who are not intended to serve a sentence of imprisonment at all but have been sentenced to borstal training and are waiting for a place. In addition a small number of offenders under 17 are convicted of serious offences and detained in prison under the Secretary of State's direction under the Children and Young Persons Act 1933, s. 53. The figures for these three groups remanded into prison *under the age of 17* are as follows (no figures are available for those *over 17* committed to prison to await removal to borstal):

1967	Male	Female
Sentenced to borstal training and committed to await removal	573	14
Detained during Her Majesty's Pleasure under the Secretary of State's direction	1	—
Detained for specified period under the Secretary of State's direction	3	—

Source: Prison Department, Statistical Tables, 1967, Table C.12, p. 18.

It must be borne in mind in interpreting these figures that since 1961 a network of remand centres has been opened to provide an alternative to prison for cases of young offenders remanded in custody. A few of these, like Risley, have been specially built for this purpose. For the rest, the facilities cannot be said to be ideal, and in some cases, as at Ashford, Middlesex, the buildings are extremely unsatisfactory. Moreover, the circumstances of detention are so similar to prison that it is hard to see the difference. One can say that even if these young people cannot claim to have seen the inside of one of the old fortress type prisons, they must have formed a pretty good idea what it is like to be a prisoner. Whether or not this is a beneficial experience is a moot point.

PRISON AS A SENTENCE

In 1958 the Prison Commissioners put forward proposals for revising the methods of dealing with young offenders between the ages of 16 and 21. These were submitted for approval to the

Advisory Council on the Treatment of Offenders, and the Council reported in July 1959. A White Paper called The Treatment of Young Offenders embodied its comments.[8]

There were three principal proposals:

1. To develop the system of detention centres to a point where it could replace short-term imprisonment (*i.e.* for six months or less) for young offenders;

2. To extend the principle of the indeterminate sentence, which already existed in the borstal sentence, to all young offenders for whom a court wished to provide a period of detention of between six months and two years;

3. To prohibit courts from sentencing young offenders under 21 to imprisonment unless they considered that a sentence of at least three years would be appropriate.

The Advisory Council agreed with the proposals in principle but made various detailed observations and recommendations. They considered certain criticisms which might be made of these proposals, and reached the conclusion that they were not well-founded. These included the objection that the courts would be deprived of the power to pass sentences of imprisonment in certain cases, and that the proposed methods of treatment would be regarded as too soft to provide an adequate punishment and deterrent. In the case of a young person sentenced to a custodial sentence, the Report makes the claim that in most cases such a youth requires training if he is to be diverted from crime:

"his sentence should . . . be related primarily to that need and he should be detained long enough for adequate training to be given. . . . This period cannot usually be judged before the sentence begins."

This justified in the Council's view the extension of the principle of the borstal sentence to new categories of young offender. Hitherto youths sentenced to imprisonment were allocated to a young prisoners' centre, where the régime was not very different from that found at a closed borstal institution. There would be advantages in merging the two forms of sentence, under the name of "borstal training".

---

8. Home Office, Report of the Advisory Council on the Treatment of Offenders, The Treatment of Young Offenders, 1959.

The problem of the persistent offender would be tackled best, in the Council's opinion, by providing that the courts should be empowered to impose a determinate sentence of not less than eighteen months' imprisonment, instead of ordering a further term of borstal training. This was eventually done by the Criminal Justice Act 1961, which also enacted the other proposals.

We shall discuss the Advisory Council's views about short sentences of detention (six months or less) in conjunction with the subject of Detention Centres.

It remains to mention that similar changes in the penal treatment of girls and young women in the sentence structure were thought to be appropriate.[9] Also it should be noted that the Advisory Council made certain very important recommendations concerning after-care following a sentence of borstal training under the new provisions. This should be provided for two years from the date of release, with the proviso that after one year the situation would be reviewed with a view to cancelling the licence where continued supervision is no longer considered necessary. This recommendation was eventually incorporated in the Criminal Justice Act 1961.[10]

Apart from detention centre sentences, sentences of imprisonment for six months or less are still possible for young offenders under 21. But, as we have already seen, the intention was to develop the system of detention centres to the point where it would be possible to ban any other kind of custodial sentence for six months or less. The Act of 1961 gives the Home Secretary power to make an order to this effect.[11] This has not been done, although the number of detention centres was increased to nearly twenty by the end of 1967.

The result is that many young offenders are received for short sentences of imprisonment. The Prison Department normally requires the segregation of young offenders from adults.[12] Since a reorganisation in 1965, youths serving sen-

---

9. See pp. 8 and 26 of the Report.
10. Criminal Justice Act 1961, s. 11(2).
11. Criminal Justice Act 1961, s. 3(5).
12. This was laid down in the Prison Rules 1949, r. 9(2), but the revised version adopted in 1964 simply requires prisoners to be classified, "in accordance with any directions of the Secretary of State, having regard to their age", and certain other criteria. It still remains true to say, as Sir Lionel Fox said, that it is a matter of course that young prisoners under twenty-one will be separated from all other categories (Fox, p. 141).

tences of over eighteen months are allocated to Aylesbury, Liverpool or Northallerton on a regional basis. Those serving less than six months are allocated (wherever possible) on a similar regional basis to Wormwood Scrubs, Ashford or Stafford, though many of these short-term prisoners, we are informed, in fact serve their sentences in local prisons. Some relief has been provided by allowing prison governors to reclassify the more mature and criminally sophisticated young prisoners as adults.[13]

The probation and after-care service is responsible for the supervision and after-care of young prisoners on release. This category of prisoners has always been released on licence and this arrangement continues.[14]

Some research carried out by Sir George Benson sought to compare the results of imprisonment of young persons with borstal training.[15] He found that there was little difference in terms of the reconviction rate between these two methods of disposal. The records of 300 youths discharged from the young prisoners' centre at Lewes in 1952 were used for this purpose. The technique employed was the application to these prisoners, on the basis of their personal records, of the Mannheim/Wilkins prediction scale developed in relation to borstal training,[16] and a comparison of the expected (or predicted) success rate of the different risk groups with the actual success rate. Sir George Benson summarises the results as follows:

> "the result of classifying Y.P.'s on the Mannheim–Wilkins basis is that in each of the groups the success rate coincides surprisingly closely with the success rates in the Mannheim–Wilkins Borstal tables. The only conclusion to be drawn from this was that imprisonment at Lewes gave results as good as those of Borstal training."[17]

Because the Lewes population was not entirely a random sample, cases which appeared to be less promising having been transferred to Stafford prison, it was decided to check the Lewes results by a similar analysis of the Stafford population, and also to prepare a table combining the outcome in both

---

13. Prison Department Report, 1965, Cmnd. 3088, August 1966, pp. 28–29.
14. See the Criminal Justice Act 1948, 6th Sched.
15. Sir George Benson, "Prediction Methods and Young Prisoners" (January 1959), 9 *B.J.D.*, pp. 192 *et seq.*
16. H. Mannheim and Leslie T. Wilkins, *Prediction Methods in Relation to Borstal Training.*
17. P. 194, 1955.

prisons. The results were still much the same. Sir George Benson claims that because the time spent in borstal training is very much longer than the prison sentence involved here, the imprisonment of young offenders must be regarded as considerably more efficient than Borstal. The results of this research are claimed to be disturbing, and to require further investigation.

One comment which we may make is that the research simply demonstrates the validity of the Mannheim–Wilkins prediction table when applied to a population of young prisoners. It does not demonstrate the effectiveness of the treatment programme itself. For all that appears, both borstal training and imprisonment of young offenders may be said to to be equally ineffective. Any judgment of the comparative value of the two treatment programmes is not possible by the use of these prediction tables.

Another point is that it is now recognised that "these results are probably mainly due to unsophisticated research methods which fail adequately to take account of real differences in the types of offenders given different treatments".[18] The work of the Grants and Stuart Adams in California has shown that the overall results of two treatments may be similar, but the treatments could each have successes and failures with different types of offenders.

Nigel Walker appears to regard the results of Sir George Benson's research as showing that:

> "Either borstal and prison are equally effective individual deterrents for males of this age range, in which case the effort to supplement the deterrent effect by a process of socialisation was unsuccessful; or else borstals deterred a smaller percentage of their inmates than did prisons, but made up for this by socialising some of the others."[19]

The latter hypothesis is described as more encouraging but is subject to the slightly improbable supposition that by sheer coincidence there has been a mis-classification of offenders which exactly cancels out the positive success of one treatment over another. For further discussion of the supposed interchangeability of penal methods, which seems to be suggested by the first hypothesis (see Chapter 13: Results of Prison Custody and Other Measures).

18. Roger Hood, *Borstal Re-assessed*, 1965, p. 216.
19. Nigel Walker, *Crime and Punishment in Britain*, 2nd Edn., 1968, p. 255.

CHAPTER 22

Borstal Training

HISTORY OF BORSTAL TRAINING

Before 1908

The nineteenth-century response to the need to avoid sentencing young offenders to imprisonment was the development of the reformatories and industrial schools, the forerunners of the modern approved school. Tobias has shown what a beneficial effect the introduction of these institutions appears to have had on the crime situation.[1] Many young offenders were still committed to prison, however, and there they were given special treatment and kept apart from adult prisoners. Parkhurst was originally used for such offenders, but the reformatory schools replaced it.[2] By the time of the Gladstone Committee's inquiry in 1895 there were still many young prisoners, a sizeable number being under the age of 16.[3]

The Gladstone Committee thought the minimum age should be raised to 17 but it was many years before this was done.[4] The Committee expressed great interest in the age group 16–21, and recommended "that the experiment of establishing a penal reformatory under Government management should be tried". This should be available for offenders under the age of 23, who would be committed "for periods of not less than one year and up to three years, with a system of licences graduated according to sentence, which should be freely exercised". What was envisaged was a sort of half-way house between the prison and the reformatory, with a staff capable of giving sound education and training and exercising "the best and healthiest kind of moral influence".[5]

The model for this development was undoubtedly the

---

1. J. J. Tobias, *Crime and Industrial Society in the 19th Century*, 1967, pp. 214–215.
2. Fox, p. 329.
3. *Ibid.*
4. *Ibid.*, p. 330.
5. *Ibid.*, pp. 330–331.

American penal reformatory, such as the one which had been founded in 1876 in New York State at Elmira, under the influence of Z. R. Brockway. This catered for the age group 16–30. In 1897 Sir Evelyn Ruggles-Brise, the new chairman of the Prison Commission, visited the United States to study the working of the American reformatory system. On his return he started the first experiments in this direction with young prisoners aged 16–21 drawn from London prisons.[6] At first, the prison at Bedford was used for this purpose. In 1902 the old convict prison outside Rochester, Kent, near the village of Borstal became the site of an experiment which made the name of the village famous wherever penal systems are studied and discussed. This was the origin of the borstal system. It was intended for what were called "juvenile adults" with sufficient time to serve to make it possible for them to benefit from this régime.[7] Here was applied something like that which we now know as borstal training—hard physical work, plenty of technical and educational instruction, a strong moral atmosphere (but not so strong as to be stifling) and a system of grades with increasing privileges as one progressed through towards discharge. Release would be under licence and adequate after-care would be provided.

The Prevention of Crime Act 1908

The borstal system was recognised by law in the Prevention of Crime Act 1908, the Bill being introduced by Mr. Herbert Samuel (later Lord Samuel) who was at the time a junior minister at the Home Office. He it was who suggested the name Borstal Institution in preference to the more cumbersome description "juvenile–adult reformatory"[8]—the phrase "borstal training" has endured and become so much a part of the English penal thinking that it is no longer spelled with capital letters, even in the statutes.

The Act of 1908, as amended by the Act of 1914, provided that persons aged 16–21, who had been convicted of indictable offences punishable with imprisonment, could be sent by the

---

6. In fact the first experiment was in Bedford prison, to which eight young prisoners from London prisons were transferred, there to be given separate training. See Roger Hood, *Borstal Re-assessed*, 1965, p. 14.
7. Fox, p. 332.
8. *Ibid.*, p. 335.

courts to borstal training for a period of not less than two years nor more than three years, to be followed by one year under supervision. There was power to release a youth after six months, a girl after three months.[9]

The first two borstals were in the old prison buildings, at Borstal and Portland. The third was in an old industrial school at Feltham, Middlesex. The premises were adapted for the purpose. For girls, provision was made within the old prison at Aylesbury, where the former State Inebriate Reformatory provided suitable premises inside the perimeter. Mary Size has given us a good picture of the atmosphere at Aylesbury in its early days as a girls' borstal institution.[10] Sir John Watson has recently described the borstal system of the nineteen-thirties and the impact on it made by that remarkable man Sir Alexander Paterson.[11] In 1930 a new borstal for boys opened at Lowdham Grange, in Nottinghamshire, after Colonel Llewellin had marched his boys from Feltham to camp in the grounds and build their own institution.

By the outbreak of World War II there were nine borstals for boys and Aylesbury for the girls. A recall centre was established for boys in a wing at Wormwood Scrubs prison. The war shattered the borstal system and dispersed the staff. Many of the boys were released into the armed services. After the war, there were difficulties in re-establishing borstal traditions, with many new staff and with a more difficult and criminally sophisticated population of inmates. An enormous rise in the number of intakes necessitated rapid expansion of the system. In the early 'thirties receptions were under 2,000 per annum. By the end of 1938 the population in the male institutions had already reached over 2,100.[12] Receptions during 1948 once more reached very nearly the same figure, and in the 1950s rapidly surpassed it. By 1958 receptions had passed 3,000 per annum. By 1968 they had passed the 6,000 mark.[13]

By 1950 there were, in addition to the two reception centres, 13 institutions for training boys, together with a correctional

9. *Ibid.*
10. Mary Size, *Prisons I have Known*, 1957, especially Chapters Two, Three and Four.
11. John A. F. Watson, *Which is the Justice?*, 1969, chapter IV, "Alec Paterson and Borstal Memories".
12. Fox, p. 365.
13. See Prison Department Report, 1967, Cmnd. 3774, October 1968, p. 14.

borstal and a recall centre. By 1960 there were 19 training borstals and the correctional borstal at Reading and the recall centre at Portsmouth. By 1968 there were 24 borstals for boys and 4 borstals for girls. It must be accepted that the problems which faced the borstal system in the 1950s and the 1960s were different in scale and substance from those which were faced in the foundation years of the system and in the 1930s.

The philosophy of the borstal system had been laid down in this early period and was clearly enunciated by Sir Alexander Paterson in 1932 in characteristically positive terms, which are reflected in the Borstal Rules. Basically they required the staff to treat each lad as an individual, a living organism with a life and character of his own. "The task is not to break or knead him into shape, but to stimulate some power within to regulate conduct aright." The system of training must be "based on progressive trust demanding increasing personal decision, responsibility, and self-control. These are qualities which can only be attained by practising them."[14] The conditions in borstal must be as unlike those in prison as is compatible with compulsory detention. They must be various and elastic to suit different characters and different stages of development. Borstals were organised on a house basis in order to generate strong group loyalties. Each house would have an assistant governor in charge who would provide leadership and set the standard for the boys, as well as carrying out a kind of case-work role, attending to their different problems. There is little doubt that this system achieved a considerable degree of success in the 'thirties. Its history in the 'fifties and 'sixties is less encouraging, and it is possible that new methods must be found to deal with the problems facing us today, and that the traditional methods have outlived their usefulness. Before elaborating on this theme we must trace the legal history of the borstal system from 1948 to the present day.

The Criminal Justice Act 1948

This Act replaced the provisions of the 1908 Act in relation to borstal training.[15] (This is the phrase now used in preference

---

14. Fox, pp. 356, 357 quoting from *The Principles of the Borstal System*, written in 1932 by Alexander Paterson.
15. See Criminal Justice Act 1948, s. 20.

to the 1908 Act's "Borstal detention".) Courts no longer had to specify whether they were ordering a maximum period of detention of two or three years. The maximum period of detention was now fixed at three years, the minimum period at nine months. There was no difference for boys and girls. After release there was supervision until the expiration of four years from the date of sentence. A person could be recalled during this period and detained until the expiration of the original three years or for six months from the date of his being retaken, whichever is the later. Only the higher courts (assizes or quarter sessions) could order borstal training, but provision was made for a magistrates' court which considered that borstal training might be appropriate to commit the offender to a higher court for this sentence to be considered.[16]

The Criminal Justice Act 1961

In his White Paper of February 1959, the then Home Secretary (Mr. R. A. Butler) outlined certain proposals for dealing with young offenders, which involved alterations in the borstal system. These proposals were referred to the Advisory Council on the Treatment of Offenders, which reported favourably on them in July 1959. They were then incorporated in a Bill which became the Criminal Justice Act 1961.

We have already described the main proposal, which was to integrate borstal training and imprisonment so far as terms of intermediate length were concerned (six months to three years). (See Chapter 21: Prison.)

We must now note the changes made in the borstal system. The most important of these was the substitution for the term of training of nine months to three years previously prescribed the term of six months to two years' borstal training. The period of licence and supervision is also amended, and becomes instead of licence to the end of the fourth year, as previously, a period of two years from the date of release.[17] This may be modified or cancelled at any time in the light of progress of the offender where he has made a good adjustment after release. A person

---

16. Criminal Justice Act 1948, s. 20(3), repealed by the Magistrates' Courts Act 1952, 6th Sched. See now Magistrates' Courts Act 1952, s. 28, which replaced the previous section.
17. Criminal Justice Act 1961, s. 11(1); Prison Act 1952, s. 45, as amended by the Criminal Justice Act 1961, s. 11(2). See 6th Sched. for effect of these changes on the enactments relating to borstal training.

failing after a previous sentence of imprisonment of not less than six months or borstal training may be sentenced to imprisonment for eighteen months or more, if it is thought appropriate.[18] Otherwise courts are debarred from sentencing a young person to imprisonment between 6 months and 3 years. Any sentence in this range must be a sentence of borstal training.[19] Sentences of three years or more may be imposed for serious offences. For the present, sentences of up to six months' imprisonment may also be imposed. The minimum age for borstal training was lowered from 16 to 15 years of age.[20] The Children and Young Persons Act 1969 raised it again to 17.[1]

Since the Act of 1961, administrative changes in the organisation of after-care have affected the borstal system. The old arrangement was that a Borstal Division of after-care existed under the aegis of the Central After-Care Association (a state body). The C.A.C.A. having been abolished, the work of supervising borstal after-care fell to the newly established probation and after-care division of the Home Office. But a separate borstal pre-release unit of the Prison Department was created "with the primary function of ensuring that common practice and procedure are followed in pre-release planning in boys' borstals and supervising the extension of the new arrangement for pre-release planning to all borstals".[2]

THE MODERN BORSTAL SYSTEM

Reception

For many years in the 1950s, a sophisticated classification and allocation procedure was followed with all male receptions to borstal training.[3] They were sent to one of two Reception Centres, either Wormwood Scrubs (where a separate wing houses borstal boys) or Latchmere House, near Kingston, Surrey. Here for a period of six weeks or so they were intensively studied by a team of medical, psychological and social workers. Educational and vocational guidance tests were administered,

---

18. Criminal Justice Act 1961, s. 3(3).
19. Criminal Justice Act 1961, s. 3(1).
20. Criminal Justice Act 1961, s. 1(1).
1. Children and Young Persons Act 1969, s. 7(1).
2. Prison Department Report, 1967, Cmnd. 3774, October 1968, p. 17.
3. See R. L. Morrison, "Borstal Allocation" (October 1957), 8 *B.J.D.*, No. 2, p. 95.

and the end result was to report to a classification and allocation board, which then decided on the training borstal to which the boy should be sent. This decision would depend on the boy's personality, emotional and physical maturity and intelligence, and his training needs. Some regard was also paid to considerations of geographical convenience from the point of view of his being visited by his parents, etc. Also the kind of trade or occupational training available at the borstal was considered. Above all, there was the question whether he should go to a closed or open institution. There were eleven open and eight closed institutions for boys in the late nineteen-fifties. The number is now somewhat higher.

It is possible to exaggerate the importance of this classification and allocation stage, and the degree to which a scientific assessment can be made and its indications followed. But there is clearly some value in a period of reflection before borstal training is commenced. Many youths are found on reception to have quite serious personal problems which cannot await the arrival at a training borstal. Some are married, some are sick or addicted, some are in financial trouble, or have other problems which require immediate attention. There is much to be said for this period of allocation, involving close and highly professional personal attention, before the training period begins. Alas, the 1960s saw Latchmere House converted into a detention centre, and all reception and allocation of borstal inmates concentrated in Wormwood Scrubs and Manchester prisons. The period of the allocation stage was cut to three weeks or so. There is therefore less time to do a thorough job.

THE TRAINING BORSTALS

We have witnessed a proliferation of borstal institutions in the modern period. Some are completely new establishments like Everthorpe in Yorkshire and Onley, the new Recall Centre near Rugby opened in December 1968 to replace Reading and Portsmouth, and the secure girls' borstal at Bullwood Hall in Essex. There has developed within the open borstals a considerable variety of training programmes. Pollington based itself on an intensive counselling and "therapeutic community" programme; Hewell Grange on individual case-work methods. A very sophisticated and complicated piece of research known as the Borstal Controlled Treatment Research Project has sought to compare the effectiveness of these two types of borstal training with the traditional training programme carried out at Morton Hall. The aim here is to test the comparative effectiveness of these different programmes in terms of outcome. Other studies are being made of techniques of classification and allocation.[4]

One constantly recurring theme in recent reports of the Prison Department about the borstal system has been the decline in the quality of receptions and the increase in the proportion of really difficult cases. Thus the 1960 Report[5] states that the lads committed to borstal training are worse risks than those who were committed in the years immediately after the war. This observation is based on a comparison of receptions in 1958 with the years 1946 and 1947, taking as a guide the proportion with poor prediction scores judged by the Mannheim–Wilkins prediction tables.[6] In 1961 we read that "more boys were received who needed training in closed conditions and the decline in quality, as measured by the Mannheim–Wilkins prediction ratings persisted".[7] By 1963 over two-thirds of those boys received into borstal were in the low-risk groups, according to an analysis of their prediction scores.[8] In 1965 a borstal Governor reported "we have been trying to help boys considerably more disturbed, with problems far less tractable and with much less respect for the need for good order than those we have trained in the past".[9] In 1964, 1965 and 1966 we find the first mentions of the problem of drug-taking among borstal receptions.

In 1967 "all reports from governors agree that receptions . . . included a larger proportion of disturbed and difficult boys than ever before".[10] So we can accept that not only are more youths being committed to borstal than at any time in the past, but of these a higher proportion are bad risks and present difficult if not hopeless problems in terms of training and rehabilitation.

---

4. See Aymeric Straker, "Current Research in the Prison Department, Home Office" (January 1968), 8 *B.J.C.*, No. 1, at pp. 53–54.
5. Report of the Commissioners of Prisons 1960, Cmnd. 1467, August 1961, p. 46.
6. H. Mannheim and Leslie Wilkins, *Prediction Methods in Relation to Borstal Training.*
7. Report of the Commissioners of Prisons, 1961, Cmnd. 1798, August 1962, p. 34.
8. Prison Department Report, 1963, Cmnd. 2381, June 1964, pp. 25–26.
9. Prison Department Report, 1965, Cmnd. 3088, August 1966, p. 20.
10. Prison Department Report, 1967, Cmnd. 3774, October 1968, p. 15.

The average length of time served by youths in borstal has varied over the years. It will be appreciated that there can be no set period of training followed by automatic discharge, and that the average period of training varies a good deal between institutions according to the type of youth received in each.[11]

The average over all the boys borstals in 1949 was 17·6 months. For girls it was 22 months at Aylesbury and 20 months at East Sutton Park. Since 1949 there has been a steady decline in the length of training for boys:

1956	..	..	..	20·3 months
1959	..	..	..	16·7 months
1961	..	..	..	15·6 months
1966	..	..	..	14 months

The Report of the Prison Department says that in order to achieve the acceleration of training in 1966:

> "all governors were encouraged to draw up a programme of training for each boy and to adopt a positive approach, asking themselves "How quickly can he be made fit for discharge?" rather than "How long must he serve?" As a result of this greater urgency more boys were sent out shortly after completing the minimum period of six months. Others, as in the past, needed to be kept for the major part of the maximum period of two years."[12]

It may well be concluded that the actual time inmates spent in borstal training has been reduced largely in response to pressures on accommodation and that this has occurred during a period when the quality of receptions dropped and a greater proportion of more difficult and recalcitrant youths were committed for borstal training.

The work programme

In 1962 the Advisory Council on the Employment of Prisoners issued a Report on Work and Vocational Training in Borstals in England and Wales.[13] This followed the earlier report on Work for Prisoners, which has already been described (see Chapter 9: Prison Work and Earnings). A separate report on the subject has been published by the Scottish Advisory Council on the Treatment of Offenders.

---

11. Fox, pp. 392–393.
12. Prison Department Report, 1966, Cmnd. 3408, October 1967, p. 15.
13. Home Office, Work and Vocational Training in Borstals (England and Wales). Report of the Advisory Council on the Employment of Prisoners, 1962.

The Council members visited most of the borstals and went into the question of work for borstal boys very thoroughly. They found that the conditions for work in borstals were very different from those in prisons.

"There is no shortage of borstal officers or of working space. In consequence borstal boys can be employed for a full normal working week and there are no immediate obstacles to the efficient organisation of vocational training and other employment."[14]

The Council were in no doubt that:

"work, in the sense of a steady, hard day's work at a productive or otherwise useful job, which is organised efficiently on modern industrial lines, is very helpful in turning borstal boys into good citizens."[15]

They went on to spell out the need to help boys acquire industrial skills which would enable them to fit into modern industrial society. The value of vocational training was recognised by the Council, which found that a considerable minority of borstal boys have the ability to learn a trade, and the vocational training courses have value in training boys in the use of tools and techniques, as well as in character training and generally interesting the boys in worthwhile work.

But there was room for improvement in the selection procedure for vocational training courses. The vocational guidance testers operating in the reception centres might well replace the present trade tests with general aptitude tests, on the ground that

"there must be some disadvantage in asking a boy at a reception centre what trade he would like to learn, giving him a test in it and then telling him sooner or later, that, though he may have been found suitable for a course in that trade, no such course is available in the borstal where he finds himself."[16]

The Council suggested, moreover, that some boys who are put in vocational training courses might have derived more benefit from some other form of industrial training. Although no attempt should be made to diminish the vocational training of boys with real ability to become skilled craftsmen, some types

---

14. P. 4, para. 7.
15. P. 6, para. 13.
16. P. 12, para. 39.

of boys who are at present given vocational training would benefit more from training in semi-skilled work.

> "There are many occupations which are not classed as skilled trades and do not make as great intellectual demands on trainees, but which are rewarding, well paid jobs involving a considerable degree of skill. Examples are the operation of mechanical plant, scaffolding, and steel bending. We recommend that consideration should be given to the introduction of training in such occupations where this would be practicable in borstals."[17]

The Council went on to observe that there is also much work involving simpler skills which boys can learn, including many of the semi-skilled operations in the building industry, and production work on modern machines in workshops. Training borstal boys in this manner would have relevance both to character training and to preparing them for subsequent employment upon release.

The Council had certain criticisms to make concerning the employment of boys on domestic cleaning, and made useful suggestions about the kitchen, laundry and hospital work, and farming and horticulture. Not much in the way of manufacturing work of the kind that forms the major prison industries was undertaken in borstals. There should be more of it, and it should be efficiently organised on modern industrial lines.

> "A thorough review of the pattern of industries in borstals should be undertaken in the light of our conclusions about the suitability of different types of work, the need for follow-up work for boys who have taken vocational training classes, and the development of training in semi-skilled work."[18]

One interesting suggestion was that borstal boys should be given simple handyman training, possibly in the evenings, "since it is nowadays a common necessity of domestic life to have some skill as a handyman".[19]

Steps are gradually being taken to implement the Council's recommendations. For example, recent visits to borstal institutions revealed that the vocational training progamme at Rochester borstal has been substantially modified, and there are evening courses in handyman's skills at Onley (the recall borstal). There is more effort to create a factory type situation.

---

17. P. 18, para. 68.
18. P. 25, para. 103.
19. P. 28, para. 112.

In the secure girls' borstal at Bullwood Hall there is plenty of work in the so-called factory which assembles small plastic toys, gift wrappings, pencil sets in plastic holders, etc. There is also a businesslike contract situation in the sewing-machine shop, where children's wigwams and cowboy clothes are assembled, and items of dolls' clothing as well as adult clothes are made. The industrial workshops at Onley, however, fall far short of what is desirable even in a recall centre and the existence of a traditional style prison mat-shop in a modern purpose-built borstal comes as something of a shocking surprise. Hollesley Bay takes pride in its breed of Suffolk Punch horses, and it is said many of the lads find great satisfaction in caring for animals. But if they are city dwellers this form of training is unlikely to be of any lasting value in terms of future employment, as the Advisory Council observed. The wholesale review of the work situation in borstal called for by the Council requires more than marginal improvements.

Other aspects of borstal training

It is not possible in the space available here to do justice to all the other facets of borstal training. The Prison Department Reports and other official papers must be left to speak for themselves, though the reader would do well to bear in mind such works of "fiction" as *The Loneliness of the Long-distance Runner*, and the writings of Brendan Behan and others.[20] There are also a number of more scholarly studies of borstal training, such as those of Healy and Alper, Gordon Rose and Roger Hood.[1]

A full discussion would require some reference to the special situation of the assistant governor in the borstal setting,[2] the work of the education staff, the group counselling in which many non-professional staff participate,[3] and the bold use of

---

20. Alan Sillitoe, *The Loneliness of the Long-distance Runner*, 1959; Brendan Behan, *Borstal Boy*, 1958; M. Benney, *Low Company*, 1936.
1. W. Healy and B. S. Alper, *Criminal Youth and the Borstal System*, 1940; A. G. Rose, *Five Hundred Borstal Boys*, 1954; W. A. Elkin and D. B. Kittermaster, "Borstal, A Critical Survey" 1950 (pamphlet); S. Barman, *The English Borstal System*, 1934; A. G. Rose, "The Sociological Analysis of Borstal Training" (January 1956), 6 *B.J.D.*, No. 3, pp. 202 *et seq.*; B. S. Alper, "Borstal Briefly Revisited" (January 1968), 8 *B.J. C.*, No. 1, pp. 6–20.
2. John P. Conrad, "The Assistant Governor in the English Prison" (April 1960), 10 *B.J.D.*, No. 4, p. 245.
3. Norman Bishop, "Group Work at Pollington Borstal" (1950), 10 *Howard Journal*, No. 3, p. 185; Pat Hooper, "Group Work with Borstal Girls" (1963) 11 *Howard Journal*, No. 2, p.119.

home leave, outside work parties, camping, adventure training, canoeing, voluntary help to the disabled or the aged. Above all, there should be room for a full appreciation of the work of borstal after-care, in its several incarnations. Every Prison Department Report expresses the confidence of the borstal after-care director in the inherent value of borstal training, and provides eloquent testimony of the broad scope of the after-care function. Undismayed by the depressing figures for the success of the system, he makes failures sound like muted triumphs (as indeed they often are). The figures do not lie, of course; they simply do not reveal the whole truth.

Results of borstal training

Until 1939 the borstal system appeared to achieve a remarkable degree of success, judged in terms of reconvictions. Thus nearly 60 per cent. of those discharged in 1937–1938 were not reconvicted, and a further 20 per cent. were reconvicted only once. The figures for the war years were less satisfactory, but, as Sir Lionel Fox remarks, this was only to be expected.[4] The figures for those released in 1946 and 1947 climbed back towards the high success rates of the years before the war. On the post-war figures, Sir Lionel Fox, writing in 1952, wished to suspend judgment. But he clearly anticipated some falling off in the rate of success. There were already some indications of this at the time when he wrote.

By 1963 the success rate, judged in terms of reconvictions, had fallen to less than 40 per cent. and some critics suggested that the borstal system must now be pronounced a failure. Dr. Little pointed out that this was despite the fact that the borstal system embodied nearly all the reforms which criminologists and penal reformers had been demanding for years.[5]

The Director of Borstal After-Care (Frank Foster) has answered these criticisms with characteristic vigour, though the disturbing deterioration in the reconviction rates is recognised frankly.[6] The Home Office Research Unit has suggested two possible explanations for the decline. The first is the higher proportion of poor risks being committed to borstal, measured

---

4. Fox, p. 400.
5. Alan Little, "Penal Theory, Penal Reform and Borstal Practice" (January 1963), 3 *B.J.C.*,No. 3, p. 257.
6. Report of the Commissioners of Prisons, 1957, Cmnd. 496, August 1958, p. 77.

according to the Mannheim–Wilkins prediction tables. The second is the "delinquent generation" argument which had been advanced by Leslie Wilkins (and is now somewhat discredited). Frank Foster's reply has always been to point out the following facts which must be considered in looking at the success rates:

1. Many of the youths committed to borstal training had already been experienced criminals;
2. Of those reconvicted in 1953, 35 per cent. had eventually become stabilised and were now leading normal lives;[7]
3. Considering the nature of the case histories, it is surprising that the results are so good. Trevor Gibbens has shown that recovery from criminal habits is for many boys a slow and difficult business lasting over many years.[8]

Nevertheless there are those, including the present author, who, while recognising the tremendous richness of the borstal tradition and the high quality and great dedication of borstal staff of all grades, believe that it is possible that the methods used are no longer appropriate to the needs of the modern criminally inclined youth, and who argue that nothing less than a drastic overhaul (or replacement) of the system will do. These arguments are to some extent supported by the conclusions of Roger Hood's excellent historical and detached survey of the borstal system. He concludes that

"although, on the surface, the borstal system has made vast progress in the last thirty years, there is little evidence to show that it has come any nearer to the solution of its major problem—the training and reformation of the 'hard-core' of its inmates."[9]

Hood believes that

"a choice has to be made between persevering with the present system of custodial training, or replacing the whole edifice with a complex and flexible range of training and treatment facilities. The latter choice implies a complete re-thinking of the principles on which borstal training has been developed over the last fifty years."[10]

---

7. This argument is repeated in the 1962 Report of the Commissioners of Prisons, Cmnd. 2030, June 1963, p. 38.
8. Quoted in Prison Department Report, 1964, Cmnd. 2708, July 1965, p. 35.
9. Roger Hood, *Borstal Re-assessed*, 1965, pp. 217–218.
10. *Ibid.*, p. 220.

There are signs that the Prison Department is aware of the dilemma. The 1957 Report said:

> "It is now almost 50 years since the Borstal System envisaged by Sir Evelyn Ruggles-Brise was established in law by the passing of the Prevention of Crime Act, 1908. Its value may be more truly assessed by the outcome of the difficult and least hopeful cases than by its immediate successes."[11]

The 1962 Report appears to have accepted the case for retention of the existing system:

> "The traditional method of borstal training, based on the house system with its competitive features, a good day's work, education and recreation in the evening, the grade system which allows increased responsibility and trust to those in the later stages, and, running through all, the interest and attention of the staff, is still followed by many borstals particularly those dealing with a large roll and difficult training material. It is a good training structure, which has spread to many countries of the world, and still produces results. It is sufficiently elastic to be capable of expansion and adaptation . . . the past few years have seen much experimentation and development of borstal training."[12]

It is quite possible to accept this line of argument and believe that the system is flexible enough to adapt to changing needs. But to many people the basic assumptions made about the roots of moral training seem somewhat dated. As Roger Hood says:

> "The boys received after the war were tougher and more undisciplined than those who had been to borstal in the thirties . . . there were some more fundamental changes in the problems and personalities of post-war youth, and in their reaction to a middle-class moralizing system."[13]

Despite the refreshing frankness of the admissions made by the authorities concerning the difficulties of managing the present-day borstal population, and the welcome lack of any doctrinaire approach, and the considerable latitude for experiment permitted within the borstal system, there is still a sameness about each of the different institutions which gives borstal training a certain indefinable character.

---

11. Cmnd. 496, p. 77.
12. Cmnd. 2030, pp. 28–29.
13. Roger Hood, p. 141.

Hood comments that since 1952 (when Fox wrote his authoritative statement of borstal training principles):

> "there have been no revolutionary changes in the system. But there has been an increasing awareness on the part of the Commissioners of the need to challenge the relevance of ideas and methods developed in the thirties. The reports of the Commissioners in the early sixties show a complete lack of dogmatism about the nature of the problem and its solution. Nevertheless, despite the appearance of group counselling, and some important shifts of emphasis, the basic structure has remained much as it was when Sir Lionel wrote."[14]

To some extent this is inevitable since the public and Parliament have insisted on retaining a somewhat narrow concept of borstal training, and the anxieties engendered by absconders and borstal failures have led to reassurances that the discipline is strict and the régime a demanding one. Hood says:

> "the Commissioners are aware that borstals are viewed as penal establishments, and that public opinion would not tolerate institutions which lacked what is traditionally thought of as 'discipline'."[15]

The basic commitment of borstal to *institutional* training, Hood maintains, blocks experimentation with novel treatment methods such as small intensive therapeutic units or entirely educational groups.[16] Gordon Rose made much the same point in 1960.[17] Hostels such as Southfields, the work of which has been described by Derek Miller,[18] are likely to remain exceptional and to develop outside the borstal system unless some new impetus or thrust is given, for example, by a report from the Advisory Council on the Penal System.

Hood suggests that the distinction between short-term training such as is provided in detention centres and long-term custodial training such as is provided in borstal institutions should be abolished, leaving the penal administrators free to choose, within a maximum sentence of two years (or a lower maximum for more trivial offenders) what kind of "training" the offender should undergo. The choice for the court should be

---

14. Roger Hood, p. 142.
15. *Ibid.*, p. 160.
16. *Ibid.*, p. 218.
17. A. G. Rose, "Penal Practice in a Changing Society: A Critical Examination of the White Paper Policy" (1960), I.S.T.D. pamphlet, p. 14, quoted by Hood, p. 160.
18. Derek Miller, *Growth to Freedom*, 1964.

between a period of community training or custodial training.[19]

Various other suggestions have been made for change in the system of borstal training. The prison medical officers asked for at least one borstal institution under medical direction.[20] The Magistrates' Association felt that the first part of borstal training should be more strictly disciplinary "for those who at present would be deemed suitable for closed conditions, or have already had one borstal sentence".[1] They also considered that special measures should be introduced for dealing with young adult offenders of the 21 to 25 age-group.[2] This last suggestion echoes a remark made by Lord PARKER, the Lord Chief Justice, a few years ago, when he is reported to have said he would not be at all opposed to the extension of the indeterminate sentence principle to some higher age-group of young adult offenders.[3]

When all the criticisms and suggestions have been considered, one feature of the borstal system remains which should never be overlooked or underestimated. Over the years, by developing traditions and a style of its own, however imperfectly, it has contributed enormously to the capital of the English penal system judged in terms of the training of staff of all grades, many of whom later find themselves posted to work in prisons. The "borstalisation" of the prison service, while never complete, has been a gradual process: not a time-bomb ticking in the cell but rather a gradual steady drip of progress making a lasting impact on the whole of the prison scene.

The borstal system, although it has many critics, has attracted many imitators. Denmark, Canada and the federal system in the United States in particular have followed the system rather closely. Sir Lionel Fox records with obvious pride the great interest and admiration which the borstal system had aroused among visitors from abroad, a fact noted by Grünhut, whose conclusion was that he had "a feeling that it is something to be proud of".[4] My own limited experience with the overseas

---

19. Roger Hood, p. 219, cf. Nigel Walker's views, expressed in 67 *The Listener* 1099.
20. Royal Commission on the Penal System in England and Wales, Written Evidence, Vol. III, Memorandum submitted on behalf of the Full-time and Part-time Medical Officers in the Prison Medical Service in England and Wales, 1967, p. 116.
1. Royal Commission, Written Evidence, Vol. II, p. 13.
2. P. 17.
3. House of Lords Debates, 1 May 1961, Vol. 230, col. 1103, See also J.P.J. & Local Government Review, 7 December 1963; *The Times*, 10 December 1963.
4. Fox, p. 401; M. Grünhut, *Penal Reform*, 1948, p. 382.

visitors who come to study the borstal system is that they are in general most envious and full of admiration especially of the educational and training facilities and the generally constructive atmosphere. If our prisons were as good as our borstals we should have less cause for concern. Many of them are almost as good and are becoming in many respects indistinguishable from borstal institutions.

CHAPTER 23

Detention Centres

Among the more controversial of the innovations introduced by the Criminal Justice Act 1948 was the detention centre. This was intended to provide a short-term disciplinary training experience for offenders under 21. It has been frequently characterised by the phrase "short, sharp shock", and is said by some to be modelled on the army disciplinary centres known as "glass houses", which practised a strict régime.

HISTORY OF THE IDEA

The Criminal Justice Bill of 1938, on which the Act of 1948 was modelled, had not contained any such proposals. It had envisaged a system of residential hostels, to be known as Howard Houses, coupled with attendance centres for non-residential training.[1] But by 1948 the approach was somewhat different, and the Government's Bill proposed the setting up of the detention centre. There appears to have been little discussion of the idea at the time of the legislation,[2] but since 1952, when the first detention centre was opened at Campsfield House, Kidlington, Oxfordshire, there has been a good deal of discussion, much of it critical, of the régime provided by the detention centre.

The idea behind the adoption of the detention centre was undoubtedly to provide a strict disciplinary régime, intended largely as a deterrent punishment, to take the place of imprisonment for short periods for young offenders under the age of 21. The origin of the notion of the "short, sharp shock" as a suitable means for bringing young offenders to their senses is not at all clear. Sir Lionel Fox mentions pressure from many magistrates, supported by the Advisory Council, for firmer sanctions, and the conclusions of Mr. J. H. Bagot in a research study of the

1. Gordon Rose, *The Struggle for Penal Reform*, 1961, p. 227.
2. Anne B. Dunlop and Sarah McCabe, *Young Men in Detention Centres*, 1965, p. 1.

use of remand homes for detention as a punishment, under s. 54 of the Act of 1933.[3] The latter appears to have approved of a suggestion made by John Watson in 1942[4] echoing the view of the Magistrates' Association in the immediate pre-war period. As Rose puts it, "the experience of the war and post-war years sharpened the feeling that punitive measures were needed, and this is reflected in the Criminal Justice Bill, which appeared in October 1947".[5] He also says:

> "It is not often that one can see as clearly as in the comparison of the 1938 and 1947 Bills the change of opinion over a period. The 1947 Bill is more inclined towards punishment than was its predecessor, as one might expect."[6]

It should not escape notice in this connection that the Criminal Justice Act of 1948 abolished the sanction of corporal punishment except for grave offences in prison.[7] This reform, which had been vigorously contested in Parliament during the debate in 1938 on the ill-fated Criminal Justice Bill,[8] was now accepted with comparatively little opposition,[9] possibly because by now the main interest lay in the capital punishment issue. Part of the explanation for the lack of opposition to the abolition of corporal punishment may perhaps lie in the diversion of interest to the latest idea of deterrent punishment, the detention centre.

THE LEGAL PROVISIONS

The Criminal Justice Act of 1948 provided this régime for persons not less than 14 but under 21 years of age, where the court had power to impose imprisonment and had been notified by the Secretary of State that a detention centre was available.[10] The basic provision was for a term of three months, but where the maximum term of imprisonment was less than that, the court could sentence for a term equal to that maximum, and if the maximum exceeded three months, and the court was of the opinion that, having regard to any special circumstances,

---

3. Fox, p. 340. J. H. Bagot, *Punitive Detention*, 1944.
4. John A. F. Watson, *The Child and the Magistrate*, 1942.
5. Rose, pp. 231–232.
6. P. 234.
7. Criminal Justice Act 1948, s. 2.
8. Rose, p. 212.
9. P. 214.
10. Criminal Justice Act 1948, s. 18.

a term of three months' detention would be insufficient, the court could sentence up to six months or the maximum term whichever was the shorter. In the case of an offender of compulsory school age, the term of detention could be less than three months but must be at least one month, and this could only be ordered where the court was of the opinion that a term of three months, or the maximum term permitted, as described above, would be excessive.[11]

An offender who has previously been sentenced to imprisonment or borstal training may not be sentenced to a detention centre sentence, nor may a person over seventeen years of age who has previously been sentenced to a detention centre since attaining that age.[12] But there is nothing to prevent boys with previous approved school experience being sentenced to a detention centre, and many have been so sentenced.

The court must consider every other method (except imprisonment) before choosing to sentence an offender to a detention centre, and may only choose a detention centre sentence when it is of the opinion that none of those other methods is appropriate.[13] An offender may be sentenced to a detention centre in default of payment of a sum of money, *e.g.* a debt or fine.[14] The Act also provided that an offender not under 14 might be ordered to be detained in a detention centre in lieu of detention in a remand home under s. 54 of the Children and Young Persons Act 1933, provided that the Secretary of State has notified the court that a detention centre is available for this purpose.[15]

THE PROVISION OF DETENTION CENTRES

At first only two detention centres were set up, one, a junior centre (14–17) at Campsfield House, Kidlington, near Oxford, opened in 1952, and the other, a senior centre (17–21) at Blantyre House, Goudhurst, Kent, opened in 1954; and courts in the south of England were notified of their availability. Later two further centres were opened for the use of courts in the Midlands and the North, viz. Foston Hall, Derby and

---

11. Criminal Justice Act 1948, s. 18(1).
12. Criminal Justice Act 1948, s. 18(2).
13. Criminal Justice Act 1948, s. 18(2).
14. Criminal Justice Act 1948, s. 18(3).
15. Criminal Justice Act 1948, s. 18(4).

Werrington House, Staffordshire (opened 1957). By the time of the White Paper on penal policy of February 1959[16] there were six detention centres already included in the current building programme and a further six were foreshadowed, so that the whole country would eventually be served by these centres. It was hoped that in this way the difficulties which magistrates had experienced in finding a place for an offender in such a centre would be overcome. Most of the detention centres accommodate about 100 boys each, in secure conditions. There is one open centre for boys.

In the late 1950s the question of corporal punishment was raised again, and the Home Secretary referred the question to the Advisory Council. In 1960 the Report of the Advisory Council confirmed the conclusions of the 1938 Cadogan Committee,[17] and there was no longer any likelihood of altering the law to put the clock back. But interest in the subject continued in some quarters, and it is in this light that the detention centre policy adopted by Mr. Butler when he was Home Secretary begins to make sense, politically if not penologically.

THE ADVISORY COUNCIL'S REPORT (1959)

In May 1958 the Advisory Council on the Treatment of Offenders were asked to consider certain proposals put forward by the Prison Commissioners for dealing with young offenders between the ages of 16 and 21. The Advisory Council's Report was published in 1959.[18] On the subject of detention centres, the proposal was that the system of detention centres should be developed to the point at which it could replace short-term imprisonment (*i.e.* for six months or less) for young offenders. The Advisory Council welcomed these proposals, which would enable more young offenders to be kept out of prison. It pointed out that so far as magistrates' courts were concerned, s. 107(4) of the Magistrates' Court Act 1952 had provided for the Home Secretary eventually to prohibit the imprisonment of persons under 21, when he was satisfied that adequate alternative

---

16. Penal Practice in a Changing Society, Aspects of Future Development (England and Wales), Cmnd. 645, February 1959.
17. Home Office, Report of the Advisory Council on the Treatment of Offenders, Corporal Punishment, Cmnd. 1213, November 1960. Report of the Departmental Committee on Corporal Punishment, Cmd. 5684, February 1938.
18. Home Office, The Treatment of Young Offenders, Report of the Advisory Council on the Treatment of Offenders, 1959.

M

means were available for dealing with such persons. This contemplated the use of detention centres as an alternative to imprisonment.[19] The policy was right, but the Advisory Council thought that certain modifications would be necessary in the law and practice to make the system wholly effective. They recommended as follows:

(i) There should be two standard sentences of detention of three months' and six months' duration;

(ii) Provision should be made to enable a youth over the age of 17 to be sentenced to more than one period of detention in a detention centre. Under the Act of 1948 such a youth could not be sentenced twice to detention centre, and the only alternative to the Advisory Council's recommendation would be to order a term of borstal training;

(iii) A youth who fails to pay all or part of a sum of money, after all proper methods of persuasion have been tried, should not be sent to a detention centre but should still be sent to prison for a period proportionate to the amount outstanding;

(iv) All sentences of detention in a detention centre should be followed by a period of statutory after-care for one year after release (subject to review after six months to see whether discharge should be recommended).[20]

For girls, the Advisory Council had recommended similar changes in the penal system, but the numbers were small and it recognised that "it would be clearly impracticable to set up a detention centre for such a small number of offenders".[1] They accepted the Prison Commissioners' view that suitable training could be devised for this purpose in special units inside selected women's prisons. There had until then been no provision of detention centres for girls, it being thought unsuitable to subject girls to this kind of disciplinary training. During the discussions on the Criminal Justice Bill in Parliament it was announced that the Government would be setting up one detention centre for girls,[2] and this was eventually opened at Moor Court in

---

19. P. 5, para. 8.
20. See pp. 26 and 27 for a summary of the conclusions and recommendations.
1. P. 8, para. 19.
2. House of Lords Debates, 16 May 1961, Vol. 231, cols. 482 *et seq.* (discussion of Lord Stonham's amendment).

Staffordshire. The experiment was not successful, and the Advisory Council has now accepted the official view that the detention centre for girls should be closed.[3] (See Chapter 16: Female Prisoners, and Chapter 22: Borstal Training.)

MR. BUTLER'S POLICY, ITS SUPPORTERS AND CRITICS

Mr. Butler described his policy as one under which young offenders would be "subject to more energetic and bracing forms of discipline" which would constitute "a suitable deterrent for the young".[4] A Conservative M.P who is a specialist in penal affairs described the future detention centres as "very important indeed":

"The detention centre and the short, sharp shock is, after all, the main substitute for the birch. It is the capacity of the detention centre, by means of a short, sharp shock, to do what the birch used to do which is the factor which decides in my mind against corporal punishment."[5]

Later in the same speech he described the detention centre as "the civilised alternative to the birch".[6]

There was spirited opposition in the House of Lords to the idea of providing a detention centre for girls, based on the different needs of girls from boys, which necessitated a different approach.[7] In the course of these discussions, a good deal is said about detention centre philosophy and, in particular, the remarks of Lady Wootton are most illuminating.[8] She noted that there was a special language for detention centres, the appropriate adjectives being "brisk", "bracing", "energetic" and the appropriate noun always "discipline". While she accepted there might be a great deal in the virtues which detention centres are supposed to inculcate, she doubted whether the emphasis on tidiness, punctuality, smartness, response to brisk discipline, and physical achievement, were relevant to the rehabilitation of offenders. There were other important virtues which equally deserved to be stressed, such

3. Home Office, Detention of Girls in a Detention Centre, Interim Report of the Advisory Council on the Penal System, 1968.
4. House of Commons Debates, 17 November 1960, Vol. 630, col. 562.
5. Cols. 632–633.
6. Cols. 635.
7. House of Lords Debates, 16 May, Vol. 231, cols. 482 *et seq.*
8. Cols. 487 *et seq.*

as kindness, consideration for other people, sympathy, generosity, help to others who are weaker, or who are in a weaker position than oneself. The questions raised by Lady Wootton, while they have particular relevance to the training of girl offenders, go to the root of the "training" philosophy of the English penal system. We need to do a great deal of serious thinking about the kind of training which young offenders need, she says. Moreover,

> "psychologists long ago disposed of the theory that if one is highly trained in one thing it enables one automatically to excel in others—the theory of the transference of mental training."[9]

She goes on to point out that:

> "A man who is detained in any kind of penal institution lives a life which is wholly artificial and far removed from any environment to which he is to be returned; and the transfer of what he learns in prison to what he is going to do outside is a transfer which is very unlikely to take place in the sense that the prison authorities wish."[10]

As has been mentioned, the discussion in Parliament in 1960 and 1961 about the extension of the detention centre principle contained in the Criminal Justice Bill took place against the background of a revival of interest in the question of corporal punishment. The matter had only recently been the subject of an Advisory Council Report. Lord PARKER, the Lord Chief Justice, clearly looked on detention centres as "places of discipline and punishment".[11] He said:

> "the prime object of a detention centre, I should have thought, was to submit a man to harsh discipline as a punishment."[12]

He described himself in the very next passage as a "reluctant advocate of corporal punishment".

In the House of Commons in November 1960 in the Second Reading debate on the Criminal Justice Bill, Mr. T. L. Iremonger, M.P., argued that

> "we should be a little careful in putting too high a value on the detention centre as an alternative to the birch. . . . although I am sure that there will be a very valuable disciplinary element

---

9. House of Lords Debates, 1 May 1961, Vol. 230, col. 1155.
10. *Ibid.*
11. Col. 1105.
12. Col 1106.

in the detention centres, we should not imagine that this will be the complete answer to the vicious young thug who has beaten up the old lady in the sweet shop. . . ."[13]

This judgment is now fairly widely accepted, and alternative means of dealing with difficult young offenders are being sought.

THE CRIMINAL JUSTICE ACT 1961

This Act implemented the new arrangements relating to the methods of dealing with offenders between the ages of 16 and 21, which had been examined and reported on by the Advisory Council in 1959. But in regard to detention centres, two out of four of the Advisory Council's recommendations described above ((i) and (iii)) were not accepted. The detention centre term remains variable in the range one month to nine months, rather than there being a choice between two standard sentences, of three months' and six months' duration. Fine defaulters may now be sentenced to detention centres. The aftercare arrangements proposed were accepted and came into effect on 1 January 1964.[14]

THE PRESENT POSITION

Since the Act of 1961 the number of detention centres has increased to eighteen, and the number of boys in detention has risen to close on 1,500. The system has an annual capacity of over 4,000 boys, so there is now some spare capacity, and many detention centres have empty places. The reasons for this are somewhat obscure, but it may stem from the early difficulties which courts experienced in finding places in detention centres, which led to a good deal of frustration and annoyance among magistrates, and to a general feeling of declining confidence in the system.

THE NATURE OF THE RÉGIME

It remains to describe the actual nature of the régime provided in detention centres and the results of the system. Sir Lionel Fox in 1952 outlined the official thinking on the subject as follows:

---

13. House of Commons Debates, 17 November 1960, Vol. 630, col. 649.
14. Criminal Justice Act 1961, (Commencement No. 3 Order) S.I. 2070 (c. 20), bringing into force s. 13 of the Act and Sched. 1.

M*

"*Ex hypothesi*, the primary purpose of the centres is deterrence, nor does the very short period of the sentence offer the possibility of constructive training; indeed it is a second hypothesis that an offender who really needs such training ought not to be committed to a centre, but to an approved school or borstal. And it is certainly a third hypothesis that these centres shall not be prisons for young people under a new name.

"To devise a régime which will comply with these intentions, in such buildings as may be found, will not be easy. It must clearly be such that the youngster who has been through it will leave with the feeling that he would rather not do it again. Yet so purely negative an attitude to the task is unthinkable. Some constructive and formative influences must be brought into play, though it may be granted at once that among these the insistence on a brisk and disciplined activity will itself rank high. Further, for those of compulsory school age, provision for their continuing education will be essential."[15]

Sir Lionel seems to have placed great reliance in finding a solution to this problem in the "sympathetic and well-selected staff",[16] and there is much testimony to the effect that, whatever the success or failures of the detention centre, the attitude and approach of the staff has been devoted and inspired by humane and enlightened considerations. Mr. Iremonger, M.P., and Mr. Deedes, M.P., are eloquent testimony to this. The former quotes one detention centre warden as saying to him "You cannot do anything by mere discipline".[17] A great emphasis is placed on getting the boys to achieve standards which they thought were impossible for them. That seemed to Mr. Iremonger to be something very different from "sterile square-bashing". Mr. Deedes pointed out that there had been modifications from the early days, when "the first idea was a short, sharp shock, what was called the brisk tempo".[18] It is well known that the tempo has relaxed somewhat, compared with the early days, if only because the staff could not sustain the pace. There is now less movement around the camp at the double, less needless clothes changing, and a little more emphasis on the positive training aspects. Serious criticism by social workers and penal reformers has often missed the vital points that should be the target of criticism.[19] These were firstly, the

15. Fox, p. 342.
16. P. 343.
17. House of Commons Debates, 17 November 1960, Vol. 630, col. 648.
18. Col. 632.
19. See, for example, Donald Ford, *The Delinquent Child and the Community*, 1957, pp. 53 *et seq.*

absence of any proper screening process to assist the courts, especially the magistrates' courts, in their selection of boys for detention centres, which has often led to boys quite unsuitable for physical or mental reasons being committed. There is some improvement here since the extension of the requirements for pre-sentence reports, however, and it is claimed that very few unsuitable boys are received in detention centres today. The other point of criticism, the absence of any after-care arrangements, a point made by the Howard League concerning the 1948 Act's provisions,[20] was remedied by the Act of 1961, as we have seen. Even before this, detention centre wardens were in the habit of making arrangements for an offender on release to see a probation officer if he agreed and it was felt he needed such supervision. Now that welfare officers have been appointed in all detention centres the attention given to the after-care arrangements has improved.

The régime is still a strict and vigorous one, the highest possible standard of achievement and behaviour being sought from the boys. There is a full working week, plenty of physical exercise, and P.T., and a good deal of educational activity. Boys of compulsory school age receive full-time education, and classes of further education are provided in the evening. At first, remission of one-sixth of the term was given for good behaviour. Now the remission is one-third.[1]

The main deterrent element lies in the fact of detention, the sudden isolation from familiar surroundings and associations. This is itself a considerable shock to many young offenders, but it is right for some offenders to be compulsorily removed from their surroundings in this way for a short period.

The Advisory Council on the Penal System has recently reviewed the operation of the senior detention centres. This followed mounting pressure from various quarters including the Howard League and the Society of Friends.[2] Changes are likely in the system, designed to keep the best features of it and eliminate the worst. The latter include the long detention centre sentences which are permitted by the present law, the

---

20. Gordon Rose, *The Struggle for Penal Reform*, 1961, p. 234.
1. House of Commons Debates, Written Answers, 1 July 1968, effective 1 August 1968.
2. Detention Centres, A Report by a sub-committee of the Friends Penal Affairs Committee, January 1968. The Advisory Council's Report was published in February 1970.

sentences of six and nine months. Another likely reform is the encouragement of more open detention centres. At present North Sea Camp, which is pretty inaccessible, is the only open detention centre. The Children and Young Persons Act 1969 provides for the eventual replacement of detention centres for the younger age group 14–17 by the local authority "community homes" and other arrangements.

RESULTS OF DETENTION CENTRE SENTENCES

From the beginning, detention centre sentences have been the subject of research studies designed to assess the success of the régime. Dr. Max Grünhut of Oxford reported in March 1958 on his research into the work of the first two centres. This research is summarised in the 1957 Prison Commissioners' Report, published in August 1958.[3] He studied 434 boys discharged from the Junior Centre at Campsfield House during its first two years, with a two-year period of follow-up to assess success and failure, the criterion being reconviction. He found that, counting offences of any kind, 48 per cent. were found guilty by courts at least once during the two-year follow-up period. Two out of three first offenders were not reconvicted, while two out of three of those with three or more previous offences were reconvicted. Over 60 per cent. of those with previous institutional experience were reconvicted. Considering the background of the more difficult boys, Dr. Grünhut thought the experience was not discouraging. With regard to the 144 boys from Blantyre House Senior Centre studied, who had also been at risk for at least two years, "comparison of this group with the one at the junior centre disclosed similar patterns in respect of the contribution of first offenders, recidivists and those with or without previous forms of treatment", though less of the senior boys had good backgrounds. In both centres the risk of relapse was highest in the first months after release.

Dr. Grünhut's conclusions were that "punitive detention appears suitable for boys with a more or less substantial criminality not due to deep-rooted personal factors or seriously adverse home conditions, for whom detention is the first experience of any form of institutional treatment". He considered that

---

3. Report of the Commissioners of Prisons, 1957, Cmnd. 496, August 1958, pp. 85 *et seq.* See also M. Grünhut, "After-Effects of Punitive Detention (January 1960), 10 *B.J.D.*, No. 3, p. 178, and the same author's "Juvenile Delinquents under Punitive Detention" (January 1955), 5 *B.J.D.*, No. 3, p. 191.

"detention in a detention centre has a legitimate place in a differentiated system of penal and corrective methods for juvenile delinquents and adolescent offenders".[4]

The White Paper of February 1959 quoted these encouraging results and announced the intention to develop the detention centre system further, as we have noted.[5]

Dunlop and McCabe completed and published in 1965 a more detailed study of the work of the senior detention centres, using a different method of measurement and assessment than the crude reconviction rates. They used a series of carefully designed interviews at different stages of sentence, administered to young men at Werrington House and Aylesbury Detention Centres. (The latter detention centre has since been closed.) The interviews were carried out at the stage of first arrival at the detention centre, and immediately prior to discharge, and in addition some follow-up study was attempted by correspondence with the young men three or four months after their discharge. These interviews were supplemented with case histories of each young man obtained from the files at the detention centres.

The young men studied showed certain characteristics which indicate the problem facing the authorities. There was a "high degree of illegitimacy, of absence from the family home, of unsatisfactory family relationships, of poor educational attainment and of employment that was sporadic, aimless and some times dull".[6] It was noticed that the offenders who were sentenced to detention by midland and northern courts were different in many ways from those who came from the south, being more honest but more violent, more attached to their families and homes, and more able and willing to keep their jobs.[7] On reception they were apprehensive and resentful. At discharge many were still critical but "dislike of individual parts of the régime had been replaced by dislike of detention in itself and the loss of freedom which this entailed".[8] In the review which the researchers were able to conduct of the behaviour of the

---

4. Cmnd. 496, p. 87.
5. Penal Practice in a Changing Society, Aspects of Future Development (England and Wales), p. 9.
6. Anne B. Dunlop and Sarah McCabe, *Young Men in Detention Centres*, 1965, p. 134.
7. P. 135.
8. P. 136.

young men during the first six months period after release, they found that those reconvicted in this period(15 out of 101) were on the whole younger, more dishonest and less violent than the sample group as a whole. Naturally they contained a disproportionate number of young men with a long history of previous proved offences. This must be considered significant in the light of the further finding that there has been a sharp rise in the proportion of offenders committed to detention centres with a record of more than four previous offences. There is also evidence of the considerable influence which the more sophisticated offenders exert over those who are less delinquent. The researchers conclude that detention centres "may have some value for a small proportion of offenders, the younger and less sophisticated".[9] It will be seen that this conclusion falls far short of Dr. Grünhut's more fulsome praise of the detention centre.

The need for careful selection of offenders for this kind of sentence is stressed by Dunlop and McCabe, as well as the need for maintaining a regional basis of allocation and for developing the after-care and welfare services.[10]

One fear which has been expressed is that the attempt to develop the detention centre provision to the point where it may take the place of short-term imprisonment may lead to more difficult and criminally sophisticated youths being committed to the detention centre. Dunlop and McCabe express their misgivings about the results which might follow from such a development.

Charlotte Banks has studied the problem more recently than Dunlop and McCabe. Her figures show that "between 1961 and 1964, the number of boys received into detention centres nearly trebled".[11] She found "about twenty per cent. of those we saw unsuitable for the regime, either because their offences were very minor ones or because they were not physically or mentally fit enough".[12] She discovered that many of the boys sent to detention centres were suffering from physical handicaps or from severe psychological handicaps, and were unsuited to

9. P. 139.
10. P. 138.
11. Charlotte Banks, "Borstal, Prison and Detention Centres", in *Changing Concepts of Crime and Its Treatment*, ed. Hugh Klare, 1966, p. 118.
12. P. 122.

the tempo, strict discipline and vigorous athletics of the detention centre régime.[13] The Council of Europe, in its Report on "Short-Term Methods of Treatment for Young Offenders," has given the English detention centre system a favourable report.[14]

---

13. Charlotte Banks, "Boys in Detention Centres", in C. Banks and P. L. Broadhurst (eds.), *Stepahnos: Studies in Psychology*, 1965. See also C. Banks, "Reconviction of Young Offenders" *Current Legal Problems*, 1964, ed. G. W. Keeton and G. Schwarztenberger.
14. European Committee on Crime Problems, Council of Europe, *Short-Term Methods of Treatment for Young Offenders*, 1967.

CHAPTER 24

Approved Schools and Fit Person Orders, Detention in Remand Homes, etc.

In order to complete the account of the courts' powers in relation to convicted offenders it is necessary to mention (1) approved school orders, (2) fit person orders, and (3) detention in remand homes; (4) we must also consider the powers of courts to order the detention of a child in a place approved by the Secretary of State. But it is not proposed to give a full description of any of these institutions nor to explain all the details of the legal powers. Adequate discussions of these matters are readily available, and these are matters more for the specialist in child care and juvenile court law, which is outside our chosen field.[1] Moreover, there is much that will be changed in relation to the means of institutional handling of offenders as a result of the Children and Young Persons Act 1969.

1 APPROVED SCHOOL ORDERS

Any court before which a child or young persons stands convicted of an offence, punishable in the case of an adult with imprisonment, may make an approved school order.[2] This has the effect of committing him to a school approved by the Home Secretary for an indefinite period, within the limits laid down by the law. It is very complicated to explain the period for which a person may be committed to an approved school, as it varies with the age on committal. John Watson has put it concisely thus:

---

1. Gordon Rose, *Schools for Young Offenders*, 1967; John A. F. Watson, *The Child and the Magistrate*, 1965; J. Gittins, *Approved School Boys* (H.M.S.O.), 1952; Home Office, Making Citizens (pamphlet); Home Office, Reports of the Children's Department; Helen J. Richardson, *Adolescent Girls in Approved Schools*, 1969.
2. Children and Young Persons Act 1933, s. 57 and 107.

"The maximum periods of detention in an approved school may be stated as follows. For juveniles under fifteen when committed, three years or until four months after their fifteenth birthday—*whichever is the longer*. For juveniles over fifteen when committed, three years or until their nineteenth birthday—*whichever is the shorter*."[3]

The actual length of time a person will spend in an approved school depends on the type of school he is sent to, and the progress made during training. The schools are classified into junior, intermediate and senior schools. Again, to quote John Watson, the release position may be described thus:

"Rarely does a juvenile remain in an approved school for the maximum statutory period. The average training of boys released from approved schools during 1963 was as follows: juniors, 27 months; intermediates, 20 months; seniors, 15 months. For girls the average periods were: juniors, 22 months; intermediates, 18 months; seniors, 16 months."[4]

Indeed the complaint which is made is that the period of training is often too short to be effective. At a recent conference of experts on the subject at Cambridge, it is reported that

"almost all of those taking part in the conference felt that the amount of time which children now spend in Approved Schools (on average, about eighteen months) is insufficient, and that a much longer period of institutional treatment is called for."[5]

One reason for this is that many disturbed and delinquent children are committed to approved school too late, and only after other non-institutional methods have failed. The case for detaining them longer must surely rest on the degree to which it can be shown that this aids their rehabilitation. The evidence here tends to show that there is no correlation between length of stay in institutions and rehabilitative outcome. Moreover, already the powers exercised over approved-school discharges by way of supervision give the possibility of a long period of supervision, similar to that for borstal training, two years or until 21 years of age, whichever is the shorter, and during this period there is the possibility of recall for further training for a substantial period of time (until the end of the original statutory period, or for six months from recall).

The approved-school system dates from 1933 when it

3. J. A. F. Watson, *The Child and the Magistrate*, 1965, p. 261.   4. *Ibid.*, p. 266.
5. University of Cambridge, Institute of Criminology, "The Residential Treatment of Disturbed and Delinquent Boys", Papers presented to the Cropwood Round-Table Conference, edited by R. F. Sparks and R. G. Hood, 1968, p. 10.

replaced the reformatory and industrial schools of the nineteenth century which had been reorganised in 1908. These reformatory and industrial schools had a long and interesting history which it would not be appropriate to pursue here.[6]

There are at present over 120 approved schools in England and Wales, 90 for boys and 33 for girls. At any time there are approximately 7,000 boys and 1,000 girls in these schools, mostly between the ages of 13 and 17.[7] There is a denominational split—Roman Catholic schools being separately provided. There is some evidence of a continuing shortage of accommodation, especially for girls, despite an extensive new building programme. A special drive is being made to provide units for seriously disturbed adolescents.[8] This may be due to the recognition that approved schools are being required to deal nowadays with a much more difficult population. As the Children's Department has said:

> "It is generally agreed by those who have long experience of approved schools that the schools are now receiving an increasing proportion of boys and girls who are more highly disturbed, and less responsive to therapy, than were the most difficult children received 20, or even 10, years ago."[9]

Approved schools are supervised and inspected by the Children's Department of the Home Office, but have been mostly provided by various voluntary societies—religious bodies, voluntary organisations or committees formed for this purpose by interested local people. Only one-quarter were provided by local authorities. There have been several periods of growth and decline, of discovery and disillusion, in the history of the approved-school movement. Many were closed in the early 1950s before the recent surge in the crime figures. The Carlton Approved School Inquiry, and the more recent inquiry into the Court Lees Approved School,[10] led to grave suspicions

6. See R. S. E. Hinde, *The British Penal System*, 1951; J. J. Tobias, *Crime and Industrial Society in the Nineteenth Century*, 1967.
7. See Home Office, Report on the Work of the Children's Department, 1964–1966, H.C. 603, 25 July 1967, Chapter VII.
8. Lady Serota, House of Lords Debates, Vol. 302, cols. 1205–1206, 19 June 1969,
9. H.C. 603, 1967, p. 53.
10. Home Office, Disturbances at the Carlton Approved School on August 29 and 30th, 1959. Report of Inquiry by Mr. Victor Durand, Q.C. Cmnd. 937, January 1960. Home Office, Administration of Punishment at Court Lees Approved School. Report of Inquiry by Mr. Edward Brian Gibbens, Q.C. Cmd. 3367, August 1967. Home Secretary's statement, 7 August 1967. See also Mr. Gibbens' address in April 1969 to the Medico-Legal Society on "Discipline in Approved Schools", printed in 37 *Medico-Legal Journal* 110.

about the quality of the staff and the nature of the programme in certain establishments. Neither the boards of managers nor the Home Office system of inspection appeared to be able to prevent isolated cases of abuse and brutality. It is too early to say whether the solution now adopted of merging the approved school system into the local authority and providing a wide range of different kinds of institutions for offenders and others, including community homes, will prove to be a satisfactory solution. Some would argue in favour of a more centralised system of organisation and control, others for a regional system which is not local-authority based.[11] It will be interesting to see how the new arrangements work out.

It should be noted that the present arrangements reverse the proposals in the 1965 White Paper on The Child, The Family and The Young Offender. This had proposed:

> "to merge and reorganise the present borstals and senior approved schools into a comprehensive system of residential training catering for a wide variety of types coming before the courts."[12]

Under those proposals the Home Office would have taken over responsibility for the senior approved schools. Under the new Children and Young Persons Act 1969, however, the trend is in the other direction. Borstal age is to be raised to 17, and approximately 500 boys per annum presently committed annually to borstal training between the ages of 15 and 17 will have to be accommodated in and assimilated by "the community homes". Some of these will be difficult youths, requiring close attention in secure conditions. It is a question how far the community homes will be able to provide such facilities.

The way in which approved schools have been organised so as to provide classifying schools, to which the courts can commit offenders, instead of leaving them to select the appropriate school, is an interesting feature of approved-school history. The first classifying school was established at Aycliffe, County Durham, and dates from 1943. Although the system was never universal, four classifying schools catering for boys of all ages, except Roman Catholics, were provided. There is also one classifying school for girls in the north.[13] A further development

---

11. See the arguments in favour of each solution in Gordon Rose, *Schools for Young Offenders*, 1967.
12. Cmnd. 2742, August 1965, p. 11, para. 39.
13. John A. F. Watson, *The Child and the Magistrate*, 1965, pp. 257–258.

was the designation of certain remand homes as classifying centres. Thus Stamford House (for boys) and Cumberlow Lodge (for girls) function in this way, as does a classifying centre for girls in the north. Although there are different views about the advantages of combining classification with the remand stage, John Watson is of the opinion that "a physical association of the two types of institution is desirable, as has happened in London."[14]

The only other feature of the approved-school system, apart from their success rates, which it is desirable to emphasise is the remarkable richness in the variety of provision which is available. Almost every kind of régime imaginable is somewhere to be found within the many different kinds of approved schools, and overseas observers have been surprised and pleased to find such a variety of provision. Thus there are three schools run on naval cadet lines, and other schools with a homely family-based régime; completely open schools where many outside activities are encouraged, and relatively closed schools. Persistent absconders and otherwise intractable boys are kept in special secure units in three of the classifying schools, but there are no similar secure units for girls.[15]

The crucial test of any system is its success rate, and here, judged by the conventional standard of reconvictions within three years of discharge, the record of the approved schools for boys in recent years has been disappointing. Well over half the boys offend again. Nearly half of these are not recommitted under a new approved-school order or sent to some other form of custodial training, but are dealt with by some other means, which suggests that their offences were not really serious.[16] For girls, the approved-school system can claim a much higher rate of success, over 80 per cent., and here the vast majority of those reconvicted are dealt with by other methods than a further period of custodial training.[17]

Finally, one feature of the approved-school system must be mentioned. These institutions have never existed solely for the custody and training of delinquents, and in the case of girls, a

14. *Ibid.*, p. 260.
15. H.C. 603, 1967, p. 53.
16. The "other means" referred to comprise absolute discharge, conditional discharge, probation, fine, recall to approved school, and proceedings under the mental health legislation.
17. See Tables in the Children's Department Report, H.C. 603, 1967, pp. 51–52.

very high proportion of admissions have been "care, protection or control" cases. It was therefore somewhat absurd for so much fuss to be made recently about the committal by Kidderminster magistrates of a girl to an approved school who had not been the subject of a criminal charge.[18] The matter was challenged at quarter sessions, which confirmed the original decision in favour of commital.[19] A similar case in the west country attracted much publicity.

One can perhaps conclude from the public anxiety concerning these cases that may well be difficulties in store for those who seek to implement the policy expressed in the Children and Young Persons Act 1969, in so far as the boundaries between delinquents and others are blurred. However desirable it may be not to draw lines in this way the public will insist on making these discriminations unless an adequate and effective campaign of public explanation and persuasion converts the prevailing ethos to something rather different from what it is.

2 FIT PERSON ORDERS

We have already seen that a probation order may be made with a condition as to residence. This is one way of securing the removal of a child or young person from his home, and is appropriate where a relative or foster-parent is available or a probation home or hostel is thought to be the right solution, and the aim is to provide a short-term answer to the problem.

A fit person order is really a long-term method of dealing with the problem,[20] and is available wherever a person under the age of 17 is found guilty of an offence for which an adult may be sentenced to imprisonment.[1] It may be combined with a probation order, and this is not infrequently done.

The result of such an order is to remove the child or young person from his home until he reaches the age of 18 unless the order is revoked sooner. The "fit person" named in the order may be (and usually is) a local authority, which thus assumes the responsibility for the child's upbringing and education and maintenance. Where the court intends to make a local authority

---

18. *The Times*, 12 June 1969, 19 June 1969.
19. *The Times*, 28 June 1969.
20. John A. F. Watson, *The Child and the Magistrate*, 1965, pp. 214–215.
1. Children and Young Persons Act 1933, s. 57. Home Office, *The Sentence of the Court*, 2nd Edn., 1969, pp. 14–15.

responsible, and the child or young person is already the subject of a probation order or supervision order, or it is proposed to make a probation order, the consent of the local authority must be obtained. This is to avoid a conflict of jurisdiction between the probation officer and the children's officer of the local authority.[2]

Many children subject to "fit person" orders are boarded out by local authorities with foster parents, who receive a small financial subvention towards the cost. In recent years the emphasis has been strongly in this direction and against accommodating children in children's homes. The only difficulty has been the shortage of suitable foster-parents.

At any time either the parent or guardian of the child or young person, or the "fit person", may apply to the court to vary or revoke the order. An approved school order or a "supervision order" may be substituted. When it revokes a fit person order the juvenile court has power to make a supervision order for not more than three years. A supervision order is similar to a probation order, but the subject being under 17 cannot consent to a probation order, and the description "supervision order" is thought to be more appropriate.

At this point the overlap between children in care and children under "fit person" orders should be explained. The former are not necessarily committed in care for criminal offences. The overriding consideration is their need for "care, protection or control". In future the boundaries will become even more indistinct, since no one under 14 will be prosecuted for criminal offences (except homicide), and very few of those aged between 14 and 17 will be prosecuted. It follows that the overwhelming majority of persons under 17 will be dealt with under the civil jurisdiction of the juvenile court as being in need of "care, protection or control".

3 DETENTION IN REMAND HOMES

Section 54 of the Children and Young Persons Act 1933 provided that an offender under 17 could be committed to the custody of a remand home if his offence is one for which the court could sentence an adult to imprisonment, and the court considers that no other way of dealing with him is suitable. The

---

2. John A. F. Watson, *The Child and the Magistrate*, 1965, p. 217.

term must not exceed one month or the maximum sentence available for the offence, whichever is the shorter.

A very small number of children are committed to remand homes under this heading, and there is usually no special regime available to deal with them. It is provided that the power under s. 54 may not be exercised where the court has received formal notification from the Home Office that a detention centre is available for offenders of his age or description.[3]

4 DETENTION IN A PLACE APPROVED BY THE SECRETARY OF STATE

Where a child or young person is convicted of a serious offence, such as murder (up to the age of 18) or one of the offences contained in s. 53(1) of the Children and Young Persons Act 1933, as amended (up to the age of 17), he or she may be ordered to be detained in a place approved by he Secretary of State. The period of detention must be specified in the order of the court, and may be life imprisonment or such term within the maximum term of imprisonment for the offence as the court sees fit.[4]

Sometimes prison is the only suitable place for the detention of such persons, but in the case of the very young, every effort is made to find an alternative solution. One recent example was the case of the 11-year-old girl who was convicted of murdering two little children.[5] A place was eventually found in a secure wing of a classifying school in the north of England, but such cases underline the poverty of our arrangements—fortunately they are of rare occurrence.

The Parole Board is now charged with the duty to advise with regard to the release of such young offenders on licence and under what conditions this may be recommended.[6]

---

3. See Leon Radzinowicz and J. W. C. Turner, (eds), *Detention in Remand Homes*, 1952; *The Sentence of the Court*, pp. 20–21.
4. *The Sentence of the Court*, pp. 35–36.
5. *The Times*, 18, 19 December 1968, 12 February 1969; Terence Morris, *The Observer*, 22 December 1968; *R.* v. *X* (*An Infant*) (1969), *Times*, 22 July.
6. Criminal Justice Act 1967, s. 61.

CHAPTER 25

Non-Custodial Methods, Including Attendance Centres

Many of the non-custodial methods of treatment of offenders are in common use both for adult offenders and for offenders under the age of 21. For example, fines, discharges (absolute and conditional) and probation are extensively used for young offenders. No separate discussion of these methods is required for young offenders. It is sufficient simply to note the statistical facts revealed in the tables on the opposite page, which show the heavy preference of the courts for using non-custodial methods in the case of offenders under 21. These tables are derived from the Home Office Criminal Statistics (England and Wales).

ATTENDANCE CENTRES

There is one kind of non-custodial measure which is applicable only to offenders under the age of 21, and that is the Attendance Centre, introduced by the Criminal Justice Act 1948. This is a place run by the police or local social-service workers, and open only at week-ends, usually for two hours on Saturday afternoon, to which the courts can order the offender to go for a required number of hours, which means on a number of successive occasions.

THE ORIGIN OF THE IDEA

The origin of the idea is not altogether clear, but Rose has pointed out that Sir Alexander Paterson "threw out the idea of attendance centres in evidence given to the Persistent Offenders Committee", and he may well have known of their

TABLES SHOWING HOW THE COURTS DEALT WITH PERSONS
FOUND GUILTY OF INDICTABLE OFFENCES

Fines: 1968

Percentage of the total number dealt with in the age group

Age Group	Male	Female
Under 14	17·7	20·8
Age 14 and under 17	31·2	31·8
Age 17 and under 21	48·2	39·1
Age 21 and over	46·7	53·1

Probation: 1968

Percentage of the total number dealt with in the age group

Age Group	Male	Female
Under 14	32·2	36·3
Age 14 and under 17	28·7	35·4
Age 17 and under 21	17·1	35·6
Age 21 and under 30	8·1	22·7
Age 30 and over	6·8	12·9

Conditional Discharge: 1968

Percentage of the total number dealt with in the age group

Higher Courts	
Age under 17	5·7
Age 17 and under 21	5·1
Age 21 and over	3·5

Absolute and Conditional Discharge: 1968

Percentage of the total number dealt with in the age group

Magistrates' Courts	Absolute Discharge	Conditional Discharge	Total
Age under 14	2·6	29·0	31·6
Age 14 and under 17 ..	1·9	20·6	22·5
Age 17 and under 21 ..	0·8	10·8	11·6
Age 21 and over	0·9	10·7	11·6

use for adults in the colonies.[1] McClintock observes that as early as 1927 "reformers had been feeling after some such scheme".[2] The Departmental Committee on the Treatment of Young Offenders had sympathetically considered the suggestion that the courts might be given authority to order the intermittent detention of persons aged between 17 and 21 in police cells for consecutive week-ends.[3] Mrs. Le Mesurier made a similar suggestion in her book published in 1931.[4] At least one bench of magistrates were doing something along these lines informally for young offenders under 16 before the 1948 Act, according to Lord Goddard's testimony.[5] The attendance centre featured in the 1938 Criminal Justice Bill, largely through the efforts of Lord Templewood (formerly Sir Samuel Hoare). "He wanted to provide a form of punishment which would avoid the pitfalls of a short prison sentence and in which the punitive element would lie solely in the curtailment of the offender's leisure", says Rosemary Braithwaite.[6] The 1948 Bill dropped the idea "mainly owing to the obstacles foreseen in the acquiring of suitable accommodation and staff".[7] It was these practical difficulties which had prevented the 1927 Committee on Young Offenders from espousing the idea. But in the House of Lords, Lord Templewood succeeded in amending the Bill to include provisions concerning attendance centres.[8]

THE PROVISIONS OF THE CRIMINAL JUSTICE ACT 1948

The Act provided for magistrates' courts, sitting as courts of summary jurisdiction, to have power to order a person aged between 12 and 21, in regard to whom they had the power to impose imprisonment, to attend at an approved attendance centre for up to twelve hours in the aggregate, as specified in the order, but not in school or working hours.[9] No more than

---

1. Gordon Rose, the *Struggle for Penal Reform*, p. 227, quoting S. K. Ruck, *Paterson on Prisons*, 1951, p. 60.
2. F. H. McClintock, *Attendance Centres*, 1961, p. 3.
3. *Ibid.*
4. L. Le Mesurier, *Boys in Trouble*, 1931, p. 265.
5. McClintock, *op. cit.*, p. 3, footnote 4.
6. R. M. Braithwaite, Note on Attendance Centres (January 1952), 2 *B.J.D.*, p. 242 at p. 243.
7. McClintock, p. 5.   8. *Ibid.*
9. Criminal Justice Act 1948, s. 19(1).

one attendance a day and no more than three hours' attendance at a time could be required.[10] Provision is made for discharging the order or varying its detailed requirements.[11] There is also a procedure laid down for dealing with breach of an attendance centre order, either by failing to attend without reasonable excuse, or serious breach of the rules while attending.[12] In the event that such a breach is proved, the court may revoke the order requiring attendance and deal with the offender "in any manner in which he could have been dealt with by the court which made the order if the order had not been made".[13] This gives the magistrates' court considerable power to supervise the enforcement of the order.

The making of an attendance centre order does not require any special procedure and the court does not have to receive any report about the suitability of the offender for such an order. But there is an important proviso in s. 19(1) of the Criminal Justice Act 1948, whereby no order can be made in the case of a person who has been previously sentenced to imprisonment, borstal training or detention in a detention centre, or has been to an approved school.[14] This was "designed to minimise at the centre the risk of the recidivist and the more unmanageable types of offender contaminating the impulsive and purely mischievous sort".[15]

The Act limited the number of hours' attendance to twelve hours in the aggregate. The original proposal in the 1938 Bill had been for an aggregate of not more than sixty hours' attendance. As we shall see, the Criminal Justice Act of 1961 altered the permitted number of hours.

THE EARLY PERIOD

The years from 1950 to 1961 can be regarded as the early period in the history of the attendance centre. The first centre was opened in July 1950 at Peel House, in the Metropolitan Police District, a hostel and training centre for young police

---

10. Section 19(2) proviso.
11. Section 19(3).
12. Section 19(7).
13. Section 19(8).
14. Section 19(1) proviso.
15. F. H. McClintock, *Attendance Centres*, 1961, pp. 5–6.

officers. A number of such centres were opened in this period, mainly run by police officers, and providing for the age group 12–17. They were open on Saturdays for two or three hours, and the régime devised included a period of strenuous physical exercise, followed by a period of elementary handicraft instruction or some educational activity. By 1960 over forty attendance centres had been provided for boys under 17, and about 3,000 orders were made annually.

McClintock points out that there are many areas of the country not provided with attendance centres. "Their establishment has in the main been limited to the larger urban and industrial areas."[16] One difficulty about expansion is the distance which a boy might have to travel for the purpose of attendance. This has been a problem in a large metropolis like London, and would inhibit the extensive use of this method in rural areas. McClintock makes the interesting suggestion that some sort of simplified system might be introduced where the numbers are necessarily small and sporadic.[17] The Advisory Council may deal with this in its Report on non-custodial penalties.

THE PROVISIONS OF THE CRIMINAL JUSTICE ACT 1961

The Criminal Justice Act of 1961 effected two major changes in the system of attendance centres:

1. The minimum age for attendance was reduced from 12 to 10 years;[18]
2. The permitted hours were increased to twenty-four hours in the aggregate, where the court is of the opinion, having regard to all the circumstances, that twelve hours would be inadequate.[19]

Provision is also made that the aggregate number of hours attendance shall not be less than twelve unless the offender is under 14 and the court is of the opinion that twelve hours would be excessive, having regard to his age or any other circumstances.

---

16. F. H. McClintock, *Attendance Centres*, 1961, p. 9.
17. *Ibid.*, pp. 10–11.
18. Criminal Justice Act 1961, s. 10(1).
19. Criminal Justice Act 1961, s. 10(2).

The origin of this change in the law is to be found in the 1957 Advisory Council's Report on The Alternatives to Short Terms of Imprisonment.[20] This recommended the lengthening of the permitted hours of attendance for the senior age group, 17–21,[1] and suggested that an experiment should be made with a senior attendance centre catering for males of this age group.[2] This suggestion was made in the context of the discussion of the proposal to institute adult attendance centres. The Advisory Council thought that a start should be made with the 17–21 age group, and in the light of the experience gained the question of extending the centres to further age groups, say, up to the age of 25 years, could be reconsidered.[3] The fear is that mature adults might respond unfavourably to the requirement of attendance at an attendance centre.

One might comment that this depends on the type of régime provided. The Prison Department has since set up a senior attendance centre at Manchester in December 1958 which has been running for several years, and this is apparently regarded as quite successful, though it has not often been used to full capacity by the courts. A second senior attendance centre, run by police officers, was opened at Greenwich in April 1964. Various different kinds of activity are required at these centres, including cleaning, scrubbing, carrying out internal decoration, first aid and physical education and competitive games, and simple handicraft work.[4]

If adults were to be provided for, careful consideration would have to be given to the kind of activities to be prescribed. For motoring offenders, possibly some intruction in the care and maintenance of cars and motor-cycles, and driving instruction, could be introduced. The possibility of using the existing network of extra-mural and extension classes might be considered. Instead of looking on the attendance centre as an enforced deprivation of leisure, which was the somewhat negative view of its innovators,[5] it could perhaps be viewed as an enforced

---

20. Home Office, Report of the Advisory Council on the Treatment of Offenders, Alternatives to Short Terms of Imprisonment, 1967.
1. P. 8.
2. P. 7, para. 21.
3. P. 8, para. 22.
4. For an account of the work of the senior attendance centres, see Prison Department Reports.
5. Including Fox, p. 339.

N

introduction to ways and means of making the best use of
leisure, a more positive goal. Looked at in this light the making
of an order for attendance might not become so much an
object of scorn and ridicule, as the Advisory Council appear
to have feared in their Report of 1957. In its Report of 1962
the Council did consider that there was scope for experiments
in the field of further education in the direction of providing
for the needs of difficult and disturbed young people.[6] But the
Council's view was that voluntary attendance was preferable to
attendance being made a requirement of a probation order,
though the law would permit the latter course to be adopted.[7]
Obviously what can be done in this direction depends a great
deal on local initiative and the co-operation of the probation
service and the local education authority and the centre organ-
izer. The Advisory Council considered that there was plenty of
room for imagination and inventiveness in this matter. It
would be interesting to know what the response has been to
this challenge since the publication of the Advisory Council's
Report in 1962.

THE POSSIBLE EXTENSION OF THE EXISTING IDEA

Sir Basil Henriques, in one of his last acts before his death,
wrote to *The Times* in November 1960 suggesting that a more
intensive and prolonged form of compulsory citizenship training
along the lines of the Boston scheme should be introduced in
Britain. The question was referred to the Advisory Council, and
its Report of July 1962 rejected the suggestion for a Boston-type
scheme. The details of that scheme are printed in an Appendix
to the Report,[8] and it appears to involve required attendance
for two hours a day, five days a week, for a period of twelve
weeks. This is for boys aged 12–17, and the attendance takes
place after school hours (in the late afternoon). Such a scheme
could not be introduced here, the Advisory Council thought,
because of a number of factors, including the shortage of suitable
personnel to man the centres, the problem of premises, the
danger of contamination of the boys by such prolonged association together, and the fact that in this country the centres

---

6. Home Office, Report of the Advisory Council on the Treatment of Offenders,
    Non-Residential Treatment of Offenders under 21, pp. 16–17, paras. 51–52.
7. Pp. 17–18, paras. 53–57.
8. Appendix C, Advisory Council's Report of 1962.

would have to meet in the evening, and release the boys at a late hour, "when those attending would be more likely to remain together and drift into mischief".[9]

So the suggestion fell on stony ground. The Advisory Council did support strongly the efforts made by some probation officers to guide their probationers towards a more constructive use of their leisure, especially by participating in youth clubs and similar activities.[10] The Council felt that scope existed, in the youth service, for developing the idea of projects of service to the community, which might be of benefit to delinquents and those on the verge of delinquency.[11]

RESEARCH ON ATTENDANCE CENTRES

McClintock's study of the work of the junior detention centres gives them a reasonable bill of health. When applied to a young offender with little or no previous experience of crime, coming from a fairly normal background, attendance centre orders are found to be "quite effective". However, when applied to the recidivist with two or more previous offences, especially one who has already failed to respond to probation, the results are "not at all encouraging".[12]

In other words, as the Advisory Council put it, the attendance centre is designed to deal with a strictly limited class of young delinquents:

"Those whose minds are still, as the Ingleby Committee put it, open to the effects of punishment and the influence of the attendance centre staff in teaching them to respect the law and the property of others'. The effectiveness of the attendance centre should be judged in relation to the class of offender for which it was designed; and by that standard the centres seem to have achieved a fair measure of success."[13]

What McClintock's study does demonstrate most convincingly is the wide divergence of policy on the part of sentencers towards the making of attendance centre orders,[14] and the almost equally wide variations in the emphasis placed on the punitive and reformative elements of treatment, as between

---

9. P. 14, para. 42.
10. P. 15, para. 45.
11. P. 16, para. 48.
12. F. H. McClintock, *Attendance Centres*, 1961, p. 99.
13. Advisory Council's Report of 1962, p. 8, para. 21.
14. *Op. cit.*, pp. 15–16, 25.

the different centres.[15] Hitherto it seems that the attendance centre has been all things to all men. McClintock's plea might well be repeated:

> Without forgoing the usefulness of particular local adaptations which occur in some régimes, it might perhaps be possible now, after ten years of development, to state a general policy which would give a greater definiteness to the aims of this measure of treatment, which would act both as a guide to the staff of the centres and to the magistrates of the juvenile courts.[16]

THE END OF THE SECOND PERIOD

We are now approaching the end of the second decade of the history of the attendance centre. Since McClintock wrote in 1961 there have been few striking developments. The senior centres are the main new development. These appear to be used mainly for boys of 17 and 18 guilty of offences of breaking and entering or theft, and taking and driving away. A few boys are ordered to attend in respect of offences of drunkenness. Neither centre has often been full to capacity.[17]

The future of the attendance centre system is now in doubt. The intention seems to be to replace it as it exists at present by the new arrangements under the Children and Young Persons Act 1969. Local authorities will be responsible for providing intermediate forms of treatment, according to the White Paper "Children in Trouble". These new arrangements are discussed further below. (See Chapter 26: Reform Proposals for Young Offenders.)

In this connection, the view expressed by the Advisory Council when rejecting the suggestion for introducing a Boston-type citizenship-training scheme is of considerable interest. The Council said it had come to the conclusion "that any new kind of non-residential training centre that might be introduced ought to be distinct from the attendance centre as it has been developed in this country".[18]

New Zealand has been experimenting with periodic detention at week-ends for up to 60 hours a week covering a period of up to one year.[19] This represents a much more onerous obligation than either the English attendance centre or the Boston citizen-

---

15. P. 49. 16. *Ibid.*
17. See Reports of the Prison Department.
18. Advisory Council's Report of 1962, p. 8, para. 22.
19. J. A. Seymour, "Periodic Dentention in New Zealand" (April 1969), 9 *B.J.C.* 182.

ship training scheme. It is really a form of modified detention centre which allows the offender to keep his employment and enjoy freedom during the week, but which causes his week-end leisure to be forfeited more or less completely for a prolonged period. Such experiments deserve careful consideration. At the very least they demonstrate that the possible alternative solutions are not limited to the present choice between detention centre, attendance and probation or some form of discharge.

CHAPTER 26

Reform Proposals for Young Offenders

A good deal of pressure has built up in recent years for the complete remodelling of our measures for dealing with offences committed by children and young persons, and young adult offenders under 21. Some thoughts about the latter group were expressed in the evidence before the Royal Commission on the Penal System, some ideas about the former in the two Government White Papers on children and young persons, which have now led to legislation. The Advisory Council has reviewed the place of the detention centre in our penal system. A more elaborate review of custodial methods for dealing with young offenders aged 17 and over has been promised, with particular reference to the system of custodial treatment.[1]

Among the suggestions made to the Royal Commission on the Penal System with regard to the handling of young offenders under 21, there is one theme which constantly recurs, viz. the need to provide a special kind of régime for chronically disturbed youths who cannot be effectively handled within the present system and whose presence is a constant source of disruption. Thus the Society of Civil Servants (Prison and Borstal Governors' Branch) would like to see "an establishment organised to cope with the chronically disturbed", where the emphasis would be on "treatment within a medical context".[2] The prison medical officers would like to see at least one borstal under medical direction, "especially for disturbed boys".[3]

The Magistrates' Association in their evidence said that "much of the remedial work in penal institutions is being sabotaged by a small minority who appear to resist every effort to help them and derive morbid satisfaction from making life

1. Rt. Hon. James Callaghan, House of Commons Debates, 25 July 1969, Vol. 787, col. 527. *The Times*, 26 July 1969. This will be carried out by the Advisory Council on the Penal System.
2. Royal Commission on The Penal System, Written Evidence, Vol. III, pp. 39–40.
3. *Ibid.*, p. 116.

unbearable for others . . . only by segregating the unco-operative minority . . . who have wilfully committed themselves to a life of crime, and subjecting them to a régime of strict discipline and hard work, can an enlightened system of treatment do justice to those who have the will to benefit".[4] The memorandum went on to express full support for the principle that the treatment of young offenders should be reformative, but contended that it was unreasonable "to lay down that in dealing with thugs of nineteen and twenty the court's primary consideration should be their welfare".

Whereas the treatment personnel appear to be calling for a more understanding, sympathetic and medically oriented régime for troublemakers, the magistrates appear to be asking for a tougher more disciplinary régime for young thugs. The prison and borstal governors are against the automatic expulsion of inmates with a high nuisance value to special establishments for intransigents, and while realising that every institution "will have its small percentage of difficult or intransigent inmates", they accept in principle "that each establishment should make its own arrangements for coping with and, where possible, re-training this minority".[5]

Whereas the magistrates would like to see the borstal régime "strengthened" by providing for the first part of training "to be more strictly disciplinary", for those who are suitable for closed conditions or have already had one borstal sentence, the governors stress the need for more preventive work in the early stages of a child's career, and generally appear to be more "treatment" oriented, as might be expected.

Both the magistrates and the governors speak of community service as something which should be encouraged, though the former are thinking primarily in terms of attendance centre type citizenship-training, while the latter are directing their minds to schemes for borstal training. The Advisory Council is engaged on an examination of the possibilities, including such ideas as week-end training centres.

The Magistrates' Association thought that "special measures should be introduced for dealing with young adult offenders of the twenty-one to twenty-five age group", though they do not say what measures they would regard as appropriate.

---

4. Vol. II, p. 2.
5. Vol. III, p. 40.

THE CHILDREN AND YOUNG PERSONS ACT 1969

It is necessary to consider the effect of the Children and Young Persons Act 1969 on the treatment of young offenders. This Act is mainly concerned with the handling of children in trouble, as the White Paper title indicates.[6] The Home Secretary, moving the Second Reading on 11 March 1969, said its basic principles were simple:

> "Its aim is to prevent the deprived and delinquent children of today from becoming the deprived, inadequate, unstable or criminal citizens of tomorrow."[7]

It seeks to achieve this aim by providing families and parents who cannot bring up their children properly with effective support and help through the social services, and, where this fails, by providing an effective range of community services of a remedial and custodial nature.

The law relating to court proceedings concerning children and young persons had remained basically unaltered since 1933, when the Children and Young Persons Act enacted the recommendations of the Departmental Committee of 1927.[8] It is true that modifications were made by more recent Acts, in particular the Children and Young Persons Act 1963, but, as the Home Secretary explained, "the law has not yet caught up with the development of a variety of less formal methods for dealing with child offenders" which had been introduced in modern times.[9]

In future, children or young persons may be brought before a juvenile court only where it is alleged one of the conditions in s. 1 is satisfied. These include the commission of a criminal offence (excluding homicide).

The orders which a court may make in such proceedings are prescribed in s. 7 as well as in s. 1(3). These give the courts three basic options which are available in all care or control proceedings and which apply to all children up to the age of 17:

1. To bind over the parents (with their consent);
2. To make a supervision order;
3. To make a care order.

---

6. Home Office, Children in Trouble, Cmnd. 3601, April 1968.
7. House of Commons Debates, Vol. 779, col. 1176, 11 March 1969.
8. Report of the Departmental Committee on the Treatment of Young Offenders, Cmd. 2831, 1927.
9. Col. 1177.

Safeguards.—In all cases there is a right of appeal to quarter sessions,[10] and in the case of a care or supervision order a right is given to apply to the juvenile court for a revocation or variation of the order with, again, appeal to quarter sessions against refusal of an application.[11]

The courts will retain their powers in criminal cases to fine, to order the payment of compensation, to discharge conditionally or absolutely, and, in the case of older young persons, to order a disqualification or endorsement in motoring cases. There will be some changes in the institutions to which a court may commit young persons. Approved schools will eventually be absorbed into the new system of community homes, and so will remand homes but not remand centres. The detention centre is unlikely to survive the impending report of the Advisory Council without drastic modification. The attendance centre will be replaced by the new arrangements to be provided by local authorities for forms of intermediate treatment.[12] The minimum age for borstal training will be raised from 15 to 17, but not many young persons are sent to borstal at this early age.

A probation order will be available for dealing with a person aged 17 or over, but not otherwise. The supervision of children under supervision orders will become the responsibility of the local authority children's service, but between 14 and 17 the courts will have a choice of either a probation officer or the local authority children's officer. The supervision order may include requirements of residence or attendance at a specified place for specified periods, and to participate in specified activities.[13] Residence shall not be required for a total in excess of ninety days, and there are a number of similar limitations. A supervision order may include a requirement to attend for mental treatment.

---

10. Section 2(8).
11. Section 21(4).
12. See the White Paper, Children in Trouble, Cmnd. 3601, paras. 25–29.
13. Section 12.

PART VI

Future Trends

CHAPTER 27

A Look Ahead

The publication in November 1969 of the White Paper relating to England and Wales, entitled "People in Prison", Cmnd. 4214, and in December 1969 of the Report on the work of the Prison Department for 1968, Cmnd. 4186, provides an opportunity to bring up to date this account of the English penal system, and also to take a look forward and discern some of the main lines of likely future developments.

As the White Paper says, in its concluding sentence,

"A society that believes in the worth of individual human beings can have the quality of its belief judged, at least in part, by the quality of its prison and probation services and of the resources made available to them."

"People in Prison" aims to inform us fully about the present position in the English prisons. It does not claim to give a complete picture, but the many substantial changes in our prisons in the post-war years are recorded, together with the more recent developments. There is a section devoted to outlining the strategy of the prison system, which is a most welcome departure, since in the past there has too often appeared to be no coherent strategy but instead a policy of drift or response to recurring crisis situations. Both buildings and staff comprise the prison service, and careful assessments are here made of the role of each in the work that is to be done.

The task faced by the prison service is fairly described. Its complexity is stressed, the problem being to provide for upwards of 35,000 men, women and young persons, in a range of 111 establishments, with a turnover of 1,500 persons a week. There are now 15,000 staff employed at different levels to cope with this large and varied task. The growth in the size of the prison population has led to a large increase in the number of staff employed in recent years, as well as in the number of institutions and the annual expenditure. Compared with 1950 the growth of staff is nearly threefold (1950: 5,500), the number of institutions has increased from 57 to 111, and the annual expenditure from £6 million to £50 million per annum.

The pressure on the prison system has been slightly eased by the combined operation of the new suspended sentence provisions and by the parole scheme. There has also been some decline in the use of custody before sentence and for fine defaulters, but it is too early to judge the success of the Criminal Justice Act 1967 in all these matters. It is clear that the number of very long sentences (fourteen years and over) has been rising, and since the abolition of capital punishment the number of life prisoners has risen dramatically, as was to be expected, and of these many have to be detained for very long periods.

The evidence about the increased length of sentences of intermediate duration appears to be equivocal. It seems that the proportion of offenders received into custody with sentences of more than five years is greater now than before the war or in 1948, and one might say the same for receptions with sentences of over three years. But the White Paper argues that there has been no great change in the last decade, and any shift which has occurred may be more a result of the decline in the use of short sentences rather than any other factor. This part of the White Paper discussing changes in the prison population and length of sentences may be usefully compared with Chapter 5 on The Use the Courts Make of Prison.

The White Paper makes it clear that the training and treatment of offenders in custody is not to be regarded simply as some kind of additive which can be used to supplement the prison programme. The close inter-connection between every aspect of "daily living" and training and treatment is emphasised, and it is recognised that here we have a society in miniature, severely hampered by Victorian buildings and shortages of staff.

The most dramatic developments in recent years have been in the provision of employment for prisoners. The installation of new power supplies, workshops and machinery have contributed a new look to prison industries. But it must be admitted that the "occupational" workshops are still primarily somewhere for the prisoners to go and spend their time out of the cells during the day. On the other hand, the industrial workshops have been reorganised and rationalised, as has been described in Chapter 9 (A Prisoner's Work and Earnings). "In no part of the prison system have there been greater changes", says the White Paper. The rapid turnover of the labour force creates problems, and the special constraints of the prison labour situation must be faced. For the first time we are supplied with some trading accounts and forecasts, and the economic potential of the prisons is assessed in terms of productivity. The new industrial prison at Coldingley is clearly one model for the future. A new look at the agricultural side of the prisons is to be undertaken, and it is possible that unrealistic assumptions about the training value of farm work will be replaced by a new approach to the use of prison farms, including perhaps their use as an experimental form of treatment for socially inadequate offenders. Although some progress has been made in improving prisoner's earnings through the incentive schemes, it is clear that the payment of full wages is still a very long way off. It is said that it would cost £30 million or more to pay everyone now in custody the national average wage. What is not said is how much of this would be recoverable from the prisoner as his contribution to the cost of maintenance and other expenses.

The education of prisoners is presently costing over £600,000 per annum, and a re-examination of the place of education in the treatment of offenders is now being carried out. Already the educational and vocational training units, hitherto regarded as separate, have been amalgamated in an endeavour to develop a further education service with close links with developments in this field of education outside the prisons.

Social work in prisons is developing fast, with 200 prison welfare officers now in post, which is double the 1966 figure. In three prisons in the Midlands an increase in the number of prison welfare officers has been made in connection with a research project into the place of social work in prisons.

Improvement in prisoner's contacts with the outside world is clearly recognised as most desirable. There have been changes in the rules governing letters, visits and home leave. The White Paper stresses the need to see the period inside as an interval between two periods outside. The importance of pre-release planning is mentioned, and one of the most interesing and significant developments is the expansion of the opportunities for pre-release employment on out-work schemes. Prisoners serving four years or more, together with lifers who have been given a date for their release, may work for an out-side employer in the last six months of their sentence. In this period they may or may not live in a prison hostel. Of the 1,000 prisoners eligible each year for this pre-release experience, two-thirds are selected as suitable, and at any one time there are now 375 places in the various schemes. Of course, even this expanded provision can only benefit a minority of the prison population. The great majority of prisoners never get to a training prison leave alone to such schemes. With regard to after-care, it is good to know that the official view is that the new voluntary basis for after-care (described in Chapter 11, Release) is regarded as having turned out to be more satisfac-tory than compulsory after-care. The role which the parole scheme is playing in the release of prisoners is also clearly important. The provision which has been made for regular review and the link with pre-release training are regarded as vital developments. The White Paper accepts the need to see parole as one stage in the process of rehabilitation, and to regard the whole question of release as a continuing process. It is claimed that the gloomy forecasts concerning the effect of parole on other prisoners and on those rejected have not been fulfilled, and that parole has already become an accepted part of the prison scene. This may be a questionable assumption, but in time the parole scheme may well come to be regarded as an integral part of the release arrangements, extending to many more prisoners than it is now possible to deal with.

The White Paper gives a list of research projects in progress, either by the staff of the Prison Department or the Home Office Research Unit, or by the universities with or without financial assistance from the Home Office. This impressive catalogue of research endeavour must be measured against the admission that "we have no effective means at present of measuring" many aspects of prison work. The search must go on to find ways of evaluating the system as a whole. The limited value of reconviction statistics, which was pointed out in Chapter 13: Results of Prison Custody (and Other Measures), is again underlined, but in the absence of a better measure, some attention must be given to these. The fact that the failure rate, judged by this means, is "dauntingly high" can be offset by pointing out that the changes in the reconviction rates do no more than reflect the changes in the type of offender sent to custody in the last few years. Many more offenders are received with previous institutional experience than was formerly the case. In connection with recidivism, which was discussed in Chapter 14: Recidivist Prisoners, it is said that persistent recidivism is "the most intractable problem confronting the prison system of this and other countries" (page 55). The conclusion which is drawn from the review of the evidence concerning the evaluation of the penal system is that the Government policy of keeping as many offenders out of custody as possible still seems to be the correct policy, and will be adhered to in the future.

This brings us to the discussion of the strategy of the prison system, previously mentioned. Much of what is said here summarises the previously announced policy decisions, which have been recorded at the appropriate places in the text. Thus the new policy concerning the institutional provision for women and girls is described in Chapter 16: Female Offenders. Elsewhere we have referred to the need for two new allocation centres for borstal youths, and the proposed comprehensive review of all custodial treatment measures for young offenders. There is also urgent need for more remand accommodation, especially for young male offenders. The original notion of coupling Remand Centres with observation and classification facilities for adult offenders has now been dropped in favour of developing the local prisons not only for the remand of adult prisoners but also for allocation and classification purposes and for pre-release schemes. The needs of the borstal system for more closed accommodation may be met by developing "closed units" inside open borstal institutions, as is being done at Hollesley Bay. Further experiments in placing borstal youths outside institutions may be expected, as at Ipswich.

With regard to male adult prisoners, the pressure of numbers is forcing the Prison Department to institute a massive building programme, as well as spending large sums of money on refurbishing and modernising the traditional Victorian prisons. As the White Paper observes, the prison service, unlike a theatre, cannot put up a "House Full" notice. So it has been thought necessary to seek to provide for the anticipated as well as the actual flow of offenders from the courts.

The arrangements for providing maximum security for the small proportion of high-risk (Category A) prisoners have been described in Chapter 7: Safe Custody and the Security Problem. Only 1 per cent. of all prisoners are estimated to fall in this category. Various physical improvements have been made to the prisons to increase their security, modern technical aids are now employed, more staff have been allocated and trained for security duties, and a prison dog service has been organised. The figures show that for the present the threat of escapes or attempted escapes has been contained. Moreover, and surely this is just as important, it is claimed in the Prison Department Report for 1968 that, although gloomy predictions were made following the Mountbatten Report concerning the decline in the quality of the prison programme, consequent upon the implementation of that Report's recommendations, these pessimistic forebodings have not been fulfilled. The great majority of the prisons are said to be unaffected in terms of their educational and other activities. This view is based on a survey made in the autumn of 1968, but since the scope and nature of the survey are not indicated, it is difficult to assess the correctness of this view. One may at the very least put on record the continuing concern of many persons in all ranks of the prison service about the adverse consequences of Mountbatten on the prison training programme. On the other hand, one can be grateful for the support given in the White Paper to the notion put forward in Chapter 7, that there is no necessary antithesis between security and rehabilitation, and hope that the prison staff will continue to find ways of doing useful "training and treatment" work in these more secure surroundings.

From the security angle, few offenders today are found to be suitable for open conditions (only 20 per cent.). On the other hand, the largest group are those who are suited for Category C prisons (50 per cent.), and several new prisons are to be built in the next few years for prisoners in this category. There will also be some new Category B prisons, to house the 30 per cent. thought suitable for this category of custody. The economies to be obtained by sharing common facilities may lead to a number of large-scale prison complexes being developed, instead of scattered small institutions. To replace entirely the existing prisons which are obsolete is regarded as quite out of the question. It is estimated that the cost would be around £100 million. No Government is likely to make such sums of public money available. It follows that many of the Victorian prisons are likely to be still in use at the end of the century.

It would be idle to criticise a strategy which is designed to meet the estimated needs of the prison service. One can only ask whether it is necessary to accept the projected rise in the total custodial population, approaching 40,000 in the early 1970s, with such equanimity. It is suggested the time has come to take further steps to reduce the size of the custodial population, if only to give the prison service a fair opportunity to do what it can in the training and rehabilitation of offenders. We are informed that overcrowding is regarded as the worst feature of our prison system at present, there being about 9,000 prisoners sleeping two or three in a cell. It is estimated that up to 1972 the numbers in custody are likely to rise faster than the buildings can be provided in order to accommodate them. Is it a sufficient response to this situation to say that "the Government has set in hand a regular and properly planned building programme" and to express the hope that "in the years ahead new penalties and methods of treatment, and the greater use of existing alternatives to prison, will further reduce the proportion of offenders committed to custody" (page 106)? Must we repeat the mistakes they made in California, which provided vast new institutions to meet the estimated needs of the custodial population, instead of developing viable alternative measures?

It is suggested that a most urgent and far-reaching inquiry should be instituted into possible means of reducing the custodial population. The Advisory Council on the Penal System has been looking into various aspects of the matter. Only by developing fresh alternatives to custody and by building new bridges between the custodial and non-custodial treatment of offenders can we avoid the danger of a breakdown in the penal system, and in the long run have the best chance of helping to reduce the amount of crime, which for all concerned must be and will remain our constant endeavour.

The development of the probation and after-care service in the years 1966–68 has recently been described in an official report of the Probation and After-Care Department (Cmnd. 4233, December 1969). This Report describes the changes which are taking place in the probation service in the light of modern developments. The total number of probation officers now exceeds 3,000, and the average case load of each officer is between forty and fifty cases. Much attention is now being given to improvements in the training arrangements, and four regional training officers were appointed in 1968. Experiments have been made in the appointment and use of "ancillary workers" designed "to discover whether there is a range of duties, intermediate between those of clerical assistant and the fully trained professional probation officer, which can be delegated".

Surprisingly little is said about the impact of the Children and Young Persons Act 1969 on the future work of the probation service, and it is disappointing to find that there is no discussion of the implications of the Seebohm Report. But it is recognised that the Act of 1969 "will result eventually in a significant change in the balance of the supervisory work undertaken by the probation and after-care service".

The big changes recorded in this Report have been in the development of social work in detention centres, and in the field of after-care. In January 1969 probation and after-care committees became responsible for filling social worker posts at detention centres, and this side of the work of detention centres will henceforth be carried out by probation officers, normally females. There are welcome signs that voluntary after-care is beginning to be more widely accepted by ex-prisoners. Approximately one-fifth of those under after-care supervision by the probation service are now voluntary cases (22 per cent. in 1968). The expansion of places in hostels for homeless offenders has continued, and at the end of 1968 there were 619 places in 55 hostels. A new development has been the sanctioning of special grants at higher rates from government funds towards the provision of places in hostels for persons with high dependency needs. There are four hostels for drug addicts, one for chronic drunken offenders and one for homeless borstal boys, which receive such support. In 1967 steps were taken to provide help in the purchase of suitable houses for use as hostels, through the foundation of the Bridgehead Housing Association. A training scheme for hostel wardens has also been sponsored by NACRO. A Home Office Working Party on Habitual Drunken Offenders was set up in June 1967. The role of prison welfare officers was clarified in an official circular in July 1967, and arangements for training such officers are now being made at the Prison Service Staff College at Wakefield, where a three weeks' training course is provided.

The Report as a whole gives clear evidence of the broadening scope and changing nature of the work of the probation and after-care service. Others have written more authoritatively of the demands this makes upon the service at the present time. In the development of non-custodial and post-custodial treatment and supervision of offenders, the probation service undoubtedly stands in a key position. It seems likely that the 1970s will provide additional demands upon the service, and it must be in all our interests to see that the resources in the way of a well-trained and contented staff are available to meet those demands.

Index